# Leveraging Developing Economies with the Use of Information Technology:

## Trends and Tools

Abel Usoro
*University of the West of Scotland, UK*

Grzegorz Majewski
*University of the West of Scotland, UK*

Princely Ifinedo
*Cape Breton University, Canada*

Iwara I. Arikpo
*University of Calabar, Nigeria*

Managing Director: Lindsay Johnston
Senior Editorial Director: Heather A. Probst
Book Production Manager: Sean Woznicki
Development Manager: Joel Gamon
Development Editor: Myla Harty
Acquisitions Editor: Erika Gallagher
Typesetter: Nicole Sparano
Cover Design: Nick Newcomer, Lisandro Gonzalez

Published in the United States of America by
Information Science Reference (an imprint of IGI Global)
701 E. Chocolate Avenue
Hershey PA 17033
Tel: 717-533-8845
Fax: 717-533-8661
E-mail: cust@igi-global.com
Web site: http://www.igi-global.com



Library of Congress Cataloging-in-Publication Data

Leveraging developing economies with the use of information technology:
trends and tools / Abel Usoro ... [et al.], editors.
p. cm.
Includes bibliographical references and index.
Summary: "This book moves toward filling the gap in research on ICT and developing nations, bringing these countries one step closer to advancement through technology"--Provided by publisher.
ISBN 978-1-4666-1637-0 (hardcover) -- ISBN 978-1-4666-1638-7 (ebook) -- ISBN 978-1-4666-1639-4 (print & perpetual access) 1. Technological innovations--Economic aspects--Developing countries. I. Usoro, Abel.
HC59.72.T4L38 2012
303.48'33091724--dc23

2011050299

British Cataloguing in Publication Data
A Cataloguing in Publication record for this book is available from the British Library.

## Editorial Advisory Board



## List of Reviewers

# Table of Contents

# Detailed Table of Contents

Knowledge sharing and re-use by both human and computer agents can suffer from the difficulty of having a shared understanding. Ontology and the study of semantics endeavour to tackle these difficulties. Osofisan moves the search for common understanding by combining both graphical and mathematical models to rigorously develop formal definitions and mapping functions derived from the extension of the axiom of selection (or choice) and Object-Attribute-Relation (OAR) model. He terms the new model he develops Knowledge Reconciliation (KNOWREM). Though highly theoretical, this paper finds its relevance in targeting knowledge sharing which is very important in developing economies where cultural factors may play introduce imprecision in information. Thus, Osofisan's future research direction is using fuzzy logic to tackle more the problem of ill-defined decision-making problems.



The importance of knowledge management in the hospitality industry is well established in the research literature. However, apparently all the studies are in developed economies and in big hotels whereas the important economic role of hospitality industry in developing countries is not disputed. This chapter develops a conceptual model of intention to adopt knowledge management in developing economies, using the constructs of developmental factors, information technology and culture. The underlying theories are from developmental studies, technology acceptance model (TAM) and Hofstede's (1980) Culture Model.



Cloud computing has tremendous economic potential to developing countries because of the reduction of the need to own computer infrastructure, platform, storage or even software. Using the web, one of its mean features is to deliver computing and storage as a service. It therefore builds on the concepts of Web Services and Quality of Service (QOS). This chapter describes web services and presents a novel game theoretical approach using genetic programming for composition of web services.

# Foreword

The book is timely, authoritative and comprehensive through a detailed view of recent Information Technology (IT) 'trends and tools' which may be exploited for the benefit of developing countries. Few agendas are more important within our globally engaged world where experience, expertise and examples may be translated and adopted from mature economies to less advantaged areas of our planet. These critical gains can be realised to support all citizens and provide universal opportunities for improved health, education and well-being facilitated by new IT. This is particularly evident through the development and diffusion of the internet which has evidently transformed societies through the application of sophisticated web-enabled systems. Many governments have recognised these trends and are seriously implementing relevant applications in this respect for economic development. This is also apparent through the emergence of eGovernment where online services are provided to improve service delivery agendas. In addition, private providers and commercial enterprises are also increasingly engaging with eBusiness systems as they recognise the opportunities for competitive advantages. In this respect a combined awareness of IT, in whatever guise, represents a valuable resource for developing countries in their efforts to maintain and sustain the quality of life for citizens.

The book usefully demonstrates the extent of the 'digital divide' between developed and developing nations and represents an important example of how imaginative IT initiatives may be leveraged to overcome physical obstacles and potentially generate significant market access and competitive stimulus. The content includes the interesting notion of 'knowledge reconciliation' which may be applied to developing countries in an attempt to capture the cultural dimensions generated from imprecise information in these contexts. A few chapters also conceptualise the concept of knowledge management within developing countries which offer insights and opportunities for commercial organisations.

In keeping with the theme of the book there is an example of the exploitation of 'web service composition' to support the enactment of high quality service applications. Most usefully the notion of cloud computing is discussed and how these innovations may again be adapted to developing country contexts. Any serious adoption of IT systems is wholly dependent upon how the systems are diffused and implemented and these issues are instigated through an assessment and role of IT training in a developing public sector context. The examples are chosen from the Nigerian Immigration Service but are again applicable and translatable to other areas of similar concern. A broader more generic perspective is also provided where national policies, social economic factors, national culture and network readiness are examined in Africa. The extent, capabilities and level of preparation are assessed to determine network opportunities. The book exposes a number of relevant areas to achieve readiness in this respect most importantly, educational systems, transparency (corruption) levels, regulatory frameworks, and cross-cultural dimensions.

Another excellent feature of the book is its demonstration of career orientations and turnover of IT personnel in Africa which is critically important where skill shortages may be exacerbated through labour transfers which are clearly instigated through lack of attention to career 'anchors'. A valuable insight is gained from a need to ensure organisational stability (job security) and sense of service initiatives. Further reports consider the adoption of eCommerce systems and present an analysis of the emergence of these systems which may enable and support revenue generation from non-traditional resources. The research models proposed are particularly helpful based upon the Diffusion of Innovation and Technology-Organisation-Environment frameworks. Culturally sensitive issues are also addressed through reference and empirical evaluation of gender differences and self-efficacy through the adoption of eBanking. The book identifies that females are disadvantaged compared with their male counter parts with respect to IT usage and acceptance. This is a complex area which clearly deserves more research attention given the value and equitability necessary for gender equality.

A further common concern relative to eCommerce systems is the apparent lack of trust in their adoption. A series of initiative to enhance the extent of trust within developing environments are suggested which will certainly engage more users in electronic exchanges. The report of the Chinese economy is a welcome addition to the experiences of larger developing countries. Evidence and evaluations clearly present important lessons for IT adoption for obtaining personal credit as an engine of economic activity and sustainability. In addition, issues and advise on the translation of Western methodologies through the application of robust credit procedures enabled from IT are discussed. eLearning applications are addressed and the opportunities to enhance literacy and library use facilities are reported. This is again a critically unique and important area of concern in developing countries to ensure the right skills are achieved in the use of IT and the available resources provided through libraries. The final chapters consider these systems and experiences of higher education. They provide a useful explanation of how and why eLearning are important particularly in relation to the educational transmission of information, knowledge, values and attitudes. The opportunity is also taken to outline the challenges associated of carrying out IT measurements in developing countries as they are different from those in developed countries. This also relates to the methods for selecting appropriate IT content. The results reveal significant differences between the academic use of IT by students and faculty members which has implications for researchers, education practitioners, planners, policy makers and government – a main objective of the book.

The richness and diversity of coverage in the book is highly commendable and it should become a critically useful resource for anyone involved with or is dependent upon the exploitation of IT systems within developing countries.

*Professor Raymond A Hackney*
*Brunel University, UK November, 2011*

**Professor Ray Hackney** *is Chair in Business Systems, Director of the Doctoral Programme and Head of the Information Systems Evaluation research group at Brunel University, UK. He has contributed extensively to research in information systems and management with publications in numerous national and international conferences and journals. He has taught and examined Doctoral and MBA programmes including Manchester Business School and the Open University. He is Associate Editor of the JGIM, JEUC, JLIM, ACITM, EJIS and case editor for IJIM. His research interests: the strategic management of information systems within a variety of organisational contexts, with an increasing speciality in government sectors; and has contributed to several EPSRC and European funded research projects. He was President of the Information Resource Management Association (IRMA) 2001/2002 and is now an Executive Member of the Information Institute www.information-institute.org; and serves on the European Doctoral Association for Management & Business Administration (EDAMBA) Executive Committee.*

# Preface

There is no doubt that IT has contributed a lot to the growth of the developing countries. Further improvement of the living conditions would be hard to imagine without the use of modern communication technologies. Although a lot has been said about the role of IT in the development of developed economies, there is still a shortage of studies on how IT can help developing economies. This book will try to fill this gap by providing a broad view of the present state in this field as well as presenting specific conceptual and empirical studies whose findings contain important policy implications for international bodies, governments, businesses and academia. Before we highlight the different chapter of this book, a brief description of developing economies will be presented.

Figures do not tell the full story but 85% of the world's population is said to live in developing countries and earns only 20% of the world's income. The gross national income (GNY) per head of the 20 poorest countries in 2003 averaged only £110 which is less than £10 per month. For the richest countries, it was put at £14,550. In 10 of the poorest countries, life expectancy is 42 years only whereas in the 10 richest countries, 79 is the figure.

It can be understood from the foregoing why developing economies need development. 'Development' is something we can feel but cannot always agree on its meaning, at least the list of items that are needed for it to happen. A list by Sloman (1991) taking from the view of various economists include:

1. Adequate food, shelter, warmth and clothing.
2. Universal access to education.
3. Availability of adequate health care.
4. Availability of non-demeaning jobs.
5. Sufficient free time to be able to enjoy social interaction.
6. Freedom to make one's own economic decisions.
7. Freedom for people to participate in the decisions of government and other bodies that affect their lives.

The problems of quantification so as to arrive at comparative values have prompted the development and use of gross national product (GNP) or gross national income (GNY) to measure the state of development. Yet such measures are still seen as inadequate for many reasons including the difficulty of including the economic value of a father personally giving all his children a hair-cut, for instance; and in developing economies, there are many personal services performed as a result of the extended family system which is not so strong in the developed economies. An improved measure for economic development published by the United Nations Development Program (UNDP) in 1990 is the Human Development Index (HDI) which actually is a composite index for (a) life expectancy, (b) school enrolment and adult literacy (c) GDP per capita.

You may agree that it does not matter which of the three approaches we use in thinking about economic development and indeed, we may bear all of the 7 items of Sloman (1991), the GNY and the HDI in mind. All are desirable for inhabitants of developing economies. Governments and scientists of various shades and colours have contributed many views. For instances, economists have proposed various trade strategies such as exploiting comparative advantage, or substituting imports to exporting manufactures. It is not the intention of this book to go through all the recipes but to focus on a very current phenomenon that has significantly affected both developed and developing economies in the past decade especially. That phenomenon is information and communication technology.

I have been privileged to spend the first 32 years of my life in a developing economy and 23 subsequent years in a developed economy. I went through education up to a Masters level, and lecturing, in a University in a developing economy, without using even an electric typewriter let alone a computer. The same snail mail (postal services as contrasted with today's emails) that delayed my admission letter to City University in London also delayed the next letter from that university that advised me not to come that year because I was too late for the three weeks' intensive programming course in Cobol (DOS- instead of Window-based) that preceded the course on Business Systems Analysis and Design. When I gave "No" answers to the two questions: "Have you used a computer before?" and "Do you know the difference between a hardware and a software," the programme leaders could not but insist before I attended the first class (despite my enthusiasm to jump into the class) that both my sponsor (the European Economic Commission) and myself sign an undertaking that I was taking a risk and that I was most likely to fail the course.

Within the 23 years, significant changes have taken place in me, in developed economies as well as developing economies. I try not to say more about myself here. For developed economies like UK, 23 years ago, most programmes did not have the GUI interface and the browser was not invented to give a "human face" to the internet. Laptops were non-existent and nearly every home did not have a computer with broadband internet connection. Mobile phones, sleek and with many computer facilities including global positioning systems (GPS), and other applications like mobile internet were not popular. All these are common today.

Researchers have agreed that much of modern economic development in developed countries are accounted for by their application of ICT to the creation of a knowledge-based economy (KBE) (Rivard et al, 2004; Olszak & Ziemba, 2011) which many experts believe is the only effective way of improving the competitiveness of countries, regions and businesses in the modern global economy (Godin, 2006, Hanna, 2010). We also have the example of China that has experienced significant economic growth in the last 30 years. Apart from human capital[1], the existence of functioning market institutions to reward hard work, technological advances adopted from developed countries (Chow 2010, pp. 43-46) along with good communication infrastructure in their urbanization policy (Song, 2011) have accounted for the rapid economic growth in China. Similarly, Techatassanasoontorn et al (2011) found out in their research that the future economic growth of Thailand would depend on increased investment and improvement in ICT and innovation.

The developed economies have not stood still either. While land telephone lines had been the asset of only the very few in developing economies, the mobile technology explosion has placed mobile phones in the hands of millions in these economies. Though not always up to the standard of developed economies, the quality of mobile phones has improved over the past years. For instance, in Nigeria, it would usually take more than 6 attempts at dialling before one could get a connection. The situation has much improved. There are also abundant internet cafes (though with slow connections because of inadequacies in the communication infrastructure) in most of the cities of developing economies. Most universities in developing economies provide some level of computer training though the computers may not be networked (as I observed in one university in Nigeria) and it may be a bit difficult for the facilities to meet the demand.

As far back as 1955, Lewis observed that "economic growth depends both upon technological knowledge about things and living creatures, and also upon social knowledge about man and his relations with his fellowmen" (1955). This book focuses on information technology. The question that this book tries to answer is how to harness the current state of ICT to achieve economic development in developing countries. How can it improve the food, shelter, warmth and clothing situation of these countries? How can it impact on education, health care, quality of job, social interaction, level of economic freedom and interaction with business and governmental organisations? How can it increase the income per capita and life expectancy? Most parts of these questions are tackled by this book as will soon be discussed. In addition, there are many other advantages: for example, the mere availability of mobile telephones helps to cut down unnecessary trips to do face-to-face personal and business meetings. This may reduce road accidents that often results in loss of life in some of these developing economies.

The provision of communication infrastructure, which is part of ICT, has been found to lead to the generation of employment (Osotimehin et al, 2010), the opening of opportunities for foreign investment (Aitken and Harrison, 1999), better education and training facilities, a boom in private sector development, improved overall regional productive capacity, a reduction in poverty (Calderon and Serven, 2004), expansion in economic activities (World Bank, 1991), and a larger spill-over to other sectors of the economy as it has a larger impact on aggregate output compared to other kinds of infrastructure (Canning, 1999). This book presents opinions, conceptual and research papers from authors situated in developing economies and in US, Canada, Greece, Thailand and UK on the trends and tools of information and communication technology for improving developing economies. Here is a summary of each section of the book and its 15 chapters.

## CHAPTER ONE: BRIDGING THE DIGITAL DIVIDE: LEVERAGING EARLY STRIDES IN NIGERIA

Arikpo, Osofisan and Usoro explain one concept of the digital divide, namely the ICT gap between developing and developed countries. It uses Nigeria as a case study in presenting several ICT initiatives and the role of some ICT bodies there. These initiatives and roles are meant to bridge the digital divide between Nigeria and the developed world. The authors also discuss the challenges facing the use of information technology for socio-economic development.

## CHAPTER TWO: THE DIGITAL DIVIDE AND DISADVANTAGED POPULATIONS IN E-TOURISM

The digital divide contributes negatively to the economic growth of e-tourism could bring to a nation because their inhabitants are denied access to adequate information technology with associated efficiencies that would benefit both tourists and the tourism industry. The resulting imbalance in technology between countries may threaten good relationships because of feelings of insecurity and jealousy. Yfantis, Usoro and Tseles discuss how the introduction of mobile technology reduces the digital divide and offers abundant opportunities to developing countries and human minorities to benefit from tourism, share knowledge and enjoy a better quality of life. The attractive features of mobile devices include their small size, low cost, ease of use and familiarity to most people.

## CHAPTER THREE: KNOWREM: FORMAL DEFINITIONS AND ONTOLOGICAL FRAMEWORK FOR KNOWLEDGE RECONCILIATION IN ECONOMIC INTELLIGENCE

Knowledge sharing and re-use by both human and computer agents can suffer from the difficulty of having shared understanding. Ontology and the study of semantics endeavour to tackle these difficulties. Osofisan moves the search for common understanding by combining both graphical and mathematical models to rigorously develop formal definitions and mapping functions derived from the extension of the axiom of selection (or choice) and Object-Attribute-Relation (OAR) model. He terms the new model he develops Knowledge Reconciliation (KNOWREM). Though highly theoretical, this paper finds its relevance in targeting knowledge sharing which is very important in developing economies where cultural factors may play introduce imprecision in information. Thus, Osofisan's future research direction is fuzzy logic to tackle more the problem of ill-defined decision-making problems.

## CHAPTER FOUR: A CONCEPTUAL VIEW OF KNOWLEDGE MANAGEMENT ADOPTION IN HOSPITALITY INDUSTRY OF DEVELOPING ECONOMIES

The importance of knowledge management in the hospitality industry is well established in the research literature. However, apparently all the studies are in developed economies and in big hotels whereas the important economic role of hospitality industry in developing countries is not disputed. Usoro and Abiagam develop a conceptual model of intention to adopt knowledge management in developing economies, using the constructs of developmental factors, information technology and culture. The underlying theories are from developmental studies, technology acceptance model (TAM) and Hofstede's (1980) Culture Model.

## CHAPTER FIVE: WEB SERVICE COMPOSITION, OPTIMIZATION AND THE IMPLICATIONS FOR DEVELOPING ECONOMIES

Cloud computing has tremendous economic potential to developing countries because of the reduction of the need to own computer infrastructure, platform, storage or even software. Using the web one of its mean features is to deliver computing and storage as a service. It therefore builds on the concepts of Web Services and Quality of Service (QOS). Osofisan, Eteng, Arikpo and Usoro describe web services and present a novel game theoretical approach using genetic programming for composition of web services.

## CHAPTER SIX: ASSESSING THE ROLE AND FUNCTION OF IT/IS TRAINING AND DEVELOPMENT AND POLICY IMPLEMENTATIONS IN A PUBLIC SECTOR ORGANISATION

Ololube, Ajayi, Kpolovie and Usoro explore the experiences of employee technological training and development and how these impact on their performance. A well reported empirical work was carried out on the Nigerian Immigration service using a sample of 82 respondents. The research framework and implication of the study emphasises the importance of information technology training to workers in developing countries if improvement in the economy is to be achieved.

## CHAPTER SEVEN: THE INFLUENCE OF NATIONAL IT POLICIES, SOCIO-ECONOMIC FACTORS, AND NATIONAL CULTURE ON NETWORK READINESS IN AFRICA

Prior studies have shown that network readiness has significant influence on how countries benefit from the use of information technology for economic development. However, research on this topic with data from Africa is rare. Therefore, Ifinedo and Ifinedo examine network readiness index of 20 diverse African countries against their national IT policies, socio-economic and cultural factors. This cross-sectional study suggests variability in the use of information technology for economic development since African countries are not seen to be a monolith. Variations that have to be taken into consideration are each country's educational system, its transparency (corruption) level, its information technology regulatory framework, and its cross-cultural dimension of power distance (PDI). African national governments and several bodies such as the World Bank and the UN ICT Task Force should focus attention on these factors which were seen to significantly relate to e-readiness index. Thus will the index improve for developing countries.

## CHAPTER EIGHT: AN EMPIRICAL STUDY OF CAREER ORIENTATIONS AND TURNOVER INTENTIONS OF INFORMATION SYSTEMS PERSONNEL IN BOTSWANA

Existing career orientation studies of information systems (IS) personnel are focused on developed economies. Mgaya, Uzoka, Kitindi, Akinnuwesi and Shemi investigate career orientations (anchors) of IS personnel in a developing country, Botswana. The findings confirm earlier ones in literature but with some variations which are attributed to cultural and socio-economic peculiarities. For example, life style is not significant but the dominant career anchors include organizational stability (security) and sense of service (service). Gender, age and education tend to moderate the anchors significantly. The major contributors to turnover intentions of IS personnel in developing economies tend to be job satisfaction and growth opportunities whereas career satisfaction, supervisor support, organizational commitment, length of service and age did not contribute significantly. One of the recommendations of this empirical study is to encourage females from secondary school level to opt to study mathematics and other sciences to provide a sound platform for IS career.

## CHAPTER NINE: E-COMMERCE ADOPTION IN NIGERIAN BUSINESSES: AN ANALYSIS USING TECHNOLOGY-ORGANIZATION-ENVIRONMENTAL FRAMEWORK

E-commerce adoption is crucial to income generation in modern businesses. Ekong, Ifinedo, Ayo and Ifinedo are contributing to recently emerging studies on e-commerce (EC) adoption in Sub Saharan Africa (SSA). They use Nigeria as an example to investigate factors that impact on acceptance of EC in small businesses. They developed a research model based on Diffusion of Innovation (DIT) and Technology-Organisation-Environment (TOE) frameworks to guide their investigation. The model is composed of factors such as relative advantage, compatibility, complexity, management support and organisational readiness. The research supports relative advantage of technologies, management support and IS vendor support as significant predictors of EC adoption in Nigerian small businesses. Other factors like organizational readiness, complexity and compatibility of technology were found to be not only insignificant but also inhibitors to EC adoption.

## CHAPTER TEN: AN EMPIRICAL EVALUATION OF THE EFFECTS OF GENDER DIFFERENCES AND SELF-EFFICACY IN THE ADOPTION OF E-BANKING IN NIGERIA: A MODIFIED TECHNOLOGY ACCEPTANCE MODEL

Considerable research interest and attention have been given to gender disparity in the usage and acceptance of information technology (IT). Most research findings indicate females to be disadvantaged with males being more proficient in IT skills. Such research concentrates in developed economies with very little done in the developing parts of the world. Ayo, Ifinedo, Ekong and Oni perform an empirical evaluation of this gender disparity in the context of e-banking in Lagos (Nigeria – a developing country) and its environs. They extended Technology Acceptance Model (TAM) to guide their study. Their finding is that gender differences moderates the acceptance of e-banking. Computer self-efficacy and perceived ease of use were concerns to females than males who were most influenced by perceived usefulness of e-banking. Their research model provides a platform for further research and their findings implies that e-banking system developers should continue to improve the ease of use of their systems if females are to be encouraged to use them more.

## CHAPTER ELEVEN: ENHANCING TRUST IN E-COMMERCE IN DEVELOPING IT ENVIRONMENTS: A FEEDBACK-BASED PERSPECTIVE

The current expansion of e-commerce has been accounted for by its ability to reduce transaction cost and to promote speed and efficiency. Nonetheless, one of its key challenges is trust. Thus much research and professional interests had been focused on this challenge. However, such focus is mainly in developed economies with advanced information technology (IT) infrastructural environments. Arikpo, Osofisan and Eteng present a unique approach by taking into consideration less-advanced IT environments that exist in developing economies. The perspective of the empirical study presented is on feedback mechanisms in e-commerce websites. The findings support the importance of feedback in enhancing trust in less-developed IT environments.

## CHAPTER TWELVE: BUILDING A CONCEPTUAL MODEL OF FACTORS AFFECTING PERSONAL CREDIT AND INSOLVENCY IN CHINA BASED ON THE METHODOLOGIES USED IN WESTERN ECONOMIES

The demand for personal credit has dramatically increased as China is embracing Western values. This has presented a challenge to financial institutions to ensure they have a workable lending system that would avoid the increasing repayment failures. In most cases, financial institutions use Western lending methodologies. The drawback is failure to take into consideration the Chinese society and culture. In an initial attempt to address this drawback Majewski, Usoro and Chumnumpan develop a research model that endeavours to express the contributing factors to the present increase in bad debts. The authors believe that once the model is empirically tested, it would contribute to automation of the lending system that would take into consideration the peculiar conditions of China as an emerging economy.

## CHAPTER THIRTEEN: INTEGRATING INFORMATION AND COMMUNICATION TECHNOLOGIES (ICT) WITH INFORMATION LITERACY AND LIBRARY-USE-INSTRUCTIONS IN NIGERIAN UNIVERSITIES

A sample of three Nigerian universities is used to study how computer literacy is incorporated into use of library course. Ntui, Ottong and Usoro compared their curriculum contents and found that students were loaded with unnecessary library technicalities. They recommend the giving of more attention to information and technology literacy and presented curriculum structures that can improve the situation.

## CHAPTER FOURTEEN: E-LEARNING IN HIGHER EDUCATION: THE NIGERIAN UNIVERSITIES' EXPERIENCE

Learning is one the key areas where recent advances in information technology have impacted. Usoro and Akuchie explore the extent of e-learning application in Nigerian Universities with a sample of four public universities. Their findings were that lecturers were better exposed to information technology than students. Most of the e-learning facilities available in the universities are neither entirely functional nor adequate. Therefore, computer facilities application in teaching and learning is very low. Their recommendations range from university to government policies for e-learning provision in higher education.

## CHAPTER FIFTEEN: THE ISSUES OF DIGITAL NATIVES AND TOURISTS: EMPIRICAL INVESTIGATION OF THE LEVEL OF IT/IS USAGE BETWEEN UNIVERSITY STUDENTS AND FACULTY MEMBERS IN A DEVELOPING ECONOMY

Ololube, Amaele, Kpolovie and Egbezor derived 11 dimensions for measuring the use of computer systems. They applied these dimensions on a sample of 191 questionnaire respondents in Nigerian universities. Their findings indicate that there is no sharp contrast between "natives" and "tourists" but that students were more of the former and academic staff were more of the latter. This is accounted for by the greater exposure (including at home) of youths (students) to computers than the adults (lecturers) are. One implication of this finding is that faculty members cannot provide the expected level of computer literacy to students. Thus, more effort should be made to equip the lecturers and update their skills so that they can impact sound knowledge including computer skills in such a way that greater economic development can be achieved.

In 2007 and 2008, I chaired in Nigeria an international Conference on Information Technology and Economic Development. In 2009, IGI requested that a book be put together on that theme. The chapters we have reviewed are not all from that conference, as an opportunity was given to a wider audience of authors. It is evident from the above synopsis of their chapters that the book has a lot to offer to policy makers, businesses, educational institutions. To the latter, there are implications to the administrative, to the academics as well as students. Apart from the discussions and recommendations, the research methods used by many of the authors are very instructional and researchers can use the material as a platform for further studies. The book is a very good teaching material and informative for anyone interested in developmental studies.

*Abel Usoro*
*MSc, PhD – Lead Editor*

## REFERENCES


Aitken, B. J., & Harrison, A. E. (1999). Do Domestic Firms bene□t from Direct Foreign Investment?: Evidence from Venezuela . *The American Economic Review, 89*(3), 605–618. doi:10.1257/aer.89.3.605

Calderan, C., & Serven, L. (2004). The Effect of Infrastructure Development on Growth and Income Distribution, *Central Bank of Chile* working Paper 270, Retrieved from: http://www.bcentral.cl/eng/stapub/studies/workingpaper/pdf/dtbc290.wfChow, Gregory C (2010). *Interpreting china's Economy* London: World Scientific.

Canning, D. (1994). Infrastructure and Growth . In Baldassarri, M., Paganetto, L., & Phelps, E. (Eds.), *International Differences in Growth Rates* (pp. 113–147). New York: Macmillan Press.

Godin, B. (2006). The knowledge-based economy: Conceptual framework or buzzword? *The Journal of Technology Transfer, 31*(1), 17–30. doi:10.1007/s10961-005-5010-x

Hanna, N. K. (2010). *Enabling enterprise transformation. Business and grassroots innovation for the knowledge economy*. New York, NY: Springer.

Lewis, W. Arthur (1955). *Theory of Economic Growth* London, UK: George Allen & Unwin Ltd.

Olszak, Celina M and Ziemba, Ewa (2011). The use of ICT for economic development in the Silesian Region in Poland, Interdisciplinary *Journal of Information, Knowledge and Management, 6* 198-216.

Osotimehin, K. O., Akinkoye, E. Y., & Olasanmi, O. O. (2010). *The Effects of Investment in Telecommunication Infrastructure on Economic Growth in Nigeria* (1992-2007), Paper for the Oxford Business and Economic Conference.

Rivard, S., Aubert, B. A., & Patry, M. (2004). *Information technology and organisational transformation. Solving the management puzzle*. New York: Elsevier.

Roztocki, N., & Weistroffer, H. R. (2009a). Information and communications technology in developing, emerging and transition economies: An assessment of research, *Proceedings of the Fifteenth Americas Conference on Information Systems.* San Franscisco, August 6 – 9. Retrived November 23 October 2011 from: http://papers.ssrn.com/sol3/papers.cfm?abstract_id=1457439

Sloman, J. (2006). *Economics*. London: Prentice Hall.

Song, C. (2011). *The Regional Macroeconomic effects of public infrastructure in China*, PhD Thesis from George Masion University, USA.

Techatassanasoontorn, Angsana A, & Huang, Haiyan; Trauth, Eileen M and Juntiwasarakij, Suwan. (2011). Analyzing ICT and development: Thailand's path to the information economy. *Journal of Global Information Management, 19*(1), 1–29. doi:10.4018/jgim.2011010101

Whitehead, G. (1994). *Economics*. London: Butterworth-Heinemann Ltd.

World Bank Report. (1991). *The Challenge of Development*, New York: The World Bank Group World Bank (2011). Retrieved 30 October 2011 from http://info.worldbank.org/etools/kam2/KAM_page 5.asp

## ENDNOTE

1 Measured not so in the traditional number of years spent in education but by work ethics which have been shaped by Chinese cultural history over the years and passed on in families from generation to generation.

# Acknowledgment

My consolation for running what seemed as endless errands for my parents was that when I am their age, I would have others run errands for me and thus will be less busy than I saw them in my little eyes. My dream is yet to come true and is quite the opposite as I see myself much busier as I grow up. Thus, when IGI approached me to put this book together, I am happy that I appointed three co-editors – Grzegorz Majewski, Professor Princely Ifinedo and Iwara Arikpo. I am very grateful for the hard work they have put not only to contribute articles, but also to help coordinate the rest of the authors. Without their efforts, this book would not be at this quality and completed now. I am very grateful to them.

I am also very grateful to each of the authors for persisting to the end. Some dropped out by the roadway and some were unfortunately dropped at the beginning after reading their proposals. For 15 chapters with joint authorship for most of them, I cannot list the names of the authors but I do acknowledge their work and help in the review process. Others who participated in the review process are members of the editorial advisory board (EAB). They participated in the review process and their useful feedback helped the authors to improve the quality of their work. For their help, am particularly grateful to Professor Malcolm Crowe and Dr Mark Stansfield of University of the West of Scotland, Dr Rosemary Burnley of University of Bedford, Dr Christina Koutra of Bournemouth University, Professor Matthew Kuofie of Central Central Michigan University and Dr Vincent Ribiere of Bangkok University. May I also express my gratitude to our Foreword Author – Professor Ray Hackney of Brunel University.

I must mention the University of Calabar for happily hosting the Conference on Information Technology and Economic Development (CITED) which attracted the IGI publishers to invite me to do this book. I am particularly grateful to the then Vice-Chancellor Professor Bassey Asuquo and the LoC (Local Organising Committee) that he appointed for the conference. I am grateful to Professor Lipcsey (the Chair of the Committee) and other members of the Committee. My visits to University of Calabar as well as Bangkok University have been generously sponsored by the Royal Society, the Royal Society of Edinburgh (different from the first one) and Carnegie Trust. I am very grateful for their support which resulted in the collaborations which is at the foundation of this book's concept. I also want to be grateful to one of the Directors of the Bangkok University research centre, Dr Lugkana Worasinchai, for receiving both my student and myself on the research visit. My University including my School of Computing and its Head, Professor Christos Grecos are to be appreciated for the support for CITED. I should also appreciate Alison Anderson (and her boss and the Head of Corporate Marketing, Marcus Ross) for accompanying me to represent the University of the West of Scotland at the first CITED and signing on behalf of the University the communiqué to be repeating the conference.

I cannot also fail to mention the team of well-wishers both in UK and outside who did so well to keep my sanity long enough to complete this task. Among them are (and the list is not in the order of importance) my PhD research students, Leonard Bloom, Mrs Evelyn Fitzpatrick, Johnson Opigo, Ezendu Ariwa of London Metropolitan University, Dr Rosemary Galli in Oxford, my brothers and their wives – Paul Usoro SAN (Senior Advocate of Nigeria), Mrs Mfon Usoro, Dr Nathaniel Usoro and Dr Chinyere Usoro. My daughter's Emem Usoro persistence to complete her medical studies next year also inspired and drove me on to the completion of this book.

I should not forget to mention Myla Harty and IGI Global for giving the opportunity to do what I have not done before and I hope there will be a better repeat performance.

*Abel Usoro*
*Lead Editor*

# Section 1
# Information Technology and Economics Issues

# Chapter 1
# Bridging the Digital Divide:
## Leveraging Early Strides in Nigeria

**Iwara I Arikpo**
*University of Calabar, Nigeria*

**Adenike Osofisan**
*University of Ibadan, Nigeria*

**Abel Usoro**
*University of the West of Scotland, UK*

## ABSTRACT

*Information and Communications Technology (ICT) has become a fundamental global phenomenon today. It has provided developing countries with a unique opportunity to compete in a global economy that was hitherto beyond their reach. ICT has greatly reduced physical obstacles, increased market access and trade efficiency, and provided a competitive stimulus among countries in a global information society. Digital divide is the ICT gap between developing and developed countries.*

*This paper outlines the current state, opportunities and potentials in the use of ICT for education, R&D, and governance in Nigeria. It presents several ICT initiatives and the roles of some ICT bodies capable of bridging the digital divide between Nigeria and the developed world. Challenges facing the continuing development of ICT in the country are identified, and solution strategies to harness the full potential of ICT as an indispensable vehicle for socio-economic development in Nigeria are also discussed.*

## INTRODUCTION

The global nature of Information and Communications Technology (ICT) provides developing countries with a unique opportunity to compete in a global economy that was hitherto beyond their reach. ICT has become a vital engine of any economy, be it developing or advanced. It is an essential infrastructure that promotes the development of other sectors such as agriculture, education, industry, health, banking, defence, transportation and tourism. It is indispensable in times of national emergencies or natural disasters

DOI: 10.4018/978-1-4666-1637-0.ch001

(as we saw Americans use it during the 9/11 attacks, Tsunamis, Japanese used it during the March 2011 earthquakes, etc). It considerably reduces the risks and rigours of travel and rural-urban migration. ICT has the potential to reduce physical obstacles, increase market access and trade efficiency, as well as provide a competitive stimulus among countries, in a global information society.

It is important to note that digital divide does not only refer to the information technology gap between countries, it covers the gap between individuals as well as companies. For example, for individuals, negative impacts may range from inconvenience to more serious outcomes, such as employment disadvantage due to lack of familiarity with ICT (*UNCTAD*, 2011).Over the years, several initiatives have been conceived by the government of Nigeria and other agencies to develop the ICT infrastructure so as to bridge the digital divide. Prominent among these initiatives is the licensing of the Global System for Mobile Communication (GSM) operators and Second National Operator (SNO), Public Service Network (PSNet), Nigerian Universities Network (NUNet), National Universities Commission DataBase (NUCDB) among others. There have also been massive investments in ICT infrastructure by Nigerians and non-Nigerians alike, the activities of which cover the whole country. Besides, the government of Nigeria and other agencies like the International Centre for Theoretical Physics (ICTP), Italy, NIIT, Oracle, APTECH, Microsoft, and many more, have trained thousands of professionals in ICT and related areas, to provide necessary knowledge and skills to support ICT ventures in the country.

According to the Information Economy Report – 2007/2008 (*UNCTAD*, 2008), between 2001 and 2004, the Nigerian Communications Commission (NCC) issued 523 new telecommunications licenses of various types, including many that commission companies to invest in developing parts of the physical network interconnections and exchanges. However, not all of these licenses have been fully operational and many types of licenses are held by a single company. Nigeria stands today as the most competitive fixed-line market in Africa, featuring a second national operator (SNO, Globacom) and over 80 other companies licensed to provide fixed-telephony services (Internet World Stats, 2011). A number of companies have also been licensed as GSM operators, the major ones of which are MTN, Globacom, Bharti Airtel (formerly Zain), Visafone, EMTS, M-Tel, Multi-Links, Starcomms, Reliance, M-Tel, Intercellular, etc, as well as over 100 Internet Service Providers (ISPs) and VSAT companies.

Despite these massive investments in ICT infrastructure and ICT-capacity building, Nigeria is still not fully connected to the Global Village, because it lacks the critical drive and strategies to harness the full potential of ICT for the socio-economic development of the country.

## ICT INDICATORS IN NIGERIA

Nigeria's population is estimated to reach 166 million people by October 31 (*Nigeria Daily News*, 2011), about 70% of whom live in underserved and remote areas of the country. It also has the fastest growing ICT market in Africa and its telecommunication penetration has improved from 400,000 connected lines in 1996 to 111.5 million in 2010. Teledensity rose dramatically from 0.4% in 1996 to 63.11% in 2010, exceeding the International Telecommunication Union's (ITU's) minimum recommendation of 1% (NCC, 2011). Nigeria has the most lucrative telecommunications market in Africa, growing at twice the African average (Odufuwa, 2006).

According to Nigerian Communications Commission Monthly Subscriber Report (May 2010 – April 2011), Nigeria's GSM subscriber base increased to 83,643,903 at the end of April, 2011, with an increase of over two million from the 81,195,684 recorded active subscriber base for the month of December, 2010. The latest results

*Table 1. Monthly Telecoms Subscriber Data, May 2010 – April 2011 (NCC, 2011)*

| | OPERATOR | Apr '10 | May '10 | Jun '10 | Jul '10 | Aug '10 | Sep '10 | Oct '10 | Nov '10 | Dec '10 | Jan '11 | Feb '11 | Mar '11 | April '11 |
|---|---|---|---|---|---|---|---|---|---|---|---|---|---|---|
| Connected Lines | Mobile (GSM) | 85,565,255 | 86,192,939 | 89,922,431 | 91,576,647 | 95,718,928 | 88,890,657 | 90,124,301 | 92,829,229 | 96,648,272 | 96,547,864 | 108,564,834 | 102,798,055 | 103,347,158 |
| | Mobile (CDMA) | 10,545,283 | 11,214,679 | 11,368,727 | 11,536,022 | 11,706,269 | 11,861,445 | 12,045,580 | 12,053,055 | 12,132,584 | 12,338,686 | 12,404,906 | 12,543,613 | 11,793,523 |
| | Fixed Wired/ Wireless | 2,561,923 | 2,665,043 | 2,689,933 | 2,708,136 | 2,722,322 | 2,743,207 | 2,745,319 | 2,749,993 | 2,736,373 | 2,741,983 | 1,619,907 | 2,762,047 | 2,162,479 |
| | ***Total*** | 98,672,461 | 100,072,661 | 103,981,091 | 105,820,805 | 110,147,519 | 103,495,309 | 104,915,200 | 107,632,277 | 111,517,229 | 114,628,533 | 122,589,647 | 118,103,715 | 117,303,160 |
| Active Lines | Mobile (GSM) | 69,649,955 | 70,838,612 | 71,819,711 | 72,772,059 | 74,074,793 | 75,362,600 | 77,455,491 | 78,927,333 | 81,195,684 | 82,618,510 | 83,453,999 | 83,857,798 | 83,643,903 |
| | Mobile (CDMA) | 7,745,377 | 7,495,078 | 6,833,911 | 6,693,970 | 6,616,457 | 6,531,021 | 6,406,514 | 6,280,675 | 6,102,105 | 6,186,442 | 6,114,669 | 6,128,661 | 5,985,163 |
| | Fixed Wired/ Wireless | 1,459,271 | 1,579,479 | 1,205,485 | 1,196,368 | 1,239,973 | 1,156,277 | 1,128,095 | 1,102,696 | 1,050,237 | 1,035,391 | 1,014,638 | 983,335 | 957,719 |
| | ***Total*** | 78,854,603 | 79,913,169 | 79,859,107 | 80,662,397 | 81,931,223 | 83,049,898 | 84,990,100 | 86,310,704 | 88,348,026 | 89,840,343 | 90,583,306 | 90,969,794 | 90,586,785 |
| Installed Capacity | Mobile (GSM) | 124,125,308 | 134,025,308 | 134,025,308 | 134,025,308 | 134,025,308 | 130,875,421 | 130,875,419 | 131,388,654 | 131,319,542 | 131,720,867 | 132,451,211 | 132,752,542 | 134,356,690 |
| | Mobile (CDMA) | 13,148,043 | 15,362,045 | 15,247,049 | 15,363,049 | 15,415,597 | 17,077,076 | 17,146,554 | 17,146,555 | 17,172,670 | 17,187,721 | 17,187,725 | 17,232,725 | 17,232,725 |
| | Fixed Wired/ Wireless | 9,327,586 | 9,311,984 | 10,831,307 | 9,314,971 | 9,315,277 | 9,314,042 | 9,335,743 | 9,340,745 | 9,347,771 | 9,348,271 | 9,351,109 | 9,351,108 | 9,351,108 |
| | Total | 146,600,937 | 158,699,337 | 160,103,664 | 158,703,328 | 158,756,182 | 157,266,539 | 157,357,716 | 157,875,954 | 157,839,983 | 158,256,859 | 158,990,045 | 159,336,375 | 160,940,523 |
| | ***Teledensity*** | 56.32 | 57.08 | 57.04 | 57.62 | 58.52 | 59.32 | 60.71 | 61.65 | 63.11 | 64.17 | 64.70 | 64.98 | 64.70 |

*Table 2. Telecoms subscriber data from 2001 – 2010 (NCC, 2011)*

| | OPERATOR | 2001 | 2002 | 2003 | 2004 | 2005 | 2006 | 2007 | 2008 | 2009 | 2010 |
|---|---|---|---|---|---|---|---|---|---|---|---|
| Connected Lines | Mobile (GSM) | 266,461 | 1,569,050 | 3,149,472 | 9,174,209 | 18,295,896 | 32,184,861 | N/A | N/A | N/A | 96,684,272 |
| | Mobile (CDMA) | N/A | N/A | N/A | N/A | N/A | N/A | N/A | N/A | N/A | 12,132,584 |
| | Fixed Wired/ Wireless | 600,321 | 702,000 | 872,473 | 1,027,519 | 1,223,258 | 1,673,161 | N/A | N/A | N/A | 2,736,373 |
| | **Total** | **866,782** | **2,271,050** | **4,021,945** | **10,201,728** | **19,519,154** | **33,858,022** | **N/A** | **N/A** | **N/A** | **111,517,229** |
| Active Lines | Mobile (GSM) | N/A | N/A | N/A | N/A | N/A | N/A | 40,011,296 | 56,935,985 | 65,533,875 | 81,195,684 |
| | Mobile (CDMA) | N/A | N/A | N/A | N/A | N/A | N/A | 384,315 | 6,052,507 | 7,565,435 | 6,102,105 |
| | Fixed Wired/ Wireless | N/A | N/A | N/A | N/A | N/A | N/A | 1,579,664 | 1,307,625 | 1,418,954 | 1,050,237 |
| | **Total** | **N/A** | **N/A** | **N/A** | **N/A** | **N/A** | **N/A** | **41,975,275** | **64,296,117** | **74,518,264** | **88,348,026** |
| Installed Capacity | Mobile (GSM) | N/A | N/A | N/A | N/A | N/A | N/A | 76,545,308 | 95,291,096 | 121,785,526 | 131,319,542 |
| | Mobile (CDMA) | N/A | N/A | N/A | N/A | N/A | N/A | 1,540,000 | 10,611,867 | 14,829,931 | 17,172,670 |
| | Fixed Wired/ Wireless | N/A | N/A | N/A | N/A | N/A | N/A | 6,578,303 | 6,830,245 | 9,388,145 | 9,347,771 |
| | **Total** | **N/A** | **N/A** | **N/A** | **N/A** | **N/A** | **N/A** | **84,663,611** | **112,733,208** | **146,003,602** | **157,839,983** |
| | ***Teledensity*** | 0.73[2] | 1.89 | 3.35 | 8.5 | 16.27 | 24.18 | 29.98[3] | 45.93 | 53.23 | 63.11 |

1. Teledensity was calculated based on population estimate of 126 million up till December 2005; from December 2006, teledensity was based on a population estimate of 140 million.

2. Teledensity from December 2001 to 2006 was based on connected subscribers.

3. Teledensity from December 2007 is based on active subscribers.

posted on the website of the Nigerian Communications Commission (NCC) also showed that teledensity has also increased to 64.70% from 63.11% recorded at the end of December, 2010 (NCC 2011).

Subscribers' base in the country has continued to increase since 2001 when the GSM technology was introduced. The teledensity ratio, which was 0.73% in 2001, has steadily increased over the years till it hit the 64.70% in April 2011. A breakdown of the data showed that the total active subscriber base increased from 88,348,026 in December 2010 to 90,586,785 in April 2011. Out of this total, GSM recorded 83,643,903 active lines, mobile CDMA 5,985,163 and fixed wired/wireless 957,719. Still comparing with December 2010, total installed capacity also increased to 160,940,523 from 157,839,983 with mobile GSM also the highest with 134,356,690, mobile CDMA 17,232,725, and fixed wired/wireless 9,351,108. Table 1 shows NCC Monthly subscriber data (May 2010 – April 2011).

Over the years, since the introduction of the GSM technology, subscriber base has consistently showed increases quarter by quarter and year by year. Table 2 shows the NCC published subscriber information from 2001 to 2010, while Figure 1 is a chart showing Nigeria's teledensity from the same period.

In spite of this obvious and significant progress, Nigeria's performance on a global scale is still far behind countries like Sweden, which has 100% access. For example, on the global Digital Opportunity Index, as at 2006, Nigeria ranked 155$^{th}$, with an index of 0.17, South Africa ranked 86$^{th}$ with an index of 0.42 and a country like Namibia ranked 113$^{th}$ with an index of 0.35 (WISR, 2007). In the global ICT Diffusion Ranking, Nigeria ranked 161$^{st}$, staying in the same lower ranks as Ethiopia at 146$^{th}$, Senegal at 149$^{th}$ and

*Figure 1. Nigeria's Teledensity Chart from 2001 –2010*

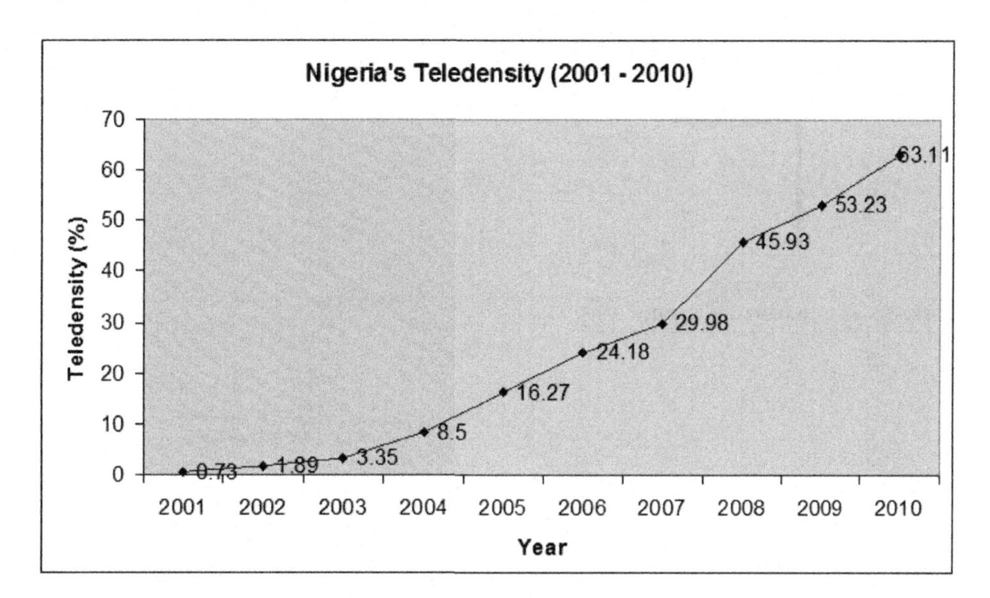


Mali at 157th (*UNCTAD*, 2005). In the global ICT Development Index 2008, Nigeria ranked 122nd behind Kenya (121st), Ghana (116th) and Gabon (113th), respectively (*ITU*, 2010). In the global networked readiness index 2009 – 2010, Nigeria ranked 99th behind Ghana, Zambia and Mali respectively (World Economic Forum, 2010).

## ICT INFRASTRUCTURE FOR EDUCATION, RESEARCH AND DEVELOPMENT

The high subscription and infrastructure costs, coupled with the poor quality of service by service providers at inception was a major hindrance to the use of ICT in education, research and development in Nigeria. To create an enabling environment for the use of ICT, foster information exchange among local scientists, and facilitate the interactions and collaboration between researchers in Nigerian institutions and their counterparts across the globe, so many initiatives had been put in place.

### Nigerian Universities Network (NUNet) Project

The National Universities Commission (NUC) started to plan an electronic communication network for Nigerian Universities on 16th October 1994, when a Committee was constituted to study the feasibility of introducing Email services.

At its conception in 1995, the Nigerian Universities Network (NUNet) was designed on the one hand to facilitate dial-up email connectivity between the National Universities Commission, NUC, and all Federally-owned universities and Inter-Universities Centres and between the Nigerian University System (NUC, Federal and State Universities and Inter-Universities Centres and other tertiary Institutions) and the outside world on the other hand using the Internet infrastructure. Figure 2 shows the initial setup of NUNet.

To achieve this, a MoU was entered into with the International Centre for Theoretical Physics (ICTP), Trieste, Italy in 1996, to:

*Figure 2. Initial setup of NUNet (NUC, 2008)*

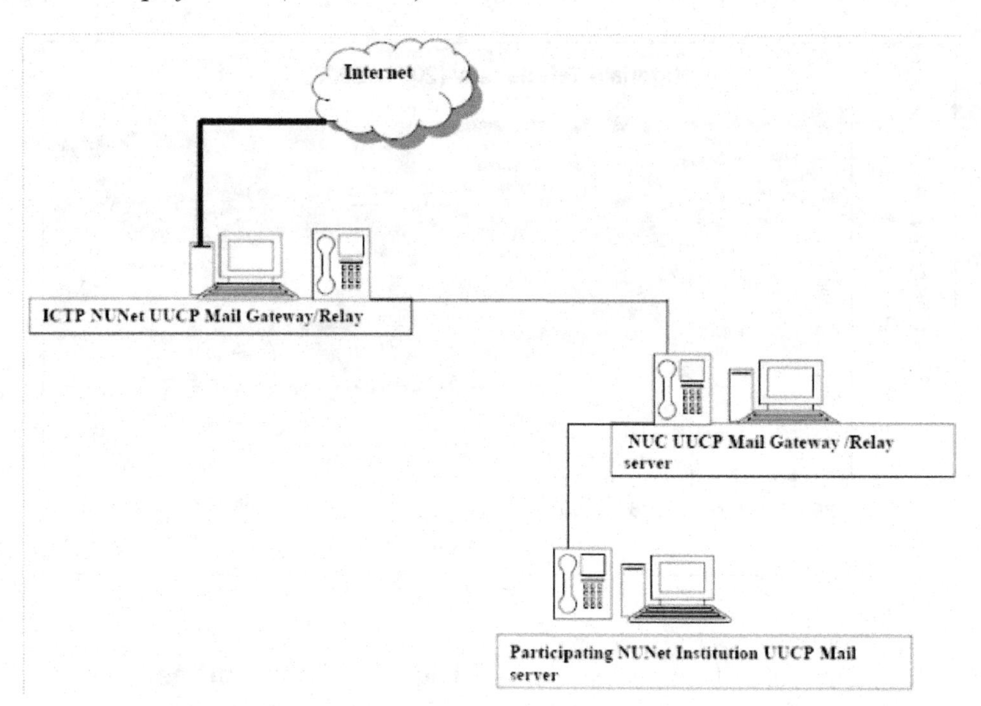


- Assist in registering domain names for the NUC and all the Federal Universities and Inter-universities centres;
- To serve as the Mail eXchanger and relay for these institutions, and
- To train Network and system administrators on Linux system and network administration.

Under this arrangement, dial-up UUCP mail servers on Linux boxes were installed at each of the initial 29 participating NUNet institutions and configured to periodically (at least 3 times daily) dial into the UUCP Email-gateway at the National Universities Commission secretariat in Abuja to forward and retrieve respective institutional mails using UUCP's "Store and Forward" mechanism. The Email-gateway at the NUC on its part was configured to periodically dial into the NUNet UUCP mail server at the ICTP, forwarding and retrieving NUNet mails.

In 2000, when the NUC acquired its own VSAT, the Email-gateways at the NUC and ICTP were reconfigured to relay outgoing and incoming NUNet mails between themselves via the VSAT link. Since then, a majority of the federally-owned universities have also deployed their own VSAT earth stations but not many of them locally host their DNS, web and SMTP web mail servers. Figure 3 shows this setup.

Wonderful as the vision of the NUNet project was, the fact that the only service provided was email, created problems for the project. Moreover, the increasing deployment of VSATs by institutions drastically reduced the institutional user-base of NUNet. At the same time, the availability of free web-based mail services and lack of intranet services in the universities has hindered the building of true network communities even within the institutions, so that most campus networks are really not more than cybercafés (Ibrahim, 2004).

*Figure 3. The NUNet topology at the inception of VSAT (Source: NUC, 2008)*

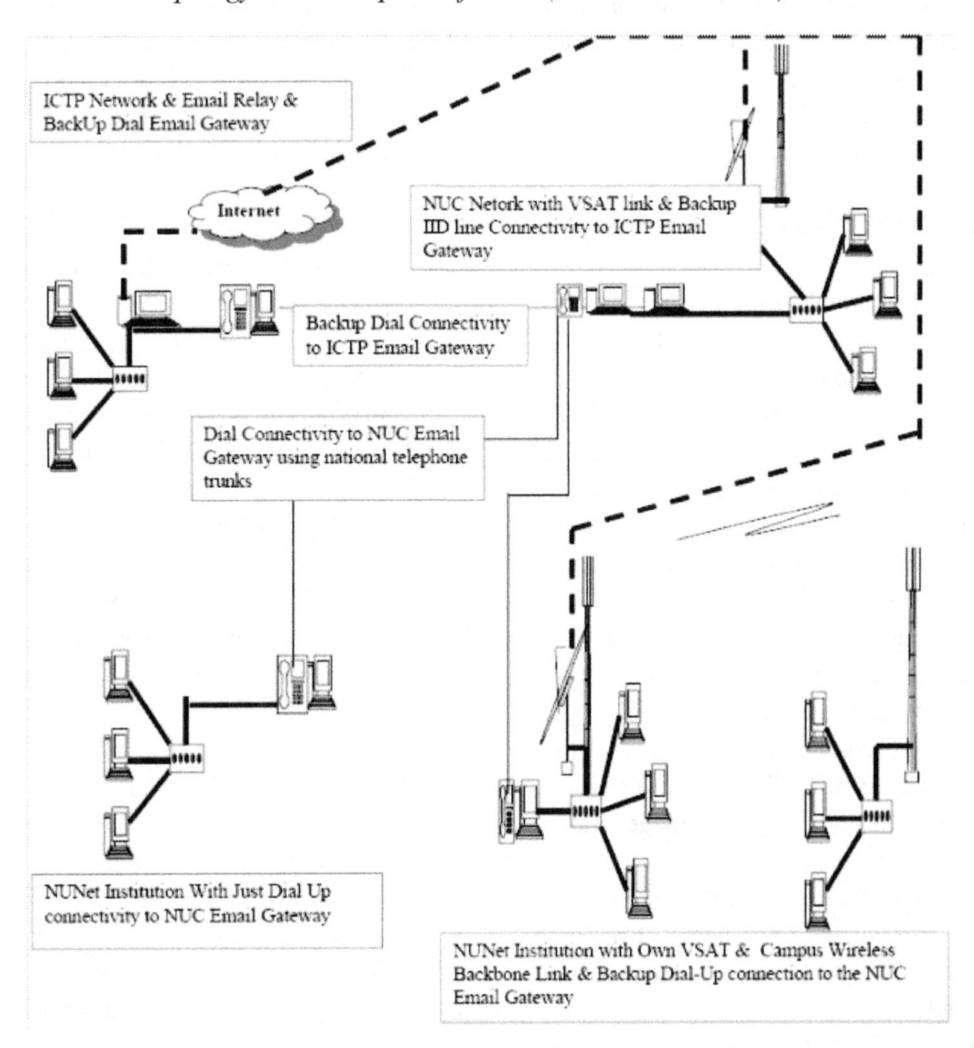


## NUCDB Project

The NUCDB (National Universities Commission Data Base) project was launched as a pilot in some Nigerian universities in 2008. It was designed to capture and process information of all Nigerian university students (past and present) in a format that will contain all students' personal information such as names, gender, photograph, date of birth, next-of-kin, parental/guardian information, among others. This format would also contain previous and present academic records, to allow for retrieval of academic history for future use by the students or interested bodies.

The project is also meant to assist in government planning, especially in the distribution of research aids and allocation of resources to each university. The complete application would enable NUC to enforce and check some of its educational policies like the "Student to Lecturer Ratio minimum standard". With the information, NUC could give accurate analysis of the comparative performance of students in all universities in Nigeria. Also corporate organisations and individuals can use the service as a search platform. Reference could be made easily on students or graduates that meet a required standard that qualifies them for particular positions or entitlement. It is worth of note that the NUCDB is still undergoing lots of refinements, even as it has been deployed in a number of universities in Nigeria (NUC, 2011). The project when fully completed will yield the following outcomes:

- A centralized, updated and replicated data repository;
- Capture and storage of biometric information of current students and all classes of university personnel;
- Failsafe, triple network-backbone, and Internet infrastructure that co-ordinates data capture and gathering at the NUC and the universities;
- Standardized students record and students result processing;
- Uniform grade point average system;
- Complete academic records for Nigerian university graduates;
- Complete personnel (academic and non academic) records for Nigerian universities;
- Automated standard transcript generation system for each university;
- Provision of academic staff web portal for online storage and referencing of research works, thesis, lecturers, academic papers, etc; and
- Provision of analytical, reporting and other rich information for government planning agencies.

## Public Service Network (PSNet)

This project, conceived by National Information Technology Development Agency (NITDA), is to address the major problem of ICT infrastructure, and to serve as a pipeline for ICT services in the Nigerian Public Service. PSNet involves the development of a National Information Backbone (NIB) for IT development in Nigeria. It is designed to form the bedrock of other technology initiatives in the country. Its vision is to provide standard best effort IP end-to-end service and offer premium mega end-to-end IP service with richer deployment of e-governance. Thus, scalability is key in its implementation (see Figure 4).

This project is ongoing and involves the deployment of:

1. A VSAT hub at NITDA's head office.
2. Wireless Hot spot in Abuja Federal Public Service (comprising Wi-Fi for phases I, II and III of the federal secretariat complex).
3. Interconnection of the above-mentioned three buildings using fibre optic cables.
4. VSAT Remote terminals in 36 states (15 states are already covered as at 2007).
5. Broad band wireless extensions in 27 states.
6. Routing and switching facilities at NITDA's Head office for the 36 states.
7. Collaboration applications video conferencing, messaging, distance learning, security, etc.

The central hub will ensure:

- Central and efficient management of bandwidth, nationwide.
- Low cost single point of interconnect to states and federal public service.
- Central consolidation for the integration of services.
- Makes for seamless integration of other IT-based programmes of the government including: Rural Internet Access, Video Conferencing, Messaging, Distance Learning, Security, etc.

Deliverables of the PSNet:

- Internet access.
- Messaging, collaboration and virtual private network.
- Switching and routing (traffic prioritizing).
- The PSNet will provide the much desired backbone infrastructure upon which e-government applications would be driven.

*Figure 4. Layout of PSNet (NITDA, 2011)*

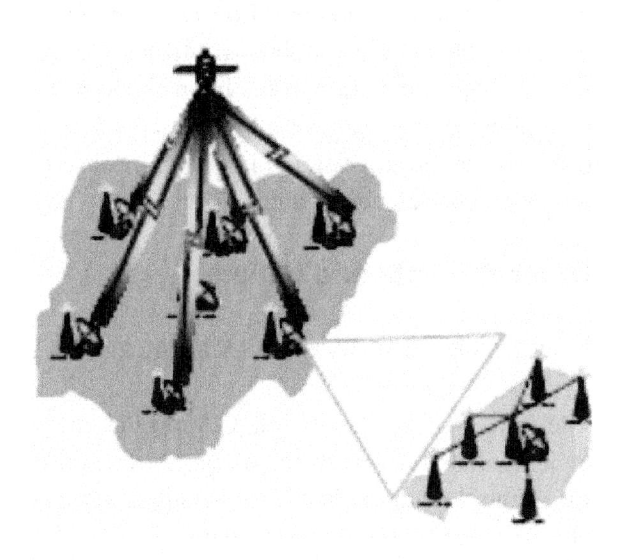

- It also will facilitate the optimal functioning and better interaction of all the institutions attached to the three major wings of government (Executive, Legislature and Judiciary).

Through this project, internet connectivity is already being provided to the Presidential Villa, National Planning Commission, and federal ministries of Finance; and Science and Technology, amongst others, in Abuja. Some are also being assisted in the development of their websites in order to have online presence. PSNet is currently operational in 15 states. Some of the states have even set up their Ministries of Science and Technology or Information Technology Units/Departments under the supervision of their respective Governors' offices (*NITDA*, 2011).

## Computers for All Nigerians Initiative (CANI)

The aim of this initiative is to improve Nigerians' access to computer hardware. It includes a funding mechanism whereby civil servants will be able to purchase computers and pay back the loan at a low rate of interest. Launched in July 2006, Computers for All Nigerians Initiative is a typical example of a public-private partnership. It is being coordinated by NITDA and involves Microsoft, Zinox and Omatek. Related to the initiative is a Petroleum Technology Development Fund (PTDF) plan to build and equip computer centres in higher educational institutions across Nigeria. However, this plan does not include internet access (*GISW*, 2007).

## National Rural Telephony Project (NRTP)

The NRTP was expected to provide 500,000 connected lines to 343 local governments in Nigeria within one year. In 2003, the Federal Government of Nigeria accessed credit from the World Bank's International Development Association (IDA), and a part of the funds obtained was to be set aside to improve national teledensity, as well as to step up telecommunication penetration in rural areas. The government also signed a memorandum of understanding (MoU) with the Peoples Republic of China, supported by a concessionary loan of USD 200 million for the NRTP. The project was to be executed in two phases by Alcatel-Shangai and ZTE. However, the project was only flagged off in August 2004. The Ministry of Communications, the supervising agency, reports that implementation is currently ongoing, although at a slow pace, in some targeted local government headquarters in Nigeria. The project is expected to combine with the Universal Service Provision Fund (USPF) to offer concessionary licensing for the providers (*GISW*, 2007).

## The Digital Bridge Institute (DBI)

The growth of the number of skilled manpower in the telecommunication industry over the years has been remarkable. The NCC took certain timely initiatives to ensure that the dearth of skilled Nigerians to run the fast expanding telecommunication industry in the country was remedied. A milestone was achieved on May 20, 2004 when the then Nigerian President, Olusegun Obasanjo commissioned an ultra modern Digital Bridge Institute (DBI) in Abuja – Nigeria, established by the NCC as an international centre for advanced telecommunication studies.

The DBI, as it is today, offers world-class training aimed at maintaining the highest standards within the dynamic ICT industry in Nigeria. The programmes are designed to be directly relevant to current business, technical, managerial and commercial operations with emphasis on "best practices" world-wide. With two more campuses (Lagos and Kano), the Institute now has ultra-modern facilities which include fully equipped training rooms, multi-media teaching aids, video conference facilities, WiFi Hotspot, a Telecom Laboratory and Digital Resource Library, guaranteeing a cutting-edge learning experience. Since 2004, the Institute has trained about 4,000 telecom professionals who are engaged in diverse sectors of the Nigerian economy (*DBI*, 2011).

## Mobile Internet Unit (MIU) Project

A project of NITDA, the Mobile Internet Unit (MIU) is a locally made bus that has been converted into a mobile training and cyber center. Its interior has 10 high-tech workstations all networked and connected to the Internet to facilitate access to several IT resources. It is equipped with printers, a photocopier and a number of multi-media facilities. Internet access is provided via a VSAT equipment with a 1.2m dish mounted on the roof of the bus. It was commissioned on 10th September, 2003, by the then President, Olusegun Obasanjo.

The unit is also equipped with a small generator to ensure regular power supply. The MIU provides everything anyone needs in a high-tech cyber centre and it has the added advantage of being mobile. It takes the Internet to places that have no other means of access such as the rural areas. It has also been deployed to various schools (primary and secondary) and the plan is to get all states and possibly Local Government Areas (LGAs) to have their own MIUs so as to facilitate the penetration of the Internet and ICT around the country (Ajayi, 2003). Figures 5 and 6 show both the exterior and interior portions of a typical mobile internet unit.

## Other Projects and Initiatives

### Universities Bandwidth Consortium

The Universities Bandwidth Consortium is a major collaborative project of the Partnership for Higher Education in Africa, an initiative that began in 2000 to build on momentum within Africa to revitalize institutions of higher education, especially the universities. The foundations – *initially Ford, MacArthur, Rockefeller, and Carnegie Corporation of New York* – invested more than $150 million USD in Partnership projects as of September 2005. as at 2010, the foundations, now joined by the William and Flora Hewlett Foundation, the Andrew W. Mellon Foundation, and the Kresge Foundation have invested an additional $200 million USD.

*Figure 5: Mobile Internet Unit bus (exterior)*

Bandwidth is a major expense for African universities, with major service currently provided by a few providers. According to a report prepared by the Bandwidth Consortium of the Partnership for Higher Education in Africa, consumers in Europe and North America typically pay $100 USD a month or less for far more bandwidth than African universities obtain for $10,000 USD per month (Bandwidth Consortium, 2011). This has drastically affected online presence for African universities, as well as affected their ranking with universities in other continents.

### National Virtual Library Project

The National Virtual Library Project was established in 2001 as one of the several strategies devised to bolster the quality of teaching and learning in Nigerian schools. A virtual library provides access to tools such as databases, electronic journals, alerting services, electronic reference, and quality-vetted e-resources. The NUC was shouldered with the task of building a National Virtual Library Project that would enhance access to locally-available resources and international library collections for sharing with university libraries all over Nigeria using digital technology (Gbaje, 2007). Other functions of the National Virtual Library Project as cited by NUC are:

- To improve the quality of teaching and research in institutions of higher learning in Nigeria through the provision of current books, journals and other library resources;
- To enhance access to academic libraries serving the education community in Nigeria to global library and information resources;
- To enhance scholarship, research and lifelong learning through the establishment of permanent access to shared digital archival collections;
- To provide guidance for academic libraries on applying appropriate technologies used in the production of digital library resources; and
- To advance the use and usability of globally distributed, networked information resources.

Unfortunately, several years after the project was launched, the Virtual Library project is yet to be fully operational. As such, none of the functions set out has been achieved. A number of studies are being conducted to forge a way forward for the project in terms deployment and sustainability (Gbaje, 2007).

## ICT ORGANIZATIONS

### National Information Technology Development Agency (NITDA)

NITDA was set up by the Federal Government on 18th April 2001 to ensure the implementation of the National Information Technology (IT) Policy and to coordinate and regulate the development and regulation of the Information Technology sector. NITDA's mandate is diverse and vast, but all their responsibilities fall under the aegis of fostering the development and growth of IT in Nigeria.

In an effort to ensure that the implementation of the IT policy proceeds with maximum effectiveness, NITDA regulates, monitors, evaluates, and verifies progress on an on-going basis under the supervision and coordination of the Federal Ministry of Science and Technology (*NITDA*, 2011).

### Computer Professionals (Registration Council of Nigeria) – CPN

The Computer Professionals Registration Council of Nigeria was established on the 10th of June,

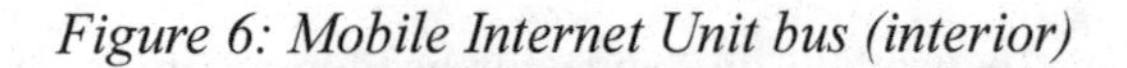

Figure 6: Mobile Internet Unit bus (interior)

1993 with a core responsibility of advancing in Nigeria the knowledge of computer science and the use of computational machinery and techniques related thereto.

## Nigerian Computer Society - NCS

The Nigerian Computer Society, NCS, is a society for Nigerians around the world in the Information Technology industry, from students to professionals. The aims of the Society include:

- Bringing together Nigerians around the globe working or interested in computer technology;
- Promoting computer and internet technologies within Nigeria;
- Promoting a forum for technology development and utilization in Nigeria;
- Helping businesses and government agencies in Nigeria better understand the benefits of today's technologies and prepare for tomorrow's advances;
- Providing an independent forum for discussion on the provision and implementation of a robust, scaleable and secure Internet infrastructure in Nigeria;
- Supporting and encouraging IT in Nigeria;
- Providing an online learning and development knowledge base accessible to all Nigerians, Ensuring that all Nigerians within Nigeria have access to computers and the Internet.

## CHALLENGES, OPPORTUNITIES AND POTENTIALS

The government's role in creating an enabling environment has faced considerable challenges, despite support by pan-African bodies like the UN Economic Commission for Africa (UNECA), with its National Information and Communication Infrastructure (NICI) process, and the New Partnership for Africa's Development (NEPAD), with its eSchools Initiative. The National Information Technology Development Agency (NITDA), which is charged with implementing ICT policy, began to work with UNECA on the country's NICI process in March 2000. While a draft ICT policy has been produced by NITDA, it has yet to be fully operational.

A Presidential Task Force on ICT Harmonization was inaugurated in August 2006. Its job is to examine the duplication of efforts and absence of cross-sectoral convergence in the government's ICT strategies. Various sub-committees have prepared reports, but it appears that their efforts have been overtaken by an unexpected announcement in December 2006 by the Federal Executive Council that several of the 27 government ministries have been merged, reducing the total number to 19. The merger of the ministries has also impacted negatively on the work of a team of Nigerian experts that has been drafting a strategic plan for 2005 to 2008, with support from an UNECA consultant. It was hoped the plan would streamline the various ICT initiatives in the country.

Another challenge facing the development of the full potential of ICT for education, research and development in Nigeria is the lack of a truly enabling environment and a sound ICT roadmap and strategies by policy makers resulting in unsustainable ICT development activities. Other challenges include:

- High running and subscription costs
- Identification of information sources that meet the needs of users
- Poor Quality of Service (QoS) of the Internet and Telecommunication services
- Regulatory issues
- High cost of hardware
- Effective management of network traffic and infrastructure.

The solution strategy for fully bridging the digital divide requires an aggressive human capacity building in ICT through training, in collaboration with local and international institutions. The capacities of relevant institutions must be strengthened and research and development must be demand-driven, focusing on the provision of products to meet local needs.

To develop and utilize the full potential of ICT in Nigeria, there is need to setup an effective ICT taskforce with representatives from all stakeholders to:

- Assist policy-makers in the formulation of sustainable ICT programmes-roadmap;
- Manage and coordinate the activities of the research and educational network;
- Develop innovative ideas for the efficient utilization of ICT infrastructure (example, distance education and virtual libraries & laboratories for teaching and research);
- To provide training in the use of new ICT-based tools, and
- To promote the use of cost-effective ICT technologies such as open source and wireless technologies.

Finally, regulatory authorities have a crucial role to play in the development and strengthening of the ICT industry. Governments of developing countries should support the establishment and development of regulatory environments that provide mobile firms, investors and consumers with the confidence and trust that will facilitate ICT-enabled development and its positive implications for overall economic development.

## CONCLUSION

Information and communications technology has become one of the most evasive phenomena in modern history. It is now the driving force and catalyst for the development of modern economies. No country can effectively participate in the new global economy without a formidable ICT base. It is this consciousness that has informed all the ICT projects and policies initiated by Nigeria as presented in this paper even though some of the actions seem to be slow.

The challenges facing the full implementation of ICT for education, research and development in Nigeria notwithstanding, Nigeria still holds promise to lead Africa in ICT, especially with the large market available.

## REFERENCES

Ajayi, G. O. (2003). *NITDA and ICT in Nigeria. Developing Countries Access to Digital Knowledge*. Trieste, Italy: ICTP.

Bandwidth Consortium. (2011). Retrieved from http://www.foundation-partnership.org/

DBI. (2011). Digital Bridge Institute. Retrieved from http://www.dbieducation.org/

Gbaje, E. S. (2007). Implementing a National Virtual Library for Higher Institutions in Nigeria. *Library and Information Science Research Electronic Journal, 17*(2), 1–15.

GISW. (2007). Global Information Society Watch. Retrieved from: www.giswatch.org/

Ibrahim, A. (2004). *NUNet topology and connectivity.* Abuja,Nigeria: National Universities Commission Internet World Stats. (2011). Retrieved from http://www.internetworldstats.com/af/ng.htm

ITU. (2010). *Measuring the Information Society*. Geneva, Switzerland: International Telecommunication Union NCC (2011). Quarterly summary of Telecom Subscribers in Nigeria. Retrieved from http://www.ncc.gov.ng/industrystatistics/subscriberdata_files/Subscriber_Quarterly_Summary_201006-201103.pdf

NCC. (2011). Subscriber Data 2001 - 2010. Retrieved from http://www.ncc.gov.ng/subscriberdata.htm

Nigeria Daily News. (2011). Retrieved from http://www.nigeriadailynews.com/latest-additions/23879-nigeria%E2%80%99s-population-to-hit-166-million-by-october,-says-npc.html

NITDA. (2011). National Information Technology Development Agency. Retrieved from http://www.nitda.gov.ng/

NUC. (2008). National Universities Commission. Retrieved from: http://www.nuc.edu.ng

NUC. (2011). National Universities Commission Data Base. Retrieved from http://www.nucdb.com/

Odufuwa, Fola (2006). *Nigeria ICT Outlook and Forecasts. Lagos, Nigeria:* eShekels Limited.

UNCTAD. (2005). *Information Economy Report*. New York, NY: United Nations Conference on Trade and Development.

UNCTAD. (2008). *Information Economy Report*. New York, NY: United Nations Conference on Trade and Development

# Chapter 2
# Digital Divide and Disadvantaged Populations in E-Tourism

**Billy Yfantis**
*University of the West of Scotland, UK*

**Abel Usoro**
*University of the West of Scotland, UK*

**Dimitris Tseles**
*Technological Education Institute of Piraeus, Greece*

## ABSTRACT

*The tourism sector has changed rapidly since the dawn of the internet revolution in the late 1990s. At the same time, the digital divide has disadvantaged many in developing economies as well as the disabled population. It is interesting to observe, however, that the emerging computer technologies, especially mobile computing, are offering significant opportunities to this disadvantaged population. This chapter discusses these opportunities that increase the participation in and reaping of benefits from tourism.*

## INTRODUCTION TO E-TOURISM

Compared to previous years, the current political and economic situation in the world has changed tourists' habits considerably. After the late 1990's, the progression and exploration of the internet has offered tourists a valuable virtual friend which has enabled them to receive more information regarding availability of services and prices that meet their individual needs (a detailed research in www.go-online.gr (2010)). The obvious difference from the pre-internet age is that the consumer now has direct contact with the tourist product producer and less intermediaries exist (Walle, 1996). Therefore the initial cost of travel goes down and the consumer has more choices available to her, being able to customize the whole travel experience (Livi, 2008).

DOI: 10.4018/978-1-4666-1637-0.ch002

Internet penetration differs from country to country and it depends on various social and political factors which impact on the citizen's access and effective use of technology with increased expected benefits to society (Xiaoming & Chow, 2004). The development of new technologies is growing at a faster rate than in the past and therefore traditional travel agencies must realize the importance of this change and adjust their philosophy accordingly to meet the needs of the new smart consumer who uses efficient technology (Swarbrooke and Horner, 1999).

The digital customer is more demanding now due to the fact that the customer is able to gather a greater amount of information which includes product availability in less time with the help of the internet. So she[1] is able to adjust her consumer buying behavior through the power of information she now owns. The comparison of prices, the customized holidays, the research through tourist travel agencies, online bids for holiday packages and information on people's travel experiences through blogs and social networking are a few of the important tools that the customer owns and uses to change (though often unconsciously) the way that the competition now operates.

The latest technologies have greatly influenced the nature of E-Tourism (Buhalis, 2003). Broadband internet connections with fast speeds have impacted the power of information which the customer finds available. The power of information depends on the quality and the quantity and these values increase as the speed of the transferred internet data increases. Moreover users are now having access in streaming sound and video which significantly affect the buying decision (Langer, 2002).

Other technologies which have helped E-Tourism progress are the wireless connections and the Wi-Fi networks. The wireless networks have helped the implementation of communication between customers and companies in any place around the world without any limitations. Wi-Fi has been very popular due to the introduction of mobile computing as a solution to use your computer facilities anytime and anywhere (Reza, 2005).

The three elements of mobile computing are ("Mobile Computing", 2010):

- Communication: Access of a network or other communication partners without a wire because it is replaced by electromagnetic waves (Schiller, 2003).
- Devices: The variety of mobile devices that exist and have access in wireless networks.
- Applications: Applications that run partially or completely on mobile devices (Amjad, 2004).

The mobile nature of computer science has been very useful for human mobility (Kim, 2001) especially when people move from one place to the other for tourism. As the years go by and public network technologies progress at a faster rate, there is an increased quantity of information exchanged between people.

## DISADVANTAGED POPULATIONS DEFINITION

The term, 'disadvantaged populations', describes the groups of people that have been denied access to the tools needed for self sufficiency. The topics that feature here are autonomy, incentive, responsibility, self respect, health, education, information, employment, capital and much more (Mayer, 2003). Self sufficiency describes the state that the human survival depends only on personal soft or hard skills and not on external factors such as support or other kinds of help. The prevention from the self sufficiency goal is usually caused by the lack of availability or low access to specific resources. The resources needed from the disadvantaged population in order to adopt self sufficiency are (Mayer, 2003):

1. Autonomy or non-dependence: Autonomy is described as the opportunity of a social group to act according to their will and be free to express themselves through their activities.
2. Incentive for development: This means that the social groups have to keep on believing that their dreams will come true and their mission will be fulfilled. They actually require a trigger which will boost their effort and cause them to try harder for personal development.
3. Decision-making responsibility: The groups should contribute within the democratic processes that leads to decision making, as this will help them to feel empowered from feeling empowered, giving them a sense of responsibility for their own lives.
4. Self-respect: People need to respect their own entity because if they respect themselves they are able to respect society and offer their knowledge towards the progress of society. Lack of self respect can prevent them from being powerful enough to offer their effort in life.
5. Community of support: Community feeling unites people under the umbrella of support and care for one another. The social groups have more chances to survive by creating communities and supporting each other, than being isolated and struggling to live in the modern world.
6. Health: Quality of health is viewed as a basic factor for safe and fast access to self sufficiency because illness can be a barrier which may hold people back from having a normal life. Disabled persons face many difficulties for self sufficiency, especially in societies where disability is considered a taboo and people tend to criticize ill persons that receive medical treatment.
7. Education: The value of learning the society's culture has a positive influence on people who want to reach a level of self sufficiency. Educated persons are capable of critically reviewing their ideas and ethics, thus they become more tolerant towards the society and fight for what they believe in.
8. Information: Awareness of information is related to the power of knowledge, as well informed people tend to adopt the knowhow of success and they are able to maintain a better quality of daily life.
9. Employment: A person in employment often feels a sense of security and is better equipped to plan for the future. When the job is promising and career oriented, additional advantages exist such as freedom of choice, spiritual satisfaction and joy.
10. Capital: Financial security tends to protect people from poverty and offers them more opportunities for a happier life than just to satisfy the basic needs of survival. Capital is the means to reach the level of hoping for the next goal unless an emotional or health barrier prevents one from that.
11. Responsive support systems: These are the systems which can support societies and give them access to resources of food, water, clothing, transportation and cultural activities.

The advantages of these resources prevent someone from being disadvantaged but in order to implement the adoption of these resources, social groups have to adjust each resource according to their culture. The diversity of cultures among the different social groups may act as a barrier to self sufficiency as each group has different beliefs and thought patterns according to factors such as sex and race.

## DIGITAL DIVIDE AND DISADVANTAGED POPULATIONS

E-Tourism depends on access and use of technology which significantly influences the progression and new trends of the tourist world (Werthner & Klein, 1999), information and communication technologies have been used as the medium to establish connection between the tourist production and the clients in an efficient way with less cost and time (Minghetti & Buhalis, 2009). During all the stages of the tourist product life cycle from the producer's side, technology delivers quicker entrance to the market through broadband connections, greater awareness through the electronic word of mouth and even a potentiality for sustainable tourist products through the use of technology (Edgell, 2006). From the client's perspective, information and communication technology provides the client with more opportunities to choose her travel arrangements among producers with different prices and different product options. Moreover, sometimes she is able to customize her preference after a direct electronic contact with the producer. It is obvious that due to these reasons, technology broadens the value and size of existing tourists markets as both clients and producers benefit from this sector (Buhalis, 1999).

Emerging economies such as exist in Africa have great potentials for E-Tourism. However, achieving E-Tourism in these economies which are characterized by the digital divide is challenging. According to the organization of E-tourism Frontiers ("What We are All About", 2010), 2% of all travel is the total online business for the African online booking because there are not enough African websites that are into online booking. Also there is no African inventory in the worldwide travel websites.

In 2008, the first ever E-Tourism conference for Kenya, held in Nairobi, drew the attention of about 150 managers from the tourism and IT sectors. The Minister for Information and Communication of Kenya, Hon. Mutahi Kagwe, stated that the real threat to the long term sustainability of the country's tourism sector is the failure to invest in and compete with technology. Kenya's competitors are taking advantage of online communication in E-Tourism, so the country is going to be left behind unless they embrace the new technologies (Mutahi Kagwe, 2008).

In Uganda, tourism is one of the main sectors for the financial growth of the country because of the wild life and the existence of rare species of gorillas. The problem in Uganda is lack of technology and the inefficient use of internet by the web viewers or even the dearth of webmasters (Baguma, 2007). In 2009, an E-Tourism conference was held in Uganda with very important visitors from the tourism industry. Moses Mapesa, the Executive Director of the Ugandan Wildlife Authority, said in the Observer newspaper that Uganda has internet connection in almost all of the country's national parks but the problem for the staff is how to use it. Also he added that the conference would be a great opportunity to learn how to use the internet and make the tourist attractions visible (Mapesa, 2009).

Despite the great importance of technology in E-Tourism, the availability, access and use of technology in a worldwide level differ from country to country. The whole phenomenon has been termed as the digital divide by experts and according to Wikipedia (2010) is defined as: "The gap between people with effective access to digital and information technology and those with very limited or no access at all. It includes the imbalance both in the physical access to technology and the resources and skills needed to effectively participate as a digital citizen."

According to a recent research from Miniwatts Marketing Group regarding Asia's Internet Usage and Population ("Internet Usage in Asia", 2010) we can view this imbalance between developed and emerging countries in the region of Asia. For instance Bangladesh that has an estimated population of 158,065,841 people in 2010, was found in 2010, to have 617,300 internet users exist with internet penetration of 0.4%. In comparison, Hong Kong which is a smaller country with an estimated population of 7,089,705 citizens, presents a significant number of 4,878,713 users and 68.8% internet penetration (refer to Table 1).

*Table 1. Asia's internet usage and population (source: Miniwatts Marketing Group).*

| ASIA - INTERNET USAGE AND POPULATION | | | | | | |
|---|---|---|---|---|---|---|
| **ASIA** | **Population (2010 estimate)** | **Internet Users (Year 2000)** | **Internet Users Feb 2011** | **Penetration (% Population)** | **User Growth (2000-2010)** | **% Users in Asia** |
| **Bangladesh** | 158,065,841 | 100,000 | **617,300** | 0.4% | 517.3% | 0.1% |
| **Hong Kong** | 7,089,705 | 2,283,000 | **4,878,713** | 68.8% | 113.7% | 0.6% |

*Table 2. Africa's internet usage and population (source: Miniwatts Marketing Group).*

| AFRICA - INTERNET USAGE AND POPULATION | | | | | | |
|---|---|---|---|---|---|---|
| **AFRICA** | **Population (2010 estimate)** | **Internet Users Dec 2000** | **Internet Users Feb 2011** | **Penetration (% Population)** | **User Growth (2000-2010)** | **% Users in Africa** |
| **Nigeria** | 152,217,341 | 200,000 | **43,982,200** | 28.9% | 21,891.1% | 39.6% |
| **Reunion (FR)** | 822,986 | 130,000 | **300,000** | 36.5% | 130.8% | 0.3% |

The same research shows that the digital divide exists in other regions of the world such as Africa ("Internet Usage in Africa", 2010) where the statistics are more impressive and representative of the digital divide: Nigeria with a population of over 150 million people has below 45 million internet users and internet penetration of 28.9% but Reunion (FR) with an estimated population of less than 850 thousand with about 300 thousand internet users has internet penetration of 36.5% (illustrated in Table 2).

The more developed countries are in a state of possessing and using technology at a larger scale than emerging countries, so the "big brother" is responsible to help the small brother in order to have a happy and balanced family. There are various factors that affect the digital divide between countries. Some of these are:

- **Income (Norris, 2001):** e.g. The monthly salary of an individual or a family not being enough for the main needs as to have money left over to purchase a computer.
- **Education (Sallis and Jones, 2002):** e.g. Countries based on agricultural production may not believe that the technological education provides skills for future human resources.
- **Geographic location (Dutton, 2005):** e.g. Countries that are located away from hi-tech countries may remain backwards in terms of technology updates.
- **Cultural (Iskander, Kapila& Karim, 2010):** e.g. Local religious beliefs may treat technology as something against their religion.
- **Political (Chadwick, 2009):** e.g. Military governments are afraid to offer citizens access to new information through the internet so as to prevent them from expressing anti-governmental ideas.

As long as the current digital divide remains, E-Tourism suffers from a shortage of potential clients that are not able to join the e-marketplace. Moreover, the tourist destinations cannot progress their service quality and develop the local economy with new work positions availability for the new services. As the cost of buying a computer and the complex education required to use it expands the digital divide (Servon, 2002), individuals are prevented from getting into internet technology which is crucial to E-Tourism. So there is a need for a device that would minimize these issues.

The devices that seem to have more opportunities to close the digital gap are the new mobile phones that have internet access and one can do almost everything that one had previously been doing with the use of a home computer (Rainer & Cegielski, 2009). Mobile phones are increasingly being used not only for voice communication but they extend the word communication by exploring all the types of communication (video, text, file sharing, etc.) that personal computer is implementing.

According to research from Pew Research Center's Internet & American Life (Horrigan, 2009):

- One third of the Americans (32%) have used a mobile phone once to access the internet.
- On a daily basis the 19% of Americans (about one fifth) use it for their internet access.

The most important findings of this research are about the minority of African Americans in the USA that use the mobile phone for internet access (Boscov-Ellen, 2009):

- 48% of African Americans have used their mobile device at least once to access the internet.
- 29% of African Americans use their mobile phones on a daily basis to access the internet regarding personal communication or finding information. In comparison with 2007, the percentage of African Americans that use the internet on a daily basis increased by 141%.

African Americans, regardless of their lower income bracket and education penetration in comparison with White Americans have managed to eliminate the digital divide between the two populations when mobile phones are taken into account regarding internet usage. The same research was conducted in other regions such as Africa, Asia or Australia and with the same results: mobile phones tend to diminish the digital divide between developed and emerging economies.

If digital divide is preventing the tourist market to grow efficiently and the local economies to benefit from this progression, then the technology's portability through the usage of mobile phones is very close to solving the problem. People with lower income are already familiar to mobile phones because they are cheap enough to use for their daily communication, cheaper than a home computer (Banks, 2008). The fact that people are familiar with mobile phones makes them more ready to accept the change in technology and brave enough to experiment with it. Moreover, the small portable device is like a toy for them so it also adds an element of entertainment to their everyday lives.

In the past there were fights among the social classes regarding the imbalance in the share of wealth and education between the poor and the rich people. Nowadays, governments are called to solve the problem of injustice in the share of technology between the nations. This is something that is already in progress with the International Finance Corporation that has spent millions of US dollars in small countries such as the Democratic Republic of Congo, Madagascar, Malawi, Sierra Leone and Uganda. The goal of this funding was the maintaining and upgrading of the existing mobile networks in a way that the smaller countries can keep in touch with the communication structure in the developed nations (Banks, 2008).

## THE SOCIAL SIGNIFICANCE OF REDUCING THE DIGITAL DIVIDE

The progress in filling the gap of the digital divide should have multiple effects on the economy and society. The solving of imbalance in the distribution and technology's usage among people should lead us to become a more democratic community where everyone, as imagined by proponents as Khosrowpour (2003), will have equal rights for access to technology society's processes such as elections and education.

The access to technology for all should offer new opportunity for scientists to rise from emerged countries and contribute to new technologies within the information society, so that they could raise the production of industry. Moreover, the country of the scientist's origination may have a competitive advantage of the human capital and knowledge management that may be exported to other countries as well (Zaqqa, 2006).

The role of exporting information (and especially the way that information is treated) is very important in current society. We live in an information society where information is considered the ultimate value for economic growth of humanity and a significant tool to build the future for the next generations ("Information Society", 2010). Information is therefore the key for raising the cultural capital that is defined as all the soft skills such as education and knowledge which lead people to move inside the hierarchy of social classes ("Cultural Capital" 2010). The movement of people within the hierarchy of the social classes is called social mobility (Devine, 1997) and the equal access to information is considered to be one of the pre-requirements for social mobility (Alonso & Oiarzabal, 2010).

The reason for considering social mobility is to review how it is related to E-Tourism. According to Wikipedia (2010) a few factors that affect the degree of social mobility are:

- The possession of economic assets that lead to a more comfortable life.
- The support on the social capital that is produced in social networks during the community's interactions.
- The definition of symbols that have meaning for people as to how they are related to society.
- The cultural capital gained through knowledge and information which is shared through human experience.

It is obvious that the relationship between social mobility and human mobility can give a boost to the market of E-Tourism and therefore beneficial for the local economies. It is therefore an effective factor in leading people towards social mobility and enabling them to move in the social hierarchy.

If we consider the foregoing discussion with the most popular triggers of social mobility then we find the social capital that is produced through virtual communities and social networking. One of the latest trends in virtual communities is the mobile social networking where groups of people with common interests are connected with the use of a mobile phone (Butler, 2006).

The extended wi-fi networks at various locations and the progressive technologies of mobile phones transfer the social networking action from the static computers to mobile computing. This trend affects the important social networking sites like Facebook, My Space, Twitter, and Go Mobile; and raises the popularity of social networking to mobile phone users who may not have had the opportunity to experience social networking before due to not owning a personal computer (Rutledge, 2008). The trend of mobile social networking is very popular in Europe and the Pacific Rim where the use of personal computers is less than the USA (Gillin, 2009). In the UK almost a quarter of all the smart phone users use mobile devices for accessing social networking ("Consumers spend", 2010). In general, portable devices are small, cheap and popular because they always come up with new software updates. The small size of the screen could be a disadvantage but there are always alternate solutions with screen projectors on large surfaces of the home, or in the office. Today there are enterprises that encourage the use of mobile social networking in the office so as to boost employee morale, create innovative ideas and unite employees under the company's internal network (Gillin, 2009). The mobile social networking within companies helps the global distribution of the work expertise and enhances the power of team working.

According to research carried out by the company, comScore, there is a rise in mobile social networking through mobile phones. Research shows that from January 2009 to January 2010, there was an increased percentage of 22.5% mobile phone users that accessed mobile social networking sites (Warren, 2010). In total, 30% of mobile phone owners accessed the mobile virtual communities, especially the popular social networks such as Facebook and Twitter that are available in mobile versions as well. There was a tremendous rise in the percentages of access through smart phones; Twitter's usage was raised by 347% from 2009 and Facebook by 112%. Twitter has created a strategy which merges the existing classical operations, such as SMS with mobile social networking. Other social network sites that maintain their original version without adding a mobile version are going down, such as MySpace where the mobile phone access has dropped to 7%.

With regards to the demographics of the mobile social networking, women tend to use the mobile virtual communities for Twitter and Facebook more than men (see research by Nielsen workgroup, (2010)). According to research by the research company Nielsen, 55% are female users and 45% are male users and the age group of 35-44 has more active users than the other age groups.

There are two types of mobile social networks regarding the access in the network. The first have collaboration with Wi-Fi companies who support these virtual communities by distributing to members the default web pages of the communities. The second category of mobile social networks operates on their own without any special promotion through other communication carriers.

Social mobility fits perfectly with human mobility because they share a common ground in movement and there is always the need for information exchange. Mobile computing is playing the role of the intermediary between the two types of mobility, with the creation of mobile communities that preserve the ethics and democracy of the community culture. The character of virtual communities in mobile social networking creates two of the requirements that society needs to lead people in the upward movement in human society: trust and e-democracy. If the mobile social networking has success in triggering social mobility, then the human mobility in E-Tourism should have a high quality result.

## RECOMMENDATIONS FOR FURTHER RESEARCH

The population of disabled people worldwide was estimated to be 650 million in 2009 (Council of Europe, 2009) and indeed they have the same rights for access to tourism services. The large number of disabled members of the society and their special needs translate to immense spending which also fulfils their entertainment and pleasure needs. According to the results of the 11th Caribbean Conference on Sustainable Tourism Development in UK alone, there are 2.7 million disabled people who travel annually and in the US there are more than 22 million people with the same consuming behavior ("Disabled people" 2010). The Canadians with disabilities are spending $25 billion annually as consumers and they also travel along with friends or relatives.

This is an important factor because apart from the predicted income from the disabled persons who travel, an additional income is going to exist from the persons that accompany the disabled community. The most important problems that disabled people encounter when they travel are classified into 3 categories:

- **Social Acceptance (Tregaskis, 2004):** Countries with low vertical social who look down on disabled people and treat them with hostility because they believe that these people cannot improve their quality of life.

- **Special Needs (Langan, 1998):** Disabled people may need special requirements such as wheelchairs in order to ease their transportation needs. Also the streets or the pavements have to be user–friendly in terms of construction. Moreover, other facilities such as elevators in high buildings have to exist.
- **Lack of Information (Turmusani, 2003):** This is a much underrated issue but surely it may be one of the reasons that prevent them from traveling. The disabilities they have may cause them insecurity about what kind of risks they may encounter or face when traveling abroad.

The disabled tourism has an emerging travel market share with special and customized needs, so it is required by the technology to play a special role and cover these special needs. E-Tourism that is based mainly on technology fits better with this group because it enables them to do all the tasks needed for their travel without them having to leave their home to deal with all the intermediaries. This is of absolute importance due to the fact that these people may be located in countries with non friendly public transportation. So they may find it difficult to get around on their own and make arrangements through a travel agency on the high street.

E-Tourism expands the more technology permeates human life and activities. Technology with its mobile computing encourages disabled people to travel with safety and leisure. The question here is, how does the digital divide affect disabled people? Have they adapted to technology or are they afraid of it? It is sure that the change in technology is going to affect them because it is a change for their life. New technology means new ways to accomplish the daily tasks so it is a time consuming method. Every person that deals with a personal change reacts in a different way so it is important to find out where a disabled person positions herself in comparison with the change.

John Fisher developed a theoretical model about how people cope with personal change and first presented this theory at the Personal Construct Congress in Berlin (1999). This model is based on the theory of Personal Construct Psychology ("Process", 2011). According to John Fisher, there is a climate of emotional stages that the person has to deal with while she faces a personal change ("Process", 2011):

1. **Anxiety and Denial:** When people do not have sufficient information about the personal change they become anxious and deny the existence of a change by continuing the use of old habits and practices.
2. **Happiness:** During this stage, people feel happy because their point of view about the disadvantages of the old habits was loud enough to persuade the insiders to change the current situation.
3. **Fear:** The potential change is going to affect the way that people are going to act after the implementation of the new tactic and practices. The new personal behavior is possibly going to change the way that the external environment of friends and colleagues view these persons, thus the question about "the day after" makes them fear.
4. **Threat:** The new environment after the change is going to affect people's lives and the old habits are going to be buried in the past. The threat here is the possibility that the new environment may not be better than the old one.
5. **Guilt and Disillusionment:** The changing environment encourages people to conduct an objective self review and decide if the new environment is close to their set of personal goals or if it alienates them from their personal beliefs. The guilt is very characteristic in the idea that with the adoption of the new

system, they may be kept away from what they want to succeed in life. If their personal beliefs do not meet the philosophy of the new system, then disillusionment occurs and people are disappointed with themselves.

6. **Depression and Hostility:** The guilt and disillusionment during the comparison between the meeting of the personal beliefs with the old habits and the disagreement of the same beliefs with the new habits causes an internal war to the affected persons. The dilemma between holding back or carrying on with the uncertainty of the new system, makes them sad and depressed. The continued effort to adjust to a new system that is unable to satisfy their personal goals can lead people return to the old system and thus underrating the new system and being hostile towards the new practices.
7. **Gradual Acceptance:** People start to realize that the change is occurring and now they position themselves in the future according to the philosophy of the new system.
8. **Moving Forward:** People realize that the change has a lot to offer for their future due to the featured advantages and they want to be part of the change by contributing in the transformation from the old system to the new one.

George Fisher's theory model makes a point by showing that each change whether it is small or big, affects people on a different level and progressively they adopt the change by moving forward and getting involved in the implementation of the change. Of course, there is always the danger for someone to get stuck at a specific stage and not adopt the philosophy of the new system. That is why it is important to detect the stage that each person or social team belongs to. A strategy then needs to be defined and to solve the issue which will make them continue to the next stage until they reach the last stage of moving forward.

Regarding the current academic effort, it is important to find in which emotional stage of the personal change the disabled people that suffer from digital divide belong to. Disadvantaged populations are considered the next big focus for E-Tourism due to the potential size of the market but digital divide is a barrier which prevents them from joining the new technology.

The lack of technology for the disadvantaged populations is usually caused by external factors that are mentioned in the analysis of the digital divide but the non efficient use of technology or lack of interest to use technology is an issue that needs further exploration. The way that people view technology and the change that is going to affect their current status of life changes their use of technology as well. If technology is a value that meets their personal beliefs and satisfies the ideal goals, then the involved persons most likely are going to adopt technology and use it efficiently by concentrating on how they can benefit from the technology's advantages. On the other hand if technology is considered as a negative value for their life then they would not care about the technology.

Disabled persons need to find technology useful in order to be motivated to take advantage of it. George Fisher's model should be applied to disabled people's point of views regarding the changes in technology and how they feel about it. The results of the research will show in which emotional stage they belong, in order to recommend a new strategy so they can reach the next stage of George Fisher's model and finally accept technology and E-Tourism.

## CONCLUSION

Digital divide is a factor that contributes negatively to the economic growth of E-Tourism by denying nations and people access to technology and associated efficiencies in its use. Most emerging economies are unable to fully embrace the internet revolution due to various issues such as unfavourable economy, culture, location, education and politics. The resulting imbalance in technology use between countries threatens the good relationships between them because of feelings of insecurity and jealousy. The increasing use of mobile computing in E-Tourism offers hope to bridge the digital divide and reduces the associated problems. The attractive features of mobile computing include their small size, low cost, ease of use and familiarity to most people.

Information and communication technology is increasingly playing a very important role with the help of mobile computing as the concept for communication and information exchange among nations is becoming a reality. We live in an information society and everything changes so quickly around us; so we do not want to lose the flow of information while the human movement is implemented. Information exchange with mobile computing should lead society to higher levels of progress. The introduction of mobile computing in the less developed countries and human minorities should have a strong impact in society's union and the humanistic mission for a democratic share of knowledge and better quality of life.

## REFERENCES


Alonso, A., & Oiarzabal, P. (2010). *Diasporas in the New Media Age: Identity, Politics, and Community*. Reno: University of Nevada Press.

Amjad, U. (2004). Mobile Computing and Wireless Communications. University of Pennsylvania: NGE Solutions, Inc.

Anonymous. (2010). E-Epiheirein. Retrieved November 28, 2010, from http://www.go-online.gr/ebusiness/specials/article.html?article_id=1561&PHPSESSID=ada989def1b7181b263c589c35cf4aec

Baguma, R., Bommel, P., Wanyama, T., & Ogao, P. (2007). Web Accessibility in Uganda: a study of Webmaster Perceptions. In *proceedings of the Third Annual International Conference on Computing & ICT Research (ICCIR 2007)*, Kampala: Uganda.

Banks, K. (2008). *Mobile Phones and the Digital Divide*. Retrieved November 28, 2010, from http://www.pcworld.com/article/149075/mobile_phones_and_the_digital_divide.html

Boscov-Ellen, D. (2009). *Mobile Internet Narrows the Digital Divide Domestically*. Retrieved November, 28, 2010 from http://www.newpolicyinstitute.org/2009/09/mobile-internet-narrows-the-digital-divide-domestically/

Buhalis, D. (2003). *eTourism: information technology for strategic tourism management*. London: Pearson Education.

Buhalis, D., & Schertler, W. (1999). *Information and communication technologies in tourism 1999*. Vienna: Springer. doi:10.1007/978-3-7091-6373-3

Butler, P. (2006). *Well connected: releasing power and restoring hope through kingdom partnerships*. Springs, CO: Biblica.

Chadwick, A. (2009). *Routledge handbook of Internet politics*. New York: Taylor & Francis.

Consumers spend almost half of their waking hours using media and communications (2010). *Ofcom. Independent regulator and competition authority for the UK communications industries*, Retrieved November 28, 2010, from http://media.ofcom.org.uk/2010/08/19/consumers-spend-almost-half-of-their-waking-hours-using-media-and-communications

Council of Europe. (2009). *Parliamentary Assembly Working Papers - 2008 Ordinary Session*, Fourth Part, 29 September-3-october 2008 - 2009, Volume 7. Retrieved from http://www.coe.int/

Cultural Capital. (2010) *Wikipedia, the Free Encyclopedia* Retrieved November 28, 2010, from http://en.wikipedia.org/wiki/Cultural_capital

Devine, F. (1997). *Social class in America and Britain*. Edinburgh, Scotland: Edinburgh University Press.

Digital Divide. (2010) *Wikipedia, the Free Encyclopedia*. Retrieved November 28, 2010, from http://en.wikipedia.org/wiki/Digital_divide

Disabled people a growing tourism market - Caribbean360. (2010). Caribbean news - Caribbean360, news around the Caribbean.Retrieved November 28, 2010, from http://www.caribbean360.com/index.php/travel/25982.html

Dutton, W. (2005). *Transforming enterprise: the economic and social implications of information technology*. Massachusetts: MIT Press.

Edgell, D. (2006). *Managing sustainable tourism: a legacy for the future*. New York, NY: Routledge.

Gillin, P. (2009). *Mobile Social Networking: The New Ecosystem*. Retrieved November 28, 2010, from http://www.virtualizationadmin.com/

Horrigan, J. (2009). Mobile internet use increases sharply in 2009 as more than half of all Americans have gotten online by some wireless means. *Pew Internet and American Life Project*. Retrieved November 28, 2010, from http://www.pewinternet.org/Press-Releases/2009/Mobile-internet-use.aspx

Information Society in Greece. (2010) Information Society: the Official Greek Portal for I.S... Retrieved November 28, 2010, from http://www.infosoc.gr/infosoc/en-UK/default.htm

Internet Usage in Africa. (2010) *Miniwatts Marketing Group*... Retrieved November 28, 2010, from http://www.internetworldstats.com/stats1.htm

Internet Usage in Asia. (2010). *Miniwatts Marketing Group*. Retrieved November 28, 2010, from http://www.internetworldstats.com/stats3.htm

Iskander, M., Kapila, V., & Karim, M. (2010). *Technological Developments in Education and Automation*. The Netherlands: Springer. doi:10.1007/978-90-481-3656-8

Khosrow-Pour, M. (2003). *Information technology and organizations: trends, issues, challenges & solutions*, Volume 1. London: Idea Group Inc (IGI).

Kim, W. (2001). The human society and the Internet: Internet-related socio-economic issues. *Proceedings of the First International Conference Human. Society @Internet 2001*, Seoul,South Korea

Langan, M. (1998). *Welfare: needs, rights, and risks*. New York, NY: Routledge.

Langer, A. (2002). *Applied ecommerce: analysis and engineering for ecommerce systems*. West Sussex, UK: Wiley.

Livi, E. (2008). Information Technology and New Business Models in the Tourism Industry. *8th Global Conference on Business and Economics*. Florence: Italy.

Mapesa, M. (2009). Uganda takes tourism trade into cyberspace. *The Observer*. Retrieved November 28, 2010, from http://www.observer.ug/index.php?option=com_content&view=article&id=3219:uganda-takes-tourism-trade-into-cyberspace

Mayer, S. E., (2003). *What is a disadvantaged group?* Minneapolis, MN: Effective Communities Project

Minghetti, V., & Buhalis, D. (2009). Digital Divide and Tourism: Bridging the gap between markets and destinations. *Journal of Travel Research*, (n.d)., 1–15.

Mobile Computing. (2010) *Wikipedia, the Free Encyclopedia*. Retrieved November 28, 2010, from http://en.wikipedia.org/wiki/Mobile_computing

Mutahi, K., & Kagwe, H. (2008). *Kenya's First E Tourism Conference Stresses the Need to Stay Competitive Online*, Retrieved November 28, 2010, from http://www.balancingact-africa.com/news/en/issue-no-333/computing/kenya-s-first-e-tourism-conference-stresses-the-need-to-stay-competit

Norris, P. (2001). *Digital divide: civic engagement, information poverty, and the Internet worldwide*. Cambridge, UK: Cambridge University Press.

Process of Personal Change. (2010) *Businessballs free online learning for careers, work, management, business training and education* Retrieved April 4, 2011, from http://www.businessballs.com/personalchangeprocess.htm

Rainer, R., & Cegielski, C. (2009). *Introduction to Information Systems: Enabling and Transforming Business*. West Sussex, UK: John Wiley and Sons.

Reza, F. (2005). *Mobile computing principles: designing and developing mobile applications with UML and XML*. Cambridge, UK: Cambridge University Press.

Rutledge, P. (2008). *The Truth about Profiting from Social Networking*. New Jersey: FT Press.

Sallis, E., & Jones, G. (2002). *Knowledge management in education: enhancing learning & education*. London, UK: Routledge.

Schiller, J. (2003). *Mobile communications*. Essex, UK: Pearson Education.

Servon, L. (2002). *Bridging the digital divide: technology, community, and public policy*. Oxford, UK: Wiley-Blackwell. doi:10.1002/9780470773529

Social Mobility. (2010) Sociology subject index and sociological subfields. Retrieved November 28, 2010, from www.sociologyindex.com

Swarbrooke, J., & Horner, S. (1999). *Consumer Behavior in Tourism*. Oxford, UK: Butterworth-Heinemann Publishing.

Tregaskis, C. (2004). *Constructions of disability: researching the interface between disabled and non-disabled people*. New York, NY: Routledge. doi:10.4324/9780203299517

Turmusani, M. (2003). *Disabled people and economic needs in the developing world: a political perspective from Jordan*. Hampshire, UK: Ashgate Publishing, Ltd.

Walle, A. H. (1996). Tourism and the Internet. Opportunities for Direct Marketing. *Journal of Travel Research, 35*(1), 72–77. doi:10.1177/004728759603500111

Warren, C. (2010). *Mobile Social Networking Usage Soars*. Retrieved November 28, 2010, from http://mashable.com/2010/03/03/comscore-mobile-stats

Werthner, H., & Klein, S. (1999). *Information technology and tourism: a challenging relationship*. Vienna: Springer-Verlag. doi:10.1007/978-3-7091-6363-4

What We are All About (2009). *E-Tourism Frontiers* Retrieved November 28, 2010, from http://www.e-tourismfrontiers.com/

Women use Mobile more than Men (2010) *Nielsen Research Group. For Social Networking*, Retrieved November 28, 2010, from http://blog.nielsen.com/nielsenwire/online_mobile/for-social-networking-women-use-mobile-more-than-men

Xiaoming, H., & Chow, S. K. (2004). *Factors affecting Internet development: An Asian survey*. Retrieved November, 28 2010, from http://firstmonday.org/issues/issue9_2/hao/

Zaqqa, N. (2006). *Economic development and export of human capital - a contradiction?: the impact of human capital migration on the economy of sending countries; a case study of Jordan*. Kassel: University Press, GmbH.

## ENDNOTE

[1] The tourism customer can be a male too but for simplicity of expression (instead of "he or she"), the female gender is consistently used.

# Chapter 3
# KNOWREM:
## Formal Definitions and Ontological Framework for Knowledge Reconciliation in Economic Intelligence

**Adenike Osofisan**
*University of Ibadan, Nigeria*

## ABSTRACT

*Although information technology is facilitating knowledge retrieval and sharing, it is sometimes difficult to adequately map the decision maker's mind-set into an appropriate object for information retrieval. Ontology potentially enables automated knowledge sharing and re-use among both human and computer agents; this is achieved by interweaving human and machine understanding through formal and real-world semantics. Thus, the combination of both graphical and mathematical model development was employed in the research with a bid to capture operational complexities and human issues and also establish rigorously defined formal definitions and mapping functions derived from the extension of the axiom of selection (or choice) and Object-Attribute-Relation (OAR) model. The research is relevant to knowledge sharing in and from developing economies where cultural factors may play their role by way of imprecision of information. Thus, the future direction of this research in fuzzy logic will tackle more the problem of ill-defined decision-making problems.*

DOI: 10.4018/978-1-4666-1637-0.ch003

## INTRODUCTION

Risk management as a particular branch of Knowledge Management employs the quality of knowledge models for insight and analysis (Allan et. al., 2007). This becomes imperative going by the fact that *within the concept of Economic Intelligence, division of labour has resulted in specialized classes of users dealing with information acquisition and its presentation, decision making and the acting agents.* The model for Knowledge Reconciliation (KNOWREM) developed in this chapter thus presents the first step towards minimizing the risk in decision making process.

Reality encompasses organizations and their environments, and we can distinguish entities, which connotes objects or events symbolically represented by their identifiers and values of their attributes. Information Values, therefore, refers to those symbolic representations of things, events, and unknown states of the environment that needs be acquired, and which can change the decision situation by itself and/or the operations results, and/or the actions that are required for successful implementation of the resultant decision (Gackowski, 2005).

## RELATED WORK

Duffing & Thiery (2005) were quick to recognize the fact that decision rationale can be measured and determined on the basis of the awareness of the challenges: risk and threat are incurable by the decision. This knowledge was used in the development of information base operating on dual-filtration towards the formation of a strategic information system. The model termed *Metiore* (Bueno & Amos, 2001) goes steps further in the context of Economic Intelligence (EI), employing the various stages in the EI process to develop a system that assists in capturing the users' objectives formulated into natural language to develop a personalized information retrieval system.

N. Bouaka & David Amos (2004) presented a model for EI decision maker, making the problem as explicit as possible. Three data categories were explained: Environmental; Organizational and Personal data. The rationale was born out of the need to juxtapose the relationship amongst the actors of EI, Information gathered and also determine who poses the problem and why. The process was represented with a flowchart. The above data categories were further broken down to constitute the decision maker problem (DMP) architecture. In their opinion, it was established that an atmosphere of confidence must be created between the decision maker and the watcher to facilitate proper information definition. Redman (1998) captured the views of executives, by defining the major problems faced by the decision makers.

These problems were posed in the form of a question: *how best can consumer satisfaction be improved; lower high cost; and complete ongoing projects*? This question has to be appropriately answered to avoid disaster for the organization. Within this lies some constrains of how best to capture the model of the real world in search for information and the utilization of such information. In view of the contribution of Risk Management from the Economic Intelligence approach, Duffing et al. (2005) submitted that appropriate economic monitoring is enhanced by information system and data warehousing. They stressed that data quality of appropriate level is the antidote for accurate decision making. The theme of the work was on the three major concepts of EI: Information; Users; and the research Processes of information whose interactions, compositions and roles were defined to determine the possibility of risk, its type, and source for any act of decision. Two broad types of risks were identified:

- **Risk Trades:** Reconciliation of knowledge and processes related to a specific concept, between two concepts, or the whole system (3-concepts);
- **Technical Risk:** Data and information processes on the data warehouse.

It can therefore be deduced from the above that the trio of Users, Information and Processes within and between these three, forms the basis for any would-be act of taking decision. This work follows closely the submissions of Duffing et al (2005) in deriving and expanding the detection and management of risk in EI, towards effective decision making.

## THE MODEL FOR KNOWLEDGE RECONCILIATION (KNOWREM)

Several attempts have been made in the last decades to formulate a decision making model aimed at solving decision making issues. Ge & Helfert (2006) reviewed a long list of decision making models based on different perspectives. Amongst these are: the Conflict model, Expected Utility model, and Accountability model. They commented that the above failed to pay attention to information quality (IQ) in decision making. In the IQ realm, (Ge & Helfert, 2006) also reviewed the Multi-input, Multi-output information systems, and others that were directed towards data quality dimension in taking appropriated decision. However, Gackowski (2004) disambiguates this notion by stating that system definition of IQ concentrates on the internal view that is intrinsic to data and information, oriented towards system design and data production, and is used independently.

This internal view is also enabling comparisons across applications, and may guide the design of IS by information quality objectives. It was opined that the completeness of information is mostly frequently unattainable; this is not due to design failure, but a result of human cognition in science and the limitation of intelligence in business and other required operations. Even when "unambiquity", "meaningful", "correct" and similar terms are used to connote whole definitions, they do not actually ensure complete contextual definitions. It was therefore reiterated that with even a perfectly meaningful and correct mapping, other important mapping information like "system states to the mind-set" of the decision maker is usually over sighted and excluded (Gackowski, 2004). The purpose-focused view of information quality (PFV/IQ) recognizes and acknowledges the importance of the ontological foundations of data/information quality. However, its emphasis was on the side of quality anchored on the teleological foundation of operation research, management science and decision making. The belief was that these views are dominant in businesses, public administration and military operations (Gackowski, 2005).

Commenting on the same vein, Ge & Helfert (2006) pointed out that even with a sterile IQ; other factors like personal preference, decision maker's experience, and the operating environment also affect the quality of decision.

The essence of the presentation thus far is not by any means trying to overlook the importance of quality in the resources (information, processes, and users) used to arrive at a logical decision. Rather, we are of the opinion and conviction that cogent factors and stages were either overlooked or completely ostracized in the process of decision making. This is sequel to the fact that quality cannot be summarily measured directly but indirectly through the measurement of its impact on operations-risk factors (Onifade, 2008) and sometimes this can even be difficult because of the corrupting effect of data manipulation (Gackowski, 2005).

The fact that decision makers never act on the basis of actual reality, for it is elusive and never fully known, makes decision a complex issue. They act on the available purported representation of reality. We therefore say that a decisional

*Figure 1. A Cause-Effect Representation of the KNOWREM Model*

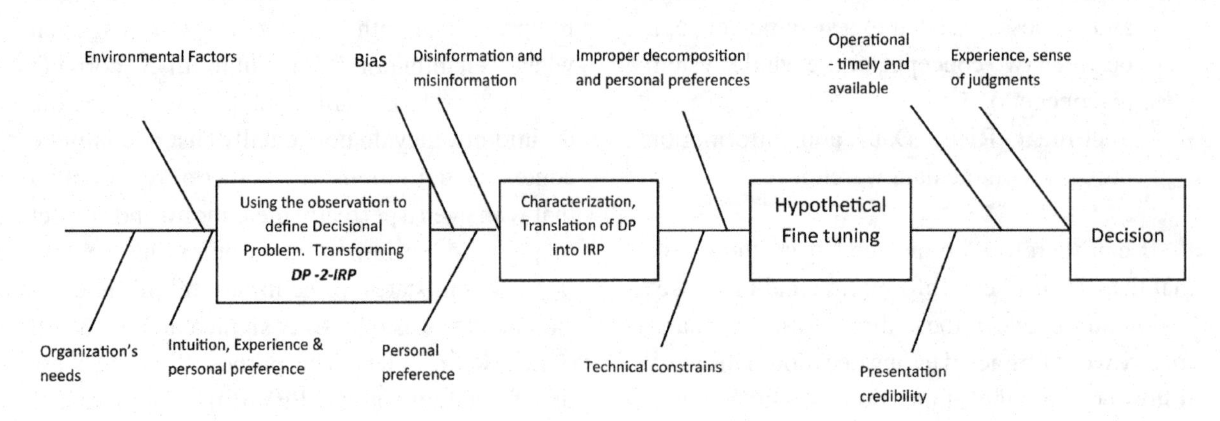


situation involves taking inventory of what is known by the decision maker (data); what is yet known and must be acquired (information) and the application of rules of reasoning (knowledge) that need be adequately reconciled for optimum efficiency.

Consequently, to further depict the importance of this particular stage of decision making process, we present the operation using a qualitative cause-effect diagram – a fishbone *(Onifade, 2008)* (see Figure 1).

A fishbone diagram is an analysis tool invented by the Japanese quality control statistician – Kaoru Ishikawa (Onifade, 2008). It is capable of systematically capturing and examining causes that affects and properly translating decisional problems. Represented by a typical fish skeleton, each bone of the fish identifies a cause (list not necessarily exhaustive) that can impair the quality of the result of the next stage under consideration (intrinsically, contextually, and possibly philosophically) and/or required actions to implement the decision made.

*Actionably Credible* is regarded as the most complex universal direct primary quality requirement of data/information values. It is defined as the degree of credibility of a data/information value at which the user/decision maker is willing to take action (Gackowski, 2006a). Contrary to other provisions of credibility, the philosophical background and the inherent roots of biases and disinformation constitute a great risk to informing – reconciling the decisional problems with the information retrieval problem. The following are definitions relevant in this context:

- **Bias:** A failure to fully inform
- **Disinforming:** Reporting untrue information as true, with knowledge that it is not true, its purpose is deceptive.
- **Misinformation:** Unintentionally misrepresenting reality. This could result from distorted acquisition, communication, storing, processing, presentation, and its interpretation.
- **Valid Information:** Faithfully representing reality. It thus amongst others are: well defined; of known variability, objective (unbiased), accurate (error free), precise, and current (up to date).

Credibility of data/information values implies whether it is true, if one may rely on the value. The word true implies consistency with reality. With this supposedly vague meaning, the users or entities informed thus have to live with either being disinformed, misinformed or with valid information (Gackowski, 2006b).

*Figure 2. The relationship between decision-making process and other processes in LRMB*

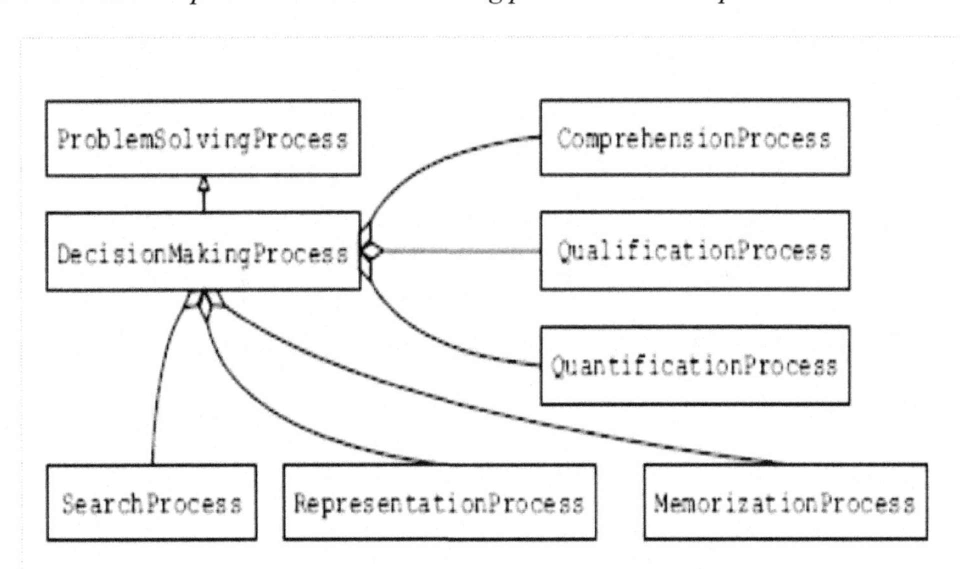


Presentation of decisional problems (as perceived by the decision maker) to the other actors of EI towards reduction of risk in the whole process, must ensure an unquestionable level of knowledge reconciliation between and amongst participating entities. Knowledge reconciliation process must match some states with their equivalent attributes or associated meaning or otherwise with any state resulting for example into automatic triggering of a sequence of operations (state transitions) in a receiving numerically controlled device.

## COGNITIVE PROCESS, ONTOLOGICAL FRAMEWORK FOR KNOWREM MODEL AND ITS MATHEMATICAL MODELS

Decision making is seen as one of the basic cognitive processes of human behavior; it involves the choice of preferred options or courses of actions from amongst sets of alternatives defined by certain criteria (Wang et. al., 2004).

It presents the process of decision making from the basis of Layered Reference Model of the Brain (LRMB) which identifies decision making as one of the 37 fundamental cognitive processes. There are two principal categories:

- Descriptive theories which are based on empirical observation and on experimental studies of choice as behaviour.
- Normative theory which assumes a rational decision maker that follows well defined, preferences that obey certain axioms of rational behaviour; these are the Utility paradigm and the Bayesian theory.

Figure 2, shows the relationship between the act of decision taking and other processes in LRMB (Wang et. al., 2004). The cognitive capacities of decision makers may be of various capacities, based on their level of exposure, environment, and other factors. However, the core cognitive processes of human brain share and exhibit similar and recursive characteristics and mechanisms.

Delivering strategic decisions, high rate performance and complex decision making are cogent features in Economic Intelligence; it is therefore appropriate to assert that appropriate method of information-sourcing for knowledge application is of utmost importance.

*Figure 3. Ontological Framework for KNOWREM Model*

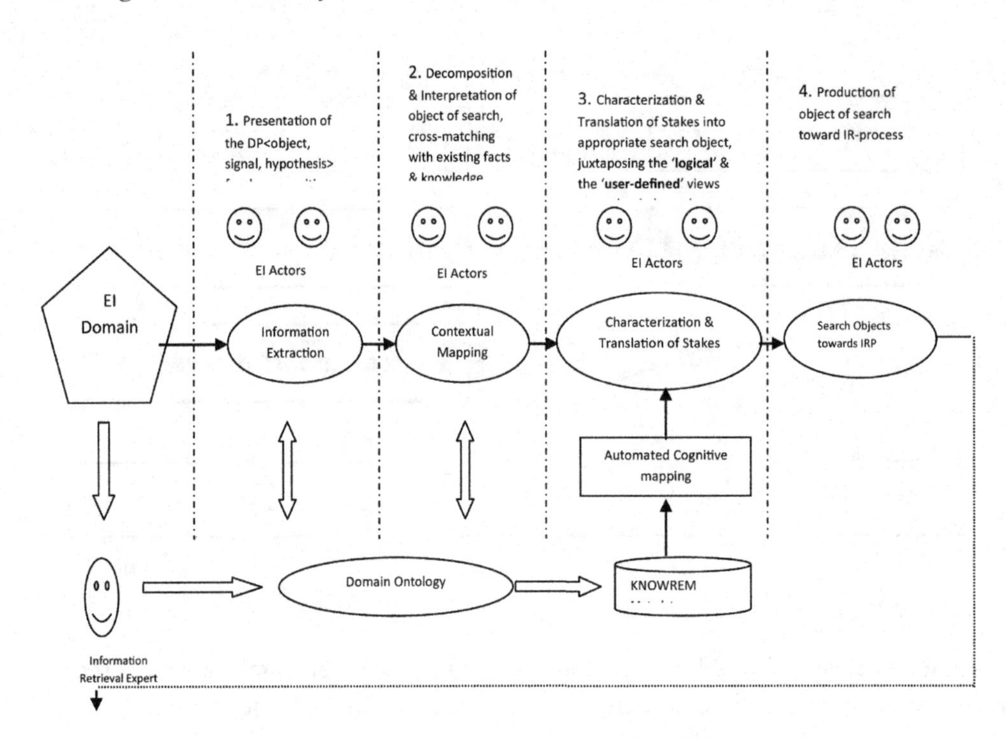


Ontology can be defined as formal vocabulary, shared by a group of people/individual, interested in a specific domain. The operation is further enhanced with a solid methodology that guarantees the collaborative engineering process. The key advantages of ontology can be summarized as knowledge sharing; reusability of knowledge and their being machine understandable.

It was argued that the basis for ontologically driven information system was the desire to incorporate knowledge from different domains into a single framework. Ontological application in risk simulation brings about the conceptual requirement of "reusability". This is because models are specified by humans to embody domain knowledge, characterized by ambiguity, thus ontology provides a profound solution in bridging the semantic-gap between the knowledge-space and the simulation model (G. M Allan et. al., 2007).

Presented Figure 3 is thus the Ontological Framework for KNOWREM Model aimed at facilitating improved classification of stakes.

The above presents a flexibly-defined and reusable framework, pedaled by ontology, and capable of capturing knowledge and modeling purposes. The framework consists of a metadata repository, where all earlier definitions and risk-factor patterns earlier captured with interpretations were kept, allowing periodical update as more risk factors are identified in the knowledge reconciliation process. It also has the domain ontology, the EI domain, and possible interactions within and amongst these entities.

## DEFINITIONS AND MATHEMATICAL MODELS

We present here some mathematical models aimed at creating an enduring foundation for the KNOWREM model. This is amongst other justifications expected to present a much deeper understanding than the contextual provisions of other types, and facilitates ease of automating the framework. In the meantime, we adopt the definitions and models presented in Wang et. al. (2004). However, a rigorous attempt was made to improve and extend these definitions to include other factors deemed necessary.

The axiom of selection (or choice) (Wang et. al., 2004) states that there exists a selection function for any nonempty collection of nonempty disjoint alternatives. Based on this, we have:

**Definition 1.1:** Suppose $\{A_i \setminus i \in I\}$ be the collection of disjoint sets $A_i \subseteq U$ and $A_i \neq \theta$, a function

$$f: \{A_i\} \rightarrow A_i, i \in I \quad (1)$$

is the *choice function* if $f(A_i) = a_i$, $a_i \in A_i$. or an element $a_i \in A_i$ may be chosen by f.

On the basis of the choice function and the axiom of selection, a decision can thus be defined:

**Definition 1.2:** A decision d, is a selected alternative $a_i$, from a nonempty set of alternatives $A_i$, $A_i \cap A_i = \theta$, $i \neq i$, $i \in I$, $A_i \subseteq U$, based on a given set of criteria, i.e.:

$$d = f(A_i, C) \quad (2)$$

$$= f: A_i \times C \rightarrow A_i, i \in I, A_i \subseteq U, A_i \neq \theta \quad (3)$$

Where C is the set of criteria for the selection of alternatives, and $\times$ represents a Cartesian product. It was pointed out that the criteria C can be a simple one or a complex one. The latter is a combination of a number of joint criteria depending on multiple factors.

**Definition 1.3:** Decision making is the process of selecting from available alternatives against the chosen criteria for a given decisional goal.

With respect to definition 1.2, the number of possible decisions, n, can be determined by the sizes of $A_i$, and C, i.e.:

$$\#(A_i) \bullet \#(C) \quad (4)$$

In this regards, # is the cardinal calculus on sets.

Considering the above equation, the case $\#(A_i) = 0$ and/or $\#(C) = 0$, implies that there is no derivable decision for such occasion.

In relation to the above mathematical definitions, we present the cognitive process of decision making (Wang et. al., 2004) and use the fundamental of Object-Attribute-Relation (OAR) model to describe our interest on the concepts of decisional problem - Decisional Problem Translation (DPT) into Information Retrieval Problem (IRP). Sequel to the diagrammatic representation of the relationship between decision-making process and the other major processes in LRMB as shown in Figure 2, it was implied that the cognitive model of human memory, particularly the long-term memory (LTM), can be described by two fundamental artifacts.

1. **Objects:** The abstraction of external entities and internal concepts. There are also sub-objects known as attributes, which are used to denote detailed properties and characteristics of an object.
2. **Relations:** Connections and relationships between object-object, object-attributes, and attribute-attribute.

The above discussion led to the development of what was referred to as an Object-Attribute-Relation (OAR) model of the memory which was described as follows:

$$OAR = \langle o, A, R \rangle \quad (5)$$

Where o is a given object identified by an abstract name, A is a set of attributes for characterizing the object, and R is the set of relations between the object and other objects or attributes of them.

Decision making process has been listed among the processes in the LRMB; thus, we adopt the pattern of definitions above presented at first to present our notion of decisional problem, the translation process and the criteria we called translation-credibility.

**Definition 1.4:** A decisional problem within the context of Economic Intelligence (EI) can be defined in terms of three principal attributes: the object, the signal, and the hypothesis.

The *Objects* are the perceptions and abstractions of both internal concepts and external entities, brought about by the presence of some *Signal(s)* generated by intuition, perception, and experience; which could be generated internally or externally, and from which some inferences in the form of *Hypothesis* could be made as to the effect of the perceived objects. We can therefore generate an *OSH* model, representing the decisional problem.

$$OSH = < o, S, H > \quad (6)$$

We can represent the decisional problem by $\delta$, o as the *object* whose identification results from the presence of some internal and external set *signals*, and by which, some sets of possible *hypothesis* could be deducted.

Let {o $\in$O, $\alpha \in$S, and $\beta \in$H}, then we can define a function $\Phi$ as follows:

$$\Phi : \{ OSH \} \rightarrow < o, \alpha , \beta > \quad (7)$$

This function maps the prompt for decision to its equivalent properties in the OSH-model.

It therefore suffices to define a decisional problem from the basis of (7) to have:

$$\Phi : \{ \delta \} \rightarrow < o, \alpha , \beta > \quad (8)$$

Translating the decisional problem into an information retrieval problem (object of search) is the next task. We reiterate here that this is usually a stage which has not been given much attention, and which could mare or make the success of any meaningful decision. This activity becomes imperative noting that sizes of many organizations have brought about division of labour resulting in specialized actors in every stage of the organization, which parallels with our concept in EI. Thus, the success of this exercise is very crucial to the decision making process.

**Definition 1.5:** Decisional problem translation or knowledge reconciliation is defined as the transformational/reconciliatory mapping which attempts to generate appropriate objects of search from the decisional problem. Hence, let a function $\Gamma$ be the transformational/reconciliatory mapping, we write:

$$\Gamma : \delta \rightarrow \Re \quad (9)$$

Where $\Re$ is the corresponding translated decisional problem (object of search). We declare that $\Gamma$ is a bijective mapping. i.e.

For $\Gamma : \delta \rightarrow \Re , \exists \partial , \tau , \ni \partial \in \delta \wedge \tau \in \Re$

$$\Rightarrow \Gamma ( \partial ) = \tau , \forall \partial \in \delta \wedge \tau \in \Re \quad (10)$$

The importance of (x) is to remove any form of ambiguity in the reconciliation.

## CONCLUSION

In this paper, we have stressed the importance of adequacy in reconciling the "mind concept" of the decision maker with users' involved in the information retrieval process. This action becomes imperative given the over flooding of available information delivery systems with different information. Since the degree of credibility of a data/information value at which the user/decision maker is willing to take action is dependent on the result of knowledge reconciliation, we proposed an ontological framework for the reconciliatory process alongside with rigorously defined mathematical models.

The need to use knowledge for decision making exists not only in developed but in developing economies. Besides, managers from both economies in this age of modern information and communication technologies tap from knowledge that comes across their economic boundaries. In this case, it is important that there is a common understanding so that useful and valid decisions can be reached. This is where ontology strives to contribute, to bring a common useful meaning. There is still much work to be done in this area because of some factors like cultural differences and meanings playing their roles (Usoro & Kuofie, 2006; Tseng, 2011). As a result some information may not be precise and well-defined. Thus, the future research effort with fuzzy logic promises to contribute to improving cross-cultural barriers in eliciting knowledge for decision making.

In the future, we hope to employ fuzzy cognitive maps (FCMs) capable of representing and capturing casual relationship and concepts made possible by fuzzy sets to implement our models. This is because it is possible to handle imprecise, ill defined, "fuzzy" problems. This factor permits the intangible expression of differences in casual relationships with introduction of partial activation of concepts as opposed to binary activation in classical cognitive maps.

## REFERENCES

Allan, G. M., Allan, N. D., Kadirkamanathan, V., & Fleming, P. J. (2007). Risk Mining For Strategic Decision Making. In Wegrzyn-Wolska, K. M., & Szczepaniak, P. S. (Eds.), *Adv. In Intel. Web, ASC 43* (pp. 21–28). Berlin Heidelberg., Germany: Springer-Verlag.

Bouaka, N., & Amos, D. (2004). A Proposal of a Decision Maker Problem for a Better Understanding of Information Needs. *IEEE Explore*, (pp 551 - 552) http://ieeexplore.ieee.org/iel5/9145/29024/01307879.pdf

CORAS -. *A platform for risk analysis of security critical systems*. (2000). Retrieved from: http://coras.sourceforge.net.

David, A., & Odile, T. (2004). *Prise en Compte du Profil de l'Utilisateur dans un Système d'Information Strategique*. [Taking into Account in the User Profile of a strategic information system] Vandœuvre-lès-Nancy, France: Publications Loria

David, B., & David, A. (2001). METIORE: A Personalized Information Retrieval System. *Proceedings of the 8th International Conference on user modeling*, (pp 168 – 177) New York, NY: Springer

Duffing, G. David, A., & Thiery, A. (2005). *Contribution de la Gestion du Risqué a la Démarché d'Intelligence Economique*.[ Contribution of the Risk Management to the economic intelligence approach] Vandœuvre-lès-Nancy, France: Publications Loria

Gackowski, Z. J. (2004). Logical Interdependence of Data/Information Quality Dimensions: A Purpose-Focused View on IQ. *In Proceedings of the Ninth International Conference on Information Quality. ICIQ – 04*, (pp 126 – 140)Washington, DC: IEEE Press

Gackowski, Z. J. (2005). Operations Quality of Data and Information: Teleological Operations Research-Based Approach, Call for Discussion. *In Proceedings of the International Conference on Information Quality*. ICIQ – 05, Boston, MA: IEEE Press

Gackowski, Z. J. (2005). Informing Systems in Business Environments: A Purpose-Focused View on IQ. *In Informing Science Journal, 8*, 101-122.

Gackowski, Z. J. (2006). Redefining Information Quality and Its Measurement: The Operation Management Approach. *In Proceedings of the International Conference on Information Quality. ICIQ – 06*, Boston, MA: IEEE Press.

Gackowski, Z. J. (2006a). Quality of Informing: Credibility Provisional model of Functional Dependencies. *Proceedings of 2006 Informing Science and IT Education Joint Conference*. (pp 99 – 114) Salford, UK: University of Salford

Gackowski, Z. J. (2006b). Quality of Informing: Bias and Disinformation Philosophical Background and Roots. *In Issues in Informing Science and Information Technology, 3*. 731 - 744.

Ge, M., & Helfert, M. (2006). A Framework to Assess Decision Quality Using Information Quality Dimensions. *In Proceedings of the International Conference on Information Quality. ICIQ – 06*, Boston, MA: IEEE

Jung, W. (2004). A Review of Research: An Investigation of the Impact of Data Quality on Decision Performance.: *International Symposium on Information & Communication Technologies (ISITC'04)*, (pp166 – 171) Washington, DC: IEEE Press

Onifade, O. F. W. (2008). Cognitive Based Risk Factor Model for Strategic Decision Making in Economic Intelligence Process. *GDR-IE Workshop*Retrieved from: http://s244543015.onlinehome.fr/ciworldwide/wp-content/uploads/2008/06/nancy_onifadeofw.pdf

Osofisan, A. O., Onifade, O. F. W., Longe, O. B., & Lala, G. O. (2007). Towards a Risk Assessment and Evaluation Model for Economic Intelligent Systems. *Proceedings of the International Conference on Applied Business & Economics*. Available online at www.icabeconference.org

Redman, T. C. (1998). The Impact of poor Data Quality on the Typical Enterprise. *Communications of the ACM, 41*(2), 79–82. doi:10.1145/269012.269025

Tseng, S.-M. (2011). The effects of hierarchical culture on knowledge management processes. *Management Research Review, 34*(5), 595–608. doi:10.1108/01409171111128742

Usoro, A., & Kuofie, M. H. S. (2006). Conceptualisation of Cultural Dimensions as a Major Influence on Knowledge-Sharing. *International Journal of Knowledge Management, 2*(2), 16–25. doi:10.4018/jkm.2006040102

# Chapter 4
# A Conceptual View of Knowledge Management Adoption in Hospitality Industry of Developing Economies

**Abel Usoro**
*University of the West of Scotland, UK*

**Bridget Abiagam**
*University of the West of Scotland, UK*

## ABSTRACT

*Existing research addresses and recognises the importance and benefits of knowledge management in the hospitality industry but especially in big hotels and in developed economies. Little or nothing has been researched in developing economies, yet the hospitality industry there is recognised in literature as a means of income redistribution and foreign currency earning. This chapter attempts to fill this gap by developing a theoretical model of KM adoption in the hospitality businesses of developing economies. The major constructs considered relevant are developmental factors, information technology, culture, and intention to adopt KM. Though at the moment a conceptual paper, the implications of the study are presented and they include the need for managers to collaboratively provide infrastructure, information technology, and training. They also have to use culture to their advantage in order to encourage KM use in their businesses.*

DOI: 10.4018/978-1-4666-1637-0.ch004

## INTRODUCTION

Hospitality industry provides accommodation, food and beverages as well as meeting arrangements for tourists, travellers and local residents (Buttle, 1986; Pizam, 2005 and Power & Barrows, 2006) and is a principal income earner for individuals, businesses and economies both in developed and developing countries. For instance, in the US more than 960,000 restaurants are expected to continue to be strong contributors to economic recovery with nearly 10% of the workforce in the industry (National Restaurant Association, 2011). In the UK, the core hospitality industry turnover, as at 2010, was £90 billion and £46 billion to the UK economy in terms of gross value added (GVA) coming from wage and profits; it also directly contributed 2.44 million jobs to the economy (Oxford Economics, 2010). In developing economies, hospitality industry helps to redistribute income among the workforce; the redistribution is through tipping, profit sharing schemes, compensation plan, benefits and others (Pizam, 2005; Walker & Miller, 2008).

Hospitality industry is knowledge intensive thereby standing to benefit extensively from the provisions of information technology, for example, for knowledge sharing which is a key knowledge management (KM) process (cf Tiedemann, Birgele & Semeijn, 2009; DiPietro & Wang, 2010). KM has the potential of providing the ethos and a set of tools as well as practices for capturing and developing individual and collective knowledge within and between organisations. Organisations that employ these techniques stand a better chance of promoting innovation through knowledge transfer and continuous learning with the result of increased effectiveness and competitiveness (Hallin & Marnburg, 2008 ). Thus, Medlik (1990) reported a few case studies in the hotel industry that use KM systems to meet the demand for quality standard though they were geographically dispersed. The same outcome was seen by Hallin and Marnburg (2008) and Bouncken (2002) gives example of Accor Hotel Group with 3,500 hotels worldwide, 130,000 employees and brands like Formula One, Ibis, Novotel and Sofitel. Hilton[1] Corporation with 2,700 hotels in over 70 countries applies its KM by implementing a university and e-learning system to consistently provide training to its staff (Baldwin, 2006). One of the new tools of KM that has been used by Sheraton hotel, Reef hotel and others is online social networks (Kasavana et al, 2010). New tools such as this should make adoption of KM in hospitality to traverse the boundaries of economic groupings.

However, much of the success stories of KM application in hospitality industry are with big companies, making hospitality industry slow compared to others in adopting this useful tool (Hallin & Marnburga, 2008). The authors have also noted that empirical research in hospitality area is lagging behind other areas. Researchers like Cooper (2006), Grizeli (2003), and Ruhanen and Cooper (2004) have given reasons for this limitation. Nonaka & Takeuchi (1995), for instance, suggested that it is because KM concepts are mostly developed from manufacturing and multi-national perspectives. Perhaps, it is the multi-national perspective that is also accountable for observed low adoption of KM in the hospitality industry of developing economies (Hallin & Marnburg, 2008). Wong (2008) and Delgado-Hernandez et al (2009) have noted the very limited study performed on developing economies in this area. This is the challenge of this paper, though at the moment, at a conceptual level.

The approach is to examine the specific factors that would influence KM adoption in hospitality of developing economies. There is, apparently, no existing model or conceptualisation of these factors and their influences. The rest of this paper will argue out a research model mainly from secondary study, present conclusions, implications and area for further investigation.

## RESEARCH MODEL

A critical consideration of existing literature has revealed factors or variables which can be organised under constructs of developmental, information technology and cultural constructs. These constructs are used to build the research model in Figure. The rest of this section presents their discussion and arguments used to derive them. The first to be discussed is the dependent variable, intention to adopt KM.

### Intention to Adoption of KM in Hospitality Industry

An organisation that adopts knowledge management would practice its processes. Therefore a culture of identifying, creating, storing and sharing knowledge, which are KM processes, would be established in the organization (Honeycutt, 2000 and Gupta et al 2000). This culture could also be seen in the leadership and behaviour of organisational members. It should be habitual to transform knowledge gained from a context into solutions in other contexts. For instance, knowledge gained from customer contact should easily translate into product design and offerings. This means that the organisation should avoid a silo mentality and also be flexible: be capable of pursuing multiple conflicting goals and adapting their actions as they learn and experience (Choo, 2002 ).

This flexibility as well implies tolerance of errors provided valuable lessons can be learned to improve subsequent performance. KM adoption can be manifest in the willingness of organisations to reward knowledge creation and sharing too. Honeycutt (2000) also made the point that information technology has to be accepted as the platform for knowledge sharing through its collaboration tools. Information technology also facilitates other aspects of knowledge management which include the capturing and storing of knowledge.

It is very impressive that tools have been developed to assess knowledge management adoption and its impacts on people, processes, performance even at the enterprise level (Becerra-Fernandez et al, 2004 ). Some of the items included in the basic assessment tool are the ease of locating information and the extent to which available knowledge improves personal effectiveness. Since this study will be directed at developing economies, such scales would have to be adjusted to indicate intention rather than actual adoption of KM. The reason is that many of the responding organisations at the empirical study stage most likely would not yet adopt KM.

As already discussed, knowledge management and its tools enable the creation, codification, storage, retrieval and sharing of knowledge. Some of these tools are information technology based, for example the ones that enable knowledge sharing. Knowledge sharing behaviour and its adoption in organisations has received much research attention (cf Usoro & Majewski, 2011; Ranjan, 2011; Friesl et al, 2011; and Chui et al, 2011). Also, much research has been carried out on the acceptance of technology tools of KM using models like TAM (Technology Acceptance Model) (Usoro & Shoyelu, 2010; Thatcher et al, 2011). However, apart from aspects like knowledge sharing, there is hardly much research on factors affecting the adoption of knowledge management. This research takes this challenge with regards to the hospitality industry of developing economies. Thus, the factors that emerge from literature analysis can be grouped into information technological, developmental, and cultural categories. The rest of this section will argue out these factors and how they affect acceptance of knowledge management in developing economies as illustrated in Figure. The discussion will begin with information technology to give a proper basis for the hypotheses that are developed with their associations with developmental factors.

## Information Technology

A World Bank (2006) study confirmed that information technology contributes to the economic growth and poverty reduction throughout the developing world where information technology originated in the first place (Kemeny, 2011). Firms in developing countries that use information technology grow faster, invest more, and are more productive and profitable than those that do not. The UN Development Programme (2001) reported that new information technologies provide opportunities in developing countries for political empowerment (such as the global email campaign that helped topple Philippine President Estrada, Egyptian President Mubarak, Tunisian President as well as putting other Arab world leaders like Colonel Gaddaffi of Libya at the edge of being toppled), health networks, long distance learning, and job creation (UNDP, 2001).

Nevertheless, OECD countries have the highest access to ICT followed by South Asia and some few other African countries. The sub-Saharan countries except for South Africa fare worst and therefore suffer from the digital divide (Arikpo et al., 2009). The consequence is the lack of and inadequate development of economic base, telecommunication networks and other technical infrastructural requirements in the developing economies (Mbarika et al., 2005). Government policies in developing countries in terms of investment and liberalisation, however, are aimed at effecting changes in accessibility and usage (Rogers, 2006).

From the foregoing, the following hypothesis can be drawn:

**$H_1$:** There is a significant relationship between developmental factors and provision of information technology.

We can also directly relate parts of developmental construct with parts of information technology as a construct. The discussion will begin with explanation of availability, perceived ease of use, perceived usefulness and perceived reliability as parts of information technology construct.

### Availability

Technology should be readily available both for personal and other usages. Availability can lead to increasing interest, desire and the habit to use technology most of the time, if not always, for searching for information and knowledge, problem solving and for many other purposes. Thus, IT availability should encourage users to adopt the KM culture of creating, storing and sharing knowledge.

### Perceived Ease of Use (PEOU)

Perceived ease of use (PEOU) is one of the constructs of Technology Acceptance Model developed by Davis (1989). It refers to "the degree to which a user expects the target system to be free of efforts" (Davis, 1989 ). Philips et al (1994, p 18) also explained it as "the degree to which the prospective adopter expects the new technology adopted from a foreign company to be free of effort regarding its transfer and utilization". Users of information or computer systems should perceive its usage to be without any or much effort (Venkatesh & Davis, 2000.

PEOU enables the measurement of attitudes with regards to the use of technology, as individuals might consider technology to be useful without being favourably disposed towards its use because of the difficulty of using it (Ajzen & Fishbein, 1975; Gefen & Straub, 2004. An easy-to-use technology is likely to be perceived as less intimidating (Moon & Kim, 2001). Technology should be easy to learn to be easy to use (Wang et al, 2003; Webber, D. & Kauffman, 2011). Thus, acceptance of technology for the usage of managing knowledge in hospitality should be encouraged by this variable because if the technology to implement KM is seen to be easy to use then employees of hospitality industry should be willing and ready to accept the computer system for implementation of managing knowledge in hospitality.

## Perceived Usefulness (PU)

Davis (1989) explained perceived usefulness (PU) as the extent or degree to which an individual believes that using a specific technology would enhance his or her job performance. Philip et al. (1994) defined this as "the prospective adapter's subjective probability that applying the new technology from foreign sources will be beneficial to his personal and/or the adopting companies' well-being". Therefore perceived usefulness refers to the user's perception of the degree to which a new technology will enhance his or her work productivity, speed, efficiency and accuracy (Abiagam, 2009). Thus, Davis (1993) and Law and Bai (2008) from their studies on consumer behaviour observed that PU influences attitude to computer system usage positively. Hence, PU would positively contribute towards the adoption of knowledge management in hospitality industry.

## Perceived Reliability

If the system of acceptance of knowledge management is not reliable and dependable then employees and staff of the hospitality industry would not use the system. Therefore the system for accepting knowledge management in hospitality should be able to perform its functions as expected without causing significant and noticeable failures thereby making it trustworthy for its users to depend upon.

## Cost

Cost deals with affordability of technology. The system for accepting knowledge management in hospitality industry should be affordable or inexpensive in terms of the purchase price and maintenance. This factor can have a significant impact on small businesses and users in developing economies.

Information technology constitutes an underlying tool to KM since it provides knowledge codification, storage, sharing and collaborative support to knowledge workers. If these technology-based KM tools are available, perceived to be easy to use, useful, reliable and cost effective (affordable), KM in hospitality industry should be accepted. Thus the following hypothesis can be formulated:

**$H_2$:** There is a positive correlation between information technology provision and adoption of KM in hospitality industry of developing economies.

## Developmental Factors

Developmental factors are often associated with metrics and indices that indicate whether a country is rich or poor, developed, developing or less developed (Worldbank, 1994). These matrices are differently perceived by researchers and experts in developmental studies. For instance, as far back as 1959, Lipset included political and legal factors. More recently, Ozturk (2007) includeed economic, health measures, educational, health, cultural and global factors as indicators of development level. Furthermore, the late Pakistani economist Mahbub ul Haq with the collaboration of the Nobel leaureate Amartya Sen developed the Human Development Index (HDI) as a summary index that measures the health, knowledge and incomes in different economies (UNDP, 2010). Their measure is used by the United Nations. Yet, other researchers include electricity and level of infrastructure like roads and railways (Song, 2011).

Some of the factors, such as social, mentioned by researchers and experts are not directly related to the acceptance of knowledge management which is the theme of this research. What is common though is that developmental factors are perceived as conditions that aid growth, increase, progress or expansion. Thus, this study has decided to focus on electricity, communication infrastructure and education which should be directly relevant to the context of our research. These factors are explained in the rest of this section.

## Electricity

Physical infrastructure sometimes termed as public capital has long been considered an important determinant of economic growth. Aschauer (1989), for example, found very large returns to public capital in the United States. Canning (1994) estimated large growth effects of physical infrastructure. Easterly and Rebelo (1993) found that public investment in transportation and communication was consistently correlated with economic growth. Physical infrastructure provision affects all aspects of any economy, for instance agricultural productivity in developing countries (Antle, 1983). Conversely, grossly inadequate (and in some cases, lack of) infrastructure imposes a major economic constraint on organizations in countries like Nigeria (Lee & Anas, 1992). Electricity supply is often epileptic in this country.

According to the World Bank (1998), for telephone and electricity generating capacity, the stock of infrastructure rises proportionately with population and more than proportionately per capita income. As the population increases, there is a tendency to have large infrastructural stock which will be proportionate with the per capita income. So the more the population the more their stock of infrastructure grows as well as the income per capita generated. This is because economies of scale push down the unit cost of infrastructure.

The demography in which the world population has been forecasted by US census bureau will increase from 6.5 billion in 2006 to 7.9 billion in 2025 (Oh & Pizam, 2008). Much of this increase is expected from developing countries like those in Asia, Africa and Latin America. All structures should be seriously impacted. Thus, increased investment in electricity is needed so as to reap its positive benefits.

Electricity supply is a problem in developing economies. For example South African electric power consumption was put at 3882 Kwh per capita but Nigerian at 85KwH per capita while the OECD recommended 85000 Kwh per capita (Raji et al, 2006 ). Constant electricity supply is necessary to reap the best benefits from the current information age. As with other infrastructure, their inadequacy can also affect the cost of doing business and technology provision in an economy (Luiz, 2010, p512). Thus it is possible to formulate the following hypotheses:

**$H_{1a}$:** There is a positive relationship between electricity and availability of information technology.

**$H_{1f}$:** There is a positive relationship between electricity and reliability of information technology.

**$H_{1i}$:** There is a positive relationship between electricity and cost of information technology.

## Communication Infrastructure

As far back as 1958, Hierschman (1958) included communication as part of infrastructure or capital goods which offer public service. Communication infrastructure refers to the backbone of communications system upon which various broadcasting and telecommunication services are operated (Gillwald, 2008). This can be built from copper cable, fiber optics and wireless technologies using radio frequency spectrum such as microwave and satellite. Recently too, electricity has been used as a communication medium. In modern internetworks, fiber optic cables are commonly relied upon for speedy backbone communications infrastructure. However, because of little or no installation of these cables in developing countries like Nigeria, there is high dependence on satellite communicate which does not convey as much bandwidth and speed.

The modern information age very much relies on communication infrastructure to upstream and downstream players on the supply chain who need upstream production of audio, data and video. Moreoever, the current customer relationship management empowers the modern customer as a major source of knowledge and intellectual capital to organizations; thus resulting in the flow of much communication upstream from consumers to organizations. Besides, both consumers and organizations need to collaborate and communicate much between themselves and for this they are being helped with the social networking tools of KM powered by the Web 2.0 facilities (Bebensee et al., 2011).

Communication infrastructure has a pervasive effect on almost all other sectors of an economy (Roller & Wavernman, 2001; Ding & Haynes, 2006; and Osotimehin et al, 2010). Thus, its function in any economy is strategic for promoting economic growth and linkages to other sectors. For example, Osotimehin et al (2010) found in their research that investing in telecommunication infrastructure can lead to generation of employment. Other gains are opening of opportunities for foreign investment (Aitken & Harrison, 1999), making possible better education and training facilities, bringing a boom in private sector development; improving the overall productive capacity at the regional level; combating of poverty (Calderon & Serven, 2004) promoting expansion in economic activities (World Bank, 1991); and generating of larger spillover to other sectors of the economy as it has a larger impact on aggregate output as compared to other kinds of infrastructure (Canning, 1999). With these gains, there is no doubt that communication infrastructure should have a direct impact on economic and social growth rate of a country.

Moreover, the World Bank (1998) demonstrated a positive correlation between urbanization and the number of telephones in poorer countries, while country size is negatively correlated with the number of telephones in richer countries. This is to say that urban development is impacted by the number of telephones in poorer (developing) countries while richer (developed) countries possess a significant number of telephones disproportionately compared to their size. Increase in the availability of telephones is associated with industralisation and modernization. Countries, like China, that pursue rapid economic development include communication infrastructure in their urbanization policy (Song, 2011). The availability of telephone lines has been relatively poor in developing economies but the boom of mobile technology and phones is rapidly bridging the digital divide (Webber & Kauffman, 2011). However, the mobile phone provision in developing countries is still in some cases not very reliable (with inadequate mobile stations with some suppliers) and is still relatively costly (Rashid & Elder, 2009). The more these communication infrastructures (which is more than the telephone system) are improved, the more will developing economies, which are classified by the UNDP as the most populous part of the world, be able to increase their development pace and register a stronger presence in the modern information age.

The internet, for instance, operates with universal basic technology but if communication network, say at the internet cafes, is epileptic and very slow, the user would not perceive the information technology easy to use, useful or reliable. Thus, while majority of populations in developed countries use the internet daily their counterpart in developing countries may use less than once in a week. Also, because of the lack of economies of scale when there is low provision of any infrastructure (such as communication infrastructure) as mentioned before, its cost would be high. It has to be noted that the recent development in mobile computing and wireless technology has put telephones and PDAs in the hands of many in developing economies thus endeavouring to reduce the problem of communication infrastructure. However, it would still be interesting to investigate the extent to which provision of communication infrastructure affects the availability, perceived ease of use and reliability of information technology in developing countries (Curwen & Whalley, 2011). These hypotheses will enable this investigation:

$H_{1b}$: There is a positive correlation between provision of communication infrastructure and availability of information technology.

$H_{1c}$: There is a positive correlation between provision of communication infrastructure and perceived ease of use of information technology.

$H_{1h}$: There is a positive correlation between provision of communication infrastructure and perceived reliability of information technology.

$H_{1i}$: There is a positive correlation between provision of communication infrastructure and cost of information technology.

The constructs of perceived ease of use and perceived usefulness are borrowed from the TAM (Technology Acceptance Model) originally developed by Davis (1989) as an extension of the Theory of Reasoned Action (TRA) that was created by Fishbein and Ajzen in 1975. The validity and reliability of TAM measures have been widely tested beginning from Davis (1989) himself with 152 respondents whose computer acceptance was being measured. Compared to other technology acceptance models, TAM is believed to be more cost effective, predictive, and robust (Venkatesh & Davis, 2000). TAM has been used in the service industry (Curran & Meuter, 2003) and has been adapted to different technology scenarios like teleworking (Perez et al, 2004); and online retailing of financial services (McKechine et al, 2006). Heijden et al (2003) proposed that TAM can be expansively applied to World Wide Web (WWW) and a few studies have done that but very little has been done to apply to KM tools in hospitality industry. This study will provide an opportunity for this with the above hypotheses.

## Education

Quality education develops cognitive skills and impacts on economic development and individual earnings (Hanushek & Wößmann, 2007a and 2007b). In a study of African countries, education by way of computer and technical skills were seen to determine the usage and adoption of information technology (Ndubuisi & Jantan, 2003). This finding suggests that the skills developed by quality education influences the users' perception of the usefulness and easy of use of information systems. Thus, it is possible to formulate the following hypotheses:

$H_{1d}$: Level of education is positively correlated with perceived ease of use of information technology for knowledge management.

$H_{1g}$: Level of education is positively correlated with perceived usefulness of information technology for knowledge management

Available measures of school attainment uniformly indicate that developing countries lag dramatically behind developed countries (Hanushek & Woessmann, 2007). This fact has driven a variety of efforts to expand schooling in developing countries by organizations including the Education for All initiative (Levin & Lockheed, 1993) and University of the People developed in 2009 based on computers and the Internet[2]. Yet, much of the discussion and much of the policy making has tended to downplay the issues of quality. International testing indicates that, even among those attaining lower secondary schooling, literacy rates (by international standards) are very low in many developing countries. By reasonable calculations, a range of countries has fewer than 10 percent of its youth currently reaching minimal literacy and numeracy levels, even when school attainment data look considerably better (Barro & Lee, 2010). Nonetheless, good quality education should be a requisite for acceptable KM operation since KM as previously discussed puts premium on knowledge workers and their understanding and ability to create, externalize and share knowledge which requires cognitive, analytical and perceptive skills. Therefore, this hypothesis can be formulated:

**$H_3$:** Quality and relevant education is positively correlated with intention to KM adopt in hospitality industry of developing economies.

Education should play a vital role in the acceptance of knowledge management in the hospitality industry as through education, skills, including cognitive and technical, can be acquired and used for management of knowledge. What can be concluded is that education should relate directly with intention to adopt KM as well as indirectly through the information technology construct.

## Culture

Geert Hofstede (2003) described culture as "the collective programming of the mind which distinguishes one group or category of people from another" (2003). The inclusion of the mind in the description indicates that culture influences thinking and how knowledge is developed and shared. Knowledge management recognizes tacit knowledge in individuals and endeavours to make it explicit so that it can be shared. Knowledge management also aims to support collaborative work. The way the group works may be influenced by their individual or collective cultural backgrounds irrespective of the universality of technology, globalization and professionalism (Root, 1994 and Huntington, 1996). The economic historian David Landes cited in Harrison and Huntington (2000) also linked culture to economic development.

From the foregoing discussion, it can be concluded that culture may or may not have a significant effect on adoption of KM in hospitality of developing economies. Thus, the following hypothesis can be formulated:

**$H_4$:** There is a significant positive relationship between culture and adoption of KM in the hospitality industry of developing economies.

Hofstede (1980) whose work on culture is most cited, initially classified the concept into (a) power distance, (b) uncertainty avoidance, (c) individualism vs collectivism, and (d) career success vs quality of life[3]. In 1991, he added a 5th dimension – long term orientation to short-term orientation (to life).

## Power Distance

Power relations shape economic exchanges and vice versa (Granovetter, 2005). World Bank (2006) stated that to approach the relationship between equity and development from this perspective, one needs to account for as many aspects of social diversity as possible so as not to miss any essential aspects of discrimination that limit the potential of individuals and social groups to choose or create. In a society in which cultural bias has no reflection on economic and political life fewer barriers to social mobility would exist and an optimal system of allocation could be achieved.

With a particular society or culture, power distance can be described as the socially accepted distribution of power among individuals and institutions within that culture. Ifinedo and Usoro (2009) describe it as "the degree of equality, or inequality, between peoples in the country's society" (2009). A society is ranked high on power distance by the extent to which the inequalities of power and wealth have been allowed to grow within the society or if the majority of its members support this distribution of power; and low if it is the minority that supports the social barriers (Usoro and Kuofie, 2008).

At organisational level, power distance would be exhibited in the employees' fear or ease of expressing views to their managers; subordinates' perception of their super ordinate's decision-making style – autocractic, democratic or laissez-faire; and their preference of the style (Hofstede, 2005). While it may be argued that people can be forced to share knowledge in an autocratic system, it may also be reasonable to conceive that better knowledge sharing occurs in less intimidating and close relationships that are likely to prevail in low power distance environment. Similarly, other knowledge management processes such as knowledge creation could be reasoned to thrive more in low power distance environment. Thus, we can formulate the following hypothesis:

**$H_{4a}$:** There is a negative relationship between power distance and intention to adopt knowledge management in hospitality industry of less developed economies.

## Individualism vs Collectivism

This dimension refers to the degree to which society reinforces individual or collective achievement and interpersonal relationships. A culture with close social networks and with focus on the good of the group practices collectivism. In such a culture individuals are encouraged to be loyal to the good of the group. To the contrary, a society ranks high on individualism when individuality and individual rights are considered paramount. In a KM context, it is important for individuals to develop and build their performance knowledge stock but the collective behaviour of knowledge sharing is essential for KM efforts to thrive. Which in these two extremes or mix thereof is ideal for encouraging adopting of KM? This will be verified with the following hypotheses:

**$H_{4b}$:** There is a positive relationship between individualism and intention to adopt knowledge management in hospitality industry of less developed economies.

**$H_{4c}$:** There is a positive relationship between collectivism and intention to adopt knowledge management in hospitality industry of less developed economies.

## Uncertainty Avoidance

Uncertainty avoidance focuses on the extent to which a society tolerates uncertainty and ambiguity (Hofstede, 1980). Do they cope well with unstructured situations? A high uncertainty avoidance ranking shows that the society has a low tolerance for uncertainty and ambiguity and therefore cannot cope well with unstructured situations. A low uncertainty avoidance ranking indicates the reverse and also means that the society can tolerate a variety of opinions. For knowledge management to thrive, it is essential that a variety of opinions and some errors of judgment be allowed, thus arguing for the following hypothesis:

**$H_{4d}$:** There is a positive relationship between individualism and intention to adopt knowledge management in hospitality industry of less developed economies.

## Career Success vs Quality of Life

Career success emphasises on assertiveness and wealth accumulation without much regard to quality of life or nurturing (Hofstede, 1980; Usoro & Kuofie, 2008). Both qualities are needed for a healthy development and operation of KM. It will be interesting to find out which of them has a stronger influence on adoption of KM in hospitality industry of developing economies. Where the balance should be drawn between the two qualities would be good to determine. Thus, the following hypotheses:

**$H_{4e}$:** There is a positive relationship between career success and intention to adopt knowledge management in hospitality industry of less developed economies.

**$H_{4f}$:** There is a positive relationship between quality of life and intention to adopt knowledge management in hospitality industry of less developed economies.

### Orientation

Hofstede added the long-term orientation vs short-term orientation to life when he observed that Western societies tend to focus on solving immediate problems whereas Eastern societies, typified by Japan, take a long-term view of situations such that organizations there tend to tolerate current problems as long as there are incremental improvements that would bring significant gains in the long run.

Both short and long term approaches to problem solving are necessary in KM environments. It would be interesting to see which of these approaches are more related to adoption of KM in hospitality businesses of developing economies. The following hypotheses will help the investigation:

**$H_{4g}$:** There is a positive relationship between long-term orientation and intention to adopt knowledge management in hospitality industry of less developed economies.

**$H_{4h}$:** There is a positive relationship between short-term orientation and intention to adopt knowledge management in hospitality industry of less developed economies.

The research model that represents all the constructs, variables and the hypotheses that link them is in Figure. Some dimensions, eg career success vs quality of life, of culture have two hypotheses connecting them with intention to adopt KM because of their dual foci. Future study will operationalise the model for empirical research so as to validate it. The research will reveal which of the hypotheses are significant and therefore needs to be countenanced and which ones are not.

## SUMMARY, IMPLICATIONS AND AREAS FOR FURTHER INVESTIGATION

Knowledge management is a proven modern tool that aids organisations to learn and significantly improve their performance because it encourages the culture of creating, storing and sharing knowledge. While KM is more researched and accepted in developed economies and especially with big hospitality organisations, it is not so done with small enterprises and in developing economies. This chapter tried to develop a conceptual model of KM adoption in hospitality industry of developing economies. Mainly from literature, developmental factors, culture and technology were considered relevant factors that not only inter-relate but also eventually affect intention to adopt KM in hospitality industry of developing economies.

The study reported in this paper is at the moment at a conceptual level meaning that empirical work is yet to be carried out to validate the theoretical model. Notwithstanding, the work so far done has important implications to managers and owners of hospitality organisations in developing economies. They have to recognise and be able to manage the developmental factors that would impinge on their operations. They should not be certain of availability of constant electricity and communication infrastructure. For big organisations, especially franchise, they have to self-provide these facilities eg generators for electricity. The smaller organisations should consider collaborating with either peers or their big organisations to benefit from their externalities. For their staff, they have to invest in constant training. Use should be made of internet-based educational materials which are increasingly be-

*Figure 1. Research model – Factors affecting intention to adopt KM in hospitality industry*

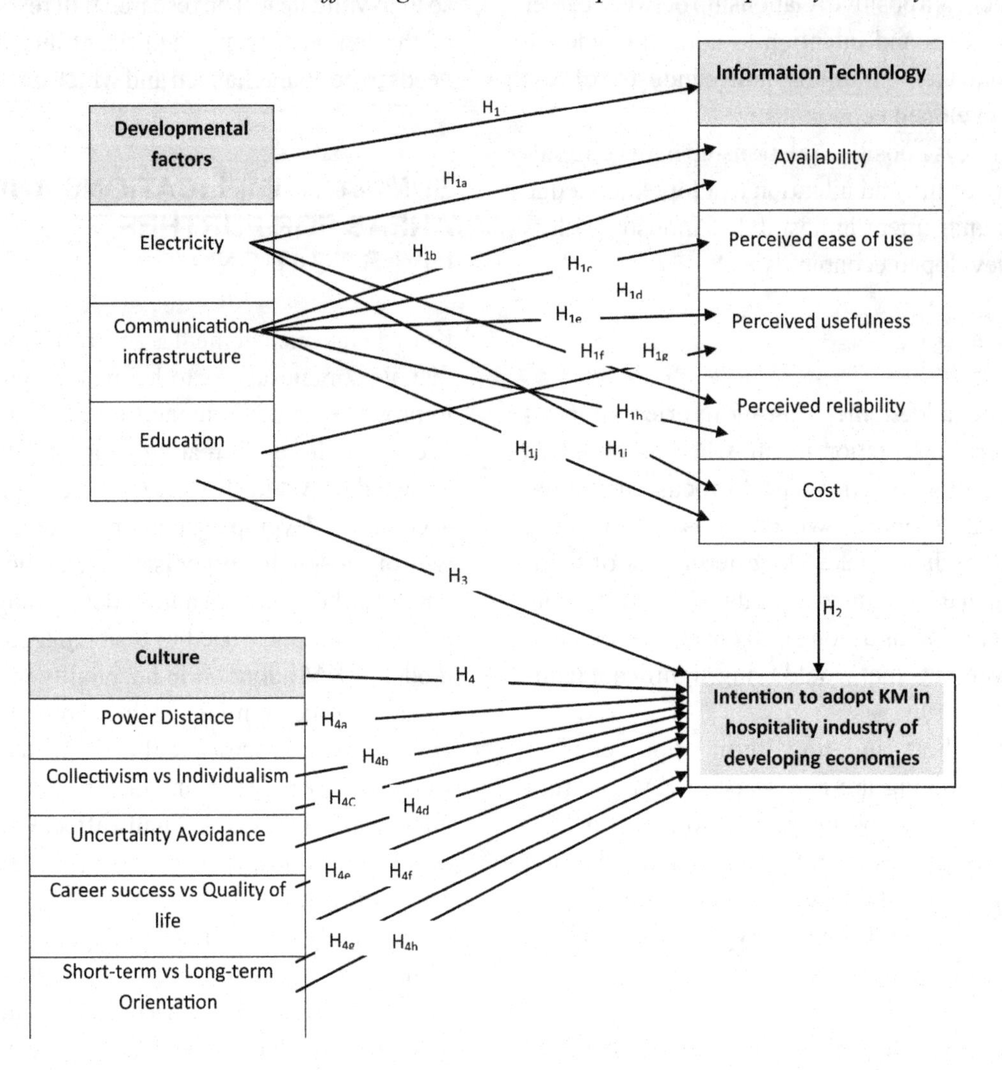


ing offered free eg on YouTube (www.youtube.com). Included in the training should be culture of externalising and sharing tacit knowledge.

Provision of electricity, communication infrastructure and education will open the opportunity for using information technology-based KM tools for knowledge storage, discovery and sharing. Data warehousing with its on-line analytics processing can provide business intelligence and data mining to discover demand patterns (Ranjan & Bhatnagar, 2011). On a basic level, even small hospitality businesses can have an effective web front and perform on-line marketing and business. If the organisation is able to bear the cost of these technologies and ensure that they are useful, easy to use and reliable, the workers will be encouraged to use them and help the local hospitality outfit to be able to tap into international markets, therefore improving their profit potentials.

A key KM tool that managers should encourage is communities of practice (CoP) especially the on-line ones since they have been found to be effective in exposing implicit knowledge and encouraging knowledge sharing (Usoro & Majewski, 2011).

CoPs cross organisational boundaries and their on-line versions also cross national boundaries. Through them, employees can tap into the brains of their colleagues virtually from any part of the world. Increasingly, the platform of Web 2.0 is used to build these CoPs in the form of social networking (Razmerita et al, 2009; Taylor, 2011). However, they are not only for social purposes but can be for serious professional purposes making them to qualify as CoPs. By using them, external knowledge can be injected into the organisation. It would counteract the isolated nature of small hospitality businesses of developing economies by significantly broadening their knowledge base.

Another KM tool that should be used is databases and document management systems that would power intranets for distribution of knowledge including best-practices and e-learning materials.

Managers of hospitality industry should be sensitive to and be smart in using the local culture of their employees to advantage. For instance, the 'collectivism' culture of developing economies should easily encourage knowledge sharing. If an employee or a group of them are oriented towards career success, this can also be harnessed. Tying knowledge creation and sharing to rewards can benefit both the organisation and individuals who seek to improve themselves.

In conclusion, it can be said that knowledge management adoption would benefit hospitality industries of developing economies. However, it should be noted that the research model of this paper is yet to be empirically validated. This validation will reveal the specific contribution of each variable to the KM adoption in hospitality of developing economies. This is an area for further studies.

## REFERENCES


Abiagam, B. (2009). *The use of the Internet in arranging travels in the United Kingdom with some implication for Nigerian Tourism.* Thesis Project, University of the West of Scotland.

Aitken, B. J., & Harrison, A. E. (1999). Do Domestic Firms bene□t from Direct Foreign Investment?: Evidence from Venezuela. *The American Economic Review, 89*(3), 605–618. doi:10.1257/aer.89.3.605

Ajzen, I., & Fishbein, M. (1975). *Belief, attitude, intention and behaviour*. Reading, UK: Addison-Wesley.

Antle, J. (1983). Infrastructure and Aggregate Agricultural Productivity: International Evidence. *Economic Development and Cultural Change, 31*(3), 609–619. doi:10.1086/451344

Arikpo, I. I., Osofisan, A., & Usoro, A. (2009). Bridging the digital divide: the Nigerian journey so far. *International Journal of Global Business, 2*(1)181-204, available at: http://gsmi-ijgb.com/Documents/V2%20N1%20IJGB%20-P08%20-Arikpo%20%20Bridging%20the%20Digital%20Divide%20-June%202009.pdf, retrieved on12/2/2011.

Aschauer, D. A. (1989). Is Public Expenditure Productive? *Journal of Monetary Economics*, (n.d). 177–200. doi:10.1016/0304-3932(89)90047-0

Baldwin, E. (2006). Hilton Highlights link between staff loyalty and e-learning. *Human Resource Management International Digest, 14*(1), 36–38. doi:10.1108/09670730610643990

Barquin, R. C. (2001). What is Knowledge Management? In Barquin, R. C., Bennet, A., & Remez, S. G. (Eds.), *Knowledge Management: the Catalyst for Electronic Government* (pp. 3–24). Vienna, Virginia: Management Concepts.

Barro, R. J., & Lee, J.-W. (2010). A New Data Set of Educational Attainment in the World, 1950–2010. *The national bureau for economic research (NBER)*, working paper no. 15902.

Bebensee, T., Helms, R., & Spruit, M. (2011). Exploring Web 2.0 Applications as a Means of Bolstering up Knowledge Management. *Electronic Journal of Knowledge Management*, *9*(1), 1–9.

Becerra-Fernandez, I., Gonzalez, A., & Sabherwal, R. (2004). *Knowledge Management: Challenges, Solutions and Technologies*. Upper Saddle River, NJ: Prentice Hall.

Bellinger, G., Durval, C., & Mills, A. (1997). Data, Information, Knowledge, and Wisdom, available at: http://www.outsightscom/systems/dikw/dikw.htm, retrieved on 18/10/2010.

Bouncken, R. (2002). Knowledge management for quality improvements in hotels. *Journal of Quality Assurance in Hospitality & Tourism*, *3*(3-4), 25–59. doi:10.1300/J162v03n03_03

Buttle, F. (1986). *Hotel and food service marketing: A Managerial Approach*. England: Continuum International Publishing.

Canning, D. (1994). Infrastructure and Growth. In Baldassarri, M., Paganetto, L., & Phelps, E. (Eds.), *International Differences in Growth Rates* (pp. 113–147). New York, NY: Macmillan Press.

Canning, D. (1999). A Database of World Stocks of Infrastructure, 1950-95. *The World Bank Economic Review*, *12*(3), 529–547.

Choo, C. W. (2002). *The strategic management of intellectual capital and organisational knowledge*. Oxford: University Press.

Chui, C.-M., Wang, C., Eric, T. G., Shih, F.-J., & Fan, Y.-W. (2011). Understanding knowledge sharing in virtual communities: An integration of expectancy disconfirmation and justice theories. *Online Information Review*, *35*(1), 134–153. doi:10.1108/14684521111113623

Cooper, C. (2006). Knowledge Management and Tourism. *Annals of Tourism Research*, *33*(1), 47–64. doi:10.1016/j.annals.2005.04.005

Curran, J. M., Meuter, M. L., & Surprenant, C. F. (2003). Intentions to use self-service technologies: a confluence of multiple attitudes. *Journal of Service Research*, *5*(3), 209–224. doi:10.1177/1094670502238916

Curwen, P., & Whalley, J. (2011). The restructuring of African mobile telecommunications provision and the prospects for economic development. *Info*, *13*(2), 53–71. doi:10.1108/14636691111121638

Davis, F. D. (1989). Perceived usefulness, Perceived ease-of-use, and User acceptance of Information Technology. *Management Information Systems Quarterly*, *13*(3), 319–339. doi:10.2307/249008

Davis, F. D. (1993). User acceptance of information technology: system characteristics, user perceptions and behavioral impacts. *International Journal of Man-Machine Studies*, *38*, 475–487. doi:10.1006/imms.1993.1022

Delgado-Hernandez, D. J., Wong, K. Y., De-La-Torre-Rivera, S., Rigaud-Tellez, N., Velarde, J. I. S., Gaxiola, D. M., et al. (2009). *Computer Science and Information Technology (IACSITSC) - Spring Conference*,(pp. 313 – 316.) Washington, DC: IEEE Press

Ding, L., & Haynes, K. (2006). The role of telecommunications infrastructure in regional economic growth in China. *Australasian Journal of Regional Studies*, *12*(3), 281–302.

DiPietro, R. B., & Wang, Y. R. (2010). Key issues for ICT applications: impacts and implications for hospitality operations. *Worldwide Hospitality and Tourism Themes*, *2*(1), 49–67. doi:10.1108/17554211011012595

Easterly, W., & Rebelo, S. (1993). Fiscal Policy and Economic Growth: An Empirical Investigation. *Journal of Monetary Economics*, *32*, 417–458. doi:10.1016/0304-3932(93)90025-B

Fishbein, M., & Ajzen, I. (1975). *Belief, Attitude, Intention and Behaviour: An Introduction to Theory and Research*. Reading, MA: Addison-Wesley.

Friesl, M, Sackmann, S. A. & Kremser, S. (2011). Knowledge sharing in new organizational entities: The impact of hierarchy, organizational context, micro-politics and suspicion in *Cross Cultural Management: an international Journal, 18*(1) 71-86.

Gefen, D., & Straub, D. W. (2004). Consumer trust in B2C e-commerce and the importance of social presence: experiments in e-products and e-services. *Omega*, (n.d). 32407–32424.

Gillwald, A. (2008). *International Encyclopaedia of Communication* available at: http://www.communicationencyclopedia.com/public/tocnode?id=g9781405131995_yr2 011_chunk_g97814051319958_ss78-1, retrieved on 21/3/2011.

Granovetter, M. (2005). The Impact of Social Structure on Economic Outcomes. *The Journal of Economic Perspectives*, *19*(1), 33–50. doi:10.1257/0895330053147958

Grizeli, F. (2003). Collaborative Knowledge Management in Virtual Service Companies-Approach for Tourism Destinations. *Journal of Tourism*, *51*(4), 371–385.

Gupta, B., Iyer, L. S., & Aronson, E. J. (2000). Knowledge management: practices and challenges. *Industrial Management & Data Systems*, *100*(1), 17–21. doi:10.1108/02635570010273018

Hallin, C. A., & Marnburga, E. (2008). Knowledge management in the hospitality industry: a review of empirical research. *Tourism Management*, *29*, 366–381. doi:10.1016/j.tourman.2007.02.019

Hanushek, E. A., & Wößmann, L. (2007a). *The role of School Improvement in Economic Development*, NBER Working paper No. 12832.

Hanushek, E. A., & Wößmann, L. (2007b). *Education Quality and economic growth*. Washington, DC: The World Bank. doi:10.1596/1813-9450-4122

Harrison, L. E., & Huntington, S. P. (2000). *Culture matters: how values shape human progress*. USA: Basic books.

Heijden, H. V., Verhagen, T., & Creemer, M. (2003). Understanding online purchase intentions: contributions from technology and trust perspectives. *European Journal of Information Systems*, *12*, 41–48. doi:10.1057/palgrave.ejis.3000445

Hierschman, A. O. (1958). *The Strategy of Economic Development*. New Haven, CT: Yale University Press.

Hofstede, G. (1980). *Culture's consequences*. London, UK: Sage.

Hofstede, G. (2005). Cultural constrains in management theories. In Redding, G., & Stening, B. (Eds.), *Cross-cultural management* (*Vol. II*, pp. 61–74). Cheltenham: Edward Elgar Publishing Limited.

Honeycutt, J. (2000). *Knowledge Management strategies*. Canada: Microsoft press.

Huntington, S. (1996). *The clash of civilizations: remaking of world order*. New York, NY: Simon and Schuster.

Ifinedo, P., & Usoro, A. (2009). Study of the relationships between economic and cultural factors and network readiness: a focus on African's regions, in *International Journal of Global Business, 2* (1)101-123, available at: http://gsmi-ijgb.com/Documents/V2%20N1%20IJGB%20-P04%20-Ifenedo%20%20Economic%20and%20Cultural%20-June%202009.pdf.

Kasavana, M., Nusair, K., & Teodosic, K. (2010). Online social networking: Redefining the human web. *Journal of Hospitality and Tourism Technology, 1*(1), 68–82. doi:10.1108/17579881011023025

Kemeny, J. (2011). Are international technology gaps growing or shrinking in the age of globalization? *Journal of Economic Geography, 11*(1), 1–35. doi:10.1093/jeg/lbp062

Law, R., & Bai, B. (2008). How do the preferences of online buyers and browser different on the design and content of travel websites. *International Journal of Contemporary Hospitality Management, 20*(4), 388–400. doi:10.1108/09596110810873507

Lee, K.-S., & Anas, A. (1992). *The Impact of Infrastructure Deficiencies on Nigerian Manufacturing, Infrastructure Department working Paper, No INU 98*. Washington, DC: World Bank.

Levin, H. M., & Lockheed, M. E. (1993). *Effective schools in developing countries*. London, UK: Routledge.

Lipset, S. M. (1959). Some Social Requisites of Democracy: Economic Development and Political Legitimacy. *The American Political Science Review, 53*(1), 69–105. doi:10.2307/1951731

Luiz, J. (2010). Infrastructure investment and its performance in Africa over the course of the twentieth century. *International Journal of Social Economics, 37*(7), 512–536. doi:10.1108/03068291011055450

Mbarika, V., Okoli, C., Byrd, A., & Datta, P. (2005). Neglected Continent of IS research. *Journal of the Association for Information Systems, 6*(5), 130–170.

Medlik, S. (1990). *The Business of Hotels*. Oxford: Heinemann.

Moon, J. W., & Kim, Y. G. (2001). Extending the TAM for a World Wide Web Context. *Information & Management, 38*(4), 217–237. doi:10.1016/S0378-7206(00)00061-6

National Restaurant Association. (2011). Available at: www.restaurant.org/forecast, retrieved on 20/2/2011.

Ndubuisi, N. O., & Jantan, M. (2003). Evaluating IS usage in Malaysia small and medium-sized firms using the technology acceptance model. *Logistics Information Management, 16*(6), 440–450. doi:10.1108/09576050310503411

Nonaka, I., & Takeuchi, H. (1995). *The Knowledge-Creating Company: How Japanese Companies create the dynamics of Innovation*. Oxford: University Press.

Nusair, K. K., Hua, N., & Li, X. (2010). A conceptual framework of relationship commitment: e-travel agencies. *Journal of Hospitality and Tourism Technology, 1*(2), 106–120. doi:10.1108/17579881011065029

Oh, H., & Pizam, A. (2008). *Handbook of Hospitality marketing management*. London, UK: Butter-Heinemann.

Osotimehin, K. O., Akinkoye, E. Y., & Olasanmi, O. O. (2010). *The Effects of Investment in Telecommunication Infrastructure on Economic Growth in Nigeria (1992-2007),* Paper for the Oxford Business and Economic Conference.

Oxford Economics for the British Hospitality Association. (2010). Available at: http://www.baha- uk.org/OxfordEconomics.pdf, retrieved on 3/3/2011.

Ozturk, S. G. (2007). *Classifying and predicting country types through development factors that influence economic, social, educational and health environments of countries*, SWDI Proceedings paper S759, (p 665-674), JEL classification: N01, N70, O15, O19.

Perez, M. P., Sanchez, A. M., Carnicer, P. L., & Jimenez, A. I. (2004). A Technology Acceptance Model of Innovation Adoption: The Case of Teleworking. *Journal of Innovation Management, 7*(4), 280–390. doi:10.1108/14601060410565038

Philips, L. A., Rodger, C., & Ming-Tong, L. (1994). International Technology Adoption: Behaviour Structure, Demand Certainty and Culture. *Journal of Business and Industrial Marketing, 9*(4), 347–362.

Pizam, A. (2005). *International encyclopedia of hospitality management*. London, UK: Butterworth-Heinemann.

Powers, T., & Barrows, C. W. (2006). *Introduction to Management in the Hospitality Industry*. London, UK: John Wiley.

Raji, M. O., Ayoade, O. B., & Usoro, A. (2006). The prospects and problems of adopting ICT for poverty eradication in Nigeria. *The Electronic Journal of Information Systems in Developing Countries, 28*(8), 1–9.

Ranjan, J. (2011). Study of sharing knowledge resources in business schools. *The Learning Organization, 18*(2), 102–114. doi:10.1108/09696471111103713

Ranjan, J., & Bhatnagar, V. (2011). Role of knowledge management and analytical CRM in business: data mining based framework. *The Learning Organization, 18*(2), 131–148. doi:10.1108/09696471111103731

Rashid, A. T., & Elder, L. (2009). mobile phones and development: an analysis of IDRC-supported projects. *The Electronic Journal on Information Systems in Developing Countries, 2*, 1–16.

Razmerita, L., Kirchner, K., & Sudzina, F. (2009). Personal knowledge management: The role of Web 2.0 tools for managing knowledge at individual and organisational levels. *Online Information Review, 33*(6), 1021–1039. doi:10.1108/14684520911010981

Rogers, A. (2006). ICT will ultimately bridge the digital and poverty Divides, UNCDF, available at:http://www.uncdf.org/english/local_development/uploads/thematic/2006-11-ICT%20will%20ultimately%20bridge%20the%20digital%20and%20poverty.pdf, accessed on 14/5/11.

Roller, L. H. & Wavernman, L. (2001). Telecommunications Infrastructure and Economic Development: A Simultaneous Approach. *American Economic Review Journal, 91* (4).

Root, F. (1994). *Entry strategies for international markets* New York, NY: Lexington.

Ruhanen, L., & Cooper, C. (2004). Applying a knowledge management framework to tourism research. *Tourism Recreation Research, 29*(1), 83–88.

Song, C. (2011). *The Regional Macroeconomic effects of public infrastructure in China*, PhD Thesis George Masion University, USA.

Taylor, C. (2011). Web 2.0 Knowledge technologies and the enterprise. *Library Review, 60*(2), 168–169.

Teidemann, N, Birgele, M. & Semeijn, J. (2009), Increasing hotel responsiveness to customers through information sharing in *Tourism Review, 64*(4) 12-26.

Thatcher, J. B., McKnight, D. H., Baker, E. W., Arsal, R. E., & Roberts, N. H. (2011). The Role of Trust in Postadoption IT Exploration: An Empirical Examination of Knowledge Management Systems. *IEEE Technology Management Council, 58*(1), 56–70.

UNDP. (2001). *Human Development Report: making new technologies work for human development*. New York, NY: Oxford University Press.

UNDP. (2010). Human Development Report, The *Real Wealth of Nations: Pathways to Human Development* available at: http://www.hdr.undp.org/en/reports/global/hdr2010/, retrieved on 20/12/2010.

Usoro, A., & Kuofie, M. (2008). Conceptualization of cultural dimensions as a major influence on knowledge-sharing. In Jennex, M. E. (Ed.), *Current Issues in Knowledge Management* (pp. 119–130). San Diego, CA: Information Science Reference. doi:10.4018/978-1-59904-916-8.ch009

Usoro, A & Majewski, G. (2011). Intensive knowledge sharing: Finnish Laurea lab case study in *Journal of Information and Knowledge Management Systems, 41*(1) 7-25.

Usoro, A., & Shoyelu, S. (2010). Task-technology fit and technology acceptance models applicability to e-tourism in *Journal of Economic Development, Management, IT, Finance and Marketing*, Volume 2, No 1, pp 1-32, available at: http://gsmi-jedmitfm.com/Documents/N2%20V1%20JEDMITFM%20-P01%20-Usoro%20-Task%20Technology%20Fit.pdf, accessed 2/2/2011.

Venkatesh, V. (2000). Determinants of perceived ease of use: integrating control, intrinsic motivation, and emotion into the technology acceptance model. *Information Systems Research, 46*, 342–365. doi:10.1287/isre.11.4.342.11872

Venkatesh, V., & Davis, F. D. (2000). A Theoretical Extension of the Technology Acceptance Model: For Longitudinal Field Studies. *International Journal of Management Science, 46*(2), 186–204.

Walker, J. R., & Miller, J. E. (2008). *Supervising in the hospitality industry: Leading Human Resource*. London: John Wiley.

Wang, Y., Wang, Y., Lin, H., & Tang, T. (2003). Determinants of User Acceptance of Internet Banking: An Empirical Study. *International Journal of Service Industry Management, 14*(5), 501–505. doi:10.1108/09564230310500192

Webber, D., & Kauffman, R. J. (2011). *What drives global ICT adoption? Analysis and research directions, Electronic Commerce Research and Applications, Article still in press*. London, UK: Elsevier

Wong, K. Y. (2008). An exploratory study on Knowledge management adoption in the Malaysian Industry. *International Journal of Business Information Systems, 3*(3), 272–283. doi:10.1504/IJBIS.2008.017285

World Bank. (2006). *Information and Communications for Development: Global Trends and Policies*. New York, NY: The World Bank Group.

World Bank Report. (1991). *The Challenge of Development*. New York, NY: World Bank Group.

World Development Report. (1991). *Infrastructure for Development*. Washington, DC: The World Bank.

World Development Report, (1998). *Knowledge for Development*, London, UK: Oxford Press.

## ENDNOTES

1. http://www.hrmguide.net/hrm/knowledge-management.htm
2. http://www.uopeople.org/
3. Hofstede initially labelled this masculinity vs femininity.

# Chapter 5
# Web Service Composition, Optimization and the Implications for Developing Economies

**Adenike O Osofisan**
*University of Ibadan, Nigeria*

**Idongesit E. Eteng**
*University of Calabar, Nigeria*

**Iwara I Arikpo**
*University of Calabar, Nigeria*

**Abel Usoro**
*University of the West of Scotland, UK*

## ABSTRACT

*The emergence of the Service Oriented computing paradigm with its implicit inclusion of web services has caused a precipitous revolution in software engineering, e-service compositions, and optimization of e-services. Web service composition requests are usually combined with end-to-end Quality of Service (QoS) requirements, which are specified in terms of non-functional properties e.g. response time, throughput, and price. This chapter describes what web services are; not just to the web but to the end users. The state of the art approaches for composing web services are briefly described and a novel game theoretic approach using genetic programming for composing web services in order to optimize service performance, bearing in mind the Quality of Service (QoS) of these web services, is presented. The implication of this approach to cloud computing and economic development of developing economies is discussed.*

DOI: 10.4018/978-1-4666-1637-0.ch005

## INTRODUCTION

According to Erl (2009), contemporary SOA (Service Oriented Architecture) represents an open, agile, expensive, federated and composable architecture comprised of autonomous, (quality-of-service) QoS-capable, vendor diverse, interoperable, discoverable, and potentially reusable services, implemented as web services. Service Oriented Architecture is therefore an architecture consisting of a collection of services. These services communicate with each other either by passing simple data or by involving in complex interactions. The services can be used within multiple separate systems from several business domains. Therefore, a deployed SOA-based architecture will provide a loosely-integrated suite of services that can be used within multiple business domains. This could be of great benefit to developing economies as will be shown later. SOA also defines how to integrate widely disparate applications for a world that is Web based and uses multiple implementation platforms; this also is a major benefit.

Service-oriented architectures have been implemented in older platforms. Such platforms include Distributed Component Object Model (DCOM) or Object Request Brokers (ORBs) based on the CORBA specification. DCOM is an extension of the Component Object Model (COM). DCOM was introduced in 1996 and is designed for use across multiple network transports, including Internet protocols such as HTTP (Hypertext Transfer Protocol). It works primarily with Microsoft Windows. CORBA (Common Object Request Broker Architecture), on the other hand, was developed under the auspices of the Object Management Group (OMG) as a middleware that allows for interoperability of programs across vendors, computers, programming languages, networks and operating systems.

The implications of a Service Oriented Architecture include the following:

A. Interoperability is a key goal and technological differences must not inhibit the performance of services.
B. Services and applications must make their capabilities publicly known so that other existing or new services can take advantage of their existence. This also implies that it must be possible to compose complex and varied services from simple ones. The composed services are known as composite services.
C. Clients must have the opportunity of selecting the optimal (best) services that must be composed to meet chosen Quality of Service (QoS) criteria.

The concept of service orientation as a design paradigm therefore stipulates the necessary foundation for simplifying the enormous convolution and integration of system development. This is made possible because service orientation takes advantage of the autonomy of existing services and developers do not need to bother about developing systems from the scratch. This has obvious economic benefits especially where funds are limited and systems development expertise is scarce.

Service Oriented Architecture can be better understood when web services are understood. A web service is a piece of software that can be defined, described and discovered by XML artifacts Ouzzani (2004). We define Web services simply as application components that communicate using open protocols and can be used by other applications. They are self-contained and self-describing applications that can be discovered, used and composed into complex services. Quality of service attributes can be used for selecting and composing appropriate web services.

According to Liu &Baras (2004), in the Service Oriented Community, Quality of Service (QoS) comprises all non-functional attributes of a service, ranging from performance-specific attributes to security and cost-related data. In general, QoS can be grouped into deterministic and non-deterministic attributes. Deterministic attributes are the attributes whose values can be determined before runtime, e.g. cost; while for non-deterministic attributes, values can only be determined at runtime.

Several authors including (Mani &Nagarajan, 2002; Platzer et al., 2009; Ran, 2003) have deliberated on the importance of QoS in the area of service-oriented systems. Quality of service issues in service oriented architecture (SOA) is still a new area of research and particularly QoS-aware service selection and composition have been core areas of research.

The need for efficient QoS-aware composition which is the major concern of this chapter has over the years become a very important concept. QoS enables a QoS-aware dynamic binding of needed services (chosen by end users, web applications or other services) to concrete services that are available in registries (UDDI) known at runtime. QoS also enables the service requestor to be able to compose services in such a way as to attain optimality in the choice of composed services. Above all, QoS offers a dynamic platform for change of choice whenever the attributes change.

This chapter will review the state of the art approaches for composing web services and will present a novel approach for composing web services in order to optimize service performance bearing in mind the Quality of Service (QoS) of these web services. This should ultimately leverage developing economies because businesses from any part of the world (whether developed or still developing) have access to building newer robust and complex applications from existing applications and these can be done with limited expertise, in a short duration and with little financial outlay.

Therefore, our approach aims at achieving the following:

A. Modeling the fitness value by bringing into consideration quality of services attributes and domain specific attributes as specified by the service composer.
B. Achieving scalability by employing a context free grammar for the genetic programming algorithm where the structure of repository of the web services are immaterial since the control structures are described in a general way.
C. Building into the architecture a monitor for run-time updates of QoS attributes. This monitor will be connected to a sequenced cache.
D. Describing a robust architecture for web services composition.
E. Quality of services attributes with their metrics are presented.
F. Modeling a game theoretic approach into genetic programming to guarantee the construction of a generic fitness function that can be used for testing several criteria.
G. Most importantly, discussing the economic implications of web service composition and cloud computing on Business Creation and employment in developing countries.

## LITERATURE REVIEW

The development and adoption of web services can, to a large extent, be traced to the same driving factors that have led to the development of the service-oriented approach and Service Oriented Architecture (Bertino et al, 2010). From an IT (Information Technology) point of view, the main vision has been to exploit methods, tools and techniques enabling businesses to build complex and flexible business processes.

Web Services are interfaces that describe a collection of operations that are network-accessible through standardized web protocols. When a required operation is not found, several services can be compounded to get a composite service that performs the desired task. (Rodrı´guez-Mier et al., 2010), Therefore, a web service is simply a software component stored on one computer that can be accessed by an application (or other software components) on another computer over a network. A web service is said to be published when it is enabled to receive client requests; and the service is said to be consumed when it is used by a client application. Practical examples of web services include: airline reservation services, weather forecast, real estate agency, and "attend a conference planner".

It is obviously common knowledge that businesses and business process models are getting complicated by the day. Business processes supported by information communication and technology should be able to adapt to changing policies, platforms and expectations and should also cope with the pervasiveness of the Internet. Web services are the answer to these challenges because they utilize existing IT infrastructures and platforms and allow businesses to wrap legacy applications in a standardized, consistent and reusable format. The result of this is that every investment can be leveraged (used and re-used). Web services therefore provide a low-cost way to connect internal applications and collaborate among business partners (Erl, 2009).

Most often than not, business processes may need to deploy several web services in order to accomplish a particular task. For example, service composition is used to describe a composite relationship between collections of web services. Several other terms are used for describing service compositions. These include "aggregating web services" and "federating web services."

## Review of Composition of Web Services

### Integer Programming

Two general approaches exist for the QoS-aware service composition and these are local selection and global optimization (Alrifai & Risse, 2009). The two methods have their distinct strengths and weaknesses and the choice of approach depends on several factors such as:

A. Nature of optimization environment such as a centralized or decentralized.
B. Nature of Quality of Service sought, e.g. single quality of service or combined quality of service.
C. Architecture employed.

### The Local Selection Approach

Using the local selection approach, a candidate service is selected in a group of related services. This selection is done independently from services in other groups. In this case, there is no need for a global or central quality of service (QoS) management. Distributed service brokers manage each group of services (Benatallah & Rachid, 2003; Li et al., 2007). According to Alrifai & Risse (2009), the idea is to select one service from each group of service candidates. Using a given utility function, the values of the different QoS criteria are mapped to a single utility value and the service with maximum utility value is selected.

The advantages of this method include that:

A. It is useful for distributed environments where central Quality of Service (QoS) management is not desirable and groups of candidate web services are managed by distributed brokers (Alrifai & Risse, 2009).
B. The approach is efficient in terms of computation time because the time complexity of the local optimization approach is O(t) where t is the number of service candidates in each group (Alrifai & Risse, 2009). Over time, the service candidates in each group are minimal.

The disadvantages of this method however make this approach not very efficient especially as it pertains to end-to-end QoS constraints. The basic disadvantages are that:

A. The local selection approach is not suitable for QoS based service composition with end to end constraint. The reason for this is simple: it is not possible to verify global constraints.

B. Another disadvantage of this approach is that it requires that the QoS data of available web services be imported from the service broker into the MIP (mixed integer programming) model of the service composer, which raises high communication (Alrifai & Risse, 2009).

## The Global Optimization approach

Several recent authors (Ardagna et al., 2007; Zeng et al., 2003; Zeng et al., 2004) have adopted the global optimization approach as a solution to the QoS aware service composition problem. This approach also has its strengths and weaknesses.

The basic advantage of this approach is that it supports QoS based service composition with end to end constraint as the problem can be modeled as an integer programming problem and global constraints can be easily verified.

The approach however has several disadvantages and these include that:

A. The problem is known to be NP-hard (Non-deterministic Polynomial-time) since it is most often modeled as a multi-choice, multidimensional knapsack problem and this is known to be NP-hard (Pisinger, 1995).
B. The optimal solution may not be found in a reasonable amount of time (Maros, 2003).
C. The proposed solution has a time complexity that is exponential (Ardagna et al., 2007; Zenget al., 2003; Zeng et al., 2004).
D. Consequent upon the reason above, the exponential time complexity of the proposed solution is only acceptable if the number of service candidates is very limited (Alrifai & Risse, 2009).
E. Most real-life composition problems such as web services for real estate agency and airline reservation systems employ several categories of web services and each of these services may have several thousands of candidate web services offering similar services and a choice of one of these must be made with QoS satisfaction in mind.

## Combining Global Optimization with Local Selection

Due to the shortcomings of the above mentioned approaches, hybrid approaches have been adopted by some authors. The approach adopted by (Alrifai & Risse, 2009) combines global optimization with local selection techniques. This solution is achieved in two basic steps; first, an integer programming algorithm is used to find the decomposition of global QoS into local constraints, and secondly the services that best meet the local constraints are selected. The selection is done using a distributed approach.

## Genetic Algorithms and Genetic Programming Approaches

Earlier in this chapter, it was pointed out that Quality of Service (QoS) aware composition can be modeled as an optimization problem. Canfora et al. (2005) propose Genetic Algorithms for modeling the QoS composition problem. A genetic algorithm is a stochastic hill climbing search in which a large population of states is maintained. New states are generated by mutation and by crossover, which combines pairs of states from the population. Canfora et al. (2005) argue that even though genetic algorithms are slower than integer programming methods, they however represent a more scalable choice and are more suitable to handle generic QoS attributes.

Genetic algorithms are typically implemented using computer simulations in which an optimization problem is specified. For this problem, members of a space of candidate solutions, called *individuals*, are represented using abstract representations termed *chromosomes*. The genetic algorithms (GA) consist of an iterative process that evolves a working set of individuals called a *population* toward an objective function, or fitness function (Goldberg, 1989; Wikipedia, 2004). According to (Hsu, 2003), traditionally, solutions are represented using fixed length strings, especially binary strings, but alternative encodings have been developed. The evolutionary process of a GA is a highly simplified and stylized simulation of the biological version. It starts from a population of individuals randomly generated according to some probability distribution, usually the uniform distribution. The algorithm then updates this population in steps called generations. In each generation, multiple individuals are randomly selected from the current population based upon some application of fitness, bred using crossover, and modified through mutation to form a new population.

Some genetic algorithm operators include:

A. **Crossover:** Exchange of genetic material (substrings) denoting rules, structural components, features of a machine learning, search, or an optimization problem.
B. **Selection:** The application of the fitness criterion to choose which individuals from a population will go to the next phase to reproduce new offspring.
C. **Replication:** The propagation of individuals from one generation to the next.
D. **Mutation:** The modification of single individuals in the chromosomes.

Canfora et al. (2005), in using genetic algorithms in their approach, assume that the problem is encoded with a suitable genome. Their genome is represented by an integer array with a number of items equals to the number of distinct abstract services composing the service. The crossover operator is the standard two-point crossover, while the mutation operator randomly selects an abstract service and randomly replaces the corresponding concrete service with another one among those available. The problem can now be modeled by means of a fitness function which needs to maximize some QoS attributes (e.g., reliability), while minimizing others (e.g., cost).

According to Li et al. (2005), genetic algorithms are widely applied to searching optimal solutions in many problem domains. Also, evolutionary algorithms (EAs) are generic, population-based meta-heuristic optimization algorithms that use biology-inspired mechanisms like mutation, crossover, natural selection and survival of the fittest. "The advantage of evolutionary algorithms compared to other optimization methods is that they make only few assumptions about the underlying fitness landscape and therefore perform consistently well in many different problem categories" (Weise & Geihs, 2006).

Several other authors (Aversano & Pent, 2006; Rao et al., 2006) have also employed genetic algorithms in solving web composition and optimization problems. By our assessment, the basic drawback of these methods is the fact that several repositories of web services were not used to test the robustness and scalability of the approach. Also, the calculation of the fitness of each individual of the population is done only based on quality of Service (QoS); other criteria like generated outputs and used input which indicate the degree to which a valid solution has been found were not included in the fitness function calculation.

Several recent authors have taken a further step by employing the use of genetic programming techniques in solving composition and optimization problems. The field of genetic programming is closely related to genetic algorithms. The principal difference is that the representations that are mutated and combined in genetic programming are programs rather than bit strings. The programs are represented in the form of expression trees. In genetic programming, the crossover operation involves splicing together sub trees rather than substrings. As a result of this, off springs are guaranteed to be well formed expressions.

Genetic programming offers several advantages for web services composition basically because it can deal with solutions with different kinds of structures. Here are some of the approaches that basically employ genetic programming approaches. Most of the approaches have employed a planning-based approach in which the web composition problem is being modeled as a planning problem (Klusch & Gerber, 2006). The basic sequences of activities in this approach include:

A. The designation of an initial set by a set of inputs and preconditions. These preconditions must be verified by the composite service.
B. The description of a set of services that are executed to obtain new and intermediate states.
C. The definition of a final state defined by a set of both outputs and preconditions that must be verified by a solution of the service composition problem.

Variances of different planners have been applied. Nau et al. (2003) and Sirin et al. (2004) employ hierarchical planners. Klusch & Gerber (2006) and Wu et al. (2007) apply a graph analysis based planner; and Rao et al. (2006) employ a logic-based planner. These approaches however have a drawback of scalability when there is a large space to be searched for services and these shortcomings have been addressed by few authors like Oh et al. (2008).

Other genetic programming approaches however do not consider the problem as just a sequence-based planning approach composition problem. Rather they employ automatic workflow composition approaches where the end result of the composition is a workflow composed of a set of control structures that decide, determine and coordinate the execution of the services. Several authors (eg Aversano et al., 2006) employ this approach. Rodrignez-Mier et al. (2010) however have done a thorough work of composition of web services through genetic programming. The strength of their approach includes the following:

A. The development of a context free grammar for generating new individuals and producing right structures for individuals after crossover and mutation.
B. The development of a genetic programming approach that adequately handles the web services composition problem. This algorithm employs the use of the context free grammar explained above.
C. A novel method for updating attributes at each node.
D. An approach that tries to minimize the number of services that looks for composition with the minimum execution path.
E. A full experimental validation with four different repositories showing great performance in all the tests.

The basic shortcoming of this work, however, is the fact that quality of service attributes which we have seen to be a basic contribution to the satisfactory composition of web services for end users is not modeled. Suffice it to say that this may not have been a major objective for the authors as it is to us.

## Games Theory

The novelty introduced in this work is the employment of concepts from the theory of games in the genetic programming implementation of the problem of service composition and optimization. It is therefore important to introduce the concept of games theory. Games theory attempts to mathematically capture behaviour in strategic situations, or games in which an individual's success in making choices depends on the choices of others (Myerson, 1981).

### Representation of Games

A game therefore can be formally defined as a kind of search problem with the following components:

A. An initial state
B. A successor function which returns a list of (move, state) pairs, each indicating a legal move and the resulting state.
C. A terminal state which determines when the game is over. States where the game has ended are called terminal states.
D. A utility function (also called an objective or payoff function) which gives a numeric value for the terminal states. In chess, the outcome is a win, loss or draw, with values +1, -1, or 0.

The games studied in game theory are well defined mathematical objects. A game consists of the following:

A. A set of players: these are the agents that make decisions. You can either have 2-player games or n-player games, where n > 2.
B. A set of actions, moves or strategies available to those players. The players may or may not have the same set of actions available.
C. A specification of payoffs for each combination of strategies. This gives the utility to each player for each combination of actions by all the players.

### Optimal Strategies

In a normal search problem, the optimal solution would be a sequence of moves leading to a goal state, that is, a terminal state which is a win. For a game, it is a lot more complex than that. In games theory, the initial state and the legal moves for each side define the game tree for the game. Therefore, given a game tree, the optimal strategy can be determined by examining the minimax value of each node, which can be written as minimax-value (n).

# RESEARCH FRAMEWORK AND ARCHITECTURE

In this chapter, a novel approach for composing web services in order to optimize service performance bearing in mind the Quality of Service (QoS) of these web services will be described. Models for the proposed approach will be proposed and the advantages of the proposed approach and models will be analyzed.

## The System Architecture

The architecture for the proposed system for service composition is shown in Figure 1.

## Description of Components

### The Requestor Service

The requestor service is the end user or service composer who makes a request. The request might be to satisfy some business models or may need a combination of several services. The requestor can either provide an abstract process model in the form of a state chart, workflow diagram or the user types his request e.g. "I need to attend CITED 2011 Conference" into an intelligent interface. In the latter case, the interface will prompt the requestor for detailed information such as quality of Service (QoS) requirements and domain specific QoS (if any). The request is sent to the composer and optimizer. The service requestor is also responsible for receiving results.

In order for the requestor to be able to send a composed message, state chart diagrams of the needed compositions must be drawn. Parameters from the state chart diagrams such as type of service e.g. AIRLINESERVICE and QoS eg, cost and reputation is supplied into the Graphical User Interface (GUI) of the composer toolkit. These parameters are then sent to the composer & optimizer and selector respectively for further processing.

*Figure1. The proposed system architecture*

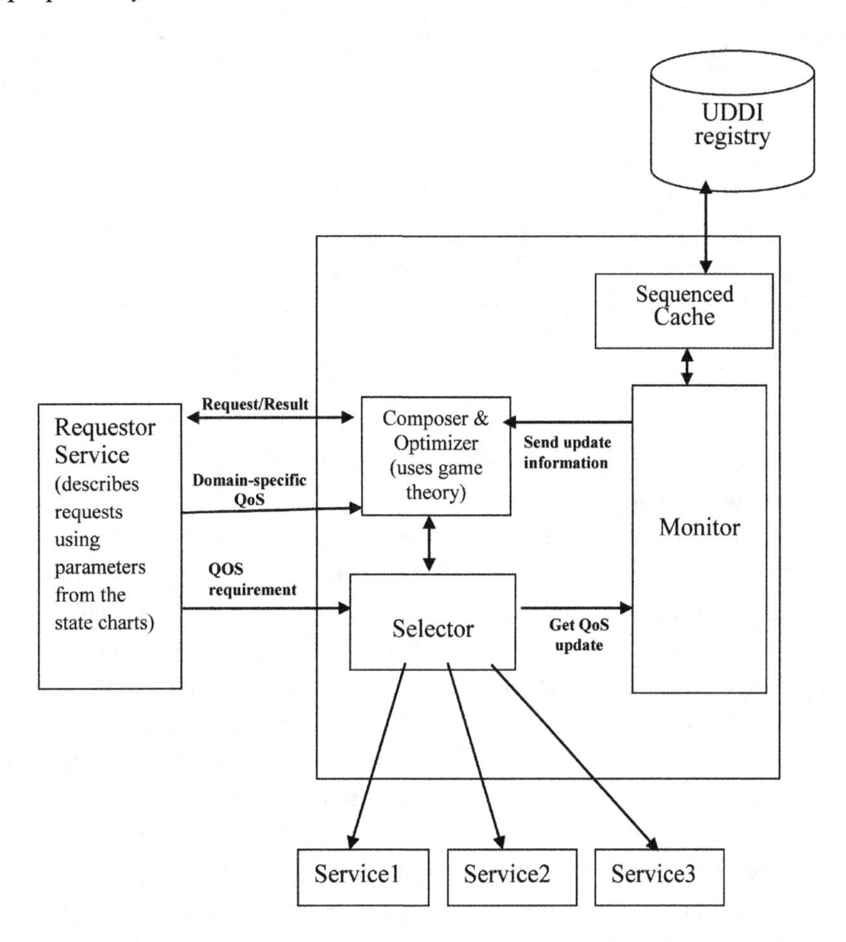


## Composer and Optimizer

A typical composed service could be an "Attend a conference planner". The planner performs sub-tasks beginning from advert-checking; this sub-task checks the advert for attending the conference and this can be published on several web sites. The next task may be conference-registration. Here, the user may need to register for the conference and he can either register with a credit card or with the nearest and convenient bank. A search for attraction and shopping can be performed in parallel with airline reservation and accommodation booking. After the searching and booking are completed, the distance from the hotel to the conference centre is calculated and depending on the distance, a call-a-cab-service or bus services can be employed. In this case, a composition model may state those tasks in that order. After the selector has looked up the services providing the same functionalities as each task specified, the composer generates various combinations of discovered services, and then chooses the best combination that gives the highest quality (optimizes). The optimizer evaluates the selected services execution plans based on their quality of service attributes and domain specific Quality of Service, and selects the best pareto set of optimal solutions.

The quality of service parameters are supplied as values as specified in Table 2. This is to enable the requestor supply the values in a form he/she is used to. However, these values are varied and the composer has to normalize them using the steps

*Table 2. Fitness Function Table*

| Attributes | Individual1 | Individual2 | Individual3 | Individualn |
|---|---|---|---|---|
| Execution Price | 150 dollars/sec | 470 dollars/sec | 360 dollars/sec | 555 dollars/sec |
| Response Time | 67 secs | 15 secs | 36 secs | 5 secs |
| Availability | 21% | 13% | 89% | 89% |
| Reliability | 90% | 56% | 82% | 71% |
| Throughput | 0.8 | 0.1 | 0.8 | 0.9 |
| Reputation | 68% | 82% | 90% | 78% |
| | Min $P_1$ | Min $P_2$ | | Min $P_{last}$ |

described in 3.5 below. The normalized values are then used by the composer. For the purpose of validating the approach, and for the genetic algorithm to be able to have as many values as needed, the needed values are generated and then the reproduction operators (mutation and crossover) are used to reproduce more values that are now tested using the fitness function.

## Selector

The service selector is responsible for selecting the best set of services discovered. It does this by giving consideration to the execution order of the services. The selected services must maximize the overall utility and quality of service of the resulting composite service.

## Monitor

This component monitors services and compositions for runtime updates and sends the relevant information to the composer and optimizer

## Sequenced Cache

The sequenced cache works with the monitor to keep records of update information in a cache. The information is stored based on time of notification.

# Problem Description

In this chapter, we consider that web services are characterized not only by their functional features. Inputs and outputs which are semantically described through ontologies or information about them are provided by the WSDL (Web Service Description Language) but also by quality of service attributes otherwise described as non-functional features.

We shall consider a composite services of n abstract services S$\Xi$ $\{S_1, S_2, ...S_n\}$ whose structure is defined by state chart diagrams. Each component Si can be bound to one of the n concrete services (Si, 1 ..., (Si, n...) which are functionally equivalent.

The functional attributes are described by state chart diagrams which model individual tasks and the control structures that combine a pair of tasks on the state chart diagram. The nonfunctional attributes are described by quality of service attributes which are either standard QoS attributes or domain specific QoS attributes as specified by the service composer.

The composition problem can be formulated as the automatic construction of a workflow (described as state charts) that coordinates the execution of a set of services that interact among them through their inputs and outputs as well as quality of service attributes. This workflow, therefore, has services and a set of control structures that define both the behavior of the execution flow and the inputs/outputs of the services related to those structures as well as quality of service attributes.

After the automatic construction of the workflow has been done and our result is a concretization of a composite service, i.e., a composite service description where each abstract service has been bound to one of its corresponding concrete services, the overall QoS can be computed by applying the rules described by Canfora et al. (2005). These rules are based on typical control structures of web services composition languages which include: sequence structure, selection structure, and parallel structure, split join structure and loop structures. A description of these structures and standard quality of service attributes are shown in Table 1. While for some standard QoS attributes the aggregation function has been explicitly specified (Benatallah, 2003 and Zeng et al., 2004) there may be other attributes (for example, domain-dependent attributes) for which the aggregation function must be specified by the service composer.

The workflow therefore has services, a set of control structures and QoS attributes description that helps in pruning out services that do not meet the user's needs. The control structures determine how the execution flow is done and also determine the input/output of services related to the structures. Below is a description of composed services (that is a combination of services to form a business process modeled as a state chart, a description of services, a description of control structures and QoS attributes.

## Composite Services Specifications

Composite services are defined as a collection of single services or tasks together with control and data flow among the services. According to Coello (2002), a composite service is similar to a workflow in many ways since a workflow has to specify the flow of work items. This research, like several others (Zeng et al, 2004) will employ state charts for representing dependencies among individual services or tasks. There are various reason for the choice of state charts. State charts are ubiquitous and easy to use and understand. State charts have well supported behaviour modeling notation and have been integrated into the unified modeling language (UML) which happens to be a *de facto* modeling language in recent times. State charts can easily be adopted and fused with other popular modeling languages such as business process execution language for web services (BPEL4WS) and web ontology language for web services OWL–S. With the use of state chart, choices such as concurrent choice of services which speeds up the service composition process can easily be demonstrated.

A state chart can be used to model members of a behavioural group, they contain graphs of state and transitions and they show the response of an object to external stimuli. A state chart is therefore made up of states and transitions. States are shown as rectangles with rounded corners. Optionally, they may be an attached name tab (OMG – UML Vl.3, 2000). A state can represent a condition during the life of an object or an interaction during which it satisfies some conditions, performs some action or waits for some event. State can either be simple or composite; some authors identify them as basic or compound (Zeng et al, 2004) respectively. A basic state may be optionally subdivided into multiple compartments separated from each other by a horizontal line. The compartments are name compartment, and internal transitions compartment.

The name compartment holds the optional name of the state, as a string. Internal transition compartment holds a list of internal actions or activities that are performed while the element is in the state.

An example of a basic state can be seen in Figure 2.

A composite state is decomposed into two or more concurrent sub states (called regions) and into mutually exclusive disjoint sub states. Com-

*Table 1. Description of QoS attributes*

| Generic QoS | Description | Unit of measure | Source | Formula |
|---|---|---|---|---|
| Response Time | Time taken to send a request and receive a response. | Millisecond | Previous execution monitoring | Response time = Response Completion Time – User Request Time |
| Availability | Number of successful invocations over total invocations. | Percent | Web services | $q_{avail}(s) = T/t$ T is the total amount of time in seconds in which service s is available over the last t seconds |
| Throughput | Total number of invocations for a given period of time. | Invocation/ second | | Max Throughput = max complete requests/unit time |
| Reliability | Ratio of number of error messages to total messages. | Percent | Data of past invocations | $q_{rel}(s) = n(s)k$ The number of times that the service s has been successfully delivered within the maximum expected timeframe. K is the total number of invocations. |
| Reputation | Measure of trustworthiness | | From user feedbacks | $Qrep = \frac{\sum_{i=1}^{n} R_i}{n}$ Ri = the end user's ranking on a service reputation. N = no of times service has been graded. |
| Duration (Execution duration) | The execution duration $qdu(s)$ measures the expected delay in seconds between the moment when a request is sent and the moment when the service is rendered. | | The execution duration is obtained from service invocation instances. Execution time is obtained via active monitoring. | The execution duration is computed using the expression $qdu(s) = Tprocess(s) + Ttrans(s)$, meaning that the execution duration is the sum of the processing time $Tprocess(s)$ and the transmission time $Ttrans(s)$. |
| Price (Execution) | Given an operation of a service, the execution price is a fee that a service requester has to pay for invoking the operation. | Valid currency | Advertised by web service providers. | nil |

pound states can either be OR-States or AND-States (Zeng et al, 2004) OR-states are used for simple grouping of tasks while AND-states are used to express concurrency. AND-states contain several regions separated by dashed lines.

Recall that state charts are made up of states and transitions. From each state comes a complete set of transitions that determines the subsequent state. A transition is a solid amount representing the path between different states of an object. Transitions are labeled with events that triggered it and the action that results from it.

- **An initial state:** Is represented by a filled circle followed by an arrow that represents the initial states.
- **A final state:** Is an arrow pointing to a filled circle nested inside another circle.

A state chart specifying an "Attend a Conference Planner" composite web services is displayed

*Figure 2. Basic State of a State Chart*

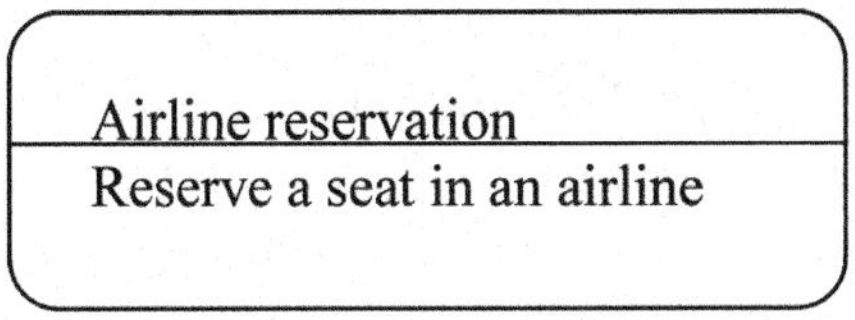

Airline reservation
Reserve a seat in an airline

in Figure 3. The composite service is made up of several tasks. If the goal of the user is to attend a conference then the user might have to carry out several tasks including getting information about the conference. This can be published on several web sites. The user may need to register for the conference and he can either register with a credit card or with the nearest and convenient bank. A search for attraction and shopping can be performed in parallel with airline reservation and accommodation booking. After the searching and booking are completed, the distance from the hotel to the conference centre is calculated and depending on the distance, a call-a-cab-service or bus services can be employed.

Note that each of the tasks modeled in the state chart can have several web services that can functionally offer the service. However, by the user choosing quality of service attributes, optimal services can be chosen that best satisfy the service composer's needs.

## Quality of Service Models and Attributes

The basic objective of quality models is to group all quality attributes into a hierarchy of related quality characteristics. According to Hilari (2009), the sum of all these quality characteristics and attributes applied to a Web Service is defined as QoS. Several QoS models that describe several attributes have been proposed by several authors. One of the earliest and most relevant was established in ISO9126, classifying the software quality in a structured set of characteristics and sub-characteristics as follows:

A. Functionality: suitability, accuracy, interoperability, compliance, security
B. Reliability: maturity, recoverability, fault tolerance
C. Usability: learnability, understandability, operability
D. Efficiency: time behaviour, resource behaviour
E. Maintainability: stability, analyzability, changeability, testability
F. Portability: installability, replaceability, adaptability, conformance

The basic limitation of this model is that most of the described attributes are not relevant to web services.

*Figure 3. An "Attend a Conference Planner"*

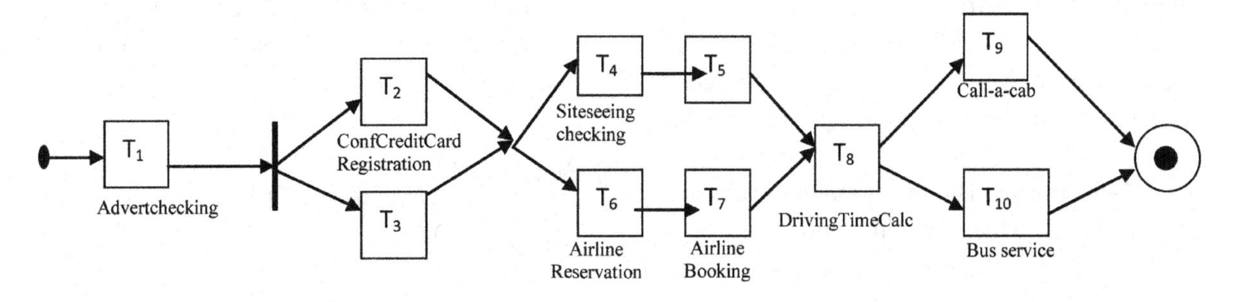

Since 2005 and based on ISO9126 (2005), the OASIS group has been developing a Quality Model for Web Services, named WSQM (Web Service Quality Model). This model is based on ISO9126 and consists of three parts:

A. Quality Factors which describe the characteristics, sub characteristics and attributes of Quality for Web Services.
B. Quality Activities which are the activities performed during the lifecycle of a web service regarding to their QoS.
C. Quality Associates which are the persons or organizations that are involved in Quality activities.

Although WSQM is the set of the three sub-models highlighted above, the part that deals with the characteristics and attributes for web services is the first part; that is Quality factors. Apart from attributes described by these standard bodies, the basic practice is for authors proposing models to choose and describe attributes that they feel are most relevant. Several authors like Canfora et al. (2005) and Zeng et al (2004) have a description of attributes.

## Description of Attributes

In this section, several relevant attributes will be described, the sources of the attributes will be stated and a computable formula of the attributes where applicable will be shown.

## Criteria for Analyzing Fitness Function

The calculation of the fitness of each individual of the population is done by analyzing some criteria:

A. **Used Input:** This criterion indicates the degree to which a valid solution has been found. This indicates the number of inputs and the QoS attributes provided by the user that have not been used.
B. **Generated Output:** This criterion indicates the degree to which a valid solution has been found. It indicates the outputs that are required to solve the composition.
C. **Execution Time:** This is the execution time of the composite service.
D. **Complexity:** This depends on the complexity of the composite service. The higher the number of atomic services in the composition, the higher the complexity of the composite service.
E. **Quality of Service (QoS)** attributes

Apart from the criteria listed above, QoS attributes are also used for evaluating the fitness function. Several attributes are incorporated in the function, some of which include: execution price, response time, availability and reliability. These attributes are disparate and their units also vary. For example, execution price can be measured in dollars per second, response time can be measured in seconds and throughput can be measured in percentage. This poses a major problem for fitness function evaluation; therefore, the values must be normalized in the interval 0...1.

In order to normalize the content of the table, some simple formulae are applied. First of all, it should be noted that some of the fitness function values are to be minimized while some are to be maximized. From the list of fitness functions given in Table 2, attributes to be maximized are: availability, reliability, throughput and reputation. These are already normalized. Response time and availability are to be minimized. A simple and straightforward way of doing this is to use the following formulae:

$$Exec\mathrm{Pr} = 1 - \frac{Exec\mathrm{Pr}}{\max(Exec\mathrm{Pr})}$$

*Table 3. Normalized Fitness Function Table*

| ATTRIBUTES | Individual1 | Individual2 | Individual3 | Individualn |
|---|---|---|---|---|
| | | | | |
| Execution Price | 0.72972973 | 0.153153153 | 0.351351351 | 0 |
| Response Time | 0 | 0.776119403 | 0.462686567 | 0.925373134 |
| Availability | 0.21 | 0.13 | 0.89 | 0.89 |
| Reliability | 0.9 | 0.56 | 0.82 | 0.71 |
| Throughput | 0.8 | 0.1 | 0.8 | 0.9 |
| Reputation | 0.68 | 0.82 | 0.9 | 0.78 |

$$rsp = \frac{rsptime}{\max(rsptime)}$$

The above formula maximizes both attributes making them comparable on the same table.

Therefore Table 1 can be replaced by the normalized Table 3.

Value must be normalized in the interval 0..1.

Min p = max min

$1 \leq i \leq$ last pi

Having normalized the table, fitness function can be found by calculating the maximin value of all normalized values. From Table 3, calculated maximin value is 0.351351351.

Therefore the fitness function is given by

FitnessFunction(indiv1)=used_input(indiv1) + generated_output(indiv1) + execution_time(indiv1) + nofatomicprocesses(indiv1) + min(attr$_i$({indiv1}| $1 \leq i \leq 6$}) *here 6 represents the number of quality of service attributes i.e. execution time, response time etc. The service composer can choose the number of attributes that are relevant.*

Max FitnessFunction(ind$_i$) where n = no. of individuals.

$1 \leq i \leq n$

## Selection

The selection mechanism to be used is the binary tournament selection. In a k-tournament selection, k individuals are randomly picked from the population with replacement, and the best of them is selected.

## Crossover

The crossover operator replaces a sub tree of an individual with a sub tree of another individual.

# THE ECONOMIC IMPLICATIONS OF WEB SERVICE COMPOSITION AND CLOUD COMPUTING ON BUSINESS CREATION AND EMPLOYMENT IN DEVELOPING COUNTRIES

Web services and composed web services can be achieved through cloud computing. According to Federico (2009) the term "cloud computing" refers to an Internet-based technology through which information is stored in servers and provided as a service (Software as a Service, or SaaS) and on-demand to clients (from the "clouds" indeed). Its impact can be spectacular on both consumers and firms. On the one hand, consumers will be able to access all of their documents and data from any device (the personal laptop, the mobile phone, an Internet Point are examples), as they already do for email services, and to exploit impressive computational capabilities. On the other hand, firms can rent computing power (both hardware and software) and storage from a service provider and to pay on demand, as they already do for other inputs as energy and electricity: thus the term *utility computing*. The former application will affect our lifestyles, but the latter will have a profound impact in terms of cost reductions on the software industry.

The introduction of a general purpose technology can provide a fundamental contribution to promote growth and competition (Acemoglu, 2009). According to Etro, (2009), the introduction of a general purpose technology can also help the economy to recover from a severe downturn as the current one. Suffice it to say that web services, web services composition and cloud computing can be described as emerging general purpose technology.

The concept of Service Oriented Architecture (SOA) and its consequent implementation through web services can have a positive impact on the economy because of the significant collaboration effect as a result of its easy integration of "business applications inside and outside of organizational boundaries" (Benatallah et al., 2003). This would enhance business to business collaborations even beyond economic boundaries which is the modern approach for organisations (Spaniol, 2004; Zeng et al., 2004). Under such situations, developing economies can drastically shorten the time to catch up with developed economies because of easily tapping into and gaining from the effects of highly developed economies with which they collaborate with the aid of SOA of cloud computing.

More on the economic implications of web services and cloud computing on a developing economy are discussed in the following subsections.

## Reduction in Initial Fixed Cost on ICT Investment

As previously discussed, web service composition results in the creation of bigger, more complex and better services. Most often than not, for new businesses to be created, the greater chunk of money goes into the purchase of hardware and software. These high up-front costs of entry constitute one of the major huddles to new market entry (Etro, 2009). The huddles can be felt more in developing economies because of their relative lack of capital. Many business opportunities are lost because of inability to invest in initial computing costs. With web services, optimally-composed services and cloud computing, potential entrants to fixed costs associated with ICT investment especially in software could be significantly reduced (Etro, 2009).

Increased input in human and physical capital has been recognized by economists as a necessity for economic growth (Edlwell et al., 2007). With web services, ICT input can be increased resulting in more investment with smaller funds that would boost economic output. A typical example is the use of cloud storage like Dropbox (www.dropbox.com) instead of spending hundreds of pounds on initial investment in local physical servers. The use of this facility can at least supplement physical and local servers thereby reducing the cost of storage. Small businesses (which are common in developing economies) can benefit a lot because Dropbox offers the first 2 gigabytes of storage free and the free space can be increased to 10.25 gigabytes when new users invited by the user register on the system. The fact that it works on the Web means that the storage is accessible from any part of the world and it is easy to invite (and drop) sharers. Besides, instead of having to attach a large document to emails and have these travel through some narrow bandwidths obtainable in some part of developing economies, a hyperlink (web link) to the document in the Dropbox (or any other cloud storage) can simply be emailed to a recipient who does not need to register on Dropbox. When he clicks on the link in his email, he will automatically obtain the required document.

## Interoperability

According to Harrington et al. (2011), one of the benefits of using web services is that they are interoperable. Web Services typically work outside of private networks, offering developers a non-proprietary route to their solutions eg the Dropbox illustrated in the subsection above. Services developed are likely, therefore, to have a longer life-span, offering better return on investment of the developed service. Web Services are virtually platform-independent. What is the implication of this to a developing economy? If services are likely to have a longer life-span and better return on investment then that should give a boost to the economy and less funds would be invested in system development and maintenance. Using the Dropbox as an example again, its servers do not need to be maintained or upgraded by the business (and private) users but by web service providers who by the way take advantage of the virtuality of cloud services to provide very high scalability to their service.

## Service Contract

Online Credit Card fraud is one of the main hindrances in promoting electronic commerce in developing countries. There are many types of card related frauds. Lost or stolen cards are most frequently used for fraud. Other kinds of fraud include skimming, identity theft and counterfeit fraud (Yufeng et al., 2011). Fraud detection and control has been a great challenge for developing countries in e-commerce. A step to minimise the rate of fraud can come from web services where human intervention is minimized and therefore cases of identity theft could be significantly reduced. According to Erl (2009), services adhere to a communication agreement, as defined collectively by one or more service descriptions and related documents. This imposes some sort of security between partner services as contracts must be fulfilled. For developing economies, there should be some reduction of identity related fraud if web services become a *defacto* for business transactions.

## Reusability

The Web offers the ability to create services that are reusable in multiple applications. This ability to re-use code is another positive side-effect of Web services interoperability and flexibility. One service might be utilized by several clients, all of whom employ the operations provided to fulfill different business objectives. Instead of having to create a custom service for each unique requirement, portions of a service are simply re-used as necessary. The economic implication of this for developing economies is obvious; services as well as codes can be created once and used several time. Instead of re-inventing the wheel for each client, one only needs to include additional application-specific business logic on the client-side. This allows development of services and/or client-side code using the languages and tools that are needed. It has to be noted that this advantage can also emanate from developing economies because the computing talents there could be used to create less expensive (because of comparatively lower labour costs) components that can be used both by developing and developed economies. Enabling talented software developers in developing economies to contribute to cloud computing can generate income to these economies.

### Discoverability

Services are designed to be outwardly descriptive so that they can be found and assessed via available discovery mechanisms. This is important to a developing economy because the extra cost of searching for a viable partner is removed. Also, the issue of fraud is minimized.

### Deployability

Web Services are deployed over standard Internet technologies. This makes it possible to deploy Web Services even over the fire wall to servers running on the Internet irrespective of what location and distance on the globe.

### Cost Saving

All these benefits add up to significant cost savings. Easy interoperability means the need to create highly customized applications for integrating data, which can be expensive, is reduced, if not removed. Existing investments in systems development and infrastructure can be utilized easily and combined to add additional value. Since Web services are based on open standards, their cost is low and the associated learning curve is smaller than that of many proprietary solutions. Finally, Web services take advantage of ubiquitous protocols and the Web infrastructure that already exists in every organization. So they require little if any additional technology investment.

### Reduced Software Development Time

Web Services are self-describing applications, which reduce the software development time. Other business partners can in turn develop application and it makes business transactions fast. Developing economies will thrive better because when software development time is reduced, business processes can be inaugurated fast with potentially better profits.

## SOLUTIONS AND RECOMMENDATIONS

From the foregoing, our proposed approach will offer the following advantages over existing methods:

A. An architecture that is adaptable to any platform.
B. A blending of the economic value of service composition and cloud computing in developing economies.
C. An approach that should deal with any type of problem and can also search from any repository. This is made possible because genetic programming can deal with solutions with very different structures since as the individuals (genomes) are usually represented by trees and these trees can have different depths and number of nodes.
D. A fitness function that will be able to analyze the individuals based on several criteria including quality of service which is a major factor leveraging developing economies when web users and composers have their QoS needs met.
E. A solution (composed service) that will always guarantee correct results (necessary outputs) because of the fact that a context free grammar will be developed for the proposed algorithm for solving the problem.
F. The maximin solution is the strategy that maximizes a player's minimum expected payoff. Therefore our approach will always guarantee a good solution. This has both architectural and financial advantages to the service composers.

G. The services can be used within multiple separate systems from several business domains. Therefore, a deployed SOA-based architecture will provide a loosely-integrated suite of services that can be used within multiple business domains. This could be of great benefit to developing economies.
H. The main vision of Service Oriented Architecture has been to exploit methods, tools and techniques enabling businesses to build complex and flexible business processes. This will be achieved using our novel architecture, approach and fitness function construction.

## FUTURE RESEARCH DIRECTIONS

Service oriented Architecture and web services development, discovery and composition are active areas of research and would be for a long time because of the explosive nature of the Internet. The following can serve as future work based on the discussions in this chapter.

A. A description of the workability, development and implementation of the un-described components (sequenced cache and monitor) of the web service composition architecture presented in this chapter.
B. Calculation and analysis of the economic impact of web services and cloud computing in a developing economy using a macroeconomic model.
C. A development of metrics for measuring trust in web services and the implementation of these metrics (this will be described in another paper).
D. A description of a context-free grammar (similar to that of Rodri´guez-mier et al., 2010) for the game theoretic genetic programming algorithm proposed in this chapter.
E. A detailed description of the implementation of the game theoretic genetic programming algorithm proposed in this chapter (this will be described in another paper).
F. Implementation and testing of the proposed methodology, architecture and concepts described in this chapter (this will be described in another paper).

## CONCLUSION

In this chapter, the service oriented architecture and its relevance to developing and developed economies was discussed. The need for web services was presented. It was reasoned out that when no single web service can fulfill the needs of a user, then several services can be composed.

Web service composition and its economic implication on developing economies were described. The need to incorporate Quality of Service (QoS) attributes while composing web services was highlighted. Standard existing QoS models and attributes were presented and it was pointed out that most solutions offered to the problem of web services composition have had authors introducing and describing relevant QoS attributes. A description of QoS attributes, their sources, description and metrics were put together and presented in a tabular form.

A robust and platform independent architecture for and several existing approaches to web services composition were described. A novel approach involving a game theoretic approach in genetic programming and its advantages were presented.

It can be concluded that QoS along with service oriented architecture which is the basis of cloud computing has the tremendous potential of reducing cost of software and hardware while enhancing reliability. Thus, they can increase the economic output of any society.

## REFERENCES


W3C Recommendation (10 February 2004), (pp. 181–190) Washington, DC, USA: IEEE Computer Society.

Acemoglu, D. (2009). *Introduction to Modern Economic Growth*. Princeton, NJ: Princeton University Press.

Alrifai, M., & Risse, T. (2009). Combining Global Optimization with Local Selection for Efficient QoS-aware Service Composition. In *International World Wide Web Conference*, (pp. 881–890) New York, NY: ACM Press

Ardagna, D., & Pernici, B. (2007). Adaptive service composition in flexible processes. *IEEE Transactions on Software Engineering, 33*(6), 369–384. doi:10.1109/TSE.2007.1011

Aversano, L., Pent, M., & Taneja, K. (2006). A genetic programming approach to support the design of service compositions. *International Journal of Computer Systems Science and Engineering, 4*, 247–254.

Benatallah, B. B., & Rachid, H. R. (2003). A Petri net-based model for web service composition. *Proceedings of the 14th Australasian database Conference, Australian Computer Society, Inc. Darlinghurst,* Australia. Retrieved July 13th 2011, from http://arxiv.org/PS_cache/cs/pdf/0406/0406055v1.pdf.

Bertino, E., Squicciarini, A., Martino, L., & Paci, F. (2010). An adaptive access control model for Web services *International Journal of Web Services Research, 3*(3), 27–60. doi:10.4018/jwsr.2006070102

Business Process Execution Language for Web Services. (n.d.) *BEA Systems, Microsoft, and IBM.* ftp://www6.software.ibm.com/software/developer/library/ws-bpel.pdf, 2002.32

Canfora, G., Penta, M. D., Esposito, R., & Villani, M. L. (2005). An Approach for QoS-aware Service Composition based on Genetic Algorithms. *Proceedings of the Genetic and Computation Conference (GECCO'05),* Washington DC, USA: ACM Press.

Coello, C. A. (2002). Theoretical and numerical constraint-handling techniques used with evolutionary algorithms: A survey of the state of the art. *Computer Methods in Applied Mechanics and Engineering*, (191): 11–12.

Elwell, C. K., Labonte, M., & Wayne, M. M. (2007). *Is China a Threat to the U.S. Economy?* Retrieved July 13th 2011, from http://www.fas.org/sgp/crs/row/RL33604.pdf.

Erl, T. (2009). *Service Oriented Architecture: Concepts, Technology and Design*. Crawfordsville, IN: Pearson Education Inc.

Etro, F. (2009).*The Economic Impact of Cloud Computing on Business Creation, Employment and Output in Europe*. Retrieved July 13th 2011, from http://www.intertic.org/Policy%20Papers/CC.pdf.

Etro, F. (2009) *The Economic Impact of Cloud Computing on Business Creation,Employment and Output in Europe*. Retrieved on 14th July, 2011, from http://www.intertic.org/Policy%20Papers/CC.pdf

Goldberg, D. E. (1989). *Genetic Algorithms in Search Optimization and Machine Learning.* Reading, MA: Addison Wesley.

Harrington, G. D., & Lipschutz, R. P. (2011). *Creating and Consuming web services* retrieved on 14th July, 2011, from http://www.blueopal.com/pdf/WebServices_tutorial_parts_1-2-3.pdf.

Hilari, M. O. (2009).Quality of Service (QoS) in SOA Systems.*A Systematic Review.Masters' Degree Thesis* retrieved on 14th July, 2011, from http://upcommons.upc.edu/pfc/bitstream/2099.1/7714/1/Master%20thesis%20-%20Marc%20Oriol.pdf

Hsu, W. H. (2003). Control of Inductive Bias in Supervised Learning using EvolutionaryComputation: A Wrapper-Based Approach. In Wang, J. (Ed.), *Data Mining: Opportunities and Challenges*. Hershey, PA: Idea Group Publishing. doi:10.4018/978-1-59140-051-6.ch002

ISO. (1991). *ISO 9126/ISO*, IEC (Hrsg.): International Standard ISO/IEC 9126, Information

ISO. (2002). *UNI EN ISO 8402* Quality Vocabulary. *Part of the ISO, 9000*, 2002.

Klusch, M., & Gerber, A. (2006).Fast composition planning of owl-s services and application. *In ECOWS '06: Proceedings of the European Conference on Web Services* Washington, DC, USA: IEEE Computer Society.

Li, C., & Li, L. (2007). Utility-based QoSoptimization strategy for multi-criteria scheduling on the grid. *Journal of Parallel and Distributed Computing, 67*(2), 142–153. doi:10.1016/j.jpdc.2006.09.003

Li, W., Jiang, X., Li, K., Moser, L., Guo, Z., & Du, L. (2005). A robust hybrid between genetic algorithm and support vector machine for extracting an optimal feature gene subset. *Genomics, 85*(1), 16–23. doi:10.1016/j.ygeno.2004.09.007

Liu, X. N., & Baras, S. J. (2004). Modeling multidimensional QoS: some fundamental constraints: *Research Articles. International Journal of Communication Systems, 17*, 193–215. doi:10.1002/dac.652

Mani, A., & Nagarajan, A. (2002). *Understanding Quality of Services for Web Services*. Retrieved Nov. 1,2010, from: www.ibm.com/developerworks/library/wsquality.html.

(1981). Maros, I., (2003).Computational Techniques of the Simplex Method.Springer. Optimal Auction Design. *Mathematics of Operations Research, 6*, 58–73.

Myerson, R. B. (1981). Utilitarianism, Egalitarianism, and the Timing Effect in Social Choice Problems. *Econometrica. Econometric Society, 49*(4), 883–897. doi:10.2307/1912508

Nau, D., Au, T.-C., Ilghami, O., Kuter, U., Murdock, W., Wu, D., & Yaman, F. (2003). SHOP2: an HTN planning system. *Journal of Artificial Intelligence Research, 20*(4), 379–404.

Oh, S. C., Lee, D., & Kumara, S. R. T. (2008). Effective web service composition in diverse and large-scale service networks. *IEEE Trans ServComput, 1*(1), 15–32.

Ouzzani, M. (2004). *Efficient Delivery of Web Services.*Unpublished doctoral dissertation, Virginia Polytechnic Institute and State University.

Pisinger, D. (1995). *Algorithms for Knapsack Problems*.PhD thesis, Dept. ofComputer Science. University of Copenhagen

Platzer, C., Rosenberg, F., & Dustdar, S. (2009). Web Service Clustering using Multi-Dimensional Angles as Proximity Measures. *ACM Transactions on Internet Technology, 9*(3), 1–26. doi:10.1145/1552291.1552294

Ran, S.A Model for Web Services Discovery with QoS.(2003). *ACM Inc., 4*(1), 1-1.

Rao, J., Kungas, P., & Matskin, M. (2006). Composition of semantic web services using linear logic theorem proving. *Information Systems, 31*(4-5), 340–360. doi:10.1016/j.is.2005.02.005

Rodriguez-Mier, P., Mucientes, M., Lama, M., & Couto, M. I. (2010). Composition of web services through genetic programming. *Evol.Intel.*, *3*, 171–186. doi:10.1007/s12065-010-0042-z

Sirin, E., Parsia, B., Wu, D., Hendler, J., & Nau, D. (2004). Htn planning for web service composition using shop2. *Journal of Web Semantics*, *1*(4), 377–396. doi:10.1016/j.websem.2004.06.005

Spaniol, O., Linnhoff-Popien, C., & Meyer, B. (2004). (Eds.) *Lecture Notes in Computer Science*, (pp. 94-107) Springer-Verlag. 1161.

Web Ontology Language Reference, O. W. L. W3C Recommendation (10 February, 2004). Retrieved on 4th June, 2011, from http://www.w3.org/TR/2004/REC-owl-ref-20040210/.

Weise, T., & Geihs, K. (2006). Genetic Programming Techniques For Sensor Networks. In Marron, P. J. (Ed.), *Proceedings of 5.GI/ITG KuVSFach gesprach Drahtlose Sensornetze* (pp. 21–25).

Wu, Z., Gomadam, K., Ranabahu, A., Sheth, A. P., & Miller, J. A. (2007). Automatic composition of semantic web services using process and data mediation. *In Proceedings of the 9th international conference on enterprise information systems (ICEIS'07).*(pp., 453–461) Funchal, Portugal: Gabler.

Yufeng, K., Chang-Tien, L., & Sirwongwattana, S. (2011). *Survey of Fraud Detection Techniques* (p. 1045). Taiwan.

Zeng, L., Benatallah, B., Dumas, M., Kalagnanam, J., & Sheng, Q. Z. (2003). Quality driven web services composition.In *Proceedings of the International World Wide Web Conference*,(pp. 411–421)

Zeng, L., Benatallah, B., Ngu, A. H. H., Dumas, M., Kalagnanam, J., & Chang, H. (2004). Qos-aware middleware for web services composition. *IEEE Transactions on Software Engineering*, *30*(5), 311–327. doi:10.1109/TSE.2004.11

# Section 2
# Information Technology and Social Issues

# Chapter 6
# Assessing the Role and Function of IT/IS Training and Development and Policy Implementation in a Public Sector Organization

**Nwachukwu Prince Ololube**
*University of Education, Nigeria*

**Oluwatosin Akinyede Ajayi**
*NOVENA University, Nigeria*

**Peter James Kpolovie**
*University of Port Harcourt, Nigeria*

**Abel Usoro**
*University of the West of Scotland, UK*

## ABSTRACT

*This study investigates the dramatic changes in the public service in recent years. The paper examines employee Information technology (IT) training and development in Nigerian Immigration services. This chapter fulfils the need for exploring the experiences in employee technological training and development and how these have impacted on their performances. Using a sample of 82 respondents, the research reported here portrays the paths which link the consequences of training and development on effective policy implementation. In this framework, IT training and development consequences in organizations represent a proxy in which employee training, actions, attitudes, and behaviours affect employees' job effectiveness. Using a multiple statistical analysis, the results indicate a mixed significance. Implications for strategic employee IT training and development policies are reported and suggestions for future research are discussed.*

DOI: 10.4018/978-1-4666-1637-0.ch006

## INTRODUCTION

In order for organizations, whether private or public, need certain inputs like human and material resources. The human side of the organization (employees) is an important component that needs to be of high quality so as to perform as an effective human capital. Although recruitment, selection and placement procedures are planned with the aim of high productivity; there arises the problem of actually ensuring that the people placed on their particular job possess the skills necessary to perform such jobs. One good attempt at ensuring that necessary job skills are available is by embarking on training and development (Kalargyrou & Woods, 2011).

Public sector employees often have a wide range of access to training and development opportunities which can increase organisations' total output hence leading to the growth of the economy. Public sector staff usually receive IT training through external courses, which are offered by the management of their particular sectors. They also benefit from the formal on the job coaching and mentoring through regular attendance of workshops which are geared towards ensuring that staff are trained (Ceriello & Freeman, 1991).

IT Training and development in public and private enterprise is very important. This is measured by the number of persons engaged whether as trainers, instructors, support personnel, or managers, the number and variety of training programmes provided, or the resources committed to it. Training is one of the most pervasive enterprise in any economy. IT Training and development are affected by demographic, political, economic and social trends. The training manager must recognize that these changes, trends, and challenges and issues must be dealt with while they can be shaped, redirected and exploited before their full effect are felt. Events have shown that many workers leave their organization because their need for training were not identified and provided for as an indispensible part of management function (Armstrong, 2004). As a result, many employees usually prefer having control of their own personal training and development. It is through this process that employees position themselves to have skills for other endeavours (Odueyungbo, 2006).

Employee's development process and training has been associated with performance improvement (Naylor, 1999; Eddie Kilkelly, 2011). Systematic IT training helps to build confidence in the workers and makes them effective on the job (Gomez-Mejia & Balkin, 2001). According to Sussman (2006), training experts help government agencies make the transition from static personnel management to incorporate modern, more efficient performance management programmes that include greater reliance, and the institution of succession planning to develop leaders for the future.

Increase in technological development is rendering existing techniques and skills of production obsolete. The modernization and technological breakthrough speeds up production process, requires new knowledge, skills and ultimately training and retraining, which is an effective way of coping with such developments. No organization can be guaranteed a permanent place in our highly competitive society and no manager can be effective unless he keeps his business competitive. Because of the dynamic nature of the business environment, it is no longer a debate whether technological training and development activities are luxuries in which organization can indulge in, only in prosperous times. It is a fact that IT training and development of an effective workforce are necessary for the spirit, survival and performance of an organization. Management must develop those who will manage the organization in the years to come (Boone & Kurtz, 1987; Clinton, Williamson, & Bethke, 1994).

According to the ILO (2000), human resources in any organisation remain the most invaluable asset for growth and development. Training and re-training are essential components of workers development. Workers development and training play a major, if not decisive, role in promoting economic growth with equity; they benefit individuals, enterprises, and the economy and society; and they can make labour markets function better.

Human resources development can be described as all efforts geared at stimulating more employment opportunities to upgrade the skills and link jobs more effectively. It is long-term and future oriented and serve the interest of the organization as well as the affected employees. Training and development although very expensive is an indispensible means of reducing obsolesces among people and an organization in the face of relentless technology innovations. It should not be seen simply as a means of improving the individual but as a continuing programme for improving the organizations in totality, allowing it to function more effectively and efficiently and so increasing its competitiveness (Clinton, Williamson, & Bethke, 1994; Akinwale, 1999).

The main objective of IT training and development in the Nigeria Immigration Services therefore is to improve current performance and provide a suitable trained staff to meet present and future needs. Therefore, research (Lewis, Goodman, & Fandt, 1995; Naylor, 1999; Odueyungbo, 2006; Schoderbek, Cosier, & Aplin, 1988; Antonios Panagiotakopoulos, 2011; Pineda-Herrero, Belvis, Moreno, Duran-Bellonch, & Úcar, 2011) has shown that for any organization to function or operate effectively, it must train and develop its employees in order to obtain the greatest benefit from their abilities. Likewise, concerns have increased over the years regarding raising standards of professional training and qualifications in order to improve employee effectiveness (Buchberger et al., 2000).

This article examines and explores the relationship between IT training and development and effective policy implementation of the Nigerian Immigration services. It seeks to find out the needs, adequacy and inadequacies of the IT training and development programmes offered in the Nigerian Immigration Services and the extent to which the programmes have improved employees job effectiveness.

## Research Questions

In order to achieve the above stated objectives, the under listed research questions were raised

1. Do Immigration officers attend IT training and development programmes?
2. How do employees adapt to IT training and development programmes?
3. How often do employees attend IT training and development programmes?
4. How does IT training and development lead to effective policy implementation?
5. How does the management's on-the-job training or off-the-job training lead to higher productivity?

## Research Hypothesis

To further verify our research questions, three hypotheses will be tested

1. $H_0$: There is no significant relationship between IT training and development and effective policy implementation.
2. $H_0$: There is no significant relationship between IT training and development and higher productivity.
3. $H_0$: There is no significant relationship in the opinions of respondents' based on their demographic information towards the variables tested.

## Research Contexts

The Nigeria Immigration Service (NIS) has witnessed series of changes since it was extracted from the Nigeria Police Force (NPF) in 1958. The Immigration Department as it was known then, was entrusted with the core Immigration duties under the headship of the Chief Federal Immigration Officer (CFIO). The department in its embryo inherited the Immigration Ordinance of 1958 for its operation. At inception the department had a narrow operational scope and maintained a low profile and simple approach in attaining the desired goals and objectives of the government. During this period, only the Visa and Business Sections were set up. On August 1st, 1963, Immigration Department came of age when it was formally established by an Act of Parliament (Cap 171, Laws of the Federation Nigeria). The head of the Department then was the Director of Immigration. Thus, the first set of Immigration officers were former NPF officers. It became a department under the control and supervision of the Federal Ministry of Internal Affairs (FMIA) as a Civil Service outfit (http://www.immigration.gov.ng/AboutUs.htm).

The resolve of NIS is to have an IT driven security outfit that can conveniently address the operational challenges of modern migration and to give the service a new sense of direction that can make it relevant at all times to the world security order and global trend http://www.immigration.gov.ng/MissionStatement.htm).

It is unfortunate, however, that most IT training programmes that have been embarked upon at the various levels of NIS in Nigeria have not produced the desired results mainly due to attitudinal problems on the part of government and the trainees and inadequate training staff and facilities in training centres. Most of the training facilities do not have modern training facilities. The use of quack consultants by government has grossly affected the quality of training given to NIS staff. High costs of training have been occasioned by lack of honesty and transparency. The cost of bribe is often built into the training costs when signing contracts with consultants. Many public servants sent for training are not allowed to utilise their skills and knowledge because of bureaucratic rigidity and unwillingness to change. Poor funding is reflected in the difference between budgetary provisions and actual funds released for training (Okotoni & Erero, 2005). The challenge before us is to investigate the training programmes of Nigerian Immigration services to see their orientations on training that will address training contents, training evaluation, attitudes to training and training utilisation.

## CONCEPTUAL FRAMEWORK

According to an online source[1], training and development are generally considered for employees to be the two ends respectively of a continuum:

- Training is imparted to a person where it is needed whereas development is a continuous process.
- Training is generally given to the operational level employees and development is done for middle level and top level executives.
- Training need analysis is done to capture the training requirements of a resource whereas development activities are based on the role of the employee.
- Training focuses on short term needs whereas development is highly focused on long term needs. For example, training is a sort of organized event whereas development takes place on a continuous basis.
- Training specially focuses on making the employee learn about a new technology or new advancements in his routine process whereas development is done for the enhancement of the personal qualities of an employee.

In addition Jones and George (2003) and Armstrong (2004) identify the differences between training and development. The differences in these two concepts are best demonstrated in four ways through the Table 1.

*Table 1. Differences between training and development*

| QUESTIONS | TRAINING | DEVELOPMENT |
|---|---|---|
| WHO | Non-Managerial | Managerial |
| WHAT | Technical and Mechanical | Theoretical and Philosophical |
| WHY | Specific job related purposes | General knowledge purposes |
| WHEN | Short –term | Long-term |

Tasks performed by employees in organizations are becoming more complex due to changes in the business environment. The importance of employee training has increased. But the rapid changes in our society have created increased pressure for organizations to re-adapt to the current business landscape. The types of jobs required and the type of skills necessary to complete these tasks are ever increasing (Armstrong, 2004). Work force IT training and development is central to all organizations and has become an improvement area of contemporary management. For any organization to survive, the need to train and develop the employees to handle the affairs of the organization is very important (Jones & George, 2003). IT training and development contributes an important backup to the recruitment and selection process in the organization. Training essentially seeks to provide the organization employees with skills necessary to achieve the organizational goals. Employee training and development is at the core of workers utilization, productivity, commitment, motivation and growth (Ceriello & Freeman, 1991).

IT training and developing internal management talent is one of the key functions of organizations (Bartol & Martin, 1998; Martin & Bartol, 2003). Training and development according to Drucker (1981) and Pineda-Herrero, Belvis, Moreno, Duran-Bellonch & Úcar (2011) is the most vital and effective strategy for achieving organizational goals because human resources planning objectives are derived from corporate strategic plan and objectives. Its benefits are greater confidence, commitment and motivation of staff; recognition and greater responsibility paralleled by improvements in pay; feelings of personal satisfaction and achievement with enhanced career prospects; and improved availability and quality of staff (Naylor, 1999, p. 498; Kalargyrou and Woods, 2011).

Thus, according to Bateman and Snell (2002) training is an ongoing process throughout an employee's tenure with the organization. Accordingly, specialized management development programmes are frequently used to improve the skills and broaden the knowledge of present and potential managers. Also, training is the development of individual skills for ultimate success. They viewed development as a collection of theoretical and practical experiences aimed at improving job function. Training and development improves employees in such a way that it enhances their performance and ability to cope with the present and the future (Akinwale, 1999). Training is an organizational efforts aimed at helping employees to acquire basic skills required for the efficient execution of the functions for which they are hired (Clinton, Williamson, & Bethke, 1994).

The primary aim of any training and development activity is to bring about desirable changes in work behaviour of the trainees (Bateman & Snell, 2002). If behaviour changes, however minor, do not follow after the training programme, it would be extremely difficult if not impossible to view training as anything but a failure (Bird, 2005). Training as any organizational planned efforts is to change the behaviour or attitudes of employees so that they can perform to acceptable standards on the job (Stone, 2002). In that way, development is an itinerary of action designed to enable the individual realize his or her potential for growth in the organization (Naylor, 1999).

Nonetheless, according to Bird (2005) many workers have failed in organizations because their need for training and development was not identified and provided for as an indispensible part of management function. Systematic training and development helps build confidence in the employee which makes him or her effective on the job. Training and development is a complex mixture of many factors aimed at increasing the ability of individuals and groups to contribute to the achievement of organizational goals. One important and interesting thing in this conception is the emphasis on the element of planning. Planning is a process for accomplishing purpose. It is a blueprint for business growth and a road map for development, which helps in deciding objectives both in quantitative and qualitative terms (Lewis, Goodman & Fandt, 1995; Aldehayyat, Khattab, & Anchor, 2011).

The relevance of IT training and development for increased productivity is related to employees' needs and job satisfaction and they are very crucial to the long-term growth of any organisation around the world. They probably rank alongside professional knowledge and skills, competencies, resources and strategies as the veritable determinants of organisational success and performance. Professional knowledge, skills and competencies occur when one feels effective in one's behaviour. In other words, professional knowledge, skills and competencies can be seen when one is taking on and mastering challenging tasks directed at organisational success and performance (Filak & Sheldon, 2003). The above factors are closely similar to efficacy, and, of course, it is well known that many employees lose or fail to develop self-efficacy within organisational settings (Dweck, 1999). In addition, needs satisfaction and motivation to work are very essential in the lives of employees because they form the fundamental reason for working in life. While almost every employee works in order to satisfy his or her needs in life, he or she constantly agitates for need satisfaction. Job satisfaction in this context is the ability of the employee job to meet employers' needs and improve their job performance (Ifinedo, 2003, 2004; Ololube, 2007).

In other words, IT training and development activities are usually planned and deliberate, which explains why organizations make deliberate efforts to train their employees to acquire relevant skills and improve their behaviour patterns (Naylor, 1999; Kalargyrou & Woods, 2011).

## METHODOLOGY AND PROCEDURE

### Research Design

The research design of this study is the logical sequence that connects the empirical data of this study to the initial research questions and hypotheses and ultimately to its conclusions. It employed a survey research design. See figure 1 for a summary of the research design.

### Population of the Study

The study is specifically based on the Nigeria immigration service, which is adopted as a case study. The research population for this study was drawn from amongst the staff of the Nigeria immigration services zonal headquarters in Lagos and Ekiti state commands of Nigeria out of the eight zones who are engaged in training and development.

### Research Instruments and Data Collection

In collecting the data for this study, both primary and secondary data were used. Questionnaires were used as the main instruments for primary data collection. It used a suitable questionnaire designed by the researcher, which was guided by Nworgu's (1991) characteristic of a good questionnaire. The characteristics as indicated by Nworgu are: relevance, consistency, usability, clarity, quantifiability and legibility. Respondents were asked to evaluate the value of the impact of the variables on employee training and development using a point likert-type scale. The questionnaire

*Figure 1. Demographic, research questions and hypotheses and ultimately to its conclusion*

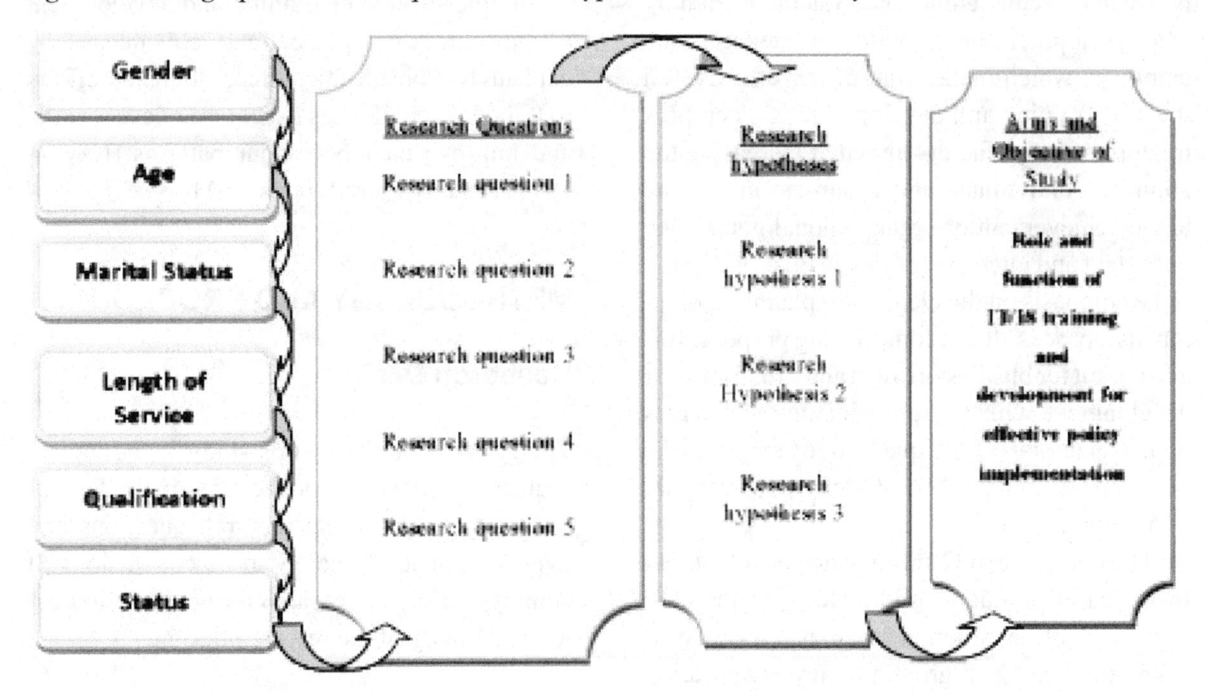


included three major sections: (a) personal data (b) training and development and higher productivity (c) training and development and organizational effectiveness. Also literature, journals and publications that are related to training and development were consulted.

## Sampling Size and Technique

The sampling technique used in this study is the non-probability sampling technique. This involves selecting samples on the basis of the researcher's judgment to the usefulness of each item. This explains that certain correspondents are skilled for participation in the study because they are presumably representative of the population of interest and meet the specific needs of the research study (Otong, 1995). The population for this study comprises of staff of 2 controls under zone A, Lagos state command and zone F, Ekiti state command of the immigration department. In these zones, 100 questionnaires (50 each) were distributed and 89 were returned from which 82 were used in the final analysis. Seven of the questionnaires were discarded because of the way they were filled out or some of the questions were not answered.

## Validity

The quality of this research is related to the possession of its quality in strength, worth, or value. The contents of the research instrument were validated by faculty members who are experienced in designing research questionnaires. The second process that was used to validate the research instrument was that the questionnaire was pre-tested outside the sample size and the responses from the respondents were used to improve on the items.

## Reliability

The strength of the research instrument used in this study was reliable because it was able to elicit the required information concerning the role and functions of IT training and development for effective policy implementation. Nonetheless, an accurate measure of reliability is supposed to be based on statistical data (Okeke & Kpolovie, 2006). Therefore, the quality of this study is in its internal consistency (Saunders et al., 2000). The coherence and reliability of the items in each variable was examined using Cronbach's alpha reliability estimates of SPSS version 18 to verify the adequacy of the measures. The reliability.846 of all the variables shows a high level of internal consistency.

## Data Analysis Techniques

Kendall's tau_b rank correlation was chosen for the analysis because it provides a distribution free test of independence and a measure of the strength of dependence between variables. In order words, it tests the strength of association of the cross tabulations when both variables are measured at the ordinal level. To tests what relationship exists between respondents background information, one way analysis of variance (ANOVA) set at $p < 0.05$ was employed (Punch, 1998).

## RESULTS AND DISCUSSION

Data from Table 2 shows that 68.3% of the respondents were male, while 31.7% were female. Likewise the information on age, revealed that 36.6% of the respondents aged between 20-30 years, 24.4% were 31-40 years, 31.7% were 41-50 years, and 7.3% were 50 years and above. At the same time, majority (65.9%) of the respondents 65.9% were married, while 34.1% were single and 0% were divorced. Table 2 further gives details of the other demographics of the respondents.

**Research Question 1:** Immigration officers attending training and development programmes

The data from Table 3, revealed that a large majority (97.6%) of the respondents attend training and development programmes whereas (2.4%) of the respondents do not.

**Research Question 2:** How do employees adapt to training and development programmes?

Table 4 shows that 65.9% of immigration officers occasionally attend training and development programmes. While 22.0% frequently attend, whereas 12.2% rarely attend such programmes

**Research Question 3:** How often do employees attend training and development programmes?

Table 5 depicts that majority 63.4% of the respondents agree that they gradually adapt to training and development programmes, while 36.6% rapidly adapt.

**Research Question 4 and Hypothesis 1:** There is no significant relationship between training and development and organizational effectiveness.

Data from the Kendall's tau_b correlations analysis for variables in Section B of the research questionnaire revealed that there is a significant relationship between Management attitude towards training and development and organizational effectiveness at.000 confidence level. The result also showed that there is a significant relationship between IT training and development facilities that are adequate for Nigerian immigration service officer's and their effectiveness on the job (illustrated in Table 6) (.001 significant level).

In the same vein, there is a significant relationship (.015) between management reimbursement on off-the-job training and development and improved job performance. Contrary to the former, there is no significant relationship between management encouragement of training and develop-

*Table 2. Demographic information and data analysis*

| Demographic variables | | F | % | Mean | SD | Variance |
|---|---|---|---|---|---|---|
| **Gender** | Male | 56 | 68.3 | 1.3171 | .46820 | .219 |
| | Female | 26 | 31.7 | | | |
| **Age** | 20-30 years | 30 | 36.6 | 2.0976 | .98895 | .978 |
| | 31-40 years | 20 | 24.4 | | | |
| | 41-50 years | 26 | 31.7 | | | |
| | 50-above years | 6 | 7.3 | | | |
| **Marital Status** | Single | 28 | 34.1 | 1.6585 | .47712 | .228 |
| | Married | 54 | 65.9 | | | |
| | Divorced | 0 | 0 | | | |
| **Length of Service** | 1-5 years | 36 | 43.9 | 2.4878 | 1.40760 | 1.981 |
| | 6-10 years | 4 | 4.9 | | | |
| | 11-15 years | 8 | 9.8 | | | |
| | 16-above years | 34 | 41.5 | | | |
| **Qualification** | WAEC/GCE | 6 | 7.3 | 2.7805 | .75399 | .569 |
| | HND/OND | 16 | 19.5 | | | |
| | BSc | 50 | 61.0 | | | |
| | MSc/MBA | 10 | 12.2 | | | |
| | PhD | 0 | 0 | | | |
| **Status** | Junior staff | 16 | 19.5 | 2.0244 | .64742 | .419 |
| | Senior staff | 48 | 58.5 | | | |
| | Management staff | 18 | 22.0 | | | |

*Table 3. Respondent answer to training and development*

| Variables | | F | % | Mean | SD | Variance |
|---|---|---|---|---|---|---|
| B1 | True | 80 | 97.6 | 1.0244 | .15521 | .024 |
| | False | 2 | 2.4 | | | |
| | **Total** | **82** | **100.0** | | | |

Key:
B1: Do immigration officers attend training and development programmes?

*Table 4. How often officers attend training and development programmes*

| Variables | | F | % | Mean | SD | Variance |
|---|---|---|---|---|---|---|
| B2 | Frequently | 18 | 22.0 | 1.9024 | .57969 | .336 |
| | Occasionally | 54 | 65.9 | | | |
| | Rarely | 10 | 12.2 | | | |
| | **Total** | **82** | **100.0** | | | |

Key:
**B2:** How often do you attend training and development programmes?

*Table 5. How officers adapt to training and development*

| Variables | | F | % | Mean | SD | Variance |
|---|---|---|---|---|---|---|
| B3 | Gradually | 52 | 63.4 | 1.3659 | .48463 | .235 |
| | Rapidly | 30 | 36.6 | | | |
| | Total | 82 | 100.0 | | | |

Key:
B3**:** How do you adapt to training and development programmes?

*Table 6. Two-tailed Kendall's tau_b Correlations for variables for Section B*

| Kendall's tau_b | | B4 | B5 | B6 | B7 | B8 | B9 |
|---|---|---|---|---|---|---|---|
| B4 | Correlation Coefficient | 1.000 | .676(**) | .319(**) | -.010 | .165 | .236(*) |
| | Sig. (2-tailed) | . | .000 | .001 | .923 | .097 | .015 |
| | N | 82 | 82 | 82 | 82 | 82 | 82 |
| B5 | Correlation Coefficient | .676(**) | 1.000 | .187 | -.014 | .146 | .246(*) |
| | Sig. (2-tailed) | .000 | . | .060 | .888 | .140 | .011 |
| | N | 82 | 82 | 82 | 82 | 82 | 82 |
| B6 | Correlation Coefficient | .319(**) | .187 | 1.000 | .000 | .309(**) | .374(**) |
| | Sig. (2-tailed) | .001 | .060 | . | 1.000 | .002 | .000 |
| | N | 82 | 82 | 82 | 82 | 82 | 82 |
| B7 | Correlation Coefficient | -.010 | -.014 | .000 | 1.000 | .178 | -.083 |
| | Sig. (2-tailed) | .923 | .888 | 1.000 | . | .069 | .384 |
| | N | 82 | 82 | 82 | 82 | 82 | 82 |
| B8 | Correlation Coefficient | .165 | .146 | .309(**) | .178 | 1.000 | .216(*) |
| | Sig. (2-tailed) | .097 | .140 | .002 | .069 | . | .025 |
| | N | 82 | 82 | 82 | 82 | 82 | 82 |
| B9 | Correlation Coefficient | .236(*) | .246(*) | .374(**) | -.083 | .216(*) | 1.000 |
| | Sig. (2-tailed) | .015 | .011 | .000 | .384 | .025 | . |
| | N | 82 | 82 | 82 | 82 | 82 | 82 |

**Correlation is significant at the 0.01 level (2-tailed).
*Correlation is significant at the 0.05 level (2-tailed).
Key:
B4. Management encourages training and development of their officers to enhance their effectiveness.
B5. Management attitude towards training and development have been favorable for improved job performance.
B6. Training and development facilities in the organization are adequate for officer's effectiveness.
B7. Organization performance and effectiveness has been adversely affected by lack of training and development
B8. Training and development has motivated employee to perform effectively
B9. Management reimburses on off-the-job training and development for improved job performance.

ment of their officers and the enhancement of their effectiveness. In the same stratum, the data revealed that organization performance and growth has been affected by lack of training and development and there is no significant relationship between IT training and development and employee motivation to perform effectively (.097). Concerns have increased over the years regarding raising standards of professional training and development in order to improve employees' effectiveness seen in Table 7. (Buchberger *et al.*, 2000)

**Research Question 5 and Hypothesis 2:** There is no significant relationship between training and development and higher productivity.

Using Kendall's tau_b to test hypothesis 2, items 1-8 of section "C" of the research questionnaire was used to test if significant relationship exists in respondents opinion on IT training and development on higher productivity. The data from the analysis shows that C1, C2, C3, C5 and C8 showed significant relationships to higher productivity. Thus, the respondents are of the view that IT training and development leads to higher productivity, positive change, improved performance, increases recognition and reduction rate of illegal immigrants by immigration officers (Naylor, 1999). On the other hand, C4, C6 and C7 showed no significant relationship to higher productivity which means that employees job dissatisfaction reduces the rate of labour and production turnover; and reduction in cost, frustration and grievances does not significantly affects higher productivity

This conclusion is evident in Filak and Sheldon (c.f., 2003), Dweck (c.f., 1999), Ifinedo (c.f., 2003, 2004) and Ololube (c.f., 2007) studies. They believe that the relevance of IT training and development for increased productivity is related to employees' needs and job satisfaction and they are very crucial to the long-term growth of any organisation around the world. They probably rank alongside professional knowledge and skills, competencies, resources and strategies as the veritable determinants of organisational success and performance. Professional knowledge, skills and competencies occur when one feels effective in one's behaviour. In other words, professional knowledge, skills and competencies can be seen when one is taking on and mastering challenging tasks directed at organisational success and performance. The above factors are closely similar to efficacy, and, of course, it is well known that many employees lose or fail to develop self-efficacy within organisational settings. In addition, needs satisfaction and motivation to work are very essential in the lives of employees because they form the fundamental reason for working in life. While almost every employee works in order to satisfy his or her needs in life, he or she constantly agitates for need satisfaction. Job satisfaction in this context is the ability of the employee job to meet employers' needs and improve their job performance (refer to Table 8).

**Hypothesis 3:** There are no significant relationship in the opinions of respondents' based on their demographic information towards the variables tested

Based on the analysis of variance conducted (see Table 8), gender as an independent variable on items 4-*9 and 1-8* in section "B and C" respectively of the research questionnaire as dependent variables, both female and male respondents have no significant gender effect on their perception of training and development and employee effectiveness.

The F-ratio.794 and significance of $p > .501$ illustrate that both male and female respondents do not have any gender differentiation in the opinions. The opinion of respondents towards IT training and development and effective job performance by different age groups also revealed that there are no significant relationships in their

*Table 7. Two-tailed Kendall's tau_b correlations for variables for Section C*

| Kendall's tau_b | | C1 | C2 | C3 | C4 | C5 | C6 | C7 | C8 |
|---|---|---|---|---|---|---|---|---|---|
| C1 | Correlation Coefficient | 1.000 | .487(**) | .577(**) | .050 | .341(**) | -.117 | .197 | .364(**) |
| | Sig. (2-tailed) | . | .000 | .000 | .632 | .001 | .236 | .051 | .000 |
| | N | 82 | 82 | 82 | 82 | 82 | 82 | 82 | 82 |
| C2 | Correlation Coefficient | .487(**) | 1.000 | .450(**) | .156 | .239(*) | .318(**) | -.010 | .058 |
| | Sig. (2-tailed) | .000 | . | .000 | .142 | .020 | .002 | .919 | .569 |
| | N | 82 | 82 | 82 | 82 | 82 | 82 | 82 | 82 |
| C3 | Correlation Coefficient | .577(**) | .450(**) | 1.000 | .311(**) | .170 | .024 | .084 | .130 |
| | Sig. (2-tailed) | .000 | .000 | . | .003 | .092 | .806 | .406 | .191 |
| | N | 82 | 82 | 82 | 82 | 82 | 82 | 82 | 82 |
| C4 | Correlation Coefficient | .050 | .156 | .311(**) | 1.000 | .033 | .198(*) | .175 | .052 |
| | Sig. (2-tailed) | .632 | .142 | .003 | . | .742 | .045 | .081 | .603 |
| | N | 82 | 82 | 82 | 82 | 82 | 82 | 82 | 82 |
| C5 | Correlation Coefficient | .341(**) | .239(*) | .170 | .033 | 1.000 | -.019 | .383(**) | .153 |
| | Sig. (2-tailed) | .001 | .020 | .092 | .742 | . | .844 | .000 | .113 |
| | N | 82 | 82 | 82 | 82 | 82 | 82 | 82 | 82 |
| C6 | Correlation Coefficient | -.117 | .318(**) | .024 | .198(*) | -.019 | 1.000 | .263(**) | .002 |
| | Sig. (2-tailed) | .236 | .002 | .806 | .045 | .844 | . | .006 | .986 |
| | N | 82 | 82 | 82 | 82 | 82 | 82 | 82 | 82 |
| C7 | Correlation Coefficient | .197 | -.010 | .084 | .175 | .383(**) | .263(**) | 1.000 | .350(**) |
| | Sig. (2-tailed) | .051 | .919 | .406 | .081 | .000 | .006 | . | .000 |
| | N | 82 | 82 | 82 | 82 | 82 | 82 | 82 | 82 |
| C8 | Correlation Coefficient | .364(**) | .058 | .130 | .052 | .153 | .002 | .350(**) | 1.000 |
| | Sig. (2-tailed) | .000 | .569 | .191 | .603 | .113 | .986 | .000 | . |
| | N | 82 | 82 | 82 | 82 | 82 | 82 | 82 | 82 |

** Correlation is significant at the 0.01 level (2-tailed).
* Correlation is significant at the 0.05 level (2-tailed).
Key:
C1. Training and development leads to higher productivity.
C2. Training and development leads to a positive change in the attitude of officers to give better satisfaction to immigrants and emigrants
C3. Training and development improves the performance of officers on the job
C4. Training and development leads to job satisfaction that leads higher productivity
C5. Training and development increases recognition and give room for promotion that leads to higher productivity
C6. Training and development reduces the rate of labour and production turnover
C7. Training and development reduces cost, frustration and grievances that affects productivity
C8. Training and development leads to greater productivity rate that reduces rate of illegal immigrants.

*Table 8. One-Way analysis of Variance (ANOVA) for respondents' perception of the variable tested*

| Demographic Information | | Sum of Squares | df | Mean Square | F | Sig. |
|---|---|---|---|---|---|---|
| Gender | Between Groups | .526 | 3 | .175 | .794 | .501 |
| | Within Groups | 17.230 | 79 | .221 | | |
| | Total | 17.756 | 82 | | | |
| Age | Between Groups | 2.938 | 3 | .979 | 1.001 | .397 |
| | Within Groups | 76.281 | 79 | .978 | | |
| | Total | 79.220 | 82 | | | |
| Maritalstatus | Between Groups | 2.550 | 3 | .850 | 4.172 | .009 |
| | Within Groups | 15.889 | 79 | .204 | | |
| | Total | 18.439 | 82 | | | |
| Lengthofservice | Between Groups | 14.493 | 3 | 4.831 | 2.581 | .059 |
| | Within Groups | 145.995 | 79 | 1.872 | | |
| | Total | 160.488 | 82 | | | |
| Qualification | Between Groups | 2.567 | 3 | .856 | 1.535 | .212 |
| | Within Groups | 43.481 | 79 | .557 | | |
| | Total | 46.049 | 82 | | | |
| Status | Between Groups | 5.426 | 3 | 1.809 | 4.946 | .003 |
| | Within Groups | 28.525 | 79 | .366 | | |
| | Total | 33.951 | 82 | | | |

perceptions. From the table, it can be seen that the F-ratio 1.001, and $p > .397$ depict likewise. Respondents' marital statuses were classified into three categories: single, married and divorced. The results indicated significant relationships in their opinions. They held IT training and development and its effects on effective job performance as important. This is shown in their F-ratio 4.172 and probability scores $p < .009$.

The opinion of respondents towards the impact of IT training and development and effective job performance based on the length of service does not have significant relationships. From the table, it can be seen that the F-ratio and probability depict likewise. From the above table, significant relationship do not exists in the F-ratio and probability scores of respondents. There is no disparity in their opinions.

Respondents' perception based on their statuses indicated significant relationships in their opinions. They held IT training and development and their effects on job effectiveness as important. This is shown in their F-ratio and probability scores.

## CONCLUSIONS, IMPLICATIONS AND RECOMMENDATIONS

The findings derived from this study confirmed Naylor (1999) and Eddie Kilkelly (2011) conclusions that the major reason for low productivity and organizational ineffectiveness is as a result of poor training and development. The quality of the employee's professional performance may result in training and development that leads to effectiveness in job performances (Kautto-Koivula, 1993, 1996; Kirschner & Thijssen, 2005).

One result of poor training and development is that immigration officers are forced to do other jobs instead of the one they are trained to do.

Based on the results in this study, a number of the immigration officers received poorer training compared to employees in other sectors of the economy, poor working conditions, and limited opportunities for professional development. The ranking of Nigerian immigration officers by the respondents may be a useful tool in providing focus for IT training and development needs which provides empirical information in getting the best out of their employees.

In view of the aforementioned findings the researchers proffer some suggestions in order to encourage IT training and development offerings in organisations. First, efforts need to be intensified towards IT training and development of employees for higher productivity and effectiveness. Second, management of the Nigeria Immigration Services should endeavour to provide their employees with adequate training and development facilities which should be a major focus of the organization to ensure effectiveness. Government needs to place high priority on the provision of equipment and facilities required for the training schools and centres.

Poor staffing for most of the training centres is a major problem. The quality of the staff available in the training schools will to a large extent determine the quality of training given to the personnel that are sent there for training. Therefore, training centres should be staffed with qualified personnels to guarantee effectiveness. If public sector staff are given proper IT training and development, it will be easier for the system to adopt modern information technology that enhances economic development because of driving down the cost of public services while significantly improving the efficiency and effectiveness of such services. For example, competent use of basic databases as well as communication technologies can reduce the time-consuming and bureaucratic paper work that is the main bain of public services in developing economies. The communication technologies can bring public services to the screens of the citizens as well as enable knowledge sharing that taps from knowledge stocks beyond the boundaries of developing economies.

Further examination of this subject matter will be in order using a carefully stratified national survey sample size to investigate the themes and concepts used in this study. A new perspective on the impact of IT training and development and its effectiveness in organization, which takes into consideration the unique characteristics of the variables used in this study and other derivations, is very much recommended. In addition, further studies could scrutinize what specific measures are taken by Nigeria Immigration Services to hasten the services rendered to immigrants and emigrants.

## REFERENCES

Akinwale, E. J. (1999) *Human Resources Management.* (An overview). (2nd Edition) Lagos: Concept Publications.

Aldehayyat, J. S., Al Khattab, A. A., & Anchor, J. R. (2011). The use of strategic planning tools and techniques by hotels in Jordan. *Management Research Review, 34*(Iss: 4), 477–490. doi:10.1108/01409171111117898

Armstrong, M. (2004). *A Hand Book of Human Resources management practice* (9th ed.). India: Kogan Page Publishers.

Bartol, K. M., & Martin, D. C. (1998). *Management* (3rd ed.). New York, NY: McGraw-Hill, Inc.

Bateman, T. S., & Snell, A. S. (2002). *Management: Competing in the New Era* (5th ed.). New York, NY: McGraw-Hill, Inc.

Bird, D. R. (2005). *Personnel management concepts and application* (10th ed.). New Jersey: Irwin McGraw Hill.

Boone, L. E., & Kurtz, D. L. (1987). *Contemporary Business* (5th ed.). Chicago: The Dryden Press.

Ceriello, V. R., & Freeman, C. (1991). *Human Resources Management Systems: Strategies, Tactics and Techniques. San Fransisco*. Jossey-Bass Publisher.

Clinton, R. J., Williamson, S. & Bethke, A. L. (1994). Implementing Total Quality Management: The Role of Human Resource Management. *SAM Advanced Management Journal, 59*.

Drucker, P. (1981). *Managing in Turbulent Times*, London: Pan.

Gomez-Mejia, & Balkin (2001). *Managing Human Resources*. (3rd Ed). New Jersey: Prentice Hall Incorporation.

Gomez-Mejia, & Balkin (2001). *Managing Human Resources*. (3rd Ed). New Jersey: Prentice Hall.

Green Paper on Teacher Education in Europe. (2000). In Buchberger, F., Campos, B. P., Kallos, D., & Stephenson, J. (Eds.), *High Quality Teacher Education for High Quality Education and Training*. Umea: TNTEE.

Ifinedo, P. (2003). *Employee Motivation and Job Satisfaction in Finnish Organizations: A Study of Employees in the Oulu Region, Finland.* Master of Business Administration Thesis, University of London.

Ifinedo, P. (2004). Motivation and Job Satisfaction among Information Systems Developers-Perspectives from Finland, Nigeria and Estonia: A Preliminary Study. In Vasilecas, O., Caplinskas, A., Wojtkowski, W., Wojtkowski, W. G., Zupancic, J. and Wryczw, S. (Eds.), *Proceedings of the 13th. International Conference on Information Systems Development: Advances in Theory, Practice Methods, and Education* (pp. 161 -172)).

ILO. (2000). *The International Labour Organization (ILO) – Activities*. Retrieved August 7, 2010, from http://www.nationsencyclopedia.com/United-Nations-Related-Agencies/The-International-Labour-Organization-ILO-ACTIVITIES.html.

Johnson, S. M. (1990). *Teachers at work*. New York: Basic Books.

Jones, G. R., & George, J. M. (2003). *Contemporary Management* (3rd ed.). New York: McGraw-Hill, Inc.

Kalargyrou, V., & Woods, R. H. (2011). Wanted: training competencies for the twenty-first century. *International Journal of Contemporary Hospitality Management, 23*(3), 361–376. doi:10.1108/09596111111122532

Kautto-Koivula, K. (1993). *Degree-Oriented Professional Adult Education in the Work Environment. A Case Study of the Mian Determinants in the management of a Long-term Technology Education Process*. Published PhD dissertation, University of Tampere, Finland.

Kautto-Koivula, K. (1996). Degree-Oriented Adult Education in the Work Environment. In Ruohotie, P., & Grimmett, P. P. (Eds.), *Professional Growth and Development: Direction, Delivery and Dilemmas* (pp. 149–188). Canada and Finland: Career Education Books.

Eddie Kilkelly, (2011). Using training and development to recover failing projects. *Human Resource Management International Digest, 19* (4).3 – 6.

Kirschner, P. A., & Thijssen, J. (2005). Competency Development and Employability. *LL in E Longlife Learning in Europe, 10* (2). 70-75.

Leino, J. (1996). Developing and Evaluation of Professional Competence. In Ruohotie, P., & Grimmett, P. P. (Eds.), *Professional Growth and Development: Direction, Delivery and Dilemmas* (pp. 71–90). Canada and Finland: Career Education Books.

Lewis, P. S., Goodman, S. H., & Fandt, P. M. (1995). *Management: Challenges in the 21st Century*. New York: West Publishing Company.

Martin, D. C., & Bartol, K. M. (2003). Factors influencing expatriate performance appraisal system success: an organizational perspective. *Journal of International Management*, *9*(2), 115–132. doi:10.1016/S1075-4253(03)00030-9

Naylor, J. (1999). *Management*. Harlow: Prentice Hall.

Nworgu, B. G. (1991). *Educational Research: Basic Issues and Methodology*. Ibadan: Wisdom Publishers.

Odueyungbo, F. (2006). *Business Management: A Practical Approach*. Lagos: Nolachid Associates.

Okeke, E. C., & Kpolovie, P. J. (2006). *Basic Research Methods and Statistics. Owerri*. Springfield Publishers.

Okotoni, O., & Erero, J. (2005). Manpower Training and Development in the Nigerian Public Service. *African Journal of Public Administration and Management*, *16*(1), 1–13.

Ololube, N. P. (2007). Professionalism, Demographics, and Motivation: Predictors of Job Satisfaction Among Nigerian Teachers *International Journal of Education Policy and Leadership*, *2*(7).

Otong, J. G. (1993). *Notes on Social Research Basic Issues*. (3rd Ed). Calabar: University of Calabar press.

Panagiotakopoulos, A. (2011) What drives training in industrial micro-firms? Evidence from Greece, *Industrial and Commercial Training43* (2).113 – 120.

Pineda-Herrero, P; Belvis, E; Moreno, V; Duran-Bellonch, M. M. & Úcar, X (2011) Evaluation of training effectiveness in the Spanish health sector, *Journal of Workplace Learning,.23* (5).315 – 330.

Punch, K. F. (1998). *Introduction to Social Research: Quantitative and Qualitative Approaches*. Thousand Oaks, CA: Sage.

Saunders, M., Lewis, P., & Thornhill, A. (2000). *Research Methods for Business Studies* (2nd ed.). Harlow: Prentice Hall.

Schoderbek, P. P., Cosier, R. A., & Aplin, J. C. (1988). *Management*. San Diego: Harcourt Brace Jovenovick Publisher.

Stone, M. H. (2002). *Management of human resources* (6th ed.). Chicago: Prentice Hall.

Sussman, D. (2006). *Public sector training: Training and development in the public sector varies among states and cities. American Society for Training & Development, Inc*. Retrieved 16th December 2009, from http://www.faqs.org/abstracts/Human-resources-and-labor-relations/Public-sector-training-Training-and-development-in-the-public-sector-varies-among-states-and-cities.html

## KEY TERMS AND DEFINITIONS

**Development:** A concept that includes the growth or change that alters the landscape in employees' mode of doing job.

**Effectiveness:** The degree to which organizational objectives are achieved, including the extent to which problems are solved to achieve goals.

**Information Systems:** It involves the gathering, processing, storing, distributing and use of information in a whole range of strategy, management and operational activities in organization. The purpose is for improving the effectiveness and efficiency of organization

**Information Technology:** Is the use of computers and softwares to manage information with the aim of processing, storing, protecting, transmitting, disseminating and retrieving information for orgamnizational purposes.

**Policy Implementation:** It is the strategy of policy-making between the establishment of a policy and the actual implementation of the policy for the purpose it was meant to serve.

**Public Sector Organization:** Often referred to as state sector, deals with the production, delivery and provision of goods and services by or on behalf of government.

**Training:** The art of teaching employees' particular skill or type of behaviour aimed at acquiring knowledge, skill and competence.

## ENDNOTE

1 http://www.citehr.com/141210-difference-between-training-development.html

# Chapter 7
# The Influence of National IT Policies, Socio-economic Factors, and National Culture on Network Readiness in Africa

**Airi Ifinedo**
*NAV Solutions, Canada*

**Princely Ifinedo**
*Cape Breton University, Canada*

## ABSTRACT

*This study examines the influence of national IT policies, socio-economic and cultural factors on the network readiness of African countries. The capability and level of preparation of a nation to participate in and benefit from information and communication technologies (ICT) for socio-development is assessed by the network readiness index. Prior studies have shown that such factors have a significant influence on how a country benefits from its use of ICT products for development. Research on this topic with data from the African continent is rare. This study serves to fill this gap. It is based on data from a cross-section of twenty diverse African countries. The data suggested variability in the use of ICT for developmental purposes among the sampled countries. To that end, Africa should not be viewed as monolithic in such respects. The study showed that all the measures used to operationalize national IT policies, socio-economic and some cultural factors are positively related to the network readiness of the sampled African countries. Importantly, the quality of each country's educational systems, its transparency (corruption) levels, its ICT regulatory framework, and its cross-cultural dimension of power distance (PDI) were found to have significant relevance to its network readiness. The implications of the study's findings for research and policy making are discussed.*

DOI: 10.4018/978-1-4666-1637-0.ch007

## INTRODUCTION

Information and communication technologies (ICT) play a vital role in the advancement of modern societies (Pohjola, 2002, 2003; Gibbs et al., 2003; Dewan et al, 2005; WEF, 2011). Countries that have realized the importance of ICT continue to benefit from such products (Dasgupta et al., 2001; Chinn and Fairlie, 2004; EIU, 2011; WEF, 2011). Indeed research has shown that countries that invest heavily in ICT products and services tend to have higher growth and developmental indicators than those with fewer ICT investments (Caselli and Coleman, 2001; Shih et al., 2002; Pohjola, 2003; Dedrick et al., 2003). The policy decisions of developed countries consistently emphasize ICT-related projects, issues and initiatives in their development plans (Jorgenson, 2001; Pohjola, 2003; Bui et al., 2003; Dedrick et al., 2003; Erumbam and de Jong, 2006).

In contrast, less developed parts of the world, including Africa, are only beginning to grasp how ICT-enabled services can be used to hasten development (Molla, 2000; G8 DOT Force, 2001; Ifinedo, 2005a). Indeed development reports (e.g. G8 DOT Force, 2001; InfoDev, 2007) and other studies (e.g. Bui et al., 2003; Mbarika et al., 2005; Langmia, 2005; Bagchi et al., 2006) indicate that several African countries are not yet quite ready to benefit from all the advances of the information age or ICT. A recent report on Africa explained "that future socio-economic development will need to embrace the use of ICT" (InfoDev, 2007, p.5).

Commentaries and research findings on how ICT diffusion is influenced by socio-economic change and development in Africa have started to emerge after a dearth of publishing from the continent on information systems (IS) (Odedra et al., 2003; Mbarika et al., 2005; Bagchi et al., 2006). Despite these efforts to disseminate new insights, most publications (e.g., Janczewski, 1992; Wallsten, 2001; Odedra et al., 2003; Roycroft and Anantho, 2003) discussing ICT-related issues in Africa tend to treat the continent as if it were a monolith. Only a handful of researchers have so far acknowledged the distinctions among Africa's separate sub-regions and countries (Darley, 2001; Straub et al., 2001; Ifinedo, 2005a; Langmia, 2005; Bagchi et al., 2006). It is important to make this clarification because ICT problems and initiatives differ among Africa's different countries (Molla, 2000; Ifinedo, 2005a; Morawczynski et al., 2006; Bagchi et al., 2006). Morawczynski et al. (2006), for example, have shown how the links between ICT acceptance and economic development vary among African countries. As Bagchi et al. (2006) explain, "[t]he diffusion of ICTs is not uniform among African nations."

Other studies on the use of ICT for development, and the diffusion of ICT innovation, have also revealed differences within countries in particular regions of the world, i.e., Europe (Pohjola, 2003; Waarts & van Everdingen, 2005; 2003; Erunbam & de Jong, 2006; Ho et al., 2007). To some degree, modernization and transformation theorists offer rationales as to why such differences arise. Gibbs et al. (2003, p.5) citing Giddens (1991) suggest that, "[t]ransformation theorists regard globalization as an *uneven process* involving elements of both convergence and divergence, in which countries around the world are experiencing a process of profound change as they try to adapt to a more interconnected but uncertain world." That is, contextual factors may account for uneven rates of adoption as each country tries to position itself within the ever-changing globalized world.

This study contends that generalizations on Africa's problems, including those related to ICT, obscure the reality of life on the continent. The study aims to increase our understanding of the factors influencing the capability of African countries to participate in and benefit from ICT use for national development and growth. In particular, it will examine the influence of national culture, national IT policies, and socio-economic factors on network readiness. This conceptual framework, highlighted in Figure 1, posits that national IT policies, socio-economic and cultural

*Figure 1. The Research Model*

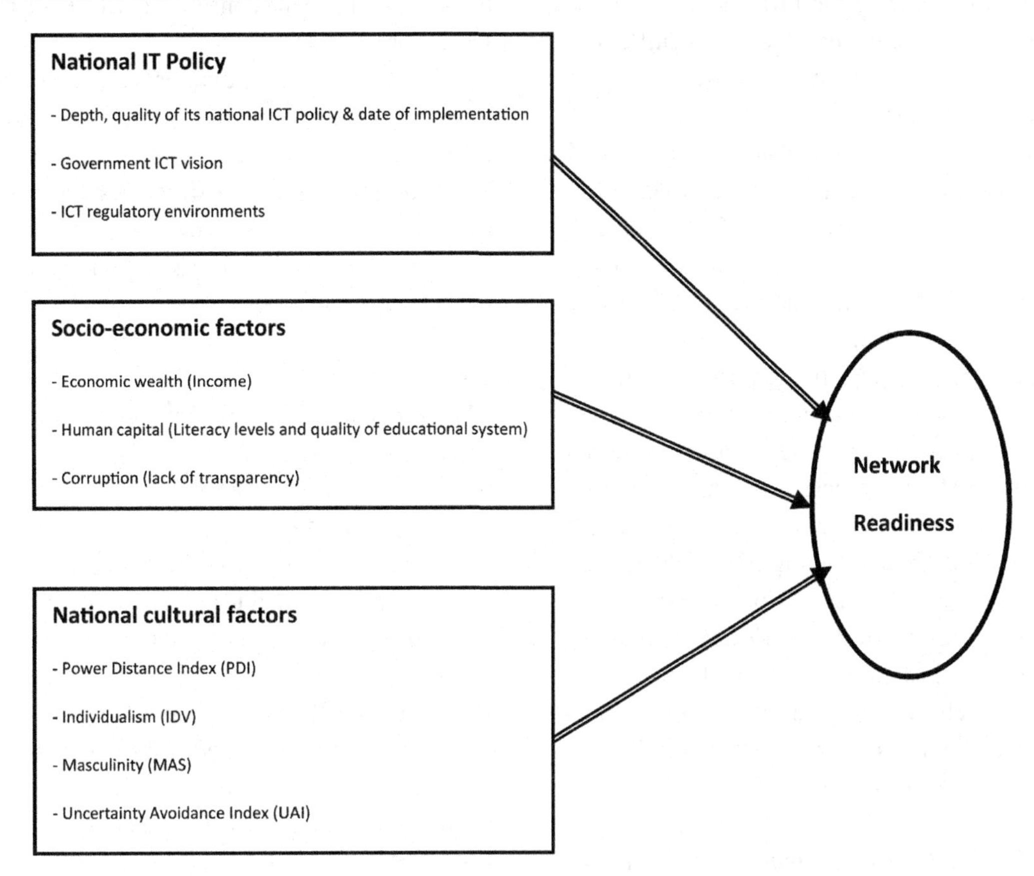


factors drive or influence the network readiness of countries. The degree of preparation of a country to participate in and benefit from ICT for socio-development is assessed by the *Network Readiness Index* (NRI) (WEF, 2011). Other organizations and researchers (e.g. EIU, 2011; Bui et al., 2003; Ifinedo, 2005a) have used *e-readiness* to describe the same concept. For simplicity's sake, we accept that both terms describe the same notion and can be used interchangeably. The EIU (2011) defines E-readiness as the "state of play of a country's information and communications technology (ICT) infrastructure and the ability of its consumers, businesses and governments to use ICT to their benefit."

As already mentioned, countries differ markedly on such issues as investment in ICT, and its general acceptance, so that nation-wide diffusion occurs at varying rates (Caselli and Coleman, 2001; Shih et al., 2002; Pohjola, 2003; Dedrick et al., 2003; Gregorio et al., 2005; Waarts and van Everdingen, 2005; Erumbam and de Jong, 2006). As Erunbam and de Jong (2006, p. 203) argue, "[w]hile some countries are receptive to [technological] changes, other countries appear to be less so." These contrasts have been attributed to a variety of influences including those stemming from economic and non-economic factors, i.e., "national culture" and policy issues. Comin and Hobijn (2004), Caselli and Coleman (2001) and Gregorio et al. (2005) suggest that national income levels and wealth could explain these differences among countries when it comes to adopting ICT products and services. Others (e.g., Nath and Murthy, 2004; Waarts and van Everdingen, 2005; Erunbam and de Jong, 2006; Leidner and Kayworth, 2006) focus on the influence of national culture. A further argument stresses the influence of human capital, as measured by literacy levels, the quality of educational systems, and higher education, on the acceptance and diffusion of ICT across countries (Kiiski and Pohjola, 2002; Gregorio et al., 2005; Bagchi et al., 2006; WEF, 2011). A positive correlation has been shown to exist between national policies and the spread of ICT (Gibbs et al., 2003; Chinn and Fairlie, 2004; Gust and Marquez, 2004). By the same token, the diffusion of ICT tends to occur more readily in less corrupt societies, with effective regulatory frameworks, than in less transparent societies with poor regulatory frameworks (Oxley and Yeung, 2001; Gust and Marquez, 2004; Langmia, 2005). Others have shown that Africa and other comparable developing regions of the world lag behind advanced regions in their use of ICT for development, and terms such as "digital divide" simply underline such differences (see e.g., Chinn and Fairlie, 2004; Mbarika et al., 2005; Ifinedo, 2005a, b; 2006).

Few studies have investigated the influence of national culture, national IT policies, and socio-economic factors on the network readiness of nations. Indeed, Bridges.org (2001) suggests that "... the unique cultural and historical environment of a region must be taken ... to truly gauge the country's e-readiness [similar network readiness] for the future." To that end, the main purpose of this study is to provide answers to the following questions: What do we know about African countries' readiness for the network world? Do all African countries display similar characteristics for such an indicator, or can we consider the African continent in its entirety with regard to network readiness? How are national culture, national IT policies, and socio-economic factors related to network readiness in African countries? Which factors or sub-measures need the most urgent attention? Suffice it to say that answers to the foregoing questions would be welcomed by policy makers on the continent and elsewhere (G8 DOT Force, 2001).

The remainder of the paper is organized as follows: Section 2 reviews the relevant literature. The research framework and hypotheses are presented in Section 3. Section 4 describes the research methodology. The data analysis is presented in Section 5. Lastly, the discussion and conclusion are set out in Section 6.

## LITERATURE REVIEW

No one theory to underpin this study's central arguments exists in the IS literature, although the accumulation of current efforts, including this work may be contributing to the development of such a theory. Nonetheless, studies using a similar conceptualization as this one abound. Dewan et al. (2005), for example, examined the effects of economic and educational variables on IT penetration rates in 40 countries. Others (e.g., Oxley and Yeung, 2001; Gibbs et al. 2003; Nath and Murthy, 2004; Gregorio et al., 2005; Waarts & van Everdingen, 2005; Bagchi et al., 2006; Kovačić, 2005; Erunbam & de Jong, 2006) have used similar frameworks. Thus the approach used in this study is not novel, but is consistent with IS studies investigating comparable themes. The research model used for study is highlighted in Figure 1.

### Network Readiness of Countries

As noted above, the capability and level of preparation of a nation to participate in and benefit from ICT for socio-development is assessed by the *Network Readiness Index* (NRI) (WEF, 2011). This indicator, developed by the World Economic Forum (WEF), accepts that ICT products and services have important roles to play in the advancement of societies and economies. The NRI provides scores for some 122 countries. It consists of three sub measures that assess: (a) the supporting environment for ICT in a country; (b) the readiness of the country's key stakeholders (individuals, business and governments]; and (c) the adoption and use of ICT by these stakeholders.

The focus of this discourse will not be on the development and strengths and weaknesses of this tool, because such analysis is available elsewhere (WEF, 2011). As noted above, other electronic (e)-readiness measurement tools exist (Bui et al., 2003; Ifinedo, 2005a; EIU, 2011). The WEF NRI index was chosen for its comprehensiveness and scope, and because scores for several African nations are included, which may not be true for other tools. For example, the EIU (2011) e-readiness Index includes scores for only 69 countries, of which only 4 are from Africa. In short, several e-readiness tools produce comparable results and interpretations (Bui et al., 2003), but the NRI is the best index for the purposes of this chapter.

## National Information Technology (IT) Policy

The UN ICT Task Force (2004) and a series of world summits on the information society (WSIS, 2007) continue to encourage developing nations, including those in Africa, to incorporate national ICT policies in their development plans. Several African countries have heeded this call, and seem to be reaping the benefits from such an exercise (InfoDev, 2007; UNECA, 2007). The UNECA (2007) study indicates that 48 African countries have such policies in place or are planning to initiate one. This trend is significant, given that only 23 countries had any national ICT policy even in 2000. The national ICT policies adopted across many African countries vary in their focus, implementation, and progress. Furthermore, a country's national ICT policy benefits from such influences as government ICT vision and efficient ICT regulatory environments. Gibss et al. (2002) and Meso et al. (2006) have shown how national ICT policies influence socio-economic development. Molla (2000) and Bagchi et al. (2006) implied that the spread of the Internet in Africa has tended to lead to greater benefits where proper national ICT policies and vision are in place.

## Socio-Economic Factors and Contexts

In general, African countries are less economically endowed than the developed West, literacy levels across Africa are lower than those of advanced societies (Molla, 2000; Ifinedo, 2005a,b; World Bank, 2007; CIA World Factbook, 2011), and the quality of educational systems on the continent are not equal to those in the developed world (CIA World Factbook, 2011). Moreover, corruption is a major cause of concern for most African countries (Transparency International, 2007).

Africa can be classified into two main regions, North Africa and Sub Saharan Africa (SSA). The northern part is comparable economically and culturally with the Middle East (World Bank, 2007; ITIM, 2011). Sub Saharan Africa is hobbled by a host of socio-economic problems, including poverty, high illiteracy levels, civil strife, corruption, and chronic under-development (Mbarika et al., 2005; Ifinedo, 2006; World Bank, 2007; CIA World Factbook, 2011). For the purposes of this study, the continent will be divided into five geographical sub-regions, that is, North Africa, West Africa, Central Africa, East Africa, and Southern Africa (Please see Figure 2). To some degree, these geographical groupings mirror the regional groupings on the continent, which include: the Economic Community of West African States (ECOWAS), East African Community (EAC), Southern African Development Community (SADC), Arab Maghreb Union (UMA), and Economic Community of Central African States (ECCAS). An equal number of countries

*Figure 2. The sub-regions / sub-groupings of Africa*

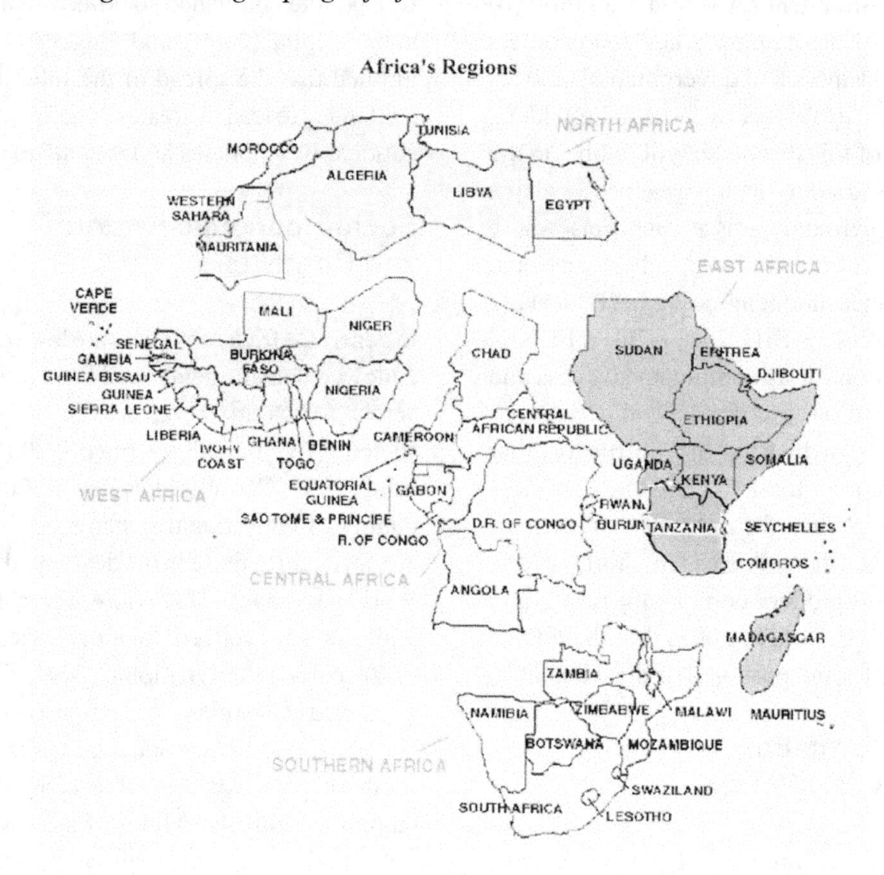


from each sub-region or sub-grouping have been selected for our analysis.

Gross Domestic Product (GDP) per capita is among the most widely used measures for comparing the wealth of nations. It refers to the value of the total goods and services produced within a nation in a given year, divided by the average population for the same year (see The World Bank, 2007). The study also uses the economic freedoms index for the selected countries to assess the extent to which the production of wealth is free from coercion (The Heritage Foundation, 2008). With regard to human capital, this study follows the example of other researchers (e.g., Gregorio et al., 2005; Bagchi et al., 2006) who used literacy rates and educational levels in countries to assess this variable. In addition, the quality of the educational system in a country was added to enhance insight. The variable of corruption (lack of transparency) was added to determine the extent to which such a factor would affect the capability of a nation to use ICT for development. The data for the selected African counties are presented in Table 1.

## National Culture (Cultural Factors)

Culture, to anthropologists, represents the fabric of meaning through which a society interprets events around them (Geertz, 1973). Bodley (1994) refers to it as the ways of life for a society. Hofstede (2001) defines culture as the collective programming of the mind which distinguishes the members of one group from another. Studies have confirmed the nexus between technological advancement, innovation and acceptance, on

*Table 1. A summary of the variables used in the study*

| Region & Country | Socio-economic indicators | | | | | National IT policy | | | National cross-cultural factors | | | | *Network readiness* (NTR) |
|---|---|---|---|---|---|---|---|---|---|---|---|---|---|
| | *GDP* | *ECO* | *LIT* | *QED* | *TPC* | *NIT-r* | *NIT-g* | *NIT-d* | *PDI* | *IDV* | *MAS* | *UAI* | |
| **SADC** South Africa | $10,600 | 63.2 | 86.4 | 2.85 | 5.1 | 4.75 | 3.73 | 5 | 49 | 65 | 63 | 49 | 4.00 |
| Zambia | $1,400 | 56.4 | 80.6 | 3.61 | 2.6 | 2.85 | 3.40 | 3 | 64 | 27 | 41 | 52 | 2.75 |
| Namibia* | $5,200 | 61.0 | 85 | 2.65 | 4.5 | 3.09 | 2.91 | 4 | 57 | 46 | 52 | 51 | 3.28 |
| Botswana* | $14,700 | 68.6 | 81.2 | 3.66 | 5.4 | 2.99 | 3.87 | 4 | 57 | 46 | 52 | 51 | 3.56 |
| **ECOWAS** Nigeria | $2,200 | 55.5 | 68 | 3.28 | 2.2 | 3.40 | 3.99 | 4 | 77 | 20 | 46 | 54 | 3.23 |
| Benin* | $1,500 | 55.0 | 34.7 | 2.92 | 2.7 | 3.07 | 4.50 | 4 | 77 | 20 | 46 | 54 | 2.83 |
| Mali * | $1,200 | 55.5 | 46.4 | 2.60 | 2.7 | 2.62 | 4.88 | 3 | 77 | 20 | 46 | 54 | 2.96 |
| Burkina Faso* | $1,200 | 55.6 | 21.8 | 2.53 | 2.9 | 2.81 | 4.30 | 3 | 77 | 20 | 46 | 54 | 2.97 |
| **ECCAS** Cameroon* | $2,300 | 54.0 | 67.9 | 3.00 | 2.4 | 2.33 | 2.92 | 3 | 71 | 24 | 44 | 53 | 2.74 |
| Chad* | $1,600 | 47.7 | 47.5 | 2.14 | 1.8 | 2.09 | 2.76 | 2 | 71 | 24 | 44 | 53 | 2.16 |
| Angola* | $6,500 | 47.1 | 67.4 | 2.59 | 2.23 | 2.19 | 2.75 | 3 | 71 | 24 | 44 | 53 | 2.42 |
| Burundi* | $800 | 46.3 | 59.3 | 2.66 | 2.5 | 2.15 | 2.56 | 3 | 71 | 24 | 44 | 53 | 2.40 |
| **UMA** Egypt | $5,400 | 59.2 | 71.4 | 2.66 | 2.9 | 3.29 | 4.47 | 5 | 80 | 38 | 52 | 68 | 3.44 |
| Algeria*† | $8,100 | 55.7 | 69.9 | 2.93 | 3.0 | 2.67 | 4.13 | 3 | 80 | 38 | 52 | 68 | 3.41 |
| Tunisia* | $7,500 | 59.3 | 74.3 | 5.13 | 4.2 | 4.60 | 5.35 | 5 | 80 | 38 | 52 | 68 | 4.24 |
| Morocco* | $3,800 | 56.4 | 52.3 | 2.94 | 3.5 | 3.19 | 4.32 | 5 | 70 | 46 | 53 | 68 | 3.45 |
| **EAC** Tanzania | $1,100 | 56.4 | 69.4 | 3.07 | 3.2 | 3.12 | 4.23 | 3 | 64 | 27 | 41 | 52 | 3.13 |
| Kenya | $1,600 | 59.6 | 85.1 | 4.20 | 2.1 | 3.34 | 4.02 | 3 | 64 | 27 | 41 | 52 | 3.07 |
| Ethiopia | $700 | 53.2 | 42.7 | 2.92 | 2.4 | 2.57 | 4.06 | 4 | 64 | 27 | 41 | 52 | 2.55 |
| Uganda* | $1,100 | 64.4 | 66.8 | 3.42 | 2.8 | 2.97 | 4.25 | 5 | 64 | 27 | 41 | 52 | 2.97 |

**Legend:** GDP = GDP per capita in US (2007 est.); LIT = National literacy level (as total %); QED = Quality of education system; TPC = Transparency and corruption index;

the one hand, and national culture on the other (e.g., Shane 1993; Png et al., 2001; Straub et al., 2001; Waarts & van Everdingen, 2005; Erunbam & de Jong, 2006). In fact the uneven spread of technological progress, as discussed by modernization and transformation theorists, seems to have a strong cultural underpinning. Steers et al. (2008, p. 1) share the same view and note, "Our thinking on this topic [the nexus between ICT and culture] would be much simpler if we could conveniently separate the artifactual components of technology and technology adoption (machines, instruments, systems, routines, and gadgets) from the axiological components (values, cultures, and worldviews). However, country-level adoptions of new technologies do not occur in a cultural vacuum."

How can cultural artefacts across countries be measured? The work of Hofstede (2001) has been widely recognized as the most dominant framework for assessing technology in the context of culture and vice versa (Myers and Tan, 2002; Ford et al. 2004; Waarts & van Everdingen, 2005). Several researchers in IS and related areas have used it (e.g., Shane, 1993; Png et al., 2001; Myers and Tan, 2002; Nath & Murthy, 2004; Erunbam & de Jong, 2006). Despite its popularity, Hofstede's cross-cultural typology has its shortcomings and has been criticized (e.g., Myers & Tan, 2002; Walsham, 2002). Nevertheless the cultural dimensions developed by Hofstede provide a lens to develop *a priori* knowledge, and compare different national cultural contexts with technology-related issues (Ford et al. 2004). The four main cultural dimensions in Hofstede's typology are briefly described below. Each is summarized using explanations taken from a web page dedicated to the works of Hofstede at: http://www.geert-hofstede.com/geert_hofstede_resources.shtml (ITIM, 2011).

- **Power Distance Index (PDI):** "Focuses on the degree of equality, or inequality, between people in the country's society. A high Power Distance ranking indicates that inequalities of power and wealth have been allowed to grow within the society" (ITIM, 2011).
- **Individualism (IDV):** "Focuses on the degree the society reinforces individual or collective achievement and interpersonal relationships. A high Individualism ranking indicates that individuality and individual rights are paramount within the society. Individuals in these societies may tend to form a larger number of looser relationships. A low Individualism ranking typifies societies of a more collectivist nature with close ties between individuals" (ITIM, 2011).
- **Masculinity (MAS):** "Focuses on the degree the society reinforces, or does not reinforce, the traditional masculine work role model of male achievement, control, and power. A high Masculinity ranking indicates the country experiences a high degree of gender differentiation. A low Masculinity ranking indicates the country has a low level of differentiation and discrimination between genders" (ITIM, 2011).
- **Uncertainty Avoidance Index (UAI):** "Focuses on the level of tolerance for uncertainty and ambiguity within the society - i.e. unstructured situations. A high Uncertainty Avoidance ranking indicates the country has a low tolerance for uncertainty and ambiguity. A low Uncertainty Avoidance ranking indicates the country has less concern about ambiguity and uncertainty and has more tolerance for a variety of opinions" (ITIM, 2011).

## RESEARCH FRAMEWORK AND HYPOTHESES

The study's research framework is illustrated in Figure 2. As discussed above, three main factors, national IT policy, socio-economic, and cultural factors (and their constituting variables) are factored into this discourse. It is worth noting here that this study does not suggest causality among the independent factors and the main construct; rather, it is accepted that such a theoretical underpinning is still evolving. Other researchers such as Kovačić (2005) have implied that relationships between some of the factors, and ICT readiness, are by no means causal. That said, the hypothesized relationships in the research model are illustrated in Figure 3. The only hypothesis with an inverse relationship with the main construct, H4d is highlighted.

*Figure 3. The hypothesized relationships in the research framework*

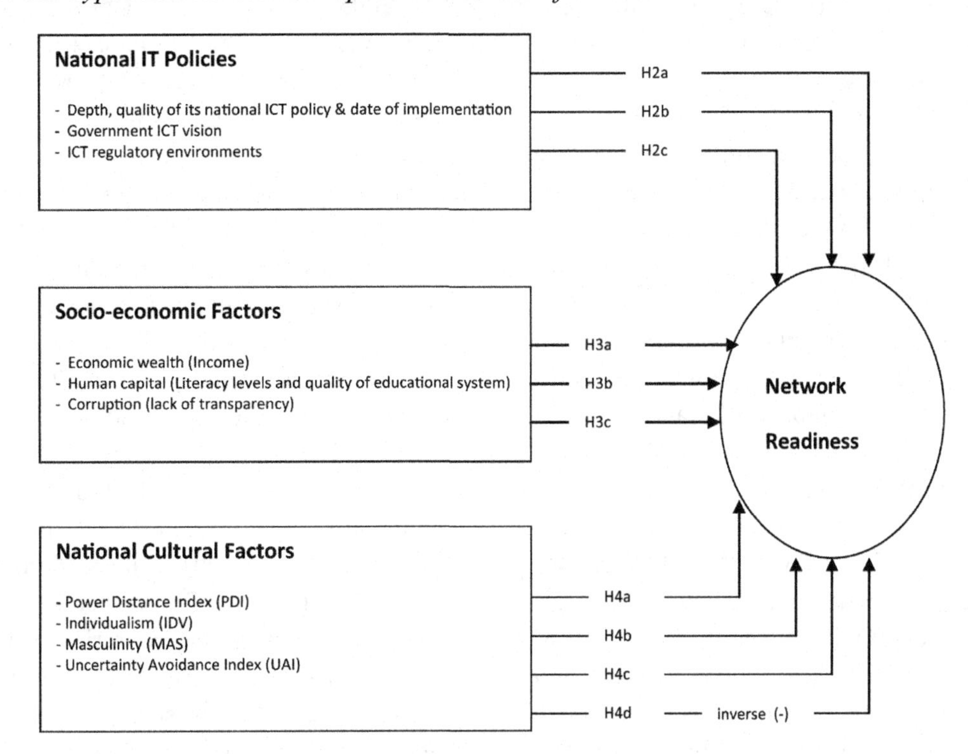


Some researchers have suggested that some countries make only uneven progress in their efforts to link up with an ever-changing, interconnected world in which the use of ICT for development is increasingly becoming crucial (Dasgupta et al., 2001; Pohjola, 2003; 2003; Chinn & Fairlie, 2004; Gibbs et al., 2003; Ho et al., 2007). In fact, the rates of technological adoption vary by country worldwide (Shane, 1993). Research findings and development reports have shown that use of ICT for development, and the diffusion of ICT innovation, varies significantly among countries on the continent of Europe (Pohjola, 2003; Waarts & van Everdingen, 2005; Ho et al., 2007; WEF, 2011; EIU, 2011). In Africa, Molla (2000), Darley (2001), and Bagchi et al. (2006) found variations for the rates of Internet diffusion across the continent as well. Ifinedo (2005a) showed that e-readiness varies by Africa's sub-regions, and Morawczynski et al. (2006) indicate that ICT investment vis-à-vis economic development differs even among countries in one sub-region of Africa, i.e. West Africa. This analysis allows us to predict that the use of ICT for development (network readiness) in African countries will differ considerably. Thus, it is hypothesized that:

**H1**: African countries' network readiness will differ significantly

Path dependency theory (e.g., Brian, 1994), which was developed to explain technological adoption processes and industry evolution, suggests that we might expect those countries which have implemented national IT policies earlier, will be better placed to reap higher rewards than those that have lagged (See also UNECA, 2007; InfoDev, 2007; Gibbs et al., 2003). Indeed, Meso et al. (2006) imply that the diffusion of national ICT policies can leverage socio-economic developments. Bagchi et al. (2006) inferred that the diffusion of ICT products especially the Internet tends to be higher in countries where quality policies are in place, compared with countries which lacked such policies.

Gust and Marquez (2002) attribute differences in adoption of ICT products to differing regulatory policies (Pohjola 2002; 2003; Chinn & Fairlie, 2004). Similarly, Gibbs et al. (2002) suggest that governments with a good ICT vision will be better prepared for a network society than those lagging behind. Such a vision might include: a) liberalized telecommunication industry sector and b) availability of ICT leadership. Caselli and Coleman (2001) showed that where quality, liberalized, telecommunication policies exist, the rates of ICT diffusion and other associated benefits tend be favorable. Similarly, favorable ICT regulatory environments tend to foster more rapid technological development (Oxley & Yeung, 2001; Gust & Marquez, 2002; Gibbs et al., 2003). Roycroft and Anantho (2003) suggest African countries with favorable policies benefit more from ICT initiatives than those lacking such. Thus, the following set of hypotheses is developed:

**H2a**: Countries in Africa with quality national IT policies (as operationalized by the depth, quality, and time of implementation) will have higher scores on the network readiness index.

**H2b**: Countries in Africa with quality national IT policies (as operationalized by government ICT vision) will have higher scores on the network readiness index.

**H2c**: Countries in Africa with quality national IT policies (as operationalized by ICT regulatory environments) will have higher scores on the network readiness index.

Over time, several studies have found a strong positive relationship between technology use, ICT use for development, and technological innovations, on the one hand, and income across countries, on the other (Dasgupta et al., 2001; Caselli & Coleman, 2001; Pohjola, 2003; Dewan et al., 2004; 2005). This result is logical and reasonable, because income is a key determinant of the demand for ICT products and services. It goes without saying that wealthier countries will be better poised to use their resources to purchase such services than their less endowed counterparts (Shin et al, 2002; Pohjola, 2003; Dewan et al., 2004).

Empirical evidence indicates that the distribution of wealth is a major inhibitor of IT usage, diffusion, and growth (Caselli & Coleman, 2001; Bagchi et al. 2006; Dewan et al., 2004; 2005). Global data on network readiness show that several high and middle-income countries have higher scores on the index than do their poorer counterparts (WEF, 2011). Other studies (e.g., Caselli & Coleman, 2001; Nath & Murthy, 2004; Comin & Hobijn, 2004; Gregorio et al., 2005) have also shown that wealthier countries tend to have more access to resources to build on the potential of ICT-enabled services, such as e-business and e-government, which invariably helps to increase their network readiness. Bagchi et al. (2006) found wealth to be one of the major factors inhibiting the growth of ICT in Africa. Given the critical importance of economic resources in enhancing a country's capability to adopt and use technological innovations for development, it is likely that wealthier African countries will have higher network readiness scores than those with lesser economic resources. Thus, it is hypothesized that:

**H3a**: Countries in Africa with higher national income levels or wealth will have higher scores on the network readiness index.

Perhaps needless to say, countries with higher levels of human capital, i.e., higher literacy levels and higher quality education, will be in a better position to benefit from the use and adoption of technological innovation, as affirmed by ample evidence (see Jorgenson, 2001; Kiiski & Pohjola, 2002; Gregorio et al., 2005; Dewan et al., 2005; Erunbam & de Jong, 2006). Indeed Comin and Hobijn (2004) found that human capital endowments affect technology adoption. Erunbam and de Jong (2006) note that technological innovations, including ICT, tend to diffuse more rapidly in societies with larger pools of human capital. The study by Gregorio et al. (2005) also showed that a positive relationship exists between literacy levels and the growth of ICT-related services across countries. Kiiski and Pohjola (2002) showed that levels of tertiary education influence ICT diffusion in countries. Reports by WEF (2011) and EIU (2011) have suggested that the capability of a nation to fully reap the benefits of ICT is undermined when literacy levels and educational systems are weak. Bagchi et al. (2006), Ifinedo (2005a), and Morawczynski et al. (2006) have all identified education as one of the major culprits holding back Africa's progress towards technological advancement. Thus, it is hypothesized that:

**H3b**: Countries in Africa with higher literacy levels and quality educational systems will have higher scores on the network readiness index.

Gust and Marquez (2004) implied that ICT initiatives thrive in an atmosphere where proper oversight is instituted. Transparent structures are significant in the development of ICT-based innovation such as e-commerce (Oxley & Yeung, 2001). Corruption, though declining in African countries, is still widespread compared with developed nations (Transparency International, 2007). To the extent that a lack of transparency or corruption hampers development on the African continent, Transparency International (2007) has indicated that it is by far the main cog in the wheel of Africa's development (see also Langmia, 2005; Ifinedo, 2005b; 2006). Langmia (2005), writing about the role of ICT in the development of Africa, suggested that scholars of development theory have suggested that African countries are unable to achieve real progress due to corruption and a lack of transparency. It is reasonable to suggest that the capability of a country to benefit from ICT will be higher in countries with transparent structures and less corruption. Thus, it is predicted that:

**H3c:** Countries in Africa with higher levels of transparency will have higher scores on the network readiness index.

Hofstede (2001) notes that technological adoption and progress is higher in countries with a low power index. However, the reality may undermine the veracity of this assertion. Ifinedo (2006) revealed that ICT-based initiatives such as e-government were able to spread after the President of Nigeria (a Sub-Saharan country) championed the cause of such an initiative. Anandarajan et al. (2002) offered a similar conclusion in their study of the acceptance of ICT products in the sub-region. The inference was that some cultures especially those in Africa might need to follow or take initiatives from those who have power or leadership roles (Hofstede, 2001; Anandarajan et al., 2002; Ifinedo, 2006). Shore and Venkatachalam (1996) citing Janczewski (1992) note "that cultural differences found in African countries [require] that information systems be modified to suit the needs of host organizations in [that continent]". Rather than predict an inverse relationship between PDI and ICT-based diffusion and acceptance, as in the studies conducted by Png et al. (2001) and others, we believe that in African cultures, predicting a positive, direct relationship between PDI and network readiness might be more appropriate. Thus, it is hypothesized that:

**H4a**: Countries in Africa with higher PDI scores will have higher network readiness index scores.

In more individualistic societies, emphasis tends to be placed on the performance of the individual rather than that of the group (Hofstede, 2001). Thus, for entities in collectivist societies, decision making is often a collective effort. Inadvertently, decision processes, including those related to the acceptance and use of technology may be delayed (Hofstede, 2001; Waarts & van Everdingen, 2005). In contrast, entities from individualistic countries may have more leeway in their decision making process, because they are freer and more agile to develop or try out new products, including ICT. Thus countries with higher IND scores might have higher network readiness scores. Thus, it is predicted that:

**H4b**: Countries in Africa with higher IND scores will have higher network readiness index scores.

The masculine/femininity (MAS) dimension describes the extent to which any society reinforces masculine achievement and control. In this way, regions where material success and achievement are valued highly might have high network readiness scores. Kovačić (2005, p. 147) notes, "it could be argued equally well that in a country with high masculinity there would also be a positive attitude toward implementing ICTs if these technologies improve performance, increase the chance of success and support competition, which are all key factors of a masculine culture." To some degree, this argument could be interpreted to mean that more masculine societies are prepared and ready to use ICT products and services for advancement. It is hypothesized that:

**H4c**: Countries in Africa with higher MAS scores will have higher network readiness index scores.

UAI refers to how a society deals with the uncertain and ambiguous situations it may confront. Hofstede (2001) suggests that technological adoption and progress is higher in countries with fewer propensities for risk taking. Nath and Murthy (2004) assert that, "A culture high in uncertainty avoidance is rule oriented, has less tolerance for opinions and behaviors different from its own, and avoids taking risks. There is also resistance to change." That is, such countries would be averse to adopting or accepting new technological products and services, including IT-related ones. On the contrary, nations with lower uncertainty avoidance scores would be more likely to adopt ICT-based initiatives for development. Png et al. (2001) showed that countries with high uncertainty avoidance scores are less likely to adopt frame relay technology. Thus, it is hypothesized that:

**H4d**: Countries in Africa with higher UAI scores will have lower network readiness index scores.

## RESEARCH METHODOLOGY

### Data

This study uses a cross-section of data collected from reputable, secondary data sources, including the World Bank, the World Economic Forum, The Heritage Foundation, and the Transparency International. The cultural dimensions of each of the countries selected for the study are from Hofstede (2001). Importantly, Hofstede (2001) provided scores for some world regions, including the Arab World (including North Africa), East Africa, and West Africa. Unfortunately, Hofstede did not provide scores for any country in Central Africa. With respect to that sub-region, an informal discussion was conducted by the author and a few IS and humanity professors of African origins. The conclusion was that there are clearly similarities, yet differences in the norms and values between the people of East and West Africa. Thus, it may not be unreasonable to use the mean scores for the cross-cultural dimensions in Hofstede for both East and West Africa as a proxy index for the sub-region of Central Africa. The logic is that numbers, which are different yet similar in both sub-regions, are used to delineate the sub-region for which no data exists. Support for this argument is available from other sources; for example, the socio-cultural parameters and contexts in Sub-Saharan Africa appeared to compare reasonably well (Mbarika et al., 2005; World Bank, 2007; CIA World Factbook, 2011).

Admittedly, the efficacy of this study's analysis will depend on variability in the selected countries. For the purposes of this study, as was indicated earlier, twenty (20) countries from each the five sub-regions were included in the analysis, that is, four countries from each. The countries (e.g., Nigeria, Egypt, and the Republic of South Africa) chosen to represent a large section of Africa's economy and population. The variables used to operationalize the national IT policy for each country was obtained from UNECA (2007) and InfoDev (2007). A subjective scale of 1 to 5, with 1 indicating poor and 5 high, was used to classify the countries. The other measures used for the national IT policy factor or variable were taken from WEF (2011). The economic (national income) variables used to gauge national wealth included the GDP per capita and the economic freedom index values. The data for GDP per capita came from the World Bank (2007) and CIA World Factbook (2011), and the economic freedom index was obtained from the Heritage Foundation (2008). The study used two measures to represent human capital: a) total literacy levels, and b) the quality of the educational system. These items are from the CIA World Factbook (2011) and WEF (2011). For the corruption variable, the study used data from Transparency International (2007). The study variables are shown in Table 1.

## DATA ANALYSIS

To test hypothesis $H_1$, we used a non parametric test, *Kruskal-Wallis H*, which was developed to assess whether differences exist among African countries with respect to their network readiness index values. A summary of the results is provided in Table 2. For the remaining hypotheses, Pearson's correlation and a series of ordinary least squares (OLS) regression models were performed using SPPS 14.0 software. The result of the *Kruskal-Wallis H* test on hypothesis $H_1$ indicated differences among the selected countries on the network readiness index. The result (Chi Square = 13.67, df = 4, p = 0.008) showed a significant difference across the countries. The data show that countries from North Africa and some from the Southern part of the continent have better network readiness scores. The results of the Pearson's correlation for the remaining hypotheses are presented in Table 2. The significant relationships – in relation to the dependent construct – are highlighted in bold print. Importantly, multicollinearity seems not to be a major problem in the study. Multicollinearity occurs when an independent measure or variable is highly correlated with one or more of the other independent variables in a multiple regression equation, which tend to undermine the statistical significance of these variables. Multicollinearity would be a concern if the correlations among the study's independent variables were above 0.8 (Kennedy, 1998). Later, regression models will be used to enhance insights. A regression model is homoskedastic if it has a constant conditional variance, which is not problematic for this study as the data used followed a normal distribution. For example, the GDP per capita was transformed and normalized with a logarithmic function, i.e., *In*.

NIT-g = ICT government vision NIT-r = ICT regulating environment; NIT-d = Depth and quality of national IT policy; NTR = networked readiness; * = countries with estimated & manipulated Hofstede's measures; † = average for sub-region (as there is no data for Angola); See the abbreviations for the cultural factors in the main text.

With respect to the hypotheses formulated to examine the relationships between the independent factors (and their sub-measures or items), i.e., H2a through H4d, the data supported eight (8) out of the ten (10) hypotheses. These results will be discussed in the next section. Importantly, the aforementioned results, though insightful are

*Table 2. The Pearson's correlation matrix*

| | lnGDP | ECO | LIT | QED | TPC | NIT-r | NIT-g | NIT-d | PDI | IDV | MAS | UAI | NTR |
|---|---|---|---|---|---|---|---|---|---|---|---|---|---|
| In-GDP | 1 | .449(*) | .548(*) | .173 | .400 | .459(*) | .047 | .392 | .654(**) | .792(**) | .345 | .359 | **.671(**)** |
| ECO | .449(*) | 1 | .475(*) | .501(*) | .548(*) | .621(**) | .454(*) | .608(**) | .482(*) | .446(*) | -.003 | -.005 | **.724(**)** |
| LIT | .548(*) | .475(*) | 1 | .438 | .058 | .413 | -.193 | .229 | .403 | .345 | .041 | -.042 | **.452(*)** |
| QED | .173 | .501(*) | .438 | 1 | .131 | .592(**) | .496(*) | .356 | .102 | .020 | .267 | .216 | **.567(**)** |
| TPC | .400 | .548(*) | .058 | .131 | 1 | .511(*) | .351 | .353 | .337 | .590(**) | -.053 | -.038 | **.633(**)** |
| NIT-r | .459(*) | .621(**) | .413 | .592(**) | .511(*) | 1 | .553(*) | .702(**) | .540(*) | .629(**) | .210 | .220 | **.883(**)** |
| NIT-g | .047 | .454(*) | -.193 | .496(*) | .351 | .553(*) | 1 | .496(*) | .094 | .145 | .465(*) | .488(*) | **.601(**)** |
| NIT-d | .392 | .608(**) | .229 | .356 | .353 | .702(**) | .496(*) | 1 | .609(**) | .479(*) | .214 | .362 | **.696(**)** |
| PDI | .654(**) | .482(*) | .403 | .102 | .337 | .540(*) | .094 | .609(**) | 1 | .658(**) | .023 | .335 | **.656(**)** |
| IDV | .792(**) | .446(*) | .345 | .020 | .590(**) | .629(**) | .145 | .479(*) | .658(**) | 1 | .286 | .241 | **.728(**)** |
| MAS | .345 | -.003 | .041 | .267 | -.053 | .210 | .465(*) | .214 | .023 | .286 | 1 | .857(**) | .404 |
| UAI | .359 | -.005 | -.042 | .216 | -.038 | .220 | .488(*) | .362 | .335 | .241 | .857(**) | 1 | .448(*) |
| NTR | .671(**) | .724(**) | .452(*) | .567(**) | .633(**) | .883(**) | .601(**) | .696(**) | .656(**) | .728(**) | .404 | .448(*) | 1 |

* Correlation is significant at the 0.05 level (2-tailed). ** Correlation is significant at the 0.01 level (2-tailed).

insufficient to provide an answer to the question: Which factors should the continent pay most attention to in order to integrate into the information age? To understand the influences of relevant factors, we must perform a series of ordinary least squares (OLS) regression models as mentioned above. To that end, the effect of each of the factors, i.e. national culture, economic wealth, and national IT policy will be regressed on the dependent construct: network readiness. Lastly, all the factors together will be regressed on the dependent variable. Thus, the four regression models to be used in the study are represented as follows:

$$NTR_j = \alpha + \beta_1 IDV_j + \beta_2 MAS_j + \beta_3 UAI_j + \beta_4 PDI_j \quad (1)$$

$$NTR_j = \alpha + \beta_1 GDP_j + \beta_2 ECO_j . \quad (2)$$

$$NTR_j = \alpha + \beta_1 NIT\text{-}g_j + \beta_2 NIT\text{-}r_j + \beta_3 NIT\text{-}d_j \quad (3)$$

$$NTR_j = \alpha + \beta_1 NIT\text{-}g_j + \beta_2 NIT\text{-}r_j + \beta_3 NIT\text{-}d_j + \beta_4 GDP_j + \beta_5 ECO_j + \beta_6 IDV_j + \beta_7 MAS_j + \beta_8 UAI \quad (4)$$

The αs and βs are parameters to be estimated, and the subscript "j" stands for countries. The above approach is similar to that followed by other researchers (see e.g., Oxley & Yeung, 2001; Nath & Murthy, 2004; Dewan et al., 2005; Bagchi et al., 2006; Gregorio et al., 2005; Waarts & van Everdingen, 2005; Kovačić, 2005; Erunbam & de Jong, 2006).

Legend:

- **PDI:** Power Distance Index
- **IDV:** Individualism
- **MAS:** Masculinity
- **UAI:** Uncertainty Avoidance Index
- **GDP:** Per capita
- **ECO:** Economic freedom Index
- **NIT-g:** ICT Government Vision
- **NIT-r:** ICT regulating environment
- **NIT-d:** Depth and quality of national IT policy
- **NTR:** Network readiness

When using equation one (1), we entered only the cultural variables as regressors on the

*Table 3. Results of national culture as the regressor on network readiness*

| | Unstandardized Coefficients | | Standardized Coefficients | t | Coefficient Sig. | Adjusted $R^2$ | F | Sig. |
|---|---|---|---|---|---|---|---|---|
| | B | Std. Error | Beta | -.231 | .821 | | | |
| (Constant) | -.235 | 1.017 | | | | | | |
| PDI | 0.20 | 0.14 | .556 | 1.459 | .165 | 0.57 | 7.29 | 0.002 |
| IDV | .025 | .029 | .271 | .861 | .403 | | | |
| MAS | .049 | .049 | .548 | .999 | .334 | | | |
| UAI | -.022 | .044 | -.273 | -.503 | .622 | | | |

main variable: network readiness. The results are presented in Table 3. The results show that all the cross-cultural measures together significantly impact the network readiness construct ($p = 0.002$). The t statistic and its significance value are used to test the null hypothesis that the regression coefficient is zero. If the significance value is small (less than $p = 0.05$) then the coefficient is considered significant. With respect to the impacts of the cross-cultural dimensions on the main dependant, it can be seen from Table 3 that none of the sub-measures have significant coefficient values.

In equation two (2), we entered only the socio-economic variables as regressors on the main variable: network readiness. The results are presented in Table 4. The measures collectively have a significant effect on network readiness ($p = 0.000$). With regard to the t statistic and its significance value, national income or wealth and the quality of educational systems were seen to be influential coefficients in the regression model.

In equation three (3) above, we entered only the national IT policy variables as regressors on the main variable: network readiness. The results are presented in Table 5. The measures collectively have a significant effect on network readiness ($p = 0.000$). With respect to the t statistic and its significance value, the ICT regulatory environment was seen to be an important coefficient in the regression model than the other two sub-measures.

In the last equation, all the factors are added into the model. However, in order to increase the predictability of the overall model, it is suggested that measures seen not to be contributing to the predictability power of the model be dropped (Kennedy, 1998). Thus, removing the measures of ECO, IND, NIT-d, NTI-g, and LIT from the model, improved its degree of freedom, and its $R^2$ as well as its overall predictability. The flip side of this procedure is that it causes the problem of missing or incomplete variables in the final model. We are satisfied with the final model because items from each of the main factors were represented. More importantly, we were assured of the high predictability of the model.

The results of the revised model are presented in Table 6. As expected, the $R^2$ of the model is significantly improved. The included measures explain 95% of the variation in the model. All the included measures collectively influence the network readiness variable significantly ($p = 0.000$). Again, regarding the t statistic and its significance value, clearly four (4) items, i.e., the quality of the educational systems, the transparency levels (corruption index), the ICT regulatory framework, and PDI were the more important coefficients in the overall regression than the remaining items.

*Table 4. Results of socio-economic factor as the regressor on network readiness*

| | Unstandardized Coefficients | | Standardized Coefficients | t | Coefficient Sig. | Adjusted $R^2$ | F | Sig. |
|---|---|---|---|---|---|---|---|---|
| | B | Std. Error | Beta | -1.400 | .183 | | | |
| (Constant) | -1.123 | .802 | | | | | | |
| InGDP | .240 | .088 | .426 | 2.723 | .017 | 0.75 | 12.14 | 0.000 |
| ECO | .020 | .017 | .209 | 1.184 | .256 | | | |
| LIT | -.002 | .005 | -.063 | -.381 | .709 | | | |
| QED | .285 | .108 | .376 | 2.653 | .019 | | | |
| TPC | .132 | .068 | .302 | 1.946 | .072 | | | |

*Table 5. Results of national IT policy as the regressor on network readiness*

| | Unstandardized Coefficients | | Standardized Coefficients | t | Coefficient Sig. | Adjusted $R^2$ | F | Sig. |
|---|---|---|---|---|---|---|---|---|
| | B | Std. Error | Beta | 2.552 | .021 | | | |
| (Constant) | .817 | .320 | | | | | | |
| NIT-r | .541 | .124 | .719 | 4.378 | .000 | 0.77 | 22.02 | 0.000 |
| NIT-g | .099 | .093 | .143 | 1.064 | .303 | | | |
| NIT-d | .068 | .089 | .120 | .764 | .456 | | | |

## DISCUSSION AND CONCLUSION

A summary of all results for the hypotheses formulated in this chapter is presented in Table 7. The discussion on each of the hypotheses follows afterward.

Hypothesis H1 was formulated to examine how far network readiness index values vary among African countries. The analysis showed that according to this index, significant differences exist among the sampled African countries. The data affirm that the processes of ICT diffusion in general and ICT use for socio-development in particular, are uneven in Africa. Thus in the context of the ever-changing globalized world, some African countries have been able to leverage ICT use for development more effectively than others. Others (e.g. Ifinedo, 2005a; Bagchi et al., 2006) have offered similar insights.

Hypothesis H2a was supported, indicating that in countries where national IT policies with depth and quality were implemented early, network readiness index values tend to be higher. This progress is less likely where poorer quality IT policies have been implemented. To some degree, this finding lends credence to the tenets of the path dependence theory. Further, Hypothesis H2b showed that where government ICT vision and focus is strong, the network readiness index is equally high. This confirmation also supports the views expressed by such agencies as UN ICT Task Force (2004), WSIS (2007), and UNECA (2007). Likewise, analysis of hypothesis H2c affirmed the notion that national IT policy which emphasizes favorable ICT regulatory environments can positively influence a country's readiness to benefit from ICT for socio-economic progress. This finding is in line with the views of Gibbs et al. (2003), Pohjola (2003), and Gust and Marquez (2004), and Meso et al. (2006).

Hypothesis H3a was developed to test the nature of the relationships between national wealth

*Table 6. Results of all the factors (and relevant sub-items) as the regressor on network readiness*

| | Unstandardized Coefficients | | Standardized Coefficients | t | Coefficient Sig. | Adjusted $R^2$ | F | Sig. |
|---|---|---|---|---|---|---|---|---|
| | B | Std. Error | Beta | -1.822 | 0.93 | | | |
| (Constant) | -.570 | .313 | | | | | | |
| InGDP | .031 | .052 | .055 | .602 | .558 | | | |
| QED | .152 | .053 | .201 | 2.878 | .014 | 0.95 | 55.0 | 0.000 |
| TPC | .135 | .028 | .310 | 4.802 | .000 | | | |
| NITr | .270 | .074 | .359 | 3.661 | .003 | | | |
| PDI | .011 | .005 | .311 | 2.437 | .031 | | | |
| MAS | .028 | .015 | .310 | 1.848 | .089 | | | |
| UAI | -.004 | .013 | -.053 | -.329 | .748 | | | |

and economic freedom, on the one hand, and network readiness, on the other. The data analysis showed that a positive relationship exists between the two constructs. This finding is consistent with the findings of researchers working with African data (e.g., Bagchi et al. 2005) and others elsewhere (e.g., Pohjola, 2003; Caselli and Coleman, 2001; Dewan et al., 2005; Gregorio et al., 2005). An additional insight to be gained from this study's analysis is that network readiness was found to be higher in countries with higher economic freedom indices. Thus we can suggest that a nation's ICT capability for development increases where the forces that influence wealth production are not perceived to be coercive.

The study provides strong support for the prediction that African countries with higher literacy levels and quality educational systems will have higher scores on the network readiness index, i.e., H3b. It is logical to expect that entities in countries where quality educational systems are established will be more likely to avail themselves of the opportunity to use ICT than those entities where such systems are lacking. The data provide strong support for this assertion. Put differently, human capital measures are highly correlated with a nation's readiness to benefit from ICT use for development. In brief, the technological progress of African countries with favorable literacy rates levels and quality educational systems are in a better position to gain the most from new innovations. In the context of African countries, Bagchi et al. (2006) offer a similar conclusion. The nexus between the levels of transparency in a country and its network readiness was examined in H3c. The data showed a strong positive relationship between the two variables. This result affirms the notion that the more open and less corrupt a country is, the more it is capable of using ICT-based initiatives such as e-commerce to enhance its socio-economic growth. On this aspect, the

*Table 7. The summary of all the results*

| | Hypothesis | Result |
|---|---|---|
| 1 | H1 | Supported |
| 2 | H2a | Supported |
| 3 | H2b | Supported |
| 4 | H2c | Supported |
| 5 | H3a | Supported |
| 6 | H3b | Supported |
| 7 | H3c | Supported |
| 8 | H4a | Supported |
| 9 | H4b | Supported |
| 10 | H4c | Not supported |
| 11 | H4d | Not supported |

study is consistent with the findings of Oxley and Yeung (2001).

Contrary to widely held views on the nature of the relationship between the cross-cultural dimension of the power distance index (PDI) and technological artefacts, this study drew from the reality of life in Africa to predict the existence of a positive relationship between PDI and network readiness, i.e., H4a. The data confirmed that a positive relationship exists between the two variables. This result lends support to the view that (in the context of Africa) ICT use for development is higher in cultures that rely on those in authority and in leadership roles to provide guidance on such issues. Hypothesis H4b states that countries in Africa with higher individualistic (IND) scores will have higher network readiness index scores. The data analysis supported this assertion.

In brief, this result allows us to suggest that network readiness in Africa tends to be higher for countries that place value on the performance of the individual rather than that of the group. As discussed, in individualistic countries, entities are more agile in trying out new innovations than those in countries where decision making may be delayed by a search for group consensus. These viewpoints must not be confused, however, with the general categorization of Hofstede (2001), who classified African societies as collective or group-oriented. Our study showed that African countries which had strongly individualistic cultural elements were more likely to be poised to benefit from ICT use for development than those without such tendencies.

Hypotheses H4c and H4d are unsupported by this study's data. It is somewhat surprising that the prediction related to the masculinity index is unsupported. This result was expected given the fact that African cultures have been categorized as masculine (Hofstede, 2001). Some African countries appear to be faring better than others regarding the diffusion of ICT and the use of such products for development (Ifinedo, 2005a; Morawczynski et al., 2006; WEF, 2011; UNECA, 2007). By the same token, it would have made more sense to see variations across African countries. Data samples different from the one used here may possibly offer more illuminating insights on these aspects of this study.

To answer the question about which factors or sub-items need the most urgent attention, we turn to the results from the regression models. As can be seen from the results tables above, each of the independent factors (with their sub-measures or items) when regressed as a single group on the network readiness construct significantly influence the main construct: network readiness. The significance values (p) of national IT policy, socio-economic factors, and national culture, for network readiness are 0.002, 0.000, and 0.000, respectively. The variation explained by these factors (with their sub-measures or items) when entered as a single group ranges from 57% to 77%. When all the relevant sub-measures or items were entered into the regression at once, the variation explained went up to 95%. This is to be expected with items being added to the model (Kennedy, 1998).

Using socio-economic factors (with their sub-measures) as the regressor on the main construct, two sub-measures, national income and the quality of educational systems, were found to be influential in the regression model (see Table 4). This result implies that the extent of wealth available to an African country and its educational systems are two important measurements that may affect its network readiness. However, the national income or wealth measure did not have a significant coefficient when regressed with other items. On the other hand, the relevance of quality of educational systems to network readiness was confirmed by its retention in the presence of other relevant measures. Similarly, ICT regulatory environment in African countries strongly influences their network readiness more than other sub-measures for the national IT policy factor. Its critical relevance was confirmed by its significant coefficient value in the overall model (see Table 5). In brief, the pertinent sub-measures that this study found deserving of attention when the independent factors (and the relevant sub-measures) were regressed on the main construct are the quality of each country's educational systems, its transparency (corruption) levels, its ICT regulatory framework, and its cross-cultural dimension of power distance (PDI).

Before discussing the implications of this study's findings, it is important to highlight its limitations. The twenty (20) countries chosen, though varied and comprehensive in range, might be limiting. Those selected countries may not unequivocally reflect patterns in their respective regions. A larger sample of countries might permit deeper insights. A fundamental flaw in Hofstede's study and typology must be acknowledged, that is, "culture" in a nation-state is assumed to be monolithic (e.g., Waarts & van Everdingen, 2005; Erunbam & de Jong, 2006). Even in one single nation there are different sub-cultures. The non-availability of cross-cultural dimension data for some parts of Africa may be limiting. Other approaches used to study the IT-national culture nexus may yield more insights (e.g., Walsham, 2002; Leidner & Kayworth, 2006). Furthermore, this study inadvertently inherits the measurement problems from the secondary sources that were used.

The results of this research provide implications for both policy makers and researchers. First, although African countries have relatively poor scores on the network readiness index, it may be misleading to lump all the countries on the continent into one pot. This study has shown that certain salient differences should not be overlooked. Second, the significance of socio-economic influences, national culture, and national IT policy for network readiness index values is underscored. To the best of our knowledge, this is among the first of such studies; its findings may form the basis for future research effort in the area. Third, this study's findings lend credence to the conclusion and observations of similar investigations (e.g. Oxley & Yeung, 2001; Caselli & Coleman, 2001; Pohjola, 2003; Dedrick et al., 2003; Gregorio et al., 2005; Waarts & van Everdingen, 2005; Bagchi et al., 2006; Gregorio et al., 2005; Langmia, 2005; Erunbam & de Jong, 2006). Importantly, the findings on the relationships between selected factors and their influences may serve as the building blocks for the development of a relevant theory. Fourth, the research community is made aware that the relationship between the cross-cultural dimension of power distance (PDI) and technological innovation may not be an inverse one for African cultures. Importantly, the nature of the various relationships between national cultural factors and network readiness is highlighted. Other studies on these themes can draw from this effort, as well as adding further insights. It must be said theoretical developments in particular, as they relate to African nations, and generally those examining the relationships between technological innovations and socio-cultural and -economic developments are still evolving.

Fifth, the subjects requiring attention by policy makers have been identified: this study contends that the quality of educational systems on the continent, favorable transparency levels, and efficient ICT regulatory frameworks would enable countries to participate in the information age. In particular, strong leadership, support, and the commitment of African national governments with respect to ICT initiatives would augur well for the development and advancement of the continent. Several bodies such as the World Bank (InfoDev, 2007), the UN ICT Task Force (2004), and WSIS (2007) have been asking: where should Africa be focusing attention with a view to improving e-readiness index scores? It is hoped that the four issues identified as significant for the network readiness index will attract the attention of governments on the continent and other external agencies. Future study on this topic is expected. Other relevant factors and sub-measures may be included. Future study should use more countries than used here. Studies of this nature may be undertaken in comparable parts of the world to facilitate comparative insights.

## REFERENCES

G8 DOT Force. (2001). *Issue objectives for the Genoa summit meeting 2001: DOT force.* Retrieved December 12, 2005 from http://www.g8.utoronto.ca/.

Anandarajan, M., Igbaria, M., & Anakwe, U. (2002). IT acceptance in a less-developed country: a motivational factor perspective. *International Journal of Information Management, 22*(1), 47–65. doi:10.1016/S0268-4012(01)00040-8

Bagchi, K., Udo, G., & Kirs, P. (2006). Global diffusion of the Internet XII: the Internet growth in Africa: some empirical results. *Communications of the Association for Information Systems, 19*(16), 323–351.

Bodley, J. H. (1994). *Cultural anthropology: tribes, states, and the global system.* Mountain View, CA: Mayfield Publishing.

Brian, A. W. (1994). *Increasing returns and path dependence in the economy.* Ann Arbor, MI: University of Michigan Press.

Bridges Organization. (2001), *Comparison of e-readiness assessment models.* Retrieved October 5, 2007, from http://www.bridges.org/ereadiness/tools.html.

Bui, T. X., Sankaran, S., & Sebastian, I. M. (2003). A framework for measuring national e-readiness. *International Journal of Electronic Business, 1*(1), 3–22. doi:10.1504/IJEB.2003.002162

Caselli, F., & Coleman, W. (2001). Cross-country technology diffusion: the case of computers. *The American Economic Review, 91*(2), 328–335. doi:10.1257/aer.91.2.328

Chinn, M. D., & Fairlie, R. W. (2004). *The determinants of the global digital divide: a cross-country analysis of computer and Internet penetration.* Retrieved October 8, 2008 from http://ssrn.com/abstract=519082.

CIA WorldFact. (2011). *Country reports.* Retrieved October 8, 2011 from https://www.cia.gov/.

Comin, D., & Hobijn, B. (2004). Cross-country technology adoption: making the theories face the facts. *Journal of Monetary Economics, 51*(1), 39–83. doi:10.1016/j.jmoneco.2003.07.003

Darley, W. K. (2001). The internet and emerging e-commerce: challenges and implications for management in Sub-Saharan Africa. *Journal of Global Information Technology Management, 4*(4), 4–18.

Dasgupta, S., Lall, S., & Wheeler, D. (2001). Policy reform, economic growth, and the digital divide: an econometric analysis. *Development Research Group, World Bank.* Retrieved October 8, 2008, from http://econ.worldbank.org /external/default/main?pagePK=64165259&piPK=64165421&theSitePK=469372&menuPK= 64216926&entityID=000094946_01032705352348

Dedrick, J., Gurbaxani, V., & Kraemer, K. L. (2003). Information technology and economic performance: a critical review of the empirical evidence. *ACM Computing Surveys, 35*(1), 1–28. doi:10.1145/641865.641866

Dewan, S., Ganley, D., & Kraemer, K. L. (2004). *Across the digital divide: a cross-country analysis of the determinants of IT penetration.* Retrieved October 8, 2008, from http://unpan1.un.org/intradoc/groups/public/documents/APCITY/UNPAN022642.pdf.

Dewan, S., Ganley, D., & Kraemer, K. L. (2005). Across the digital divide: a cross-country multi-technology analysis of the determinants of IT penetration. *Journal of the Association for Information Systems, 6*(12), 409–432.

EIU (Economic Intelligence Unit). (2011). *Global intelligence and analysis.* Retrieved March 18, 2011 from http://www.eiu.com/public/.

Erumbam, A. A., & de Jong, S. B. (2006). Cross-country differences in ICT adoption: a consequence of culture? *Journal of World Business*, *41*(4), 302–314. doi:10.1016/j.jwb.2006.08.005

Ford, D. P., Conelly, C. E., & Meister, D. B. (2003). Information systems research and Hofstede's culture consequences: an uneasy and incomplete partnership. *IEEE Transactions on Engineering Management*, *50*(1), 8–25. doi:10.1109/TEM.2002.808265

Geertz, C. (1973). *The interpretation of cultures*. New York, NY: Basic Books.

Geertz, C. (1973). *The interpretation of cultures*. New York, NY: Basic Books.

Gibbs, J. L., Kraemer, K. L., & Dedrick, J. (2003). Environment and policy factors shaping global e-commerce diffusion: a cross-country comparison. *The Information Society*, *19*(1), 5–18. doi:10.1080/01972240309472

Giddens, A. (1991). *Modernity and self-identity: self and society in the late modern age*. Cambridge, England: Polity Press.

Gregorio, D. D., Kassicieh, S. K., & Neto, R. D. (2005). Drivers of e-business activity in developed and emerging markets. *IEEE Transactions on Engineering Management*, *52*(2), 155–166. doi:10.1109/TEM.2005.844464

Gust, C., & Marquez, J. (2004). International comparisons of productivity growth: the role of information technologies and regulatory practices. *Labour Economics*, *11*(1), 33–58. doi:10.1016/S0927-5371(03)00055-1

Ho, S.-C., Kaufmann, R. J., & Liang, T.-P. (2007). A growth theory perspective on B2C E-commerce growth in Europe: an exploratory study. *Electronic Commerce Research and Applications*, *6*(3), 237–259. doi:10.1016/j.elerap.2006.06.003

Hofstede, G. (2001). *Culture's consequences: comparing values, behaviors, institutions, and organizations across nations* (2nd ed.). Thousand Oaks, CA: Sage Publications.

Ifinedo, P. (2005a). Measuring Africa's e-readiness in the global networked economy: a nine-country data analysis. *The International Journal of Education and Development using Information and Communication Technology*, *1*(1), 53-71.

Ifinedo, P. (2006). Towards e-government in a Sub-Saharan African country: impediments and initiatives in Nigeria. *Journal of E-Government*, *3*(1), 4–28. doi:10.1300/J399v03n01_02

Ifinedo (2005b). E-government initiative in a developing country: strategies and implementation in Nigeria, *In Proceedings of 6th. World Congress on Electronic Business*,(pp. 1-11) Hamilton, Ontario, Canada.

InfoDev (2007). *The information for development program*. Retrieved December 12, 2010, www.infodev.org/.

ITIM. (2011). *Geert Hofstede cultural dimensions*. Retrieved September, 6, 2006 from http://www.geert-hofstede.com /hofstede_dimensions.php.

Janczewski, L. J. (1992). Relationships between nformation Technology and Competitive advantage in New Zealand Businesses, *In Proceedings of 1992 Information Resources Management Association Charleston*, (pp. 347-364.) Hershey, PA: Idea Group Publishing

Jorgenson, D. W. (2001). Information technology and economy. *The American Economic Review*, *9*(1), 1–32. doi:10.1257/aer.91.1.1

Kennedy, P. (1998). *A guide to econometrics*. Cambridge, MA: The MIT Press.

Kiiski, S., & Pohjola, M. (2002). Cross country diffusion of the internet. *Information Economics and Policy*, *14*(2), 297–310. doi:10.1016/S0167-6245(01)00071-3

Kovačić, Z. J. (2005). The impact of national culture on worldwide e-government readiness. *Informing Science: International Journal of an Emerging Discipline*, *8*, 143–158.

Langmia, K. (2005). The role of ICT in the economic development of Africa: the case of South Africa. *International Journal of Education and Development using Information and Communication Technology*, *2*(4), 144-156.

Leidner, D. E., & Kayworth, T. (2006). A review of culture in information systems research: toward a theory of information technology culture conflict. *Management Information Systems Quarterly*, *30*(2), 357–399.

Mbarika, V. W., Okoli, C., Byrd, T. A., & Datta, P. (2005). The neglected continent of IS research: a research agenda for Sub-Saharan Africa. *Journal of the Association for Information Systems*, *6*(5), 130–170.

Meso, P., Checchi, P. M., Sevcik, G. R., Loch, K. D., & Straub, D. W. (2006). Knowledge spheres and the diffusion of national IT policies. *The Electronic Journal of Information Systems in Developing Countries*, *23*, 1–16.

Molla, A. (2000). Downloading or uploading? the information economy and Africa current status. *Information Technology for Development*, *9*(3-4), 205–221. doi:10.1080/02681102.2000.9525333

Morawczynski, O., Ngwenyama, O., Andoh-Baidoo, F. K., & Bollou, F. (2006). Is there a relationship between ICT, health, education And Development? an empirical analysis of five West African Countries from 1997-2003. *The Electronic Journal on Information Systems in Developing Countries*, *23*(5), 1–15.

Myers, M. D., & Tan, F. B. (2002). Beyond models of national culture in information systems research. *Journal of Global Information Management*, *10*(1), 24–32. doi:10.4018/jgim.2002010103

Nath, R., & Murthy, V. N. R. (2004). A study of the relationship between internet diffusion and culture. *Journal of International Technology and Information Management*, *13*(2), 123–132.

Odedra, M., Lawrie, M., Bennett, M., & Goodman, S. E. (1993). Sub-Saharan Africa: a technological desert. *Communications of the ACM*, *36*(2), 25–29. doi:10.1145/151220.151222

Oxley, J. E., & Yeung, B. (2001). E-commerce readiness: institutional environment and international competitiveness. *Journal of International Business Studies*, *32*(4), 705–723. doi:10.1057/palgrave.jibs.8490991

Png, I. P. L., Tan, B. C. Y., & Wee, K.-L. (2001). Dimensions of national culture and corporate adoption of IT infrastructure. *IEEE Transactions on Engineering Management*, *48*(1), 36–45. doi:10.1109/17.913164

Pohjola, M. (2002). The new economy: facts, impacts and policies. *Information Economics and Policy*, *14*(2), 133–144. doi:10.1016/S0167-6245(01)00063-4

Pohjola, M. (2003). The adoption and diffusion of ICT across countries: patterns and determinants. In Jones, D. C. (Ed.), *The New Economy Handbook* (pp. 77–100). New York, NY: Academic Press.

Roycroft, T. R., & Anantho, A. (2003). Internet subscription in Africa: policy for a dual digital divide. *Telecommunications Policy*, *27*(1/2), 61–74. doi:10.1016/S0308-5961(02)00091-5

Shane, S. A. (1993). Cultural influences on national rates of innovation. *Journal of Business Venturing*, *8*(1), 59–73. doi:10.1016/0883-9026(93)90011-S

Shih, C.-F., Dedrick, J., & Kraemer, K. L. (2002). *Determinants of IT spending at the country level*. Irvine, CA: University of California.

Shore, B., & Venkatachalam, A. R. (1996). Role of national culture in the transfer of information technology. *The Journal of Strategic Information Systems*, *5*(1), 19–35. doi:10.1016/S0963-8687(96)80021-7

Steers, R. M., Meyer, A. D., & Sanchez-Runde, C. J. (2008). National culture and the adoption of new technologies. *Journal of World Business*, *43*(3), 255–260. doi:10.1016/j.jwb.2008.03.007

Straub, D. W., Loch, K. D., & Hill, C. E. (2001). Transfer of information technology to developing countries: a test of cultural influence modeling in the Arab world. *Journal of Global Information Management*, *9*(4), 6–28. doi:10.4018/jgim.2001100101

The Heritage Foundation. (2008). *Index of economic freedom*. Retrieved January 17, 2007 from http://www.heritage.org/Index/

Transparency International. (2007). *Corruption perception index – 2007*. Retrieved January 27, 2007 from http://www.transparency.org /news_room/in_focus/2007/cpi2007/cpi_2007_table

UN ICT TASK Force. (2004). *The history of the United Nations information and communication technologies task force*. Retrieved January 17, 2007 from http://www.unicttaskforce.org/index.html.

UNECA. (2007). *National information and communications strategies*. Retrieved January 10, 2008 from http://www.uneca.org /aisi/nici/nici_country_pages.htm

Waarts, E., & van Everdingen, Y. (2005). The influence of national culture on the adoption status of innovations: an empirical study of firms across Europe. *European Management Journal*, *25*(6), 601–610. doi:10.1016/j.emj.2005.10.007

Wallsten, S. J. (2001). An econometric analysis of telecom competition, privatization, and regulation in Africa and Latin America. *The Journal of Industrial Economics*, *49*(1), 1–19. doi:10.1111/1467-6451.00135

Walsham, G. (2002). Cross-cultural software production and use: a structurational analysis. *Management Information Systems Quarterly*, *26*(4), 359–380. doi:10.2307/4132313

WEF (World Economic Forum). (2011). *Global competitiveness 2009-2010.* Retrieved April 2, 2011 from http://www.weforum.org/reports.

World Bank. (2007). *Development data and statistics*. Retrieved December, 10, 2007 from http://web.worldbank.org/.

WSIS. (2007). *World summit on the information society*. Retrieved April 2, 2011 from http://www.itu.int /wsis/basic/about.html

## KEY TERMS AND DEFINITIONS

**Africa:** One of the continents in the world.

**National ICT Policy:** A dedicated, well-focused statements guiding the national information and communication technology agenda of a country.

**Social Factors:** These are factors affecting the life styles of citizens of countries.

**Economic Factors:** These are basic elements related to the financial matters of countries.

**National Culture:** This refers to values and norms in a country which differentiates it from other countries.

**Network Readiness:** This refers to the capability of countries to use ICT for developmental purposes.

**Human Capital:** This refers to the literacy levels and quality of educational systems in a country

# Chapter 8
# An Empirical Study of Career Orientations and Turnover Intentions of Information Systems Personnel in Botswana

**K. V Mgaya**
*University of Botswana, Botswana*

**F. M. E. Uzoka**
*Mount Royal University, Canada*

**E. G. Kitindi**
*University of Dar es Salaam, Tanzania*

**A.B. Akinnuwesi**
*Bells University of Technology, Nigeria*

**A. P. Shemi**
*University of Botswana, Botswana*

## ABSTRACT

*A number of studies on career orientations of information systems (IS) personnel have focused on developed countries. This study attempts to examine career anchors of IS personnel from the perspective of a developing country, Botswana. The results of the study show that IS personnel in Botswana exhibit career orientations similar to those identified in literature. However, there are some variations, which are attributed to cultural and socio-economic peculiarities. The study indicates that life style does not feature as a significant career anchor in Botswana. The dominant career anchors include organizational stability (security) and sense of service (service). Gender, age, and educational qualifications tend to moderate the career anchors significantly; thus creating a partition of the anchors across demographic groups. The major contributors to the turnover intentions of IS personnel in developing economies are job satisfaction and growth opportunities. Career satisfaction, supervisor support, organization commitment, length of service, and age did not contribute significantly to turnover intention.*

DOI: 10.4018/978-1-4666-1637-0.ch008

## INTRODUCTION

Organizations all over the world are looking for information systems (IS) specialists in computing, programming, systems analysis, networking and user support. Demand exceeds supply. Scarcity of IS personnel affects both developed and developing countries albeit in differing magnitudes. Niederman *et al.* (1991) identified human resource management as one of the critical issues facing the IS profession in the 1990s. Recruitment and retention of IS personnel are the major problems affecting many organizations worldwide (Cone, 1998; Jiang, 2000). Monetary incentives tend to work during the early years of the career after which employees tend to strive for achievement and authority (Jiang, 2000). Over time, there exists a career self-concept, which results from the coalescing of the employees' motives, values and talents (control elements), moderated by environmental, socio-cultural and demographic concomitants (Beecham et al., 2007).

Research done in the developed world, especially the USA, shows that the most prevalent career orientations of Management Information Systems (MIS) employees are technical and managerial. Most systems programmers, application programmers and software engineers tend to be more technically oriented while most systems analysts, project leaders and computer managers tend to be more managerially oriented (Igbaria & Greenhaus, 1991). Schein's earlier work (Schein, 1978) had suggested the following eight major anchors that drive an individual's career decisions: 1). security and stability, 2). autonomy and independence, 3). technical/functional competence, 4). managerial competence, 5). entrepreneurial creativity, 6). service and dedication to a cause, 7). pure challenge, and 8). life style.

Closely related to career anchors are factors that affect turnover intentions of IS personnel. A number of researchers have studied IS personnel turnover intentions especially in the developed world and some Asian economies (Igbaria & Greenhaus, 1992; Lacity & Iyer, 2008; Muliawan et al,. 2009). The environmental, socio-economic, and cultural contexts of developing countries vary considerably from those of developed countries, and could probably affect the job characteristics and turnover intentions of IS personnel. It is noted by Schein (1985) that societal and organizational cultures greatly affect careers in terms of prestige, legitimacy of motives, clarity of the career concept itself, and the importance attached to career versus family and self development. The career anchors and turnover intentions of IS personnel in developing countries is less researched and under-represented in literature (Pringle & Mallon, 2003; Ituma & Simpson, 2007). This research intends to contribute to the filling of that knowledge gap and is expected to provide important information that will help employers to better understand the characteristics of their IS and potential IS staff in order to attract, motivate and retain appropriate IS personnel. Understanding the factors that could trigger employee turnover would be an important managerial information that could assist in stemming the tide of IS employee turnover, especially in a less predictive economy.

In this study, we examine the career anchors and turnover intentions of IS personnel in Botswana in the light of Schein's classifications (for careers anchors) and Igbaria's model of IS employee turnover intentions (Igbaria & Greenhaus, 1992). Botswana is a unique African country which shows a seeming alloy of characteristics of developed and developing worlds, with a number of cultural peculiarities such as high level of patriotism, contentment and a degree of xenophobia (Campbell, 2003). Botswana is a relatively small country in sub-Saharan Africa with a population of about 1.84 million ("Internet World Stats", 2008), but with one of the most thriving and well managed economies in the world. Diamond exploitation, tourism and cattle trading are the key sources of National income. The economic growth rate of Botswana is one of the highest in the world (Isaacs, 2007).

After this section the paper proceeds as follows: Section 2 examines existing works in the area of IS personnel career orientations and turnover intentions. It also outlines the model and hypotheses associated with the study. Section 3 outlines the methodology of the study. The results of the data analyses are presented in Section 4, and discussed in Section 5, while some conclusions are drawn in Section 6.

## REVIEW OF RELATED WORKS AND RESEARCH FRAMEWORK

### Career Anchors

The career anchor (also known as career orientation) theory was developed by Schein (1978) in 1960s and continued to mid 1980s. Originally, the theory was developed based on a longitudinal study of 44 MBA students at the Sloan School of Management, Massachusetts Institute of Technology. A person's career anchor is his or her self-concept, consisting of: 1) self-perceived talents and abilities; 2) basic values and the most important; 3) the evolved sense of motives and needs as they pertain to the career (Schein, 1996). Schein (1987) showed that most people's self-concepts revolved around the following eight categories reflecting basic values, motives and needs.

1. **Autonomy/independence**: Autonomy-oriented individuals seek work situations in which they will be maximally free of organizational constraints and restrictions to pursue their professional competence.
2. **Security/stability:** This anchor combines two types of securities that employees may be looking for: geographical security which relates to a desire to live and work in certain geographical areas and organizational/job security which relates to the desire to be employed by an organization that will guarantee a long term or lifetime employment.
3. **Technical/functional competence:** Employees with this anchor tend to be challenged by the work that they do in line with their technical or functional area of competence, and fear general management as too political.
4. **General Managerial Competence:** Employees with this anchor tend to be challenged by the work of leading others at a level of general manager. Such persons primarily are excited by the opportunity to analyze and solve problems under conditions of incomplete information and uncertainty, like harnessing people together to achieve common goals, and are stimulated (rather than exhausted) by crisis situations.
5. **Entrepreneurial Creativity:** Employees having entrepreneurial anchor would like to create something of their own, such as: a) developing a new product or service, b) building a new enterprise through financial manipulation, c) starting and building a business of their own.
6. **Service or Dedication to a Cause:** Employees who have service orientation are motivated by the desire to serve others and make the world a better place; they want to align work activities with personal values about helping society and are more concerned with finding jobs which meet their values rather than their skills.
7. **Pure Challenge:** This anchor is for employees who are primarily motivated to overcome major obstacles, solve almost unsolvable problems or to win over extremely tough opponents.
8. **Life Style:** Lifestyle oriented employees are those who are motivated to balance career with lifestyle, and are highly concerned with issues such as paternity/maternity leaves, day-care options.

As careers and lives evolve, most people discover that one of these eight categories is their anchor, the thing they will not give up, but most careers also permit the fulfilling of several of the needs that underlie different anchors. According to Suutari and Taka (2004) an individual can only discover his or her anchor through actual work experience. Schein (1996) opines that most people become aware of their career anchors when faced with promotion, job loss, or relocation (geographical or functional). The career anchor or career orientation is significant because it influences career choices, affects decisions to move from one job to another, shapes what is being looked for in life, determines an individual's views of the future, influences the selection of specific occupations and work settings, and affects employees' reactions to their work experiences (Schein, 1978).

It is therefore argued that organizations should analyse career orientations in order to determine which career interventions are most appropriate for each career orientation (Derr, 1986). Supervisors are urged to restructure jobs so that there is a match between the need of the organization and that of the employee, thus reducing employee turnover. Yarnall (1998) summarised the literature on organizational benefits in understanding career orientations of employees as being:

- The ability to tailor career interventions appropriately;
- The ability to offer opportunities congruent with an individual's orientation;
- The design of appropriate reward systems;
- The design of appropriate promotion systems;
- Targeted recognition systems;
- An increased understanding by managers of what drives internal career satisfaction;
- A means of understanding the overriding career culture in the organization;
- A way of structuring career discussions and particularly exit interviews.

Some studies have been carried out to find the career anchors of IS personnel (Ginzberg & Baroudi, 1992; Igbaria & Greenhaus, 1991; Igbaria et al., 1995; Igbaria & McCloskey, 1996; Crepeau et al., 1992; Ituma & Simpson, 2007; Igbaria & Baroudi, 1993; Wynne et al., 2002; Ituma, 2006) and the impact of career anchors on career satisfaction (Jiang & Klein, 2000; Hsu *et al.*, 2003). Generally, research findings have confirmed that information system personnel exhibit high incidence of technical and managerial anchors (Hsu *et al.*, 2003). Research findings in US show that the most prevalent career orientations of IS employees are technical and managerial. Most systems programmers, application programmers and software engineers tend to be more technically oriented while most systems analysts, project leaders and computer managers tend to be more managerially-oriented (Igbaria & Greenhaus, 1991).

There are, however, some exceptions to the generalisation that the dominant career anchors of IS personnel is managerial and technical. In a study by Wynne et al. (2002), in which they researched on the career anchors of United States Air Force information systems workers, the lifestyle anchor did not load as expected and the dominant career anchor was that of job security followed by service. A study by Igbaria et al. (1995) revealed that the IS employees are very much service and security oriented. Similarly a study by Igbaria and McCloskey (1996) on MIS employees in Taiwan showed that the highest orientation was job security, followed by service, challenge and life-style, respectively and the lowest orientation was technical competence, followed by autonomy and entrepreneurship. It has also been established that IS employees have diverse career orientations and organizations need to recognize this diversity so that appropriate career paths and reward systems can be developed (Igbaria et al., 1991; Baroudi and Ginzberg, 1992; Igbaria & McCloskey, 1996).

Studies on career anchors have yielded varying results. A major explanation for this diversity in research findings could be the cultural context within which the studies are conducted. As Schein (1984) points out, cultural factors do influence career patterns. Culture is considered to have a significant impact on research findings in those cases where the studies are conducted in different nations (although differences are also possible in results of studies conducted in the same nation). These studies produced dominant career anchors that were different across the studies. This difference in findings is suggestive of a strong cultural influence. Studies undertaken by Hofstede (1980, 1983, & 1984) demonstrate that groups of countries could have similar cultural traits. He was able to identify four cultural dimensions which explain the work-related values of different employees in different countries. These cultural dimensions were *individualism versus collectivism*, *large versus small power distance*, *strong versus weak uncertainty avoidance*, and *masculinity versus femininity*. Hofstede (1980) grouped several countries according to these dimensions, which were divided into four quadrants representing the cultural orientation of those countries. The African countries were classified as large power distance, low individualism, weak uncertainty avoidance and feminine (Hofstede, 1983). This means that some degree of social inequity in power is acceptable, manifested mainly in the respect given to elders and those holding positions of power. Other countries were located in different quadrants in Hofstede's paradigms. These classifications will be used to explain any differences in findings of the current study and previous studies.

## Research Questions on Career Anchors

Based on existing literature on career anchors, the researchers sought to study the career orientations of IS personnel in Botswana in order to ascertain the relevance of the career anchors identified in the literature to the motivation of IS employees in Botswana. The study attempted to provide answers to the following research questions:

**Q1:** Are the Botswana IS personnel career anchors in line with Schein's career constructs or their variants?

**Q2:** How do the career orientations correlate with each other?

**Q3:** What are the dominant career orientations of IS personnel in Botswana?

**Q4:** How do demographics such as age, gender, and educational qualifications of IS employees affect their dominant career orientations?

## Hypotheses on Career Anchors

Based on literature, especially (Igbaria et al., 1995), and the knowledge of the fact that South Africa and Botswana possess some high level of socio-cultural and economic similarities, one would expect that the dominant career anchor of IS employees in Botswana would be similar to those of South Africa. Thus the first hypothesis is proposed *a priori* as follows:

**$H_a$:** The dominant career anchor of IS personnel in Botswana is *sense of service*.

The dominance of a career anchor may not be a function of the IS personnel's personal or organizational demographics. Rather, it could be a function of some extraneous factors such as culture, national orientation, and a general sense of dignity of labour, which is very characteristic of the Botswana society. Therefore, the second research hypothesis is equally proposed *a priori* as follows:

**$H_b$:** Sense of service has strong correlations with IS personnel's demographics.

## IS Employee Turnover Intentions

The IS profession is facing a big problem of personnel turnover. This problem has been reported from many countries and for a long time. Rouse (2001) hinted that "voluntary turnover in many fields, especially in information technology is reaching epidemic proportions". The information technology trade magazines such as Computerworld and PC Computing were indicating that money was the main reason for moving into new position. Jiang and Klein (2002) reported that the "continuing challenge in information systems (IS) personnel is the high turnover rate in the profession. Ever since statistics have been kept, IS turnover has been a problem." Joseph et al. (2007) noted that the problem of IS personnel turnover has continued to persist notwithstanding the recent trend by companies to relocate IT jobs offshore.

Several factors contribute to turnover intentions of IS employees. Age, education, pay and promotion have been some of the factors which influence intention to leave. Research by Rouse (2001) showed that young entry level IS employees who were 25 years old and under were the most dissatisfied. Earlier studies found that job satisfaction and commitment to the organizational characteristics are the most substantial and the most direct influences on the turnover intentions even among IS personnel (Igbaria & Greenhaus, 1992), which is similar to other findings concerning other professions in the organizations except that job satisfaction would have more influence on turnover than organization commitment (Niederman et al., 2006; Muliawan et al., 2009). Muliawan et al. (2009) observed that factors affecting IS auditors' turnover intentions are role conflict, satisfaction with pay, and fulfilment of growth needs. They note that these factors are moderated by organizational commitment and job satisfaction as expected, and argue that the need to satisfy personal and professional growth exerts a particularly strong influence on IS auditors' turnover intentions. They also found that IS auditors share similar characteristics to other IS professionals rather than with general accountants and auditors. They suggest that organizations wanting to retain their IS auditors should provide regular opportunities for their auditors to satisfy their personal growth needs.

According to Tiedemann et al. (2006) changes in work environment introduced by globalization have brought in new concepts related to turnover and thus necessitated additional career anchors such as Creativity, Identity, Autonomy, and Variety. Research in India by Krishnan and Singh (2010) on software professionals with less than four years of experience indicated that intention to quit does lead to less performance orientation, higher organizational deviance, and less organizational citizenship behavior.

Pay and promotion is part of distributive justice (Byrne & Cropanzano, 2001). Distributive justice relates to the perceived fairness of reward allocation and has been mentioned as the beginning of organizational justice which is the employees' perceived fairness in the workplace. According to DeConinck and Johnson (2009) an employee's perceptions of equity or inequity are based on a social comparison with a reference person or group such that the "employee expects to receive similar outcomes (e.g. pay and promotion) as another person with whom he or she believes has equal inputs (e.g. the same level of education and seniority)". Igbaria and Greenhaus (1992) found that young and highly educated employees tended to hold low levels of satisfaction with their jobs and careers and tend to experience low levels of commitment to their organizations with concomitant intentions to leave.

Several researchers have underscored the contribution of role stressors (role conflict and role ambiguity) on work-related attributes (job satisfaction, career satisfaction, organizational commitment; and intention to leave) (Baroudi, 1985; Igbaria & Greenhaus, 1992; Goldstein and Rockart, 1984; Jackson and Schuler, 1985; Van Sell et al., 1981). Role ambiguity may be caused by insufficient information on how to perform a job or conflicting expectations from peers while role conflict may be caused by ambiguity of performance evaluation methods (Igbaria & Greenhaus, 1992).

Recently, Rutner et al. (2008) identified another factor which he called emotional dissonance, which works better than perceived workload, role conflict or role ambiguity. Emotional dissonance is defined as the "conflict between the way one feels toward interaction partners and the emotion one feels compelled to display toward those individuals" (Rutner et al., 2008). Many organizations may explicitly stipulate what type of emotional demeanour employees are supposed to maintain even under the strangest of the circumstances in order to maintain good customer relations. A dissonance occurs when an employee's deep felt emotions are suppressed in order to display the desirable emotions. Research by Rutner et al. (2008) found that emotional dissonance significantly contributes to work exhaustion and job dissatisfaction.

Work related attitudes which include career satisfaction, job satisfaction and organizational commitment play a major role in the intention to leave by IS personnel (Igbaria & Greenhaus, 1992). The components of job satisfaction include satisfaction with work, satisfaction with supervisor, satisfaction with co-workers, satisfaction with pay and satisfaction with promotion, while organizational commitment is the employee's identification with a particular organization and the desire to maintain the membership (Igbaria & Guimaraes, 1999).

## Employee Turnover Model and Hypotheses

A number of organizational behavior researchers have attempted to study the impact of organizational, job, and demographic factors on intention to stay on or leave a job (e.g. Martin, 1979; Igbaria & Greenhaus, 1992; Lochhead & Stephens, 2004; Muliawan et al,. 2009). Turnover and retention models mainly draw from concepts in motivational theories such as: the two factor theory (Herzberg, 1968), theory of needs (McClelland, 1961), person to organization fit theory (Argyris, 1957), and turnover models (Hackman & Oldham, 1976; Mobley et al., 1978; Igbaria & Greenhaus, 1992).

The turnover models posit that job and organizational characteristics determine job satisfaction, which in turn, determines turnover intention. Our study is based on a modified IS employee turnover model by Igbaria and Greenhaus (1992). The Igbaria and Greenhaus turnover model considers demographic variables, role stressors, and career experiences to affect work related attitudes and turnover intention. The model takes a comprehensive look at the direct and indirect effects of these variables on turnover intention. Our study replaces organizational tenure with length of employment in the present organization. This is because in Botswana, the concept of job tenure is not common, especially when majority of the national employees are on permanent and pensionable terms. We also recognize growth opportunity and supervisor support as key internal career related variables (Michaels & Spector, 1982). Our research model is presented in Figure 1.

The model predicts direct effects of demographic variables (age, length of service, and level of education), role stressors (role ambiguity, and role conflict), and career related variables (growth opportunity, supervisor support, and external career opportunities) on work related attitudes (job satisfaction and career satisfaction), as well as direct effect of the demographic, role stressors and career related variables on turnover intention. The model also suggests a direct relationship of job satisfaction on career satisfaction, job and career satisfaction on organizational commitment and direct effect of organizational commitment on turnover by Igbaria and Greenhaus (1992). The signs (+ or -) indicate the direction

*Figure 1. Employee Turnover Intention Model*

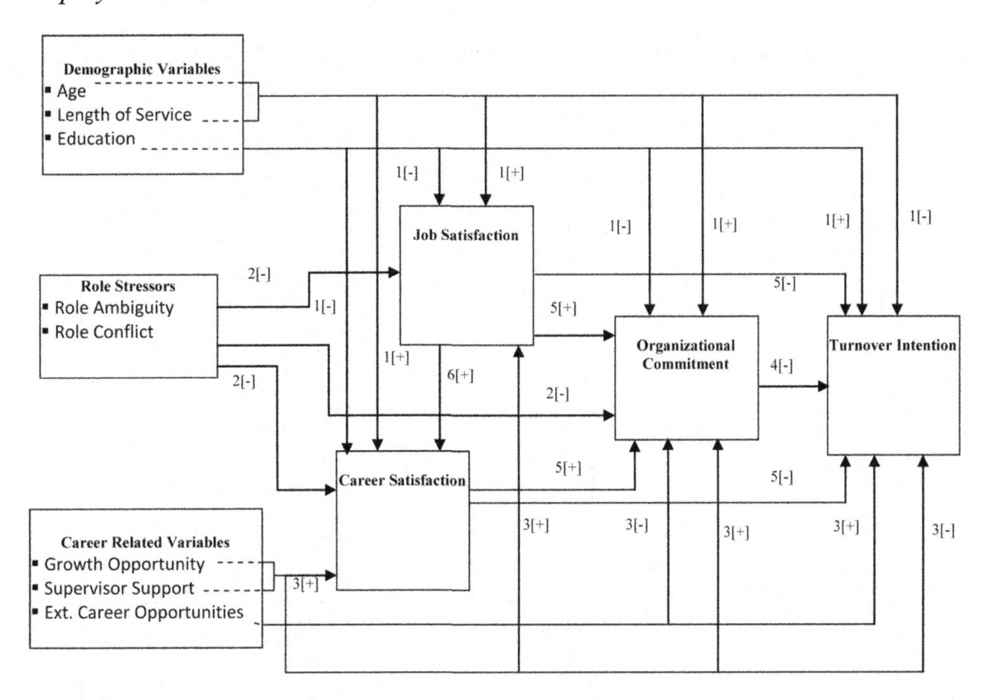


of effect of each independent variable(s) on the corresponding dependent variable. The following hypotheses and sub-hypotheses are tested, based on the results obtained (see Table 1).

## METHODOLOGY

### Sampling

The study population was all IS employees in Botswana who are employed at the technician level and above, as well as all employers of IS personnel. A list of employers was obtained from the Botswana Chamber of Commerce Industry and Manpower (BOCCIM). The list from BOCCIM had 1522 employers. Included in the list, however, was every imaginable employer in Botswana apart from the government and its parastatals. Most of the employers in the BOCCIM list were very small businesses that do not employ any IS personnel let alone use a computer. It was not possible to draw a sample from the BOCCIM list. This list was therefore used as a rough guide to employers of IS personnel. The guide was not perfect as in most cases several organizations that were expected to be heavy users of IT were either not using the technology or they outsourced it. In some cases researchers knew the existence of other employers of IS personnel through other respondents. This was very helpful as the BOCCIM list was also a bit out of date.

Data was also collected from government employees through the Government Computer Bureau. There are few parastatal organizations in Botswana. Most of them are heavy users of IT. The research tried to cover all parastatal organizations that employ IS personnel. The researchers identified 48 organizations that employ IS personnel. The research therefore concentrated on the 48 organizations. Two hundred and forty three questionnaires were administered to IS employees in 48 organizations. The questionnaires were distributed to employees who work as computer programmers and above, excluding all support staff such as technicians and computer operators.

*Table 1. Research Hypotheses*

| Hypotheses | Independent Variables | Sub-hypotheses | Dependent Variables | Effect [+/-] |
|---|---|---|---|---|
| 1 | Age | $H_{1.1.1}$ | Career satisfaction | + |
| | | $H_{1.1.2}$ | Job satisfaction | + |
| | | $H_{1.1.3}$ | Org. Commitment | + |
| | | $H_{1.1.4}$ | Turnover Intention | - |
| | Education | $H_{1.2.1}$ | Career satisfaction | + |
| | | $H_{1.2.2}$ | Job satisfaction | - |
| | | $H_{1.2.3}$ | Org. Commitment | + |
| | | $H_{1.2.4}$ | Turnover Intention | - |
| | Length of Service | $H_{1.3.1}$ | Career satisfaction | - |
| | | $H_{1.3.2}$ | Job satisfaction | - |
| | | $H_{1.3.3}$ | Org. Commitment | - |
| | | $H_{1.3.4}$ | Turnover Intention | + |
| 2 | Role Ambiguity | $H_{2.1.1}$ | Career satisfaction | - |
| | | $H_{2.1.2}$ | Job satisfaction | - |
| | | $H_{2.1.3}$ | Org. Commitment | - |
| | Role Conflict | $H_{2.2.1}$ | Career satisfaction | - |
| | | $H_{2.2.2}$ | Job satisfaction | - |
| | | $H_{2.2.3}$ | Org. Commitment | - |
| 3 | Growth Opportunity | $H_{3.1.1}$ | Job satisfaction | + |
| | | $H_{3.1.2}$ | Org. Commitment | + |
| | | $H_{3.1.3}$ | Turnover Intention | - |
| | Supervisor support | $H_{3.2.1}$ | Job satisfaction | + |
| | | $H_{3.2.2}$ | Org. Commitment | + |
| | | $H_{3.2.3}$ | Turnover Intention | - |
| | External Career opportunity | $H_{3.3.1}$ | Org. Commitment | - |
| | | $H_{3.3.2}$ | Turnover Intention | + |
| 4 | Org. Commitment | $H_4$ | Turnover Intention | - |
| 5 | Career satisfaction | $H_{5.1}$ | Org. Commitment | + |
| | Job satisfaction | $H_{5.2}$ | | + |
| | Career satisfaction | $H_{5.3}$ | Turnover Intention | - |
| | Job Satisfaction | $H_{5.4}$ | | - |
| 6 | Job satisfaction | $H_6$ | Career satisfaction | + |

One hundred and four employees from 29 organizations completed and returned the questionnaires, giving a 42.8% response rate.

## Measures

This questionnaire consisted of seven parts. The first part was used to collect demographic data of the respondents. The second part of the questionnaire had seven statements on supervisory support that employees get from their organizations, designed using a five point Likert-type scale. The third part of the questionnaire had five statements on career satisfaction. Part four of the questionnaire collected data for determining the career orientations of IS personnel in Botswana. Forty-one career anchor items were used (See appendix A). These items constitute the Career Orientation Inventory (COI) and were originally developed by Schein (1978). The fifth section of the questionnaire dealt on external career opportunities and factors that may influence IS employees to leave their current jobs. The sixth part of the questionnaire had ten items on work environment. The seventh part of the questionnaire focused on gender issues and was to be answered by female employees only. In this paper, we present the results of the analysis of the components that deal with the career orientation inventory.

## Analysis Procedure

The first part of the analysis involves the use of exploratory factor analysis to reduce the variables into few explainable internal career anchors that could motivate IS employees. This was carried out using Statistical Package for Social Sciences (SPSS) Version 16.0. Principal component analysis (PCA) was utilized as the estimation method, while *Varimax* with *Kaiser Normalization* was used as the rotation method. The initial factor extraction was achieved by N-criterion, wherein the number of factors to be retained is specified on the basis of a Social Science rule which states that only the variable with loading equal to or greater than 0.5 and percentage of variance greater than 1 should be considered meaningful and extracted for factor analysis (Uzoka & Akinyokun, 2005). Also, variables that did not load on any factor, or exhibited cross loading were excluded from the factor analysis (Elliot & Boshoff, 2005). The reliabilities of the resulting factors were measured using the Cronbach's alpha, which is based on the average correlation of items within an instrument or scale; and is regarded as an indication of internal consistency.

In utilizing factor analysis, it is important to determine the adequacy of the data and the suitability of factor analysis. The Bartlett's test of sphericity produces a $\chi^2$ of 14310.543 (>500) with a significance level of 6.14e-101 (< 0.05), which confirms the adequacy of the sample. The Kaiser-Mayer-Olkin (KMO) measure of sampling adequacy produced a value of 0.685 (> 0.5), which further confirms the adequacy of the sample. The results obtained from the Bartlett's test and the KMO test also indicate the suitability of application of factor analysis for exploratory purposes. Correlation analyses were carried out in order to understand the relationships among career anchors, and also between individual anchors and respondent's demographics. Dominant career anchors were established from the data, and further considered in terms of gender, age, and educational qualifications of respondents.

Multivariate regression analyses were carried out in order to test the hypotheses relating to employee turnover. Table 2 shows the various test constructs and the questionnaire variables that measured the constructs.

# ANALYSES AND RESULTS

Table 3 shows a summary of the demographic characteristics of IS employees in Botswana. Out of 104 respondents 83 (79.8%) were Botswana citizens and 21 (20.2%) expatriates, 26 (25%) were females and 78 (75%) males. It can be seen that the proportion of female employees in the IS profession in Botswana is still very low. Age-wise, IS employees in Botswana are very young. None of the respondents was aged more than 50 years and the highest percentage of respondents came from those aged between 20 and 30 years (57%). This shows that the profession is relatively new to Botswana. This is also supported by statistics

*Table 2. Test Constructs*

| Constructs | Variables | Reliability |
|---|---|---|
| Age (AGE) | Age | 1.000 |
| Education (EDUCATN) | Education | 1.000 |
| Length of service (LENTSERV) | Length of Service | 1.000 |
| Role ambiguity (ROLEAMB) | Duties-qualifications mismatch (dutqualmismatch) | 1.000 |
| Role conflict (ROLCNFLT) | Non- core IT duties (noncoreduties) | 1.000 |
| Growth Opportunity (GRWTOPPT) | Opportunity for promotion (promotion) | 0.739 |
| | Career development support (cardevtsppt) | |
| | Training opportunities (trainingoppt) | |
| | Fairness of annual assessment (annualass) | |
| Supervisor Support (SUPSUPPT) | Supervisor learns employee careers goals (suplearngoals) | 0.889 |
| | Supervisor cares about goal achievement (supcargoalach) | |
| | Supervisor Informs employee about career opportunities (supinfomcaropp) | |
| | Supervisor gives credit for on the job task accomplishment (supgivescredt) | |
| | Supervisor gives helpful performance feedback (supprffeedback) | |
| | Supervisor gives helpful performance advice (supgivesadvice) | |
| External Career Opportunities (EXTCAROPP) | External offer of better salary and benefits for same job (salary) | 0.631 |
| | External offer of higher position but about same benefits (higherposit) | |
| | External offer of tenured position but same salary (tenure) | |
| | External offer of more challenging job but same salary (jobchallenge) | |
| Organizational Commitment (ORGCMIT) | How loyal the individual is to the present organization (loyalty) | 1.00 |
| Career Satisfaction (CARRSAT) | Satisfaction with achieved career success (satcarsucess) | 0.808 |
| | Satisfaction with progress towards career goals (satcargoalprgrss) | |
| | Satisfaction with progress towards advancement goals (satadvcmtglprgrs) | |
| | Satisfaction with progress towards income goals (satincmeglprgrss) | |
| | Satisfaction with skills development goals (satskldvtglprgrs) | |
| Job Satisfaction (JOBSAT) | *Integration* | 0.731 |
| | No difficulty in being accepted (acceptnotdiff) | |
| | Contributions valued (contrvalued) | |
| | Interaction with internal peers (peerinteraction) | |
| | Interaction with eternal peers (peerinteractout) | |
| | *Pre-Employment Expectations* | |
| | Meeting of pre-employment expectations (jobexpect) | |
| | *Job Characteristics* | |
| | How much variety is in the job (jobvariety) | |
| | How much organizational stability is in the job (orgstability) | |
| | How much identity the job provides (jobidentity) | |
| | How much geographic security the job has (geosecurity) | |
| | How much technical competence does the job require (tchcmptence) | |
| | How much managerial competence does the job require (mgrcmptence) | |
| | How much autonomy is in the job (autonomy) | |
| | How much skill and talent related service is in the job (service) | |

*Table 3. Demographic Characteristics of the IS Employees*

| Variable | | Number of Respondents | Percent |
|---|---|---|---|
| 1. Age | 20 – 30 Years | 56 | 57 |
| | 31 - 35 Years | 20 | 20 |
| | 36 – 40 Years | 10 | 10 |
| | 41 - 50 Years | 13 | 13 |
| | | | |
| 2. Citizenship | Expatriates | 21 | 20.2 |
| | Batswana | 83 | 79.8 |
| | | | |
| 3. Gender | Females | 26 | 25 |
| | Males | 78 | 75 |
| | | | |
| 4. Education | High School or less | 10 | 9.6 |
| | Diploma | 37 | 35.6 |
| | First Degree | 42 | 40.4 |
| | Masters Degree and above | 15 | 14.4 |
| | | | |
| 5. Annual Basic Salary (in Botswana Pula (P)) | Below 50 000 | 8 | 8 |
| | 50 000-99, 999 | 25 | 25 |
| | 100, 000-149, 999 | 28 | 27 |
| | 150, 000-199, 999 | 19 | 19 |
| | 200, 000-249, 999 | 11 | 10.5 |
| | Above 249,999 | 11 | 10.5 |
| | | | |
| 6. Years in IS field | 0 – 5 Years | 48 | 51 |
| | 6 – 10 Years | 19 | 20 |
| | 10 – 15 years | 17 | 18 |
| | More than 15 Years | 11 | 11 |
| | | | |
| 7. Years in Current Organization | 0 – 3 years | 68 | 66 |
| | 4 – 5 Years | 10 | 9.7 |
| | 6 – 10 Years | 14 | 13.6 |
| | Above 10 Years | 11 | 10.7 |

which show that 51% of the respondents have less than five years in the IS field while only 11% have worked for more than 15 years in the IS field.

In the area of education, 9.6% of the respondents had attained a maximum of high school education, 35.6% had a diploma and the rest had a first degree (40.4%) or second degree (14.4%). Most of the respondents are still in the low salary bands. About 25% of the respondents earn an annual salary of between P50, 000 and P99, 999; 60% earn below P150, 000 per annum. Only 10.5% of IS employees earn P249, 999 and above per annum. One of the reasons for the large number of employees in the low salary scales could be the fact that the IS profession is still very young in Botswana. The results show that only 29% had worked for 10 or more years in the IS field.

## Career Orientations

Igbaria and Greenhaus (1991), Igbaria and Baroudi (1993) and Jiang (2000) researched on career anchors of IS personnel. The study by Jiang (2000) differs slightly from the first two because he used 36 items instead of 41 and his study excluded entrepreneurial creativity but included two different orientations, identity and variety. Career anchors used in this study were the same as those used by Igbaria and Greenhaus (1991), and Igbaria and Baroudi (1993). Since the factor structure of the Career Orientation Inventory has not been firmly established, a factor analysis (with varimax rotation) was conducted. The result produced nine factors with eigenvalues greater than or equal to 1.0 and accounted for 70.72% of the total variance. Examination of the factor results revealed that factors corresponded very closely to the results reported by Igbaria and Greenhaus (1991), and Igbaria and Baroudi (1993) except that of lifestyle integration. All the life style variables did not load on any factor. It was also observed that two of Schein's original factors were split into two. *Security* was split into *organizational stability* and *geographical stability*, while *technical and functional competence* was split into *technical and functional competence* and *specialization driven growth.*

The nine career anchors revealed by factor analysis in this study were: Entrepreneurial Creativity, Pure Challenge, Managerial Competence, Technical and Functional Competence, Autonomy, Sense of Service, Geographical Stability, Specialization Driven Growth, and Organizational Stability. Table 4 shows the results of the factor analysis, while Table 5 presents the summary statistics for the career anchors (obtained from Table 4), which are explained below:

### Entrepreneurial Creativity

This career anchor included four out of five items developed by Schein (1985) to measure entrepreneurial creativity. The items loaded under this factor point to an interest in entrepreneurship. That is, individuals exhibiting this career orientation would like to see themselves creating and overseeing the growth of their own businesses, and this is one of their main goals. The mean value for this factor was 2.05 and the internal consistency was 0.75.

### Pure Challenge

According to Schein (1996) there has always been a small group of people who defined their careers in terms of overcoming impossible odds, solving the unsolved problems, and winning over competitors. These are the ones who derive satisfaction by being able to face and overcome challenges, and would seek challenging situations whenever possible. The mean value for this factor was 2.32 and the internal consistency was 0.70.

### Managerial Competence

Managerially-oriented employees wish to supervise, influence, and lead others. They seek promotions to general manager positions as a vehicle to achieve feelings of success (Igbaria & Greenhaus 1991). Four items loaded under this factor with a mean value of 2.25 and internal consistency of 0.70.

### Technical and Functional Competence

This career anchor comprises individuals who are highly motivated by the technical nature of the work they are doing, and are generally not

*Table 4. Factor Loadings for Internal Career Anchors*

| Rotated Component Matrix[a] | | | | | | | | | |
|---|---|---|---|---|---|---|---|---|---|
| | Component | | | | | | | | |
| | **EntCreat** | **PureChalng** | **MgrlComp** | **TFunComp** | **Autonomy** | **SnsOfServ** | **GeoStab** | **SpecGrow** | **OrgStab** |
| car0040 | .783 | | | | | | | | |
| car0024 | .766 | | | | | | | | |
| car0016 | .740 | | | | | | | | |
| car0008 | .584 | | | | | | | | |
| car0014 | | .781 | | | | | | | |
| car0030 | | .732 | | | | | | | |
| car0038 | | .670 | | | | | | | |
| car0002 | | | .759 | | | | | | |
| car0034 | | | .702 | | | | | | |
| car0026 | | | .629 | | | | | | |
| car0018 | | | .607 | | | | | | |
| car0017 | | | | .851 | | | | | |
| car0009 | | | | .800 | | | | | |
| car0003 | | | | | .841 | | | | |
| car0011 | | | | | .745 | | | | |
| car0019 | | | | | .639 | | | | |
| car0005 | | | | | | .765 | | | |
| car0021 | | | | | | .740 | | | |
| car0013 | | | | | | .717 | | | |
| car0028 | | | | | | | .824 | | |
| car0041 | | | | | | | .758 | | |
| car0020 | | | | | | | .617 | | |
| car0033 | | | | | | | | .884 | |
| car0025 | | | | | | | | .790 | |
| car0004 | | | | | | | | | .814 |
| car0012 | | | | | | | | | .773 |

Extraction Method: Principal Component Analysis
Rotation Method: Varimax with Kaiser Normalization
Rotation converged in eight iterations

interested in being promoted to managerial positions outside the technical area they are in. They value the importance of knowledge and skill and focus on the exercise of technical competence. Only two items loaded under this factor (mean = 2.61, internal consistency = 0.80).

## Autonomy and Independence

Individuals who exhibit these characteristics are primarily desirable of freedom to pursue career interests that are not inhibited by organizational rules and other constraints. Such individuals, if employed, can change employment anytime they believe the organization is becoming too intrusive

*Table 5. Summary of Career Anchors*

| Factor | Description | Number of items | Reliability (α) | Mean | S.D | %variance explained | Eigenvalue |
|---|---|---|---|---|---|---|---|
| EntCreat | Entrepreneurial Creativity | 4 | 0.746 | 2.05 | 0.77 | 10.311 | 2.681 |
| PureChalng | Pure Challenge | 3 | 0.695 | 2.32 | 0.89 | 8.87 | 2.306 |
| MgrlComp | Managerial Competence | 4 | 0.701 | 2.25 | 0.85 | 8.354 | 2.172 |
| TFunComp | Technical and Functional Competence | 2 | 0.795 | 2.61 | 1.08 | 7.977 | 2.074 |
| Autonomy | Autonomy | 3 | 0.711 | 2.49 | 1.01 | 7.905 | 2.055 |
| SnsOfServ | Sense of Service | 3 | 0.651 | 1.40 | 0.52 | 7.292 | 1.896 |
| GeoStab | Geographical Stability | 3 | 0.667 | 3.42 | 0.97 | 6.992 | 1.818 |
| SpecGrow | Specialization Driven Growth | 2 | 0.729 | 2.560 | 1.110 | 6.60 | 1.716 |
| OrgStab | Organizational Stability | 2 | 0.623 | 1.550 | 0.790 | 6.419 | 1.669 |

of their private space. Many would want to completely disassociate themselves with employment and set up their own businesses instead, just to be able to exercise their freedom. Three items loaded under this factor, with mean of 2.49 and the internal consistency of 0.71.

## Sense of Service

Employees who are oriented to a sense of service are dedicated to serve people and to make the world a better place to live and work in. Such employees get gratification from the services they render, some of which may be for free. These individuals are usually characterised by membership in volunteer and other non-profit organizations. Three items loaded on this factor with a mean of 1.40 and internal consistency of 0.65.

## Geographical Security

Individuals who exhibit these characteristics feel a sense of security when they work in a geographical environment with which they are familiar, and would put much emphasis on ensuring that they remain within that environment. These individuals would rather leave their jobs than be promoted out of those areas, and they may actually change employment several times, but would join other organizations within the preferred geographical area. Three items loaded under this factor, and had a mean value of 3.42 and an internal consistency of 0.67.

## Specialization-Driven Growth

This career anchor comprises of individuals who are strongly motivated by their being able to grow along the path of their specific area of specialization. Their careers are built around their fields of specialization and are willing to sacrifice promotion if it takes them out of that specialization. Two items loaded under this factor. These had a mean value of 2.56 and the reliability was 0.73.

## Organizational Stability

Individuals under this career anchor have a strong desire for stability of employment and benefits. Although they may change employment, they would generally prefer to minimise the risks associated with frequent job changes just for the sake of increased remuneration. They prefer to work with an organization that guarantees lifetime

*Table 6. Correlations among career anchors*

| | EntCreat | PureChalng | MgrlComp | TFunComp | Autonomy | SnsOfServ | GeoStab | SpecGrow | OrgStab |
|---|---|---|---|---|---|---|---|---|---|
| EntCreat | 1.000 | | | | | | | | |
| PureChalng | .310** | 1.000 | | | | | | | |
| MgrlComp | .369** | .347** | 1.000 | | | | | | |
| TFunComp | -.144 | .121 | -.120 | 1.000 | | | | | |
| Autonomy | .336** | .073 | .232* | .037 | 1.000 | | | | |
| SnsOfServ | .110 | .177 | .168 | .172 | .185 | 1.000 | | | |
| GeoStab | .072 | .078 | .067 | .104 | .028 | -.093 | 1.000 | | |
| SpecGrow | .063 | .247* | .054 | .250* | -.092 | .013 | .101 | 1.000 | * |
| OrgStab | -.040 | .116 | .127 | .221* | .011 | .137 | .227* | .231* | 1.000 |

** Correlation is significant at the 0.01 level (2-tailed)
* Correlation is significant at the 0.05 level (2-tailed)

employment and long-term retirement benefits or a guaranteed pension. Two items loaded under this factor, with a mean value of 1.55 and reliability of 0.62.

## The Relationships Amongst the Career Anchors

Table 6 shows the correlations among the nine career anchors. In the table, "entrepreneurial creativity" is positively correlated with "pure challenge", "managerial competence", and "autonomy". This implies a relationship between a desire to be able to solve apparently unsolvable problems with the desire to create and develop new products and services. Also, an association is suggested between the desire for managerial responsibilities and the desire to create and develop new products and services. Those deriving satisfaction from being able to solve complex problems are also desirous of autonomy. The association between "entrepreneurial creativity" and the other three career anchors is significant at $p = 0.01$.

In addition to a positive relationship with "entrepreneurial creativity", "pure challenge" is positively correlated with "managerial competence" and "specialization-driven growth". This suggests that individuals who derive a thrill from work-based challenges are more likely to seek managerial positions. It could be that a management position is itself considered a challenge that needs to be conquered. This relationship between "managerial competence" and "pure challenge" was significant at $p = 0.01$. Individuals who enjoy challenges are also more likely to be interested in pursuing a career in a specific preferred specialization. The relationship between these two anchors was significant at $p = 0.05$.

A positive relationship is also indicated between "managerial competence" and "autonomy". Managerially-oriented employees were said to be those who wish to supervise, influence, and lead others, i.e. those who desire managerial responsibilities. Individuals driven by a desire for autonomy, on the other hand, derive satisfaction by disassociating themselves with employment and setting up their own businesses. The positive association with managerial competence, which is significant at $p = 0.05$, could suggest that those seeking autonomy associate managerial positions with relative autonomy since the position gives one powers to impose rules and regulations on others, but not oneself.

The results also show a positive relationship between "technical and functional competence" and "specialization-driven growth" on the one hand, and "organizational stability" on the other. This may suggest that individuals who are more concerned with the technical nature of the job, from which they derive their satisfaction, will also be keen to continue working in their particular area of specialization. More likely, those who have specialised in vocations that require a particular specialization are happy to continue practicing their vocations since it gives them great satisfaction. At the same time, the individual who enjoy the technical nature of the job are more likely to desire stability at the workplace, partly because stability will guarantee their ability to continue with the same technical jobs they perform. Both correlations were significant at $p = 0.05$.

Finally, organizational stability is shown to be positively correlated with "geographical stability" and "specialization-driven growth". This suggests that individuals seeking stability in employment are also likely to seek stability in geographical location, and vice versa. These two career anchors can both be considered as providing an element of security to the employees. Employees interested in job security are likely to be satisfied when they can be guaranteed employment in an organization located in a preferred geographical area. The relationship between organizational stability and "specialization-driven growth" also appears to be rational in the sense that a guarantee of employment in a particular organization is highly likely to lead to an assurance of continued employment in a preferred area of specialization. Both relationships were significant at $p = 0.05$.

## Correlation Between Career Anchors and Respondents' Characteristics

A research by Igbaria and McCloskey (1996) on career orientations of MIS employees in Taiwan examined the relationship between personal variables and career orientations. The personal variables included gender, education, age, and number of years in the MIS field. It was found that there was a significant negative relationship between gender and managerial and geographic security, along with significant positive relationship between gender and lifestyle. There was no significant correlation between education, age, and number of years in the MIS field with any of the career anchors.

This study also examined the correlation between the evolved career anchors and some respondents' characteristics. The correlations are shown in Table 7 below. A number of significant correlations are evident here as well. For instance, there is a significant positive correlation ($p \leq 0.05$) between "managerial competence" and the number of employers one has worked for. This appears to suggest that some respondents, in pursuit of more responsible positions up the professional hierarchy, have had to change employers. It looks like the more one yearned for such a position the more likely one was to change employment. This could refer to those who have been impatient in waiting for an opportunity to exercise power over others.

"Managerial competence" is negatively correlated ($p \leq 0.05$) with age. This is a surprising result as it suggests that the younger one is the more likely one is to desire managerial responsibilities. Normally, one would expect the older employees to have such a desire as they would most likely consider themselves as having accumulated the required experience to assume such a position. However, it is possible the younger employees have greater ambitions, perhaps due to their qualifications, to climb faster within the profession and the organizational hierarchy. The depicted positive correlation between "age" and "specialization-driven growth" is perhaps more understandable. The more one became older the more likely one was to want to continue working in one's area of specialization. This correlation is strong ($p \leq 0.01$).

"Level of education" is found to be positively correlated with "pure challenge" ($p \leq 0.01$) and "specialization-driven growth" ($p \leq 0.05$), and negatively correlated with "autonomy" ($p \leq 0.01$). Individuals who possess higher educational

*Table 7. Correlations between career anchors and some respondent's demographics*

| | EntCreat | PureChalng | MgrlComp | TFunComp | Autonomy | SnsOfServ | GeoStab | SpecGrow | OrgStab |
|---|---|---|---|---|---|---|---|---|---|
| Number of years in IS field | .003 | .062 | -.023 | -.023 | -.029 | .029 | -.033 | .117 | .126 |
| Number of employers worked for | -.020 | .038 | .134* | -.069 | -.110 | -.032 | .097 | .038 | -.035 |
| Age | .019 | .093 | -.139* | .038 | -.018 | -.069 | -.034 | .234** | .107 |
| Education-al level | .024 | .276** | .124 | .030 | -.237** | -.108 | -.031 | .184* | .123 |
| Salary | .047 | .265** | .024 | .169* | -.115 | -.088 | .048 | .287** | .106 |
| Size of IS department | .244** | .128 | .090 | -.136* | .046 | .022 | -.060 | .050 | -.044 |

** Correlation is significant at the 0.01 level (1-tailed)
* Correlation is significant at the 0.05 level (1-tailed).

qualifications are more likely to seek challenging work environments from which they derive satisfaction. This would be an opportunity to them to find out or to show how much they can do with their knowledge. These individuals are also more likely to be interested in pursuing their areas of specialization where the possibility of excelling is higher. These same individuals with higher qualifications are less likely to desire freedom to pursue career interests that are not inhibited by organizational rules and other constraints. In other words, highly qualified individuals have less desire to seek, for example, self-employment. It could be that the higher qualifications give them the confidence to stay in employment knowing that their knowledge and skills are required.

Other positive relationships are between "salary" and "pure challenge", "technical and functional competence" and "specialization-driven growth". Higher-salaried employees appear to be more inclined towards these three career anchors. Lastly, there seems to be a positive correlation between the "size" of the IS department and "entrepreneurial creativity", which might imply the employees in a large department are more likely to desire venturing out into entrepreneurship, maybe because the size of the department (and the implied number of employees therein) denies them the opportunity for their individual contribution to be appreciated at the workplace. A negative correlation is also shown between the size of the IS department and "technical and functional competence". This might also imply that employees who are highly motivated by the technical nature of the job are less likely to find a large IS department providing that opportunity to enjoy the work.

## Dominant Career Orientations

Hypothesis ($H_a$) proposed *sense of service* as the dominant career anchor. To test the hypothesis we used the chi square ($\chi^2$) statistic with ($n$-$1$) degrees of freedom at $\alpha = 0.05$. ($n$ is number of factors). The $\chi^2$ test sought to determine if the variations in values of dominant career anchors were statistically significant, or they could be attributed to experimental chance. The results of the chi square test indicate that the variations in the career orientations were statistically significant ($\chi^2_{calc}$ (172.62) > $\chi^2_{crit}$ (15.507)). Thus, hypothesis $H_a$ is supported as confirmed by the results of Table 8. The *mean absolute deviations (MAD)* were computed for the careers anchors.

*Table 8. Dominant career anchors*

| | BY GENDER (%) | | | By Age (%) | | | | | BY EDUCATIONAL QUAL (%) | | | |
|---|---|---|---|---|---|---|---|---|---|---|---|---|
| | Combined | Males | Females | < 20 | 20-30 | 31-35 | 36-40 | > 41 | ≤ High Sch. | Dip. | BS | ≥ MS |
| Autonomy | 1.9 | 2.6 | 0.0 | 33.3 | 0.0 | 0.0 | 10.0 | 0.0 | 10.0 | 0.0 | 2.4 | 6.7 |
| EntCreat | 2.9 | 0.0 | 11.5 | 0.0 | 1.8 | 10.0 | 0.0 | 0.0 | 0.0 | 0.0 | 2.4 | 6.7 |
| GeoStab | 1.0 | 0.0 | 3.8 | 33.3 | 0.0 | 0.0 | 0.0 | 0.0 | 0.0 | 0.0 | 0.0 | 6.7 |
| MgrlComp | 2.9 | 1.3 | 7.7 | 0.0 | 1.8 | 5.0 | 0.0 | 7.7 | 0.0 | 2.7 | 4.8 | 0.0 |
| OrgStab | 33.7 | 28.2 | 50.0 | 0.0 | 33.9 | 35.0 | 30.0 | 38.5 | 50.0 | 37.8 | 26.2 | 33.3 |
| PureChalng | 2.9 | 1.3 | 7.7 | 0.0 | 3.6 | 0.0 | 10.0 | 0.0 | 10.0 | 2.7 | 2.4 | 0.0 |
| SnsOfServ | 42.3 | 51.3 | 15.4 | 33.3 | 42.9 | 40.0 | 50.0 | 38.5 | 10.0 | 43.2 | 52.4 | 33.3 |
| SpecGrow | 6.7 | 9.0 | 0.0 | 0.0 | 10.7 | 5.0 | 0.0 | 0.0 | 20.0 | 8.1 | 4.8 | 0.0 |
| TFunComp | 5.8 | 6.4 | 3.8 | 0.0 | 5.4 | 5.0 | 0.0 | 15.4 | 0.0 | 5.4 | 4.8 | 13.3 |

It was realised that the variation in dominant career anchors were mostly caused by the *sense of service* anchor (MAD = 2.80), followed by *organizational stability* (MAD = 2.03). The least was *specialization driven growth* (MAD = 0.40).

According to Schein (1985) the most faithful representation of an employee's career orientation is the anchor that is most salient to the employee in relative terms. The most salient career anchor for each employee was calculated determining the percentage scores for each of the nine anchors. The dominant career anchor was one that had the highest percentage score. These percentages are summarized in Table 8 (total, and according to gender, age and education).

It is apparent that the dominant career anchor in this study was "sense of service" with a combined score of 42.3%, followed by "organizational stability" which scored 33.7%. The least dominant career anchor was "geographical stability" which had a score of 1.0%. The importance assigned to a sense of service in Botswana is in contradiction to the findings by other researchers. For example, in a study involving members of the Association for Computing Machinery in the US, Igbaria et al. (1991) found that out of the eight career orientations uncovered in their study, sense of service ranked sixth in dominance. However, that sense of service was a dominant anchor in this study is in agreement with the study by Igbaria et al. (1995) involving IS employees in South Africa which also revealed that service and security were dominant anchors. Service has an important connotation in Botswana which needs to be understood for one to appreciate the importance of this career anchor.

Organizational stability is the other dominant anchor in this study. Individuals under this career anchor have a strong desire for stability of employment and benefits. In the study by Igbaria et al. (1991) organizational stability was tied together with geographical stability (reported in the current study) to form an orientation named "security." Igbaria et al. (1991) found that this orientation was one of the least dominant in their study, seventh out of the eight orientations uncovered. However, in a recent study in Nigeria (Ituma & Simpson, 2007) being stable was the most dominant anchor out of the six anchors that emerged in that study. This anchor was the equivalent of organizational stability uncovered in this study, and applied to individuals who prioritised financial security provided by a stable employment. Thus, the finding by Ituma and Simpson (2007) with regard to the "being stable" orientation is consistent with the finding of the current study for the "organizational stability" orientation, but not with the "security" orientation in the study by Igbaria et al. (1991). On security, there is consistency in findings of this study with those of Igbaria et al. (1995).

As argued earlier in this paper, cultural differences in the locality of the study and in the study subjects may explain to a great extent these differences in findings. The classifications by Hofstede (1980) reflect the differences that exist among cultures of different countries. In those cases where countries appear in the same quadrant, it was possible that the cultural differences may not be significant. However, these cultural differences would be expected to be significant when countries appear in different quadrants. As explained earlier, USA was plotted in a different quadrant to that of countries in West and East Africa, which appeared in the same quadrant. That the findings by Igbaria et al. (1991) are different to those by Ituma and Simpson (2007) and those obtained in this study is therefore consistent with their appearance in different quadrants in Hofstede's cultural dimensions. The culture in USA is starkly different from the culture in African countries (such as Nigeria and Botswana). On the other hand, Botswana and South Africa are close neighbours sharing a common border. The similarity in the finding regarding the sense of service anchor is thus not surprising due to the enormous similarities in the culture of the people in these two countries.

It is apparent from Table 8 that career orientation was related to gender. Gender differences were seen in virtually all career orientations. Of the two significant orientations found in this study, women were concerned most with organizational stability than any of the other career anchors, while men were more into providing service to society. In both cases more than 50% of the respondents exhibited these anchors. Other studies also report gender differences in the anchors (e.g. Igbaria et al. 1991, Ituma & Johnson 2007).

Results of analysis by age show that the youngest group of IS employees in Botswana were oriented towards autonomy, geographical stability, and a sense of service. The oldest group was more oriented towards organizational stability and a sense of service. In terms of education, respondents with a high school or lesser qualification were oriented mostly towards organizational stability, but also towards specialization-driven growth, and to a lesser extent autonomy, pure challenge, and a sense of service. Those with a Master's degree or higher qualifications were also more inclined towards organizational stability and a sense of service. A noticeable percentage of the respondents were also oriented towards technical and functional competence.

To test the second hypothesis ($H_b$), a correlation analysis was conducted between the career anchors and the respondents' demographics as indicated in Table 7. The results of the analysis indicate that at 0.05 and 0.01 levels of significance, the most dominant career anchor (sense of service) did not significantly correlate with respondents' personal or organizational demographics. Moreover, there is no definite pattern of correlation between demographics and career anchors. The 'composite' correlation coefficient between *sense of service* and the demographics is 0.32, which is not significant. Therefore, hypothesis ($H_b$) is not supported. The implication is that IS personnel's personal and organizational demographics do not have significant correlation with dominant career anchors.

This study shows that IS personnel in Botswana are more oriented towards provision of service, followed by organizational stability. These two career anchors account for 76% of all respondents to this study. Other orientations, in order of percentage scores are specialization-driven growth, technical and functional competence, entrepreneurial creativity, managerial competence, pure challenge, autonomy and geographical stability. All these other orientations had percentage scores of less than 10%.

*Table 9. Results of Hypotheses Tests*

| Hypotheses | Independent Variables | Sub-hypotheses | Dependent Variables | Effect (+/-) | β | *t* | Sig | Conclusion |
|---|---|---|---|---|---|---|---|---|
| 1 | Age | $H_{1.1.1}$ | Career satisfaction | + | -.189 | -1.615 | .109 | Not supported |
| | | $H_{1.1.2}$ | Job satisfaction | + | -.197 | -1.679 | .096 | Not supported |
| | | $H_{1.1.3}$ | Org. Commitment | + | -.032 | -.267 | .790 | Not supported |
| | | $H_{1.1.4}$ | Turnover Intention | - | .101 | .866 | .389 | Not supported |
| | Education | $H_{1.2.1}$ | Career satisfaction | + | -.117 | -1.153 | .252 | Not supported |
| | | $H_{1.2.2}$ | Job satisfaction | - | -.109 | -1.071 | .287 | Not supported |
| | | $H_{1.2.3}$ | Org. Commitment | + | -.012 | -.112 | .911 | Not supported |
| | | $H_{1.2.4}$ | Turnover Intention | - | .164 | 1.612 | .110 | Not supported |
| | Length of Service | $H_{1.3.1}$ | Career satisfaction | - | .211 | 1.870 | .064 | Not supported |
| | | $H_{1.3.2}$ | Job satisfaction | - | .100 | .878 | .382 | Not supported |
| | | $H_{1.3.3}$ | Org. Commitment | - | -.030 | -.256 | .798 | Not supported |
| | | $H_{1.3.4}$ | Turnover Intention | + | -.183 | -1.624 | .108 | Not supported |
| 2 | Role Ambiguity | $H_{2.1.1}$ | Career satisfaction | - | -.225 | -2.333 | .022 | Supported |
| | | $H_{2.1.2}$ | Job satisfaction | - | -.120 | -1.216 | .227 | Not supported |
| | | $H_{2.1.3}$ | Org. Commitment | - | .095 | .957 | .341 | Not supported |
| | Role Conflict | $H_{2.2.1}$ | Career satisfaction | - | -.017 | -.173 | .863 | Not supported |
| | | $H_{2.2.2}$ | Job satisfaction | - | -.079 | -.798 | .427 | Not supported |
| | | $H_{2.2.3}$ | Org. Commitment | - | -.013 | -.126 | .900 | Not supported |
| 3 | Growth Opportunity | $H_{3.1.1}$ | Job satisfaction | + | .624 | 8.015 | .000 | Supported |
| | | $H_{3.1.2}$ | Org. Commitment | + | .190 | 1.947 | .054 | Not supported |
| | | $H_{3.1.3}$ | Turnover Intention | - | -.430 | -4.785 | .000 | Supported |
| | Supervisor support | $H_{3.2.1}$ | Job satisfaction | + | .435 | 4.884 | .000 | Supported |
| | | $H_{3.2.2}$ | Org. Commitment | + | .001 | .011 | .991 | Not supported |
| | | $H_{3.2.3}$ | Turnover Intention | - | -.349 | -3.757 | .000 | Supported |
| | External Career opportunity | $H_{3.3.1}$ | Org. Commitment | - | -.086 | -.868 | .387 | Not supported |
| | | $H_{3.3.2}$ | Turnover Intention | + | .321 | 3.407 | .001 | Supported |
| 4 | Org. Commitment | $H_{4}$ | Turnover Intention | - | -.061 | -.615 | .540 | Not supported |
| 5 | Career satisfaction | $H_{5.1}$ | Org. Commitment | + | .049 | .498 | .620 | Not supported |
| | Job satisfaction | $H_{5.2}$ | | + | .092 | .932 | .354 | Not supported |
| | Career satisfaction | $H_{5.3}$ | Turnover Intention | - | -.139 | -1.417 | .159 | Not supported |
| | Job Satisfaction | $H_{5.4}$ | | - | -.466 | -5.296 | .000 | Supported |
| 6 | Job satisfaction | $H_{6}$ | Career satisfaction | + | .169 | 1.736 | .085 | Not supported |

*Table 10. Correlation of Some Turnover Constructs*

| | JOBSAT | GRWTOPPT | CARRSAT | ORGCMIT | AGE | LENTSERV | TRNOVRINT |
|---|---|---|---|---|---|---|---|
| JOBSAT | 1 | | | | | | |
| GRWTOPPT | .624** | 1 | | | | | |
| CARRSAT | .169 | .234* | 1 | | | | |
| ORGCMIT | .096 | .193 | .051 | 1 | | | |
| AGE | -.178 | -.082 | -.116 | -.052 | 1 | | |
| LENTSERV | .000 | .080 | .115 | -.047 | .508** | 1 | |
| TRNOVRINT | -.468** | -.431** | -.139 | -.063 | .054 | -.131 | 1 |

** Correlation is significant at the 0.01 level (2-tailed).
* Correlation is significant at the 0.05 level (2-tailed).

## Turnover Intentions

The results of the hypotheses tests (using multivariate regression analysis) are presented in Table 9. The results show that demographic variables do not have a significant effect on job satisfaction, career satisfaction, organizational commitment or turnover intention. However, the effects of age on job satisfaction ($t$= -1.679) and career satisfaction ($t$= 1.615) are quite sizable, even when they are not statistically significant. The older people tend to be more satisfied with their jobs and careers than young people. Also, the effects of length of service on career satisfaction ($t$= 1.870) and turnover intentions ($t$= -1.624) are quite reasonable. The longer a person stays on the job, the more his career satisfaction and the less likely the tendency to leave the job. Growth opportunity has a reasonable (not significant) effect ($t$=1.947) on organizational commitment, and the same can be said of job satisfaction and career satisfaction ($t$=1.736). A correlation analysis was conducted on the constructs that seem to have some reasonable but not statistical effects on the corresponding dependents. The results are presented in Table 10.

From Table 9, it is evident that role ambiguity has a statistically significant negative effect on career satisfaction ($t$= -2.333, $p$ = 0.022); thus $H_{2.1.1}$ is supported. Most of the hypotheses relating to career variables are strongly supported ($H_{3.1.1,}$ $H_{3.1.3,}$ $H_{3.2.1,}$ $H_{3.2.3,}$ $H_{3.3.2}$). The effect of job satisfaction on turnover intention is equally very significant. A high level of job satisfaction leads to less tendency to leave the job ($t$=-5.296, $p$= 0.000).

The correlation analysis (Table 10) shows a positive significant relationship between growth opportunity and job satisfaction (at 99% confidence level), and between growth opportunity and career satisfaction (at 95% confidence level). Age does not have any significant relationship with any of the other constructs, while length of service has a strong significant relationship with age (almost given). Job satisfaction and growth opportunity have strong significant negative relationship with turnover intention.

## DISCUSSION OF RESULTS

### Demographics

#### Age Composition of IS Employees in Botswana

This research has established that the majority of IS employees in Botswana are of a young age. The average age of female employees is 27.1 years while that of male employees is 28.3 years. None of the respondents was more than 50 years old and more than half of the respondents were below

30 years old. More than half of the respondents have worked for less than 4 years in the IS field. The young working population is putting a lot of pressures on the organizations in which they work because, compared to their mature colleagues, they are the least stable in employment. There are a number of reasons as to why this is the case. Young employees generally tend to earn less than older employees because they have worked for a relatively shorter period of time and are therefore not as experienced as their older colleagues. They are thus more inclined to quit their current jobs in search of better remuneration elsewhere. Secondly, most of the young employees, being in the early phases of their careers, are in need of career development support, including training, from their employers. In order to ensure that these young employees are satisfied in their employment, employers should strive to put forth training programmes which would provide them with both theoretical and hands on training in aspects related to their work. On its part, government should create an environment that is conducive for employers to be able to provide this training to its young recruits.

### Educational Qualifications of IS Employees

The findings of this study seem to suggest that about 50% of the IS employees have at least a Bachelor's degree. On the face of it, this is an encouraging situation. However, the findings show also that there are a sizable number of expatriates in the profession. Although the percentage of expatriates is not too high (20.2%) it is worth considering the possibility that these could be occupying the relatively senior positions in the profession. There is need to explore the necessity for training citizens for higher qualifications so that they are prepared to occupy senior positions that may fall vacant in future. This will also be good for morale and long term stability in the profession.

## Career Anchors

### Sense of Service

According to Schein (1980) individuals with a sense of service career anchor are primarily motivated to improve the world in some way and they want to align work activities with personal values about helping society. Such individuals are more concerned with finding jobs which meet their values than their skills. Schein (1996) indicates that the number of people showing up with this anchor in USA is increasing. Hofstede (1980)'s four dimensions of culture include that of individualism versus collectivism that explain the extent to which individual members in a society consider themselves more important or less important than the society at large (such as relatives, caste, clan, and organization). Under individualism people take care of themselves and their immediate families while under collectivism identity is based on social system and absolute loyalty to the society is expected. Kanungo and Jaeger (1990) characterized the socio-cultural environment of the developing countries when compared to the developed countries, as relatively low on individualism. Mendonca and Kanungo (1996) remind us that each of Hofstede's dimensions of national culture represents a set of underlying beliefs and assumptions which people carry with them when they join an organization.

In Botswana the issue of giving back to the community is ingrained within the socio-economic and cultural environments. Giving back to the community is considered an explicit way of showing concern to other members of society. This issue manifests itself in the numerous charitable/non-governmental organizations that operate in the country. Individuals and corporate entities will usually use any opportunity available to demonstrate this care for others through monetary donations, or donations in the form of time spent on social or other committees which time is not compensated for in monetary terms.

The importance of this show of concern is demonstrated by its inclusion in Botswana's Vision 2016, which anticipates, among others, that Botswana will be a just and caring nation by the year 2016 ("BV2016C", 2004). It may therefore not be surprising that the dominant career anchor in Botswana, which is consistent across gender (especially men), age and educational qualification (other than those who did not progress beyond high school) is that of sense of service.

## Organizational Stability

In an environment where unemployment is very high organizational stability is very important. If one loses a job there is no guarantee of finding another one within a reasonably short period of time. An employer who might close business and make massive layoffs in the foreseeable future may not be attractive unless the payment is extremely good. But, as Schein (1996) points out, even the government bureaucracy as a lifetime employer can no longer be relied upon as pressures mount toward decentralization, reducing size of government, and making government more efficient. Therefore, individuals who orient themselves initially to finding a good employer and staying with that employer for the duration of their careers have to develop a new way of thinking about themselves and locate new external or internal structures on which to become dependent.

Unemployment is one of the most serious problems that Botswana is facing (Siphambe, 2003). This is a serious challenge to the government of Botswana, which has seen the economy go through various growth rates over the years that have resulted in the country being one of the few in sub-Saharan Africa now classified as a middle-income country. Unemployment has particularly affected the youth, including graduates from tertiary institutions in Botswana. In this study, except for the sense of service career anchor, the organizational stability career anchor has got the second largest percentage of respondents across gender (especially women), age and educational qualification lines. This clearly reflects the fears employees have about their employment. The reason why women employees in Botswana are more concerned with organisational stability than men could be because most of them, across all social classes, are single mothers who raise their children assisted by their parents, brothers and sisters while those who are well-off raise their own children without resorting to their parents because they can afford to employ domestic workers who take care of the children while they are at work (Mannathoko, 1999). It is surprising though that the employees in the age bracket of less than 20 years do not show concern for this career anchor. This age-group and the one above it are the ones most affected by unemployment (Siphambe, 2003).

Related to organizational stability in Schein's (1996) career anchors is that of geographic stability. Employees who prefer geographical stability like to work in particular geographical areas where they and their families feel comfortable and secure. They would rather leave their jobs than be promoted out of those areas. Overall, geographic stability scored the lowest percentage (1.0%) of the dominant career anchors. Only the very young employees (less than 20 years) exhibited this orientation, with one-third of them showing concern for this anchor. This is the same age group that is affected most by employment but whose members do not acknowledge that fact. This finding supports at least one study which shows a tendency of young labour to move from rural to urban areas (Bell 1980). It is possible that the youth seek employment in certain preferred areas, most likely in the urban areas where the social lifestyle is relatively modern and many opportunities exist for training as well as entertainment after office hours. For the other respondents, geographical stability is not a factor they can control that much. Hence, they are ready to be moved from one geographic area to another. As Bell (1980, p 409) points out, "Botswana government employees are so liable to regular posting throughout the country that, while their overall commitment to urban life may be high, integration into any one centre is difficult." This fact reinforces the observations made with regard to the absence of lifestyle as one of the career anchors.

## Lifestyle

Data analysis showed that there is no lifestyle anchor for IS personnel in Botswana. People in the lifestyle career anchor strive to balance between work and life. The particular lifestyle they look for should ensure that they earn enough through getting employed but not at the expense of sacrificing family-life relationships. Talking about career anchors of managers with global careers, Suutari and Taka (2004) elaborate that "one of the reasons that may explain the emergence of the lifestyle anchor among the most common anchors is the fact that an international assignment is not an important issue for the person himself or herself only – it is always an issue which influences the whole family". Danziger and Valency (2006) argue that individuals with a strong lifestyle anchor look for organizations that have strong pro-family values and programs.

One of the possible reasons for the lack of lifestyle career anchor in this study could be the low number of females who responded to the questionnaire. A study by Danziger and Valency (2006) showed that the percentage of women with lifestyle as their dominant anchor is almost twice the percentage among men. Suutari and Taka (2004) opined that the reason why the lifestyle career anchor was viewed as very important in Finland is because the country is a very feminine society in which social relationships and the family-life are valued.

National and organisational cultures and employer practices in Botswana could provide a second reason for the lack of lifestyle career anchor. For many years, South Africa, the biggest economy in Africa attracted many male migrant workers from Botswana and other neighbouring countries to work in its mines. Most would return to their home countries for a very brief period and go back or when they are very old and unproductive (Brown, 1983). This system completely upset the social and economic structure of the society in Botswana. Many women became single mothers and raised their children assisted by their parents and brothers and sisters. In the process women learnt to be more independent and tended to be less submissive to men (Peters, 1983). The single mother phenomenon which is currently the norm cuts across all social classes in Botswana, peasants and middle class women (Mannathoko, 1999). Many professional middle class women can raise their own children without resorting to their parents because they can afford to employ domestic workers who take care of the children while they are at work (Mannathoko, 1999). The respondents to this research may not have been directly affected by the situation described above, but the environment in which they have been raised and currently live and work would influence their points of view. This would apply to both, men and women.

A third reason for the lack of life style anchor in Botswana could also be some national and organisational employee relocation policies. For some time it was an established and acceptable practice for an employer to transfer a married person from one workstation to another without giving much consideration to whether the spouse will also be able to secure a job in the new location should the spouse chose to move with his/her partner. In this case work is given priority over family and there is absolute loyalty to the organization (Hofstede, 1980).

## Other Career Orientations

Apart from sense of service and organisational stability the study shows that IS employees in Botswana are not very much concerned with the other career anchors that were highlighted in this study. All had percentage scores of less than five percent, with the exception of specialization-driven growth (6.7%) and technical and functional competence (5.8%). Of these two, specialization-driven growth appeared to be a factor of concern mainly to employees who do not have qualifications beyond high school. Twenty percent of this employee category showed concern or interest in specialization-driven growth. This consists of those employees who are strongly motivated by their being able to continue working in their specific area of specialization. Their careers are built around their fields of specialization and are willing to sacrifice promotion if it takes them out of that specialization.

In Botswana the orientation of this group to this anchor is also reflective of the labour situation in the country. As mentioned above, Botswana is facing high rates of unemployment (Siphambe, 2003). It is very likely that this group is aware of their vulnerability in the labour market, given their relatively lower educational achievement, and would prefer the status quo rather than face uncertainties associated with new challenges. Such challenges result from moving into a new specialization area for which they may not be adequately prepared, or the responsibilities associated with a promotion or other similar movement. Both changes in the status quo may expose their weaknesses and increase the likelihood of them being replaced if need arises.

It is noted that one third of the young employees (age group less than 20 years) indicated a concern for autonomy and independence. Individuals who exhibit these characteristics are primarily desirable of freedom to pursue career interests that are not inhibited by organizational rules and other constraints. Such individuals, if employed, can change employment anytime they believe the organization is becoming too intrusive of their private space. As discussed above, this age group appears to be oblivious to the economic environment in which they are working. These employees are willing to risk their current employment for another which they are not sure of. Much as it reflects their relative attitude towards risk, it is possible that if they had a better grasp of what is happening in the economy they would have had a different attitude. The same appears to be the case with the employees who did not go beyond high school. Of these, 10% indicated concern or autonomy and independence.

## Turnover Intentions

According to the results, the major contributors to the turnover intentions of IS personnel in Botswana are job satisfaction and growth opportunities. Research by Igbaria and Greenhaus (1992) found that the immediate determinants of turnover intentions were job satisfaction and organizational commitment. Growth opportunities cover issues such as opportunity for promotion, career development, training opportunities and annual assessments. Apart from contributing significantly to turnover intentions, growth opportunity has got a direct positive impact on job satisfaction and career satisfaction. It was observed from the study that young employees have got the highest propensity to turnover. Most of the young employees are in the lower salary bands, have got one degree, and do not have enough working experience.

For a long time it has been like a culture in Botswana that most employees get sponsored for further education by their employers, especially for second degrees and short courses. The sponsorship could cover all costs such as tuition and paid leave. Those employers who cannot afford to release their employees and or pay them while they are pursuing further studies would at least make certain concessions which will allow their employees to smoothly carry on with their studies. This is engrained in the minds of employees, especially the young ones. As a result employees jump from one job to another trying to find an employer who would be willing to meet their training needs. Indeed, 46.25 percent of all employees indicated that one of the factors that would make them leave their current jobs would be if the employer does not like to sponsor them for further education or new skills development. It is further observed that employees who fail to find any growth opportunities at their places of work indicate that their careers have been a failure which in turn contributes to turnover intentions.

Benson (2006) researched on two types of employee development which can be provided to employees: on-the-job training and tuition-reimbursement which provides general or marketable skills. It was observed that on-the-job training was positively related to organizational commitment and negatively related to intention to turnover. Participation in tuition-reimbursement was positively related to intention to turnover, although the intention to turnover seemed to be reduced if after earning a degree (through tuition-reimbursement) the employees were subsequently promoted. According to Benson (2006: 185) therefore, employees who participate in on-the-job training and gain specific skills which are relevant to their current jobs "are more committed and less likely to intend to leave the firm, while employees who participate in tuition-reimbursement express higher intention to leave the firm".

According to the results growth opportunities have a major impact on job satisfaction. Items under job satisfaction cover issues such as pre-employment expectations, the ease at which a new employee gets integrated at place of work, and job characteristics. Job satisfaction is negatively correlated with intentions to turnover. This means that employers can try to reduce their employees' intentions to turnover by ensuring that the above factors are taken care of.

Sector-wise comparisons in this study show clearly that employees who work in the government sector are very happy with the career advancement support which they get from their employer, but they are the most disgruntled and would like to leave their jobs. Government employees are very unhappy with all aspects of supervisory support that they get from their employer. The inadequacy of supervisory support in the government sector can be pointing to a much complex problem. Does the government supervisor posses enough discretionary powers for motivating his/her subordinates? What is the impact of the government's bureaucratic system on the supervisory support given to its employees?

## CONCLUSION AND RECOMMENDATIONS

The findings of this study suggest that the IS profession is heavily weighted in favour of the male gender. Three-quarters of the respondents were male. An earlier study, also in Botswana, showed that the proportion of women in the IS profession was smaller than the national average of women employees (Mgaya et al., 2005). It appears nothing has changed much since that study. For a country that is promoting gender equality in employment, this disparity cannot be allowed to continue. Results of the current study seem to suggest that based on their responses on the organizational stability career anchor, women could turn out to be the most stable in employment. However, if women continue to be neglected and mistreated in employment (Mgaya et al., 2005) they may be left with no other option than to leave their employment at the earliest opportunity. The result would be a further reduction in the proportion of women in employment generally, and specifically in the IS profession. This will also create undue pressure on employers to ensure that they have the staff they need at the time they are needed.

The number of female IS employees can be increased by deliberately increasing the number of female students at tertiary education level and encouraging them to enrol in IS courses. Efforts to increase female students in IS should start by first encouraging female students in secondary schools to opt for mathematics and science subjects. These students would then provide a basis for increasing enrolments in IS and related courses at tertiary level.

This study has identified nine career anchors for employees in the field of IS. Two of these anchors, namely a sense of service and organizational stability, appear to be of most concern to IS employees. Some gender differences were observed in the results, with female employees more concerned with organizational stability while men were more concerned with the sense of service. Some differences were noted across age groups and by educational attainment. More attention, however, needs to be given to the gender differences.

The study examined the factors that affect the IS employees' intention to leave their current jobs using the Igbaria and Greenhaus (1992) model. The results of the study show that *role ambiguity* has a negative effect on career satisfaction, while supervisor support and growth opportunity have positive effects on job satisfaction. Turnover intention is influenced negatively by internal growth opportunity, supervisor support, and job satisfaction. External career opportunity tends to have a positive significant effect on the employee's intention to quit. Most of the results obtained in this study are not in consonance with the results obtained by Igbaria and Greenhaus (1992) upon which the turnover intentions study was based. For example, Igbaria and Greenhaus found strong negative relationship between organizational commitment and turnover intention, but our study found a very non significant negative relationship between the two. Some of our results have partially corroborated the Igbaria's results. For example, Igbaria and Greenhaus identified role stressors to affect turnover intentions indirectly through job satisfaction. Our study found role stressors (role ambiguity and role conflict) to have non-significant negative effects on job satisfaction, whereas, job satisfaction had significant negative effect on turnover intention.

It is expected that employers in Botswana would realise the unique career needs of IS personnel in the country and emphasize growth opportunities and supervisor support as instruments for increasing the levels of job and career satisfaction of IS employees in order to reduce the rate of turnover of IS employees. High employee turnover can be a serious obstacle to productivity, quality, and profitability at firms of all sizes (Hogan, 1992; Catherine, 2002)

## AREAS OF FURTHER RESEARCH

Based on the above findings, it would be useful to look into areas of gender differences on career anchors and turnover intentions of IS professionals. Comparative studies that focus on the private and public sector could provide more detail on the pattern of gender differences that have surfaced in this study. This is to take cognizance of the fact that unlike other countries such as the US where similar studies have been undertaken, the Botswana IS labour market heavily leans on the Government of Botswana as the largest employer. Further, a contextual view that looks into these areas with a bias towards cultural values in Botswana can greatly enhance the results of this study.

## REFERENCES

Argyris, C. (1957). The individual and organization: some problems of mutual adjustment. *Administrative Science Quarterly*, *2*, 1–24. doi:10.2307/2390587

BV2016C (Botswana Vision 2016 Council) (2004). *Towards Prosperity for All*. Retrieved January 18, 2008 from http://www.vision2016.co.bw

Baroudi, J. J. (1985). The impact of role variables on IS personnel work attitudes and intentions. *Management Information Systems Quarterly*, *9*(4), 341–356. doi:10.2307/249234

Baroudi, J. J., & Ginzberg, M. J. (1992). Career Orientation of IS Personnel. *Computer Personnel, 14*(2), 15–29. doi:10.1145/147114.147118

Beecham, S., Baddoo, N., Hall, T., Robinson, H., & Sharp, H. (2007). *Motivation in Software Engineering: A Systematic Literature Review.* Retrieved October 30, 2008 from https://uhra.herts.ac.uk/dspace/bitstream/2299/989/1/S70.pdf

Bell, M. (1980). Rural-Urban Movement among Botswana's Skilled Manpower: Some Observations on the Two Sector Model. *Africa: Journal of the International African Institute, 50*(4), 404–421. doi:10.2307/1158431

Benson, G. S. (2006). Employee development, commitment and intention to turnover: a test of 'employability' policies in action. *Human Resource Management Journal, 16*(2), 173–192. doi:10.1111/j.1748-8583.2006.00011.x

Brown, B. B. (1983). The Impact of Male Labor Migration on Women in Botswana. *African Affairs, 82*(328), 367–388.

Byrne, Z. S., & Cropanzano, R. (2001). The history of organizational justice: The founders speak. In Cropanzano, R. (Ed.), *Justice in the workplace: From theory to practice (2)*. Mahwah, NJ: Lawrence Erlbaum Associates, Inc.

Campbell, E. K. (2003). Attitudes of Botswana Citizens towards Immigrants: Signs of Xenophobia. *International Migration (Geneva, Switzerland), 41*(4), 11–71. doi:10.1111/1468-2435.00253

Catherine, M Gustafson. (2002). Staff turnover: Retention. *International Journal of Contemporary Hospitality Management, 14*(3), 106–110.

Cone, E. (1998). Managing that churning sensation. *InformationWeek, 680*, 50.

Crepeau, R. G., Crook, C. W., Goslar, M. D., & McMurtrey, M. E. (1992). Career Anchors of Information Systems Personnel. *Journal of Management Information Systems, 9*(2), 145–160.

Danziger, N., & Valency, R. (2006). Career anchors: distribution and impact on job satisfaction: The Israeli case. *Career Development International, 11*(4), 293–303. doi:10.1108/13620430610672513

DeConinck, J. B., & Johnson, J. T. (2009). The Effects of Perceived Supervisor Support, Perceived Organizational Support, and Organizational Justice on Turnover Among Salespeople. *Journal of Personal Selling & Sales Management, 29*(4), 333–351. doi:10.2753/PSS0885-3134290403

Derr, C. B. (1986). *Managing the New Careerists.* San Francisco, CA: Jossey Bass.

Elliott, R., & Boshoff, C. (2005). The Influence of Organisational Factors in Small Tourism Businesses on The Success of Internet marketing. *Management Dynamics, 14*(3), 44–58.

Ginzberg, M., & Baroudi, J. J. (1992), Career orientations of IS personnel, *Proceedings of the ACM SIGCPR Conference, April 5-7*, (pp.41-55.) New York, NY: ACM Press.

Goldstein, D. K., & Rockart, J. F. (1984). An Examination of Work-Related Correlates of Job Satisfaction in Programmer/Analysts. *Management Information Systems Quarterly, 8*(2), 103–115. doi:10.2307/249347

Hackman, J. R., & Oldham, G. R. (1976). Motivation through the design of work: Test of a theory. *Organizational Behavior and Human Performance, 16*(2), 250–279. doi:10.1016/0030-5073(76)90016-7

Herzberg, F. (1968). One more time: how do you motivate employees? *Harvard Business Review, 46*(1), 53–62.

Hofstede, G. (1980). *Culture's Consequences*. Beverly Hills, CA: Sage Publications.

Hofstede, G. (1983). Dimensions of National Cultures in Fifty Countries and Three Regions. In Deregowski, J. B., Dziurawiec, S., & Annis, R. C. (Eds.), *Expiscations in Cross-Cultural Psychology* (pp. 335–355). Lisse: Swets and Zeitlinger.

Hofstede, G. (1984). *Culture's consequences: International differences in work-related values*. Beverly Hills, CA: Sage Publications.

Hogan, J. J. (1992). Turnover and what to do about it. *The Cornell HRA Quarterly.*, *33*(1), 40–45.

Hsu, M. K., Chen, H. G., Jiang, J., & Klein, G. (2003). Career Satisfaction for Managerial and Technical Anchored IS Personnel in Later Career Stages. *ACM SIGMIS Database*, *34*(4), 64–72. doi:10.1145/957758.957766

Igbaria, M. & Baroudi J.J. (1993). A short-form measure of career orientations: A psychometric evaluation, *Journal of Management Information Systems*, Fall, *10*(2), 132-145.

Igbaria, M. & Baroudi, J.J. (1993). A short-form measure of career orientations: A psychometric evaluation, *Journal of Management Information Systems*, Fall, *10*(2), 132-145.

Igbaria, M., & Greenhaus, J. H. (1991). Career orientations of MIS employees: An empirical analysis. *Management Information Systems Quarterly*, *15*(2), 151–170. doi:10.2307/249376

Igbaria, M., & Greenhaus, J. H. (1992). Determinants of MIS Employees' Turnover Intentions: A Structural Equation Model. *Communications of the ACM*, *35*(2), 35–49. doi:10.1145/129630.129631

Igbaria, M., Greenhaus, J. H., & Parasuraman, S. (1991). Career orientations of MIS employees: an empirical analysis. *Management Information Systems Quarterly*, *15*(2), 151–169. doi:10.2307/249376

Igbaria, M., & Guimaraes, T. (1999). Exploring differences in employee turnover intentions and its determinants among telecommuters and non-telecommuters. *Journal of Management Information Systems*, *16*(1), 147–164.

Igbaria, M., & McCloskey, D. W. (1996). Career orientations of MIS employees in Taiwan. *Computer Personnel*, *17*(2), 3–24. doi:10.1145/227728.227729

Igbaria, M., Meredith, G., & Smith, D. (1995). Career orientations of information-systems employees in South-Africa. *International Journal of Strategic Systems*, *4*(4), 319–340. doi:10.1016/0963-8687(95)80002-8

Internet World Stats. (2008). *Botswana Internet Usage and Marketing Report*. Retrieved October 23, 2008 from http://www.internetworldstats.com/af/bw.htm

Isaacs, S. (2007). ICT in Education in Botswana, *Survey of ICT and Education in Africa*. Retrieved October 21, 2008 from http://www.infodev.org/en/Publication.387.html

Ituma, A. (2006). The internal career: an explorative study of the career anchors of information technology workers in Nigeria, *SIGMIS CPR '06: Proceedings of the 2006 ACM SIGMIS CPR conference on computer personnel research: Forty four years of computer personnel research: achievements, challenges & the future.* New York, NY: ACM Press

Ituma, A., & Simpson, R. (2007). Moving Beyond Schein's Typology: Individual Career Anchors in the Context of Nigeria. *Personnel Review*, *36*(6), 978–005. doi:10.1108/00483480710822463

Jackson, S. E., & Schuler, R. S. (1985). A meta-analysis and conceptual critique of research on role ambiguity and role conflict in work settings. *Organizational Behavior and Human Decision Processes*, *36*, 16–78. doi:10.1016/0749-5978(85)90020-2

Jiang, J.J. (2000). Supervisor Support and Career Anchor Impact on the Career Satisfaction of the Entry-Level Information Systems Professional, *Journal of Management Information Systems*, Winter, *16*(3), 219-241.

Jiang, J. J., & Klein, G. (2000). Software development risks to project effectiveness. *Journal of Systems and Software*, *52*, 3–10. doi:10.1016/S0164-1212(99)00128-4

Jiang, J. J., & Klein, G. (2002). A discrepancy model of information system personnel turnover. *Journal of Management Information Systems*, *19*(2), 249–272.

Joseph, D., Ng, K., & Koh, C., &, S. (2007). Turnover of Information technology Professionals: A narrative review, meta-analytic structural equation modelling, and Model development. *Management Information Systems Quarterly*, *31*(3), 547–577.

Kanungo, R. N., & Jaeger, A. M. (1990). Introduction: the need for indigenous management in developing countries. In Jaeger, A. M., & Kanungo, R. N. (Eds.), *Management in Developing Countries*. London: Routledge.

Krishnan, S. K., & Singh, M. (2010). Outcomes of intention to quit of Indian IT professionals. *Human Resource Management*, *49*(3), 419–435. doi:10.1002/hrm.20357

Lacity, R. P., & Iyer, V. (2008), Understanding turnover among Indian IS Professionals, in Lacity & Rottman (eds.)*Offshore Outsourcing of IT Work* (pp. 209-244), Palgrave, London.

Lee, P. C. B. (2002). Career Goals and Career Management Strategy among Information Technology Professionals. *Career Development International*, 7(1), 6–13. doi:10.1108/13620430210414829

Lochhead, C., & Stephens, A. (2004). Employee retention, labour turnover and knowledge transfer: A case study from the Canadian plastic sector, *Canadian Labour and Business Centre*. Downloaded on August 30, 2010 from http://www.cpsc-ccsp.ca/PDFS/CPSC%20Final%20Report%20June28%20-%207%20case%20studies2%20oct%207%2004.pdf

Mannathoko, C. (1999). What does it mean to be a middle class woman in Botswana? In Zmroczek, C., & Mahony, P. (Eds.), *Women and Social Class: International Feminist Perspectives*. London: UCL Press Ltd.

Martin, T. N. (1979). A contextual model of employee turnover intentions. *Academy of Management Journal*, *22*(2), 313–324. doi:10.2307/255592

McClelland, D. C. (1961). *The Achieving Society*. Princeton, NJ: Van Nostrand.

Mendonca, M., & Kanungo, R. N. (1996). Impact of culture on performance management in developing countries. *International Journal of Manpower*, *17*(4-5), 65–75. doi:10.1108/01437729610127640

Mgaya, K. V., Shemi, A. P., & Kitindi, E. (2005). Gender inequality in the information systems workforce: challenges and implications for management in Botswana, *World Review of Science. Technology and Sustainable Development*, *2*(2), 126–138.

Michaels, C. E., & Spector, P. E. (1982). Causes of employee turnover: A test of the Mobley, Griffeth, Hand, and Meglino Model. *The Journal of Applied Psychology*, *67*(1), 53–59. doi:10.1037/0021-9010.67.1.53

Mobley, W., Horner, S., & Hollingsworth, A. (1978). An evaluation of precursors of hospital employee turnover. *The Journal of Applied Psychology*, *63*, 408–424. doi:10.1037/0021-9010.63.4.408

Muliawan, A. D., Green, P. F., & Robb, D. A. (2009). The Turnover Intentions of Information Systems Auditors. *International Journal of Accounting Information Systems*, *10*(3), 117–136. doi:10.1016/j.accinf.2009.03.001

Niederman, F., Brancheau, J. C., & Wetherbe, J. C. (1991). Information systems management issues for the 1990s. *Management Information Systems Quarterly*, *15*(4), 475–495. doi:10.2307/249452

Niederman, F., Sumner, M., & Maertz, C. P. (2006). An analysis and synthesis of research related to turnover among IT personnel', *Proceedings of ACM SIGMIS-CPR*, Claremont, CA, (pp.130–136.) New York, NY: ACM Press

Nunnally, J. C. (1967). *Psychometric Theory* (1st ed.). New York, NY: McGraw-Hill.

Peters, P. (1983). Gender, Developmental Cycles and Historical Processes: A Critique of Recent Research on Women in Botswana. *Journal of Southern African Studies*, *10*(1), 100–122. doi:10.1080/03057078308708070

Pringle, J. K., & Mallon, M. (2003). Challenges for the boundaryless career odyssey. *International Journal of Human Resource Management*, *14*(5), 839–853. doi:10.1080/0958519032000080839

Rouse, P. (2001). Voluntary turnover related to information technology professionals: A review of rational and instinctual models. *The International Journal of Organizational Analysis*, *9*(3), 281–291. doi:10.1108/eb028937

Rutner, P. S., Hardgrave, B. C., & McKnight, D. H. (2008). Emotional Dissonance and the Information Technology Professional. *Management Information Systems Quarterly*, *32*(3), 635–652.

Schein, E. H. (1978). *Career dynamics: Matching individual and organizational needs*. Reading, MA: Addison –Wesley.

Schein, E. H. (1984). Coming to a New Awareness of Organizational Culture. *MIT Sloan Management Review*, (25), 3–16.

Schein, E. H. (1985). *Career Anchors: Discovering Your Real Values*. San Diego, CA: University Associates.

Schein, E. H. (1987). Individuals and careers. In Lorsch, J. W. (Ed.), *Handbook of Organizational Behavior* (pp. 155–171). Englewood Cliffs, NJ: Prentice-Hall.

Schein, E. H. (1996). Career Anchors Revisited: Implications for Career Development in the 21st Century. *The Academy of Management Executive*, *10*(4), 80–88. doi:10.5465/AME.1996.3145321

Siphambe, H. K. (2003). Understanding unemployment in Botswana. *The South African Journal of Economics*, *71*(3), 480–495. doi:10.1111/j.1813-6982.2003.tb00082.x

Suutari, V., & Taka, M. (2004). Career anchors of managers with global careers. *Journal of Management Development*, *23*(9), 833–847. doi:10.1108/02621710410558440

Tiedemann, J., Taylor, S., Fiorile, R., & Sciarappa, W. (2006). *Vulnerable Wetlands and Associated Riparian Areas in the Shark River Estuary Watershed. US EPA Wetlands Protection Project Grant Final Report Monmouth University Centre for Coastal Watershed Management*. N.J: W. Long Branch.

Uzoka, F. M. E., & Akinyokun, O. C. (2005). Factor Analytic Model for Evaluating the Effects of HR Profile on Organizational Productivity: Case Study of University Academic Staff. *South African Journal of Higher Education*, *19*(3), 527–538. doi:10.4314/sajhe.v19i3.25508

Van Sell, M., Brief, A. P., & Schuler, R. S. (1981). Role Conflict and Role Ambiguity: Integration of the Literature and Directions for Future Research. *Human Relations*, *34*(1), 43–71. doi:10.1177/001872678103400104

Wynne, L. A., Ferratt, T. W., & Biros, D. P. (2002). Career anchors of United States Air Force information systems workers: a turnover predictor? *In Proceedings of SIGCPR'2002*. 79-89

Yarnall, J. (1998). Career anchors results of an organizational study in the UK. *Career Development International*, *3*(2), 3. doi:10.1108/13620439810207536

# APPENDIX A

# CAREER ANCHOR VARIABLES DESCRIPTION

*Table 11 E-commerce trends in developing economies*

| Variable name | Description |
|---|---|
| car0001 | Building career around specific functional or technical area |
| car0002 | Process of managing people at all levels |
| car0003 | Having self initiative and not constrained by organizational rules |
| car0004 | Job security through guaranteed work and retirement benefits/program |
| car0005 | The use of my interpersonal and helping skills in the service of others is |
| car0006 | Working on problems that are almost insoluble is |
| car0007 | Developing a life cycle that balances my career and family needs is |
| car0008 | To be able to create or build something that is entirely my own product or idea is |
| car0009 | Remaining in my specialized area as opposed to being promoted out of my area of expertise is |
| car0010 | To be in charge of a whole organization is |
| car0011 | A career that is free from organization restrictions is |
| car0012 | An organization that will give me long-run stability is |
| car0013 | Using my skills to make the world a better place to live and work in is |
| car0014 | Competing with and winning out over others is |
| car0015 | Developing a career that permits me to continue to pursue my own life-style is |
| car0016 | Building a new business enterprise is |
| car0017 | Remaining in my area of expertise throughout my career is |
| car0018 | To rise to a high position in general management is |
| car0019 | A career that permits a maximum amount of freedom and autonomy to choose my own work, hours, etc., is |
| car0020 | Remaining in one geographical area rather than moving because of a promotion is |
| car0021 | Being able to use my skills and talents in the service of an important cause is |
| car0022 | The only real challenge in my career has been confronting and solving tough problems, no matter what area they were in |
| car0023 | I have always tried to give equal weight to my family and to my career |
| car0024 | I am always on the lookout for ideas that would permit me to start and build my own enterprise |
| car0025 | I will accept a management position only if it is my area of expertise |
| car0026 | I would like to reach a level of responsibility in an organization whereby I would supervise others in various business functions and my role would primarily be to integrate their efforts |
| car0027 | During my career I have been mainly concerned with my own sense of freedom and autonomy |
| car0028 | It is more important for me to remain in my present geographical location than to receive a promotion or new job assignment in another location |
| car0029 | I have always sought a career in which I could be of service to others |
| car0030 | Competition and winning are the most important and exciting parts of my career |
| car0031 | A career is worthwhile only if it enables me to lead my life in my own way |

*continued on following page*

*Table 11. Continued*

| Variable name | Description |
|---|---|
| car0032 | Entrepreneurial activities are the central part of my career |
| car0033 | I would rather leave my company than be promoted out of my area of expertise |
| car0034 | I will feel successful in my career only if I become a high-level general manager in some organization |
| car0035 | I do not want to be constrained by either an organization or the business world |
| car0036 | I prefer to work for an organization that provides lifetime employment [tenure] |
| car0037 | I want a career in which I can be committed and devoted to an important cause |
| car0038 | I feel successful only if I am constantly challenged by a tough problem or a competitive situation |
| car0039 | Choosing and maintaining a certain life-style is more important than is career success |
| car0040 | I have always wanted to start and build up a business of my own |
| car0041 | I prefer to work for an organization that will permit me to remain in one geographical area |

# Section 3
# E-Commerce Trends in Developing Economies

# Chapter 9
# E-Commerce Adoption in Nigerian Businesses:
## An Analysis Using the Technology-Organization-Environmental Framework

**Uyinomen O. Ekong**
*University of Uyo, Nigeria*

**Princely Ifinedo**
*Cape Breton University, Canada*

**Charles K. Ayo**
*Covenant University, Nigeria*

**Airi Ifinedo**
*NAV Solutions, Canada*

## ABSTRACT

*Business organizations around the world engage in e-commerce (EC) and e-business to support business operations and enhance revenue generation from non-traditional sources. Studies focusing on EC adoption in Sub Saharan Africa (SSA) are just beginning to emerge in the extant information systems (IS) literature. The objective of this current study is to investigate factors impacting the acceptance of EC in small businesses in SSA with Nigeria as an example. A research model based on the Diffusion of Innovation (DIT) and the Technology–Organization–Environment (TOE) frameworks were used to guide this discourse. Such factors as relative advantage, compatibility, complexity, management support, organizational readiness, external pressure, and IS vendor support were used to develop relevant hypotheses. Questionnaires were administered to respondents in Nigeria and data analysis was performed using the Partial Least Squares (PLS) technique. Predictions related to relative advantage, management support, and IS vendor support were confirmed; the other hypotheses were unsupported by the data. The study's implications for research and practice are discussed in the chapter.*

DOI: 10.4018/978-1-4666-1637-0.ch009

## INTRODUCTION

The emergence of Electronic Commerce (EC) has significantly changed the business environment for both individuals and businesses around the world (Turban et. al., 2010). EC arrangements allow sellers to access global markets and buyers have a greater choice to procure goods and services from a variety of sellers around the world at reduced costs (Turban et. al., 2010; Ifinedo, 2011). In fact, Turban et. al., (2010) and Grandon & Pearson, (2004) note that EC enhances productivity for the adopting organization in the following ways: a) it improves efficiencies through automation of transactions, b) it reduces intermediaries in the value chain to foster greater economic advantages, c) it consolidates demand and supply through organized exchanges, d) it facilitates product improvement as well as engenders innovative ways of selling existing products and services. It is safe to suggest that the benefits accruing from EC continue to fuel its acceptance around the globe (Turban et. al., 2010; Ifinedo, 2011; Grandon & Pearson, 2004; Leadpile, 2010). A recent report by Leadpile (2010) predicted that e-commerce sales around the world will likely surpass the $1 trillion mark by 2012.

It is implied that the level of commercial activities and transactions generated through EC and other online initiatives in a country has a positive correlation with the nation's overall economic growth and well-being (EIU, 2011; WEF, 2011). As such, parts of the world especially the developing countries where the expansion of EC and related activities have been slow to develop, run the risk of being marginalized in the emerging digital or network economy (EIU, 2011; WEF, 2011; Ifinedo, 2005). Widely reported reasons as to why countries in the developing world have failed to use information communication and technologies (ICT) products to integrate into the digital economy include factors such as poor infrastructure, legal, institutional, cultural, and socio-economical constraints (Hadidi, 2003; ECA, 2000; UNCTAD, 2008; Ho et. al., 2007; Ifinedo, 2008). It is easy to notice that all the aforementioned constraints are at the macro level. While emphasis on such factors may be relevant in comparative analyses that seek to highlight key facilitating and inhibiting factors across countries/regions of the world, (Kaufmann & Liang, 2007; Farhoomand, et. al., 2000; Tan et. al., 2007) the impacts arising from micro level issues tend to be downplayed and underemphasized in such approaches.

Furthermore, the literature suggests that the extent of EC adoption in the developed world where favorable macro level environments exist does not necessarily indicate that such environmental or external factors alone serve as sole determinants of EC acceptance in those contexts (Ho et. al., 2007; Gibbs & Kraemer, 2004; Scupola, 2003). For example, a lack of financial resources is often identified as an inhibiting factor to the spread of EC in the developing countries; (WEF, 2011; Ifinedo, 2005; Ifinedo, 2008) however, studies (Ifinedo, 2011; Cragg & King, 1993) in the developed world found that this particular item was not a sufficient factor to set back EC adoption in firms with interests in such platforms. With respect to the influence of culture on EC adoption, Okoli (2003) study in a Sub-Saharan African (SSA) country did not uphold the view suggesting that national cultural values inhibit EC adoption (Countries in the SSA region include Ghana, Nigeria, and Botswana; these countries are located south of the Sahara). The pertinence of legal and other institutional factors in the adoption process of EC has been reported to be problematic across contexts (Shih & Kraemer, 2005; Oxley & Yeung, 2001). Importantly, the ongoing gains regarding ICT infrastructure expansion in the developing world especially in SSA suggests that the issue of poor infrastructure that has been putatively noted as a significant inhibitor of technology acceptance in the region is fast losing its relevance. Reports from ITU International Telecommunication Union (2011) and Internetworldstats (2011) indicate that growth in Africa's Internet and broadband sector has accelerated in recent years to the extent that the process is already virtually completed in some of the more developed countries in SSA.

Researchers, including Molla, & Licker, (2005) and Uzoka et al., (2007) have suggested that it is illuminating when attention is paid to issues at the micro level or issues at the boundary of the firm (i.e. supplier/competitive pressure, government support/incentives for firms to adopt needed technologies) when discussing factors that may encourage or discourage the adoption of ICT-enabled initiatives such as EC in the developing world. This present study concurs with Molla, & Licker, 2005 viewpoint indicating that internal knowledge of the advantages of ICT products, the role of management, organizational readiness and competence, pressure from the competition/partners, among others should be duly considered in examining the factors influencing EC adoption across contexts. Indeed, other researchers in the developed West (Ifinedo, 2011; Gibbs et. al., 2004; Scupola, 2003; Al-Qirim, 2007) have examined EC adoption from such a viewpoint.

Tornatzky & Fleischer (1990) proposed the Technology-Organization-Environment (TOE) framework, which best encapsulates the approach that Molla & Licker (2005) and others Ifinedo, (2011); Uzoka et. al., (2007) have clamored for and used in that regard. To that end, this current research will draw from the TOE framework to investigate the factors affecting EC adoption in Nigerian small businesses. The country was selected because of its paramount socio-economic, technological, and political standing in SSA (WEF, 2011) It is not claimed herein that Nigeria is a perfect representative of all the countries in SSA; however, its business environment vis-à-vis EC adoption or rejection may mirror those in comparable countries in the SSA region (Ifinedo, 2006; Ayo et. al., 2008) Indeed, Ho et. al., (2007) suggest that EC adoption in a leading country in a region does influence views in other countries where its influence is being felt. Thus, insights and conclusions from this study may have useful interpretations for firms in other countries in the region. Additionally, Nigeria was chosen because recent development reports indicate that its ICT infrastructure is among the best in SSA (WEF, 2011; ITU, 2011; Internetworldstats, 2011). Further to this, its economy is the second largest in SSA, (EIU, 2011; WEF, 2011; CIA WorldFact, 2011) and its businesses have started accepting EC in greater number (Eze, 2008).

This research is significant because it seeks to contribute to the literature with information from a region of the world i.e. SSA that has not been adequately studied (Mbarika et.al., 2005). In fact, others (Farhoomand et. al., 2000,Tan et. al., J., 2007) have suggested that the diffusion of EC in organizations in developing and developed countries differs significantly. Accordingly, by focusing on EC adoption issues in the SSA region, useful insights that may enhance understanding in the area are engendered. Importantly, given that Internet-based commerce is predicted to be the new engine of economic growth for developing countries (WEF, 2011), it will be useful for research efforts to be directed toward understanding the impact of relevant micro level issues in the context of SSA's business organizations.

It is argued herein that if the knowledge of salient, relevant issues that managers and business owners of small businesses in the SSA region can deal with or relate to, are not adequately discussed, predictions made about explosion of EC in Africa in this 21st century will continue to remain elusive (Hadidi, 2003,Okoli, 2003,Uzoka et. al., 2007,Mbarika et.al., 2005). Obviously, a business executive in SSA may not be empowered to address the poor levels of infrastructure in his context nor can he enact legal frameworks to guide EC engagements; however, he is able to bring about a change in attitude for issues in his domain (the foregoing statement rests on the assumption of rationality). Thus, if the top management support for EC adoption is identified as a problem in a particular business organization, its owner(s) is able to directly react to protect his business investments and interests with more favorable disposition. That being said, this research is designed to: a) use the TOE framework to investigate factors impacting the EC adoption in Nigerian small businesses, b) qualify the relative importance of each factor in the research framework, and c) gain an understanding of what could be serve as facilitators and inhibitors of EC adoption in the study's context.

## Background Information on Nigeria

Nigeria is the most populous country both in SSA and Africa with a population of about 155 million people in 2010 (CIA WorldFact, 2011). Its Gross Domestic Product (GDP) purchasing power parity and GDP per capita in 2010 were US$369.8 billion and $2400, respectively. Broadly speaking, the country has been slow with the adoption of ICT-enabled initiatives (Ayo et. al., 2008,Ifinedo, 2009). Nigeria initiated various projects in the recent past to improve its capability to use of ICT for development; one of the recent developments was the creation of the Nigerian IT Development Agency (NITDA). The body was mandated to drive the nation's ICT policy (Ifinedo, 2005,Ifinedo, 2008). One of its objectives is to "promote electronic trade, business and commerce in the country" (Nigeria IT). Despite the concerted efforts to promote EC in Nigeria, evidence suggests that the growth of EC and associated concepts such as e-payment is still very slow to consolidate (Ayo et. al., 2008; Eze, 2008) For instance, a report indicated that the value of electronic payment and commerce in the country in 2006 stood at 360 billion naira (about US$2.81 billion) (Ayo et. al., 2008). In contrast, e-commerce trend in developed countries such as Canada, in the same year was valued at US$49.9 billion (Grau, 2008).

With respect to using ICT products to develop its economy and foster its welfare (i.e. e-readiness index), Nigeria has not fared well on this index. It ranked 61st out of 70 countries on a ranking of e-readiness produced by the Economist Intelligence Unit (EIU, 2011). Similarly, the country ranked 99th out of 133 countries on the networked readiness index for 2009–2010 that was produced by World Economic Forum (WEF, 2011) These indicators clearly show that Nigeria is not fully prepared for the digital economy. However, progress, albeit slow has been made in Nigeria since 2001. The Nigeria's telecommunication sector, which was perennially underdeveloped and unreliable has been deregulated and liberalized (Ifinedo, 2005; Ifinedo, 2008; ITU, 2011). Four GSM networks were licensed by 2002. Also, more than 400 ISPs and a number of data carriers, Internet exchange and gateway operators have been licensed in the country ("Internetworldstats", 2011). This apparent developments make Nigeria one of the fastest growing ICT markets in SSA after South Africa ("Internetworldstats", 2011).

In 2001, there were only 200,000 Internet users in Nigeria (0.1% of the population); this has jumped to 43,982,200 (28.9% of the population) in 2010 ("Internetworldstats", 2011) Nigeria has instituted lower tariffs for ICT imports and a number of local personal computers (PC) manufactures have started producing PCs in the country (Ifinedo, 2007). With such noted ongoing improvements in the technological infrastructure of the country, it comes as no surprise that EC is beginning to spread among business organizations in Nigeria (Ifinedo, 2006,Ayo et. al., 2008,Eze, 2008). As already indicated, the focus of this research will not be on macro level influences on EC adoption in Nigeria; rather this study's emphasis will be on selected micro level issues.

## Some Previous Reports and Research on E-commerce Acceptance in SSA, including Nigeria

Reports and research studies have discussed EC adoption in selected SSA countries, including Nigeria by drawing from the macro level perspectives. For example, (Ayo et. al., 2008) attributed the slow diffusion of EC in Nigeria to socio-political, economic, and technological factors. Molla & Licker (2005) examined EC adoption in South Africa and concluded that factors such as human-related skills, awareness, business readiness, and knowledge of technological resources are pertinent to the growth of EC in that country. Uzoka et. al. (2007)'s study of EC adoption in Botswana concluded that "environmental factors affecting the adoption of e-commerce include the internet marketing factor and customer/logistic factor." They also noted that management support was an important organizational enabling factor. Olatokun & Kebonye, 2010 investigated EC adoption in Botswana; they reported that organizations in their study that had adopted EC technologies did so because of pressure from customers and suppliers, and the main barrier to adoption was a lack of internal IT knowledge and knowledge. Likewise, Mutula & van Brakel, (2006) found a lack of relevant skills as an inhibitor of ICT expansion in Botswana. This current study concurs with Mutula & van Brakel, (2006) where it was stated that most studies on the adoption of ICT products, including EC by businesses and organizations in SSA have been restricted to macro (national) assessments to the extent that the importance of micro level issues are downplayed.

With respect to micro level issues, Eze, (2008) found that compatibility (fit), relative advantage, and top management support positively impact the development of electronic business in Nigerian firms. Aghaunor & Fotoh, (2006) investigated the factors influencing EC acceptance in the Nigerian banking sector. They found in decreasing order of impacts such factors as perceived complexity, perceived benefits [relative advantage], organizational competence [readiness], perceived compatibility, supporting industries e-readiness, management support, market e-readiness, IT capability, and government e-readiness [support] to influence the adoption process in their study's context. Ifinedo, (2009) showed that low levels of IT skills and knowledge about EC concepts was the main barrier to EC adoption in Nigerian small businesses. As well, Macharia, (2009) indicated that low IT skills levels among business owners and executives generally impeded the expansion of EC in SSA. Importantly, the impacts of the aforementioned issues will be discussed in this chapter.

## A REVIEW OF THE RELEVANT LITERATURE AND HYPOTHESES FORMULATION

### Background Theoretical Foundation

This current research like comparable efforts that have investigated ICT and EC adoption in organization is pursued from the perspective of an innovation (Rogers, 2003; Looi, 2005). According to Looi, 2005 innovation is the process by which any idea, practice, or object is perceived to be new. EC is a new idea to small businesses in SSA. Indeed, a fundamental approach in the study of adoption of EC in organizations involves the use of diffusion of innovation (DIT) theoretical frameworks (Rogers, 2003; Tornatzky & Fleischer; 1990; Tornatzky & Klein, 1982) theory of innovation suggests that new technologies will diffuse faster when they are perceived to possess the following five attributes: relative advantage, complexity, compatibility, trialability, and observability. However, studies using the framework indicate that three of the technical attributes—*relative advantage, compatibility*, and *complexity*—have been persistently regarded as the more important for the adoption process (Tornatzky & Klein, 1982). Moreover, deeper understanding will emerge if other relevant, contingent factors, beyond the technical features of an innovation are duly considered (Ifinedo, 2011; Tornatzky & Fleischer, 1990).

*Figure 1. The Research Model*

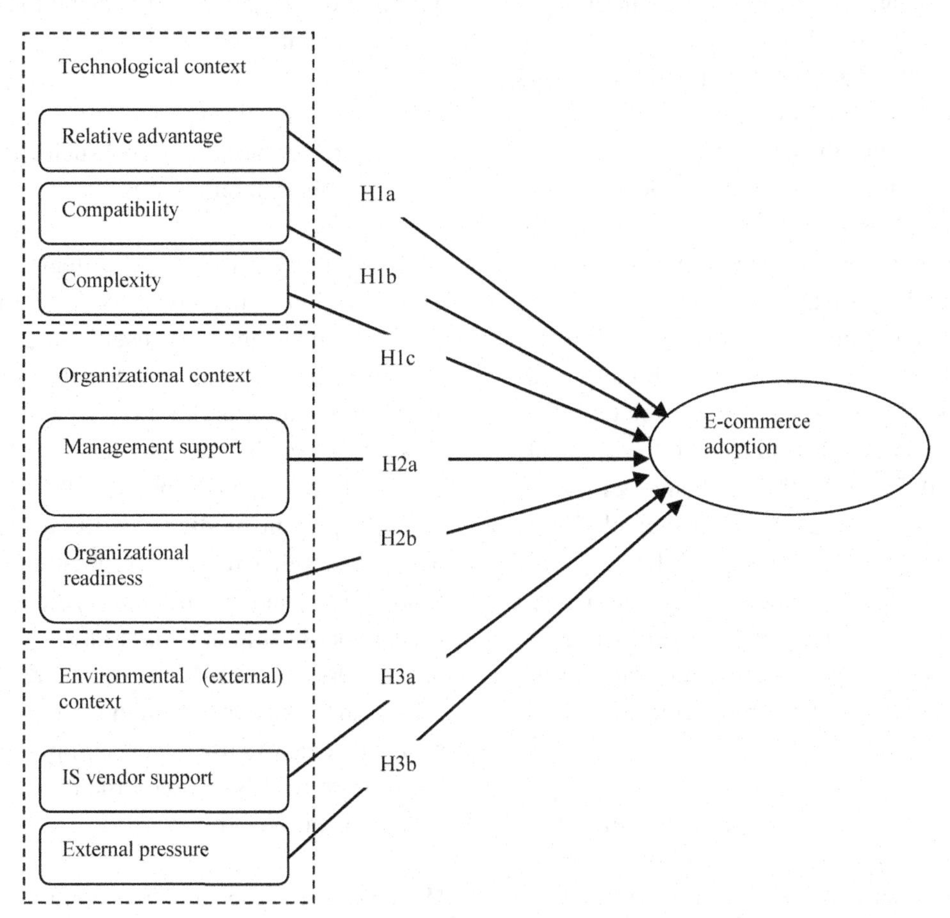


Several studies that used the TOE framework to investigate the impact of relevant organizational and environmental factors included such variables as *management support, organizational readiness, external pressure, and the availability of IT vendor support* on EC adoption. Researchers found almost all the aforementioned factors to be crucial in the adoption of EC in business organizations (Ifinedo, 2011; Gibbs et. al., 2004; Scupola, 2003; Looi, 2005; Iacovou et.al., 1995; Teo et. al., 1997; Premkumar & Roberts, 1999; Caldeira & Ward, 2002). The critical importance of the selected list of factors is offered as illustrative rather than exhaustive examples. Prior research (Kendall et. al., 2001; Jeyaraj et. al., 2006; Love & Irani, 2004; Van der Deen, 2005) has used a variety of variables, including adoption, acceptance, intention to use, receptivity, business performance, or a combination of other relevant variables as the dependent variable. In this study, the dependent variable is *adoption;* it is operationalized with measures related to the frequency, extent of use, and criticality of the use of such technologies in business operations. Other prior studies Ifinedo, (2011); Chong & Pervan, (2007) have used a similar approach to facilitate the emergence of deeper insight.

## Hypotheses Development

This study' research framework, which incorporates the factors identified as being pertinent to the discourse of EC adoption in SSA, is highlighted in Figure 1. The framework also highlights the proposed hypotheses.

Relative advantage is defined by Rogers, 2003 as "the degree to which an innovation is perceived as being better than the idea it supersedes". Thus, the adoption of an innovation will be positively encouraged if its benefits are perceived as having advantages over existing practices and systems. Prior research has examined factors impacting technology adoption with this variable (Ifinedo, 2011; Jeyaraj et. al., 2006). Several previous studies found this factor to be positively related to EC adoption in business organizations (Ifinedo, 2011; Al-Qirim, 2007; Eze, 2008; Premkumar & Roberts, 1999; Kendall et. al., 2001; Jeyaraj et. al., 2006; Chong & Pervan, 2007; Cragg & King, 1993). Indeed, Cragg & King, (1993); Ifinedo, (2011) and Jeyaraj et. al., (2006) found perceived relative advantage to be the most important factor for the adoption of IS in business organizations. Accordingly, it is predicted that:

**H1a:** Higher levels of perceived relative advantage of EC will lead to greater the adoption of such technologies by Nigerian businesses.

Compatibly is defined as "the degree to which an innovation is perceived as consistent with the existing values, past experience, and the needs of potential adopters (Rogers, 2003). It is to be expected that technological innovations will diffuse more freely and easily where such applications appear to match the adopter's processes. However, some IS researchers (Ifinedo, 2011; Gibbs et. al., 2004) did not find support for a positive relationship between this factor and the adoption of IS in organizations. Yet, others have confirmed the relationship; for example, (Cragg & King, 1993; Kendall et al.,Kendall et. al., 2001 and Saffu et al.K. Saffu et. al., 2007) found compatibility to be a significant predictor of IS innovation in adopting organizations. This insight leads to the prediction that:

**H1b:** Higher levels of EC compatibility will lead to greater the adoption of such technologies by Nigerian businesses.

Complexity refers to "the degree to which an innovation is perceived to be relatively difficult to understand and use." (Rogers, 2003). It is reasonable to suggest that the diffusion of a new innovation is inhibited or discouraged if it is perceived by the adopter to be complex. While Premkumar & Roberts, 1999 found it to be an important predictor of EC acceptance in businesses, other researchers including Kendall et. al., (2001) and Ifinedo, (2011) did not confirm such a relationship in their studies. Nonetheless, researchers such as Mirchandani & Motwani, (2001) and Grandon & Pearson, (2004) have suggested that easy to use business applications tend to be more readily adopted than complex ones. Thus, it is predicted that:

**H1c:** The lower the perceived complexity of EC, the greater the adoption of such technologies by Nigerian businesses.

Management support refers to as the "active engagement of top management with IS implementation."Thong et. al., (1996) and Jeyaraj et. al., (2006) found top management support to be one of the best predictors of organizational adoption of IS innovations. Previous studies indicate that management support generally boded well for the acceptance of technological innovations in businesses (Ifinedo, 2011; Grandon & Pearson, 2004; Al-Qirim, 2007; Iacovou et.al., 1995; Premkumar & Roberts, 1999; Mirchandani & Motwani, 2001). This is because top managers act as change agents in the adoption process of technological innovations (Thong et. al., 1996). When top managers understand the importance of technological innovations, they tend to play a crucial role in influencing other organizational members to accept it (Ifinedo, 2011 and Mirchandani & Motwani, 2001). Conversely, where management support is low or unavailable, technology acceptance and adoption tend to be less successful (Ifinedo, 2011 and Jeyaraj et. al., 2006). In Nigeria, Eze, (2008) found support for the relevance of this factor for the successful adoption of EC in the country's financial firms. Thus, it is predicted that:

**H2a:** Higher levels of management support for EC will lead greater the adoption of such technologies by Nigerian businesses.

Organizational readiness is defined by Iacovou et.al., (1995) as "the availability of the needed organizational resources for adoption." Organizational readiness of businesses is critically important for IS adoption and it encompasses not only physical assets, but also human knowledge of IS (Mehrtens et. al., 2001 Thong & Yap, 1995) found a lack of computer literacy among owners of small businesses and a lack of knowledge regarding the benefits of IS use as an inhibitor to IS adoption in small businesses. Chircu & Kauffman, 2000 found that inability to acquire skill and expertise in new technologies, and a lack of training and education form significant barriers to the adoption of EC systems. Businesses that possess adequate knowledge of the benefits of EC and have the necessary values and vision are more likely to accept EC innovations in their contexts (Teo et. al., 1997,Caldeira & Ward, 2002,Cragg & King, 1993,Pflughoeft et. al., 2003). In SSA, Saffu et. al., (2007); Ifinedo, (2006); Ifinedo, (2009); Mutula & van Brakel, (2006) and Macharia, (2009) indicated that EC thrives better where operators of business have an understanding of EC concepts. Thus, it is predicted that:

**H2b:** Higher levels of organizational readiness with EC will lead to greater the adoption of such technologies by Nigerian businesses.

Businesses can sometimes come under the pressure of their customers, partners, and competition to adopt an IS innovation (Olatokun & Kebonye, 2010,Mehrtens et. al., 2001,Poon & Swatman, 1999,Gatignon & Robertson, 1989). For example, pressure from the competitor can lead to environmental uncertainty that could increase the rates of innovation adoption in an industry (Looi, 2005; Chong & Pervan, 2007; Gatignon & Robertson, 1989). Similarly, business partners' pressure can influence a business to adopt new technological innovations (Ifinedo, 2011; Hart & Saunders, 1998). While Hart & Saunders, (1998) and Mehrtens et. al., (2001) found that business partner influence is a significant predictor of the acceptance of IS innovations. However, others did not confirm this relationship (Ifinedo, 2011). Regarding customers' pressure, Kula & Tatoglu, (2003) and Carmichael et. al., (2000) indicated that businesses innovate when they their clients demand it. In general, Jeyaraj et. al., 2006 found external pressure to be one of the most important predictors of IS adoption at the organizational level. In the context of SSA, the studies by K. Saffu et. al., (2007); Uzoka et. al., (2007) and Olatokun & Kebonye, (2010) showed that competitive pressure is positively related to EC adoption. This insight leads to the hypothesis indicating that:

**H3a:** Higher levels of external pressure from a business' partner, suppliers, and customers will lead to greater need to adopt such technologies by Nigerian businesses.

IS vendor support refers to the support for implementing and using IS that a business obtains from external sources of technical expertise (Rogers, 2003; Premkumar & Roberts, 1999; Caldeira & Ward, 2002). According to Attewell, (1992) business organizations tend to postpone technology adoption due to a lack of expertise and knowledge. Thus, the availability of external support can help businesses to bridge knowledge gaps related to IS innovation acquisitions; researchers have found this factor to be an important factor in the adoption of EC and related technologies (Scupola, 2003; Gatignon & Robertson, 1989). However, other scholars (Al-Qirim, 2007; Premkumar & Roberts, 1999) did not find support for such a proposition. A lack of external technical support can inhibit EC adoption as well as the limit the benefit realization from such initiatives (Scupola, 2003) Thus, IS vendors can act as facilitators during the EC adoption especially for organizations lacking in needed technical skills (Rogers, 2003,Attewell, 1992). As indicated above, low levels of IT skills is among the major barriers of EC growth in SSA (Ifinedo, 2008; Ifinedo, 2006; Mutula & van Brakel, 2006; Macharia, 2009) Thus, the availability of IS vendor support can mitigate this shortcoming. It is therefore predicted that:

**H3b:** Higher perception levels of the availability IS vendors support will positively influence EC adoption by Nigerian businesses.

## RESEARCH METHODOLOGY

### Data Collection

The data for this study was collected in Lagos and environs; the city is the largest commercial city in Nigeria (and in SSA) (Eze, 2008) Thus, it is hoped that the search of businesses with knowledge of EC will be easier in such a place (Ayo et. al., 2008). The targeted population comes from the list of business contacts held by a local university in the city. This approach is akin to judgmental sampling (Iacobucci & Churchill, 2009) because the researcher selects respondents based on his/her knowledge of the suitability of the participants. Other prior studies (Ifinedo, 2006,Ayo et. al., 2008) in the region have used a similar method for data collection. The identified participants who were mainly middle-level managers came from a wide range of industries in the private sector. As the unit of analysis of this study was at the organization level, the inclusion of such organizational informants would ensure that useful insights are uncovered.

To ensure content validity, six (6) knowledgeable individuals, including business managers and IS faculty members participated in a pilot test with an initial draft of the questionnaire. Comments and suggestions helped to improve the quality of the final questionnaire. The research effort identified 300 possible respondents from the contacts list and each received a copy of the questionnaire in person. Each package contained a cover letter explaining the purpose of the study. Participation in the study was voluntary. Respondents were assured that their individual responses would be treated with anonymity and confidentiality. The participants were also motivated with a promise that a summary of the results will be sent to them.

The measurement items used in the study were taken from previously validated sources. Table 1 highlights the construct's sources and their descriptive statistics. The full list of the items is provided in the Appendix. The measurement items were anchored on a 7-point Likert scale ranging from "strongly disagree" (1) to "strongly agree" (7) in which participants were asked to indicate an appropriate response. The Cronbach alpha and composite reliability scores for each factor exceeds the recommended 0.7 limit to indicate a reasonably high reliability of the research measures and constructs (Nunnaly, 1978).

### Survey Results

One hundred and fifty six (156) responses were received from the administered 300 questionnaires. Thus, the effective response rate for the survey is 52%. Self-administered surveys tend to have higher response rate than mail or telephone surveys (Hox & de Leeuw, 1994). However, 22 responses were not considered valid for the study;

*Table 1. The constructs' descriptive statistics and their reliability values*

| Construct | Items | Mean | SD | Factor loading | Cronbach's alpha | Composite reliability | Sources |
|---|---|---|---|---|---|---|---|
| Relative advantage | RAI | 4.914 | 1.11367 | 0.92238 | | | Premkumar & Roberts, 1999; Ifinedo, 2011 |
| | RA2 | 4.7448 | 1.30278 | 0.837650 | | | |
| | RA3 | 4.0597 | 1.27298 | 0.884653 | 0.912153 | 0.934445 | |
| | RA4 | 4.1045 | 1.23403 | 0.845459 | | | |
| | RA5 | 4.2403 | 1.42355 | 0.819502 | | | |
| Compatibility | CMP1 | 4.1269 | 1.65626 | 0.755943 | | | Premkumar & Roberts, 1999; Ifinedo, 2011 |
| | CMP2 | 4.2463 | 1.42711 | 0.841579 | 0.751163 | 0.843469 | |
| | CMP3 | 3.9627 | 1.78700 | 0.636067 | | | |
| | CMP4 | 4.4403 | 1.47924 | 0.788165 | | | |
| Complexity | COX1 | 3.5075 | 1.67128 | 0.893256 | | | Premkumar & Roberts, 1999; Ifinedo, 2011 |
| | COX2 | 2.5000 | 1.50063 | 0.720472 | 0.710156 | 0.807596 | |
| | COX3 | 2.3731 | 1.50023 | 0.666536 | | | |
| Management support | MGT1 | 4.6343 | 1.43815 | 0.864017 | | | Thong & Yap, 1995 |
| | MGT2 | 4.6045 | 1.45622 | 0.844151 | | | |
| | MGT3 | 4.5149 | 1.47018 | 0.877834 | 0.858450 | 0.902950 | |
| | MGT4 | 4.2985 | 1.59901 | 0.755240 | | | |
| Organizational readiness | ORG1 | 4.7985 | 1.18118 | 0.828954 | | | Iacovou et.al., 1995; Ifinedo, 2011 |
| | ORG2 | 4.8209 | 1.20681 | 0.828620 | | | |
| | ORG3 | 4.4627 | 1.52994 | 0.815981 | 0.804114 | 0.871798 | |
| | ORG4 | 4.5448 | 1.51987 | 0.695425 | | | |
| External pressure | EXT1 | 3.1567 | 1.77219 | 0.782640 | | | Premkumar & Roberts, 1999; Grandon & Pearson, 2004 |
| | EXT2 | 3.8731 | 1.80818 | 0.799226 | | | |
| | EXT3 | 4.1642 | 1.77787 | 0.778143 | 0.857066 | 0.892173 | |
| | EXT4 | 3.5821 | 1.78253 | 0.818608 | | | |
| | EXT5 | 4.1269 | 1.60554 | 0.733033 | | | |
| | EXT6 | 3.3134 | 1.78304 | 0.649308 | | | |
| IS vendor support | ISV1 | 3.9403 | 1.6578 | 0.878021 | | | Premkumar & Roberts, 1999; Thong & Yap, 1995 |
| | ISV2 | 3.4701 | 1.70664 | 0.839519 | 0.865586 | 0.918030 | |
| | ISV3 | 4.0149 | 1.38186 | 0.944272 | | | |
| EC adoption | ECA1 | 5.2239 | 1.62332 | 0.896244 | 0.851672 | 0.900523 | Chong & Pervan, 2007; Ifinedo, 2011 |
| | ECA2 | 5.2164 | 1.61825 | 0.884175 | | | |
| | ECA3 | 5.2388 | 1.62486 | 0.891323 | | | |
| | ECA4 | 5.1493 | 1.63839 | 0.896451 | | | |

these included responses from the public sector, those with a high percentage of missing entries, and those indicating non-adoption of EC in their business operations. Table 2 summarizes the profile of respondents. The participants' average work experience was 3.94 years (s.d. = 1.22). The respondents included 64% middle-level managers and 26% top managers. Seventy-two percent (74%) of the sample had at least a university/college degree. The average age of the respondents was 32.3 years. The workforce ranged from 1 to 500 employees, with a median of 6 employees. The other profiles of the responding businesses are highlighted in Tables 2 and 3.

To test for nonresponse bias, it is advised that data should be collected from respondents that are not willing to make available their opinions on the study's phenomena; their data should be compared with data of those showing a willingness to participate. This is not a simple exercise; a practical way to assess nonresponse bias is to compare the mean values of selected items for early and late respondents in a survey (Iacobucci & Churchill, 2009) Chi-square ($\chi 2$) test was used to compare the sampled firm size, annual revenue, and industry type. The results of the Chi-square tests (significant at $p < 0.05$) showed there were no significant differences along these key characteristics.

The problem of common method bias exists for studies that used single informants. The procedural remedies for controlling common method biases were followed as well. First, to increase the study's validity, clear and concise questions were used in the questionnaire. Second, to reduce apprehension, respondents' anonymity was assured. Third, a statistical procedure, i.e. the Harmon one-factor test, was used to assess if such biases were a problem in our sample (Podsakoff et. al., 2003). The test results showed that several factors with eigenvalues greater than one are present in the collected data. To that end, the most covariance explained by one factor in our data is 33.2% to indicate that common method variance is not a problem for the data.

*Table 2. The profile of the respondents*

| Profile | Frequency | Percentage (%) |
|---|---|---|
| **Gender** | | |
| Male | 94 | 70.1 |
| Female | 40 | 29.9 |
| Age | | |
| Less than 20 years | 2 | 1.5 |
| 21-30 years | 37 | 27.6 |
| 31-40 years | 67 | 50.0 |
| 41-50 years | 23 | 17.2 |
| 51-60 years | 5 | 3.7 |
| Education | | |
| Primary education | 1 | 0.7 |
| Secondary education | 4 | 3.0 |
| College/Bachelor's education | 74 | 55.2 |
| Post-graduate degree | 53 | 39.6 |
| Other | 2 | 1.5 |
| Job title | | |
| CEO | 9 | 6.7 |
| Director (e.g. Operations, Sales) | 11 | 8.2 |
| Manager (Admin, IT, Project, etc.) | 74 | 55.2 |
| Engineer<br>Assistant/Office<br>Executive<br>Other (e.g. Surveyor, Lab Technician)<br>Missing | 8<br>18<br>12<br>2 | 6<br>13.4<br>9<br>1.5 |

## DATA ANALYSIS AND RESULTS

This research used the Partial Least Squares (PLS) technique for data analysis. The PLS approach is suitable for validating predictive models and for theory building (Chin, 1998). The approach permits information about the measurement and structural models to be gathered as well. The

*Table 3. Profile of the participating businesses*

| Profile | Frequency | Percentage (%) |
|---|---|---|
| **Business type** | | |
| Adverting, Marketing, Sales | 10 | 7.5 |
| Manufacturing | 18 | 13.4 |
| Retail, Wholesale | 19 | 14.2 |
| Financial services | 35 | 26.1 |
| Pharmaceutical/Chemical | 6 | 4.5 |
| Information Technology (IT) and Telecoms | 23 | 17.2 |
| Oil and Gas Services | 8 | 6.0 |
| Hospitality | 6 | 4.5 |
| Other (e.g. Aviation, Surveying) | 7 | 5.2 |
| Missing data | 2 | 1.5 |
| Annual sales revenues | | |
| Less 500,000 naira | 3 | 2.2 |
| 500,001 - 1.0 million naira | 9 | 6.7 |
| 1.1 - 5.0 million naira | 7 | 5.2 |
| 5.1 - 10.0 million naira | 8 | 6.0 |
| 10.1 - 20.0 million naira | 15 | 11.2 |
| 20.1 - 50.0 million naira | 81 | 60.4 |
| Missing data | 11 | 8.2 |
| Workforce | | |
| 1-25 employees | 27 | 20.1 |
| 26-50 employees | 12 | 9.0 |
| 51 - 75employees | 6 | 4.5 |
| 76 -100 employees | 8 | 6.0 |
| Above 100 employees | 78 | 58.2 |
| Missing data | 3 | 2.2 |

Note: The exchange rate of the naira per US dollar is 150.48 in year 2009 when the data was collected.

specific tool used was SmartPLS 2.0, which was created by (Ringle et. al., 2005).

## The Measurement Model

The psychometric properties of the measurement model were assessed by the reliability, convergent, and discriminant validities. Essentially, the internal consistency of the data is assured when the reliability of each measure in a scale is above 0.7 (Nunnaly, 1978). As already presented above, the Cronbach alphas for the study's constructs were above the 0.7 threshold (Nunnaly, 1978,Hair et. al., 1998) to assure reliability. As well, convergent validity is assured when each item has an item loading that is greater than 0.6 on its associated construct. Additionally, the measurement item should not load highly on any other construct(s) (Chin, 1998,Hair et. al., 1998). These requirements were adequately met in this study (please see Table 1). Fornell & Larcker, (1981) recommend that the following conditions be met for adequate

*Table 4. Inter-construct correlations, AVE, and the square root of AVE*

| | AVE | 1 | 2 | 3 | 4 | 5 | 6 | 7 | 8 |
|---|---|---|---|---|---|---|---|---|---|
| 1:EC adoption | 0.698 | 0.835 | | | | | | | |
| 2:Complexity | 0.587 | 0.131 | 0.766 | | | | | | |
| 3:Compatibility | 0.576 | 0.318 | 0.201 | 0.759 | | | | | |
| 4:Competitive pressure | 0.581 | 0.263 | 0.221 | 0.309 | 0.762 | | | | |
| 5:Management support | 0.700 | 0.445 | -0.01 | 0.4284 | 0.471 | 0.837 | | | |
| 6:Organizational readiness | 0.631 | 0.382 | -0.01 | 0.310 | 0.221 | 0.596 | 0.794 | | |
| 7:Relative advantage | 0.742 | 0.300 | 0.242 | 0.023 | 0.289 | 0.224 | -0.015 | 0.861 | |
| 8:IS vendor support | 0.789 | 0.337 | 0.127 | 0.367 | 0.393 | 0.338 | 0.407 | -0.083 | 0.888 |

Note: (a) The bold fonts in the leading diagonals are the square root of AVEs,
(b) off-diagonal elements are correlations among constructs

discriminant validity to be assured: a) the square root of the average variance extracted (AVE) of all constructs should be larger than all other cross-correlations; b) the value of the AVE should be of the threshold value 0.50. Table 4 shows that the AVE ranged from 0.576 to 0.789, and in no case was any correlation between the constructs greater than the squared root of AVE (the principal diagonal element). Thus, the measurement items used for this study demonstrate good convergent and discriminant validities.

## The Structural Model

The structural model in PLS provides information regarding the path coefficients (β) and the squared R ($R^2$). While the strength of the relationship is indicated by the β, the $R^2$ highlights the percentage of variance in the model, which gives an indication of its predictive power. The path significance levels (t-values) are estimated by the bootstrapping procedure. The SmartPLS 2.0 results for the βs and the $R^2$ are shown in Figure 2

Three out of the seven hypotheses were supported; hypothesis (H1a) was confirmed to show that relative advantage of EC will facilitate greater adoption of EC. Hypothesis (H2a) was supported to affirm the view that management support is crucial in the encouragement of EC adoption by Nigerian small businesses. The result also demonstrated significant, statistical support for hypothesis (H3a), which predicted that IS vendor support will enhance EC adoption. The data did not provide support for H1b, H1c, H2b, and H3b. Contrary to the prediction made in hypothesis (H1b), compatibility did not lead to greater EC adoption in the sample. Hypothesis (H1c), which predicted that lower perceived complexity of e-commerce will result in greater adoption of such technologies by Nigerian businesses, was unconfirmed. Similarly, the prediction related to the pertinence of external pressure in the EC adoption processes of Nigerian businesses was unsupported by the data. All the variables together explain 33% of the variance in the dependent construct. This indicates that the proposed research conceptualization possess moderate predictive power to permit an understanding of EC adoption in the sampled businesses (Chin, 1998). Further discussion on the results is presented in the next section.

*Figure 2. The SmartPLS results for the data*

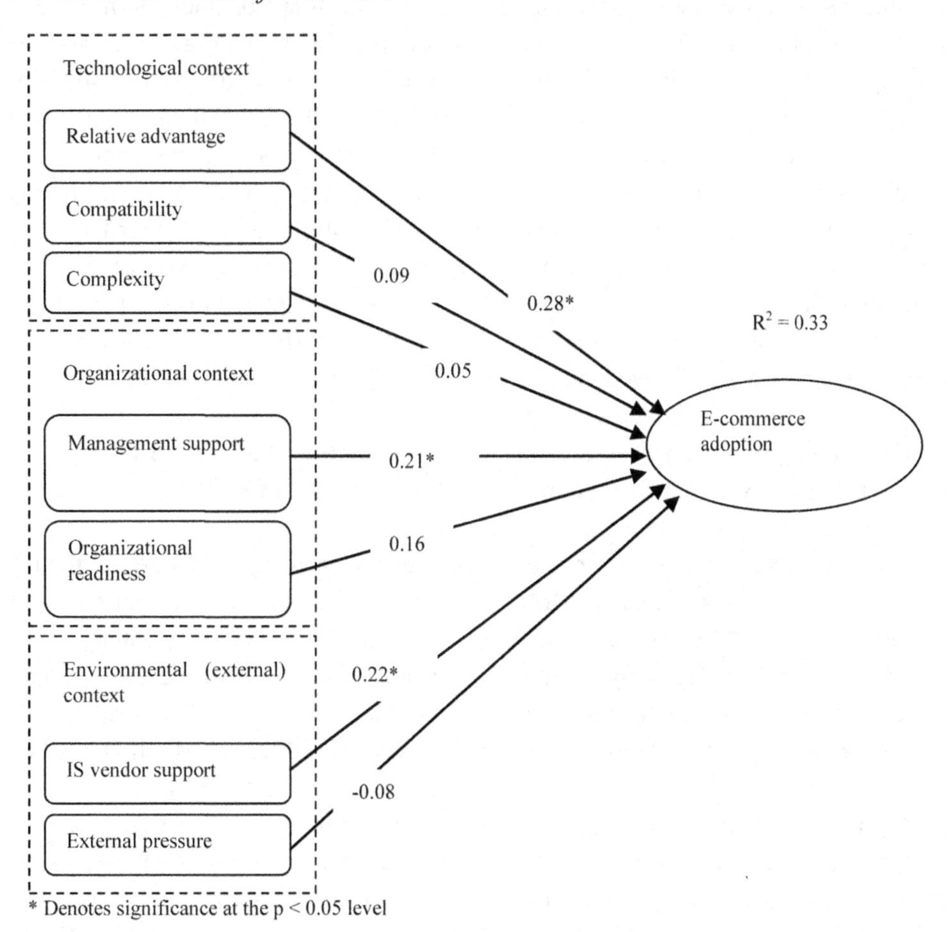


## DISCUSSION

Drawing from the DIT and TOE models, this study posits that relative advantage, compatibility, complexity, management support, organizational readiness, external pressure from, and IS vendor support will influence EC adoption in Nigerian small businesses. Subsequent data analysis confirmed the significance of relative advantage, management support and IS vendor support in the adoption of EC in the research context. In that regard, the result showed that small businesses in Nigeria are generally positively encouraged to adopt EC upon realizing the perceived benefits of such technologies over existing practices in their contexts. This finding provides support for the works of Eze, (2008) and Aghaunor & Fotoh, (2006) who showed that an understanding of the relative advantage of EC augurs well for the spread of such technologies in Nigeria. In relation to other selected factors used in this study, relative advantage was seen to be the most important predictor of EC adoption in the sampled businesses in Nigeria. This finding supports previous studies that have signified the critical importance of relative advantage in the adoption processes of technological innovations, in small businesses (Ifinedo, 2011; Gibbs et. al., 2004; Looi, 2005; Iacovou et.al., 1995; Premkumar & Roberts, 1999; Mehrtens et. al., 2001)

To the extent that management support is considered crucial for the successful adoption of EC by Nigerian small businesses, this study's findings provide empirical support for such a claim. The views in the sampled businesses indicated that the levels of EC adoption were higher where management support and commitment were relatively high. This finding lends credence to the body of work indicating that management support is positively associated with the successful acceptance of technologies in business organizations (Teo et. al., 1997; Premkumar & Roberts, 1999; Thong et. al., 1996). The study's result also showed that the availability of IS vendor support boded well for the spread of EC initiatives in businesses lacking such technical expertise. Given that prior studies have noted that low levels of IT skills and knowledge about EC concepts was the main barrier to EC adoption among small businesses in SSA, including Nigeria (Ifinedo, 2008; Ifinedo, 2006; Mbarika et.al., 2005; Olatokun & Kebonye, 2010) it is instructive to accept that external sources of technological expertise would be helpful to businesses lacking in such expertise.

The data did not support the view indicating that external pressure was an important factor that positively influences the adoption of EC by Nigerian small business. A plausible reason for this result might be the lack of critical mass among businesses in SSA (Ifinedo, 2008; Okoli, 2003; Uzoka et. al., 2007; Mutula & van Brakel, 2006; Macharia, 2009). Also, the data showed that the technological attributes of compatibility and complexity are insignificant in the adoption of EC for the sampled businesses. With respect to compatibility, the results are perhaps indicating that the Nigerian small businesses do not perceived EC to be consistent with their existing practices, and may hold a belief that such technologies do not meet their needs (Mutula & van Brakel, 2006; Aghaunor & Fotoh 2006). With respect to complexity, the result is inconsistent with the stated prediction. This particular result seems to be suggesting that practitioners in the sample may be finding EC relatively difficult to use and understand. As a consequence, the acceptance levels of EC by small businesses in Nigeria have not been positively encouraged. As well, organization readiness was found to be an insignificant predictor of EC adoption in the sample. To some extent, this particular finding corroborates observations related to the poor showing of organizational IS sophistication and computer knowledge among small businesses in SSA (ECA, 2000; Ifinedo, 2008; Okoli, 2003; Molla & Licker, 2005; Uzoka et. al., 2007; Ifinedo, 2006; Ayo et. al., 2008; Eze, 2008; K. Saffu et. al., 2007).

## Implication for Research and Policy Making

This research has implications for future study. First, the incorporation of both the DIT and TOE frameworks in this current study has engendered deeper insight regarding factors that influence the adoption of EC in Nigeria. Second, the dependent variable, i.e. adoption used in this study departs from prior research efforts that tend to operationalize such constructs with a single item of Use (Usage) or Intention to use. The utilization of such singular items may obfuscate reality and has, in fact, been criticized for limiting insight (Legris & Collerette, 2003). In that respect, the measures used to operationalize adoption in this study may be beneficial to others wishing to investigate comparable issues. Third, this research, in some respect, lends credence to findings and observations regarding the factors that influence the adoption of EC and similar innovations in SSA's business organizations. Fourth, it is possible that some of the unconfirmed hypotheses indicate issues that can be considered inhibitors of EC adoption in the country - and in the region as well - deserving of further attention.

By focusing on a less endowed part of the world i.e. SSA, this research has focused attention on possible factors or issues that could serve to inhibit/enable the adoption of e-commerce in that part of the world. Policy makers, industry leaders, and business executives wishing to have an understanding of some of the reasons why the spread of EC in the region have been minimal could benefit from the information provided in this research. Given that the study's respondents indicated a poor understanding of the compatibility of EC technologies in their business operations and they also viewed EC as a complex tool, this study recommends that more concerted efforts be made toward sensitizing business owners and their employees about the pertinence of such innovations in their business operations. In other words, there is a need to provide tailored EC mentoring, coaching, and training (Ifinedo, 2011) for such business in the region.

As relative advantage was shown to be an important factor for the adoption of EC in Nigerian small businesses, it is in order to suggest that by increasing user awareness of the benefits of EC technologies, more business would be positively encouraged to accept such technologies. IS vendor support matters in the adoption process. To that end, incentives could be provided by the authority to local IS vendors to assist more businesses acquire needed knowledge in the area. Relevant government agencies and other local sources of expertise can be marshaled towards providing such training to businesses requiring such knowledge. With this sort of support in place, it is to be expected that more and more businesses will acquire the confidence and knowledge to try out EC in their businesses. When knowledge of the relevance of technological innovations in business activities becomes deep-rooted and ubiquitous, critical mass in the acceptance of EC will accordingly follow. Ultimately, Nigerian businesses, their partners and customers will collectively be pushing and pulling themselves toward adopting EC use in their engagements and operations. Without a doubt, the Nigerian business environment and economy stand to profit hugely from the widespread use of such innovations.

## Limitations and Avenues for Future Research

First, despite the fact that common method bias was not seen to pose a problem for this study's data, it is still possible that respondents may be subject to a *halo effect*. Asking only one respondent to present a view on behalf of their organization may be problematic. Second, findings from this study cannot be generalized for the whole of Nigeria given that only one part of the country was sampled. Data from other parts of the country may be different from what is reported and discussed in this chapter. Accordingly, caution should be exercised in interpreting the results presented herein. Third, the research included the views of both owners and employees in the sampled organizations. It is possible that the views of both cohorts may differ somewhat on some of the issues presented in the questionnaire. The inclusion of the views of both cohorts might have negatively impacted the study's results.

This study opens up avenues for future research. Whenever possible some of the aforementioned limitations could be addressed in subsequent studies. This research effort can be replicated in other parts of Nigeria and in comparable SSA countries to reify or debunk claims presented in this study. The data used in this study is cross-sectional in nature; future efforts could consider using longitudinal data to facilitate more insight. Such factors as government support and the availability of financial resources not considered in this study should be explored in future research. The research framework could be used to study the impacts of similar factors in larger businesses in the country and across the region. Information from such an exercise could benefit research and policy making. Industry specific studies could also be commissioned to further enhance insight. The research framework could be further reinforced with the identification of relevant variables that could moderate the relationship between inhibiting/enabling factors and business' adoption of EC.

Future research using meta-analytic approaches could examine the enablers and inhibitors of EC in Nigeria and SSA. Knowledge from such efforts stands to consolidate theories related to the diffusion of EC and related innovations in Africa.

## CONCLUSION

This research drew from the diffusion of innovation and the TOE schema in investigating the adoption of EC in Nigerian small business organizations. The research showed that relative advantage of such technologies, management support and IS vendor support are significant predictors of the adoption of EC in Nigerian small businesses. The factors of organizational readiness, complexity, and compatibility of the technology, as well as external pressure were found to be insignificant for e-commerce adoption in the sampled Nigerian businesses. This research argued that these foregoing factors are, in fact, inhibitors of EC adoption among small business in Nigeria (and in SSA). Knowledge of the relative advantage of EC was found to be the best enabler of the adoption process of such innovations in the research context.

Overall, the study' findings enrich the discourse related to the reticence of Nigerian small businesses in adopting EC for business operations. It is hoped that the discussions and conclusions made in this study benefits practitioners and policy makers in the country and in comparable countries in SSA. Importantly, this current effort contributes to the growing body of knowledge regarding the factors influencing EC adoption in the developing parts of the world, and it seeks to complement past research efforts in the SSA region in this area of research. More work is expected.

## ACKNOWLEDGMENT

The authors are grateful to the participants of this research. Comments and suggestions received from anonymous reviewers of an earlier draft of this chapter are appreciated.

*Contributions:* Prof. C. Ayo and Mrs U. Ekong collected the data in Nigeria. Prof. P. Ifinedo and Mrs. A. Ifinedo performed the data analysis. Also, Prof. P. Ifinedo designed the research questionnaire and wrote this chapter.

## REFERENCES

Aghaunor, L., & Fotoh, X. (2006). *Factors affecting e-commerce adoption in Nigerian Banks*. Sweden: Jonkoping University.

Al-Qirim, N. (2007). The adoption of ecommerce communications and applications technologies in small businesses *in New Zealand. Electronic Commerce Research and Applications*, *6*(4), 462–473. doi:10.1016/j.elerap.2007.02.012

Attewell, P. (1992). Technology diffusion and organizational learning: The case of business computing. *Organization Science*, *3*(1), 1–19. doi:10.1287/orsc.3.1.1

Ayo, C. K., Adebiyi, A., Fatudimu, I. T., & Ekong, U. O. (2008). A framework for e-commerce implementation: Nigeria a Case Study. *Journal of Internet Banking and Commerce*, *13*(2), 1–12.

Caldeira, M. M., & Ward, J. M. (2002). Understanding the successful adoption and use of IS/IT in SMEs: An explanation from Portuguese manufacturing industries. *Information Systems Journal*, *12*(2), 121–152. doi:10.1046/j.1365-2575.2002.00119.x

Carmichael, C., Turgoose, C., Gary, M. O., & Todd, C. (2000). Innovation and SMEs the case of Yorkshire, UK. *Journal of Industry and Higher Education*, *14*(4), 244–248. doi:10.5367/000000000101295147

Chin, W. (1998). Issues and opinion on structural equation modeling. *Management Information Systems Quarterly*, *22*(1), vii–xvi.

Chircu, A. M., & Kauffman, R. J. (2000). Limits to value in electronic commerce-related IT investments. *Journal of Management Information Systems, 17*(2), 59–80.

Chong, S., & Pervan, G. (2007). Factors influencing the extent of deployment of electronic commerce for small and medium-sized enterprises. *Journal of Electronic Commerce in Organizations, 5*(1), 1–29. doi:10.4018/jeco.2007010101

CIA WorldFact. (2011). *Nigeria Reports*. Available at https://www.cia.gov/library/publications/the-world-factbook/geos/ni.html. Accessed April 3, 2011.

Cragg, P., & King, M. (1993). Small-firm computing: Motivators and inhibitors. *Management Information Systems Quarterly, 17*(1), 47–60. doi:10.2307/249509

ECA (Economic Commission for Africa). (2000). *The ECA/IDRC: Pan-African Initiative on e-Commerce*. Available at http://www.uneca.org/codi/documents/pdf/doc30en.pdf

EIU (Economic Intelligence Unit). (2011). *Global intelligence and analysis*. Available at http://www.eiu.com/public/.

Eze, U. C. (2008). E-business deployment in Nigerian financial firms: An empirical analysis of key factors. *International Journal of E-Business Research, 4*(2), 29–47. doi:10.4018/jebr.2008040103

Farhoomand, A. F., Tuunainen, V. K., & Yee, L. W. (2000). Barriers to global electronic commerce: A cross-country study of Hong Kong and Finland. *Journal of Organizational Computing and Electronic Commerce, 10*(1), 23–48. doi:10.1207/S15327744JOCE100102

Fornell, C., & Larcker, D. F. (1981). Evaluating structural equations models with unobservable variables and measurement error. *JMR, Journal of Marketing Research, 18*(1), 39–50. doi:10.2307/3151312

Gatignon, H., & Robertson, T. S. (1989). Technology diffusion: An empirical test of competitive effects. *Journal of Marketing, 53*(1), 35–49. doi:10.2307/1251523

Gibbs, J. L., & Kraemer, K. L. (2004). A cross-country investigation of the determinants of scope of e-commerce use: An institutional approach. *Electronic Markets, 14*(2), 124–137. doi:10.1080/10196780410001675077

Grandon, E. E., & Pearson, J. (2004). Electronic commerce adoption: An empirical study of small and medium US Businesses. *Information & Management, 42*(1), 197–216. doi:10.1016/j.im.2003.12.010

Grau. J. (2008). *Canada B2C e-Commerce: A work in progress*. Available at http://www.emarketer.com/Reports/All/Emarketer_2000547.aspx.

Hadidi, R. (2003). The status of e-finance in developing countries. *Electronic Journal of Information Systems in Developing Countries, 11*(5), 1–5.

Hair, J. F. Jr, Anderson, R. E., Thatham, R. L., & Black, W. C. (1998). *Multivariate data analysis*. Upper Saddle River, NJ: Prentice-Hall International, Inc.

Hart, P. J., & Saunders, C. S. (1998). Emerging electronic partnerships: Antecedents and dimensions of EDI use from the supplier's perspective. *Journal of Management Information Systems, 14*(4), 87–111.

Ho, S.-C., Kaufmann, R. J., & Liang, T.-P. (2007). A growth theory perspective on B2C E-commerce growth in Europe: An exploratory study. *Electronic Commerce Research and Applications, 6*(3), 237–259. doi:10.1016/j.elerap.2006.06.003

Hox, J. J., & de Leeuw, E. D. (1994). A comparison of nonresponse in mail, telephone, and face-to-face surveys. Applying multilevel modeling to meta-analysis. *Quality & Quantity, 28*, 329–344. doi:10.1007/BF01097014

Iacobucci, D., & Churchill, G. A. (2009). *Marketing research: Methodological foundations (with Qualtrics Card)* (10th ed.). Cincinnati, OH: South-Western College Publishing.

Iacovou, C. L., Benbasat, I., & Dexter, A. S. (1995). Electronic data interchange and small organizations: adoption and impact of technology. *Management Information Systems Quarterly, 19*(4), 465–485. doi:10.2307/249629

Ifinedo, P. (2005).Measuring the e-readiness of five Sub-Saharan African (SSA) countries: An assessment of SSA'S preparedness for the global networked economy, In Palvia P. and Pinjani, P. (Eds.), *Proceedings of the 6th. Global Information Technology Management Conference (GITM '05), Anchorage, Alaska,* (pp. 5 – 8)

Ifinedo, P. (2007). A Study of the relationships between economic climates, national culture and E-government e-readiness: A global perspective. In Kurihara, Y., Takaya, S., Harui, H., & Kamae, H. (Eds.), *Information Technology and Economic Development* (pp. 234–247). Hershey, PA: IGI Global. doi:10.4018/978-1-59904-579-5.ch017

Ifinedo, P. (2008). Internet commerce and SMEs in Sub-Saharan Africa: Perspectives from Nigeria, *Conference on Information Technology and Economic Development (CITED2008)*, (pp. 1- 8)

Ifinedo, P. (2009). The Internet and SMEs in Sub-Saharan Africa. In Mehdi, K. (Ed.), *Encyclopedia of Information Science and Technology* (2nd ed., pp. 2183–2188). Hershey, PA: Idea Group Publishing. doi:10.4018/978-1-60566-026-4.ch344

Ifinedo, P. (2011). (Forthcoming). Internet/e-business technologies acceptance in Canada's SMEs: An exploratory investigation. *Internet Research.* doi:10.1108/10662241111139309

Ifinedo, (2006). Factors affecting e-business Adoption by SMEs in Sub-Saharan Africa: An exploratory study from Nigeria. In N. Al-Qirim (Ed.), *Global Electronic Business Research: Opportunities and Directions*, (pp. 319 – 346) Hershey, PA: Idea Group Publishing,

Internetworldstats (2011). *Country Reports*. Available at http://www.internetworldstats.com/

ITU International Telecommunication Union. (2011*). Weekly Update*. Available at http://www.itu.int/en/pages/default.aspx.

Jeyaraj, A., Rottman, J. W., & Lacity, M. C. (2006). A review of the predictors, linkages, and biases in IT innovation adoption research. *Journal of Information Technology, 21*(1), 1–23. doi:10.1057/palgrave.jit.2000056

Kendall, J. D., Tung, L. L., Chua, K. H., Hong, C., Ng, D., & Tan, S. M. (2001). Receptivity of Singapore's SMEs to electronic commerce adoption. *The Journal of Strategic Information Systems, 10*(3), 223–242. doi:10.1016/S0963-8687(01)00048-8

Kula, V., & Tatoglu, E. (2003). An exploratory study of Internet adoption by SMEs in an emerging market economy. *European Business Review, 15*(5), 324–333. doi:10.1108/09555340310493045

Leadpile, (2010). *United States E-commerce Sales to Top 120 Billion, says Leadpile*. Available at http://www.leadpile.com/press/2006-10-24_press1.html.

Legris, P., Ingham, J., & Collerette, P. (2003). Why do people use information technology?: A critical review of the technology acceptance model. *Information & Management, 40*(3), 191–204. doi:10.1016/S0378-7206(01)00143-4

Looi, H. C. (2005). E-commerce adoption in Brunei Darussalam: A quantitative analysis of factors influencing its adoption. *Communications of the Association for Information Systems, 15*(3), 61–81.

Love, P. E. D., & Irani, Z. (2004). An exploratory study of information technology evaluation and benefits management practices of SMEs in the construction industry. *Information & Management, 42*, 227–242. doi:10.1016/j.im.2003.12.011

Macharia, J. (2009). Factors affecting the adoption of e-commerce in SMEs in Kenya, International. *Journal of Technology Intelligence and Planning, 5*(4), 386–401. doi:10.1504/IJTIP.2009.029377

Mbarika, V. W., Okoli, C., Byrd, T. A., & Datta, P. (2005). The neglected continent of IS research: A research agenda for Sub-Saharan Africa. *Journal of the Association for Information Systems, 6*(5), 130–170.

Mehrtens, J., Cragg, P. B., & Mills, A. M. (2001). A Model of internet adoption by SMEs. *Information & Management, 39*(3), 165–176. doi:10.1016/S0378-7206(01)00086-6

Mirchandani, A. A., & Motwani, J. (2001). Understanding small business electronic adoption: An empirical analysis. *Journal of Computer Information Systems, 41*(3), 70–73.

Molla, A., & Licker, P. S. (2005). eCommerce adoption in developing countries: a model and instrument. *Information & Management, 42*, 877–899. doi:10.1016/j.im.2004.09.002

Mutula, S. M., & van Brakel, P. (2006). E-readiness of SMEs in the ICT sector in Botswana with respect to information access. *The Electronic Library, 24*(3), 402–417. doi:10.1108/02640470610671240

Nunnaly, J. C. (1978). *Psychometric theory*. New York, NY: McGraw-Hill.

Okoli, C. (2003). *Expert assessments of e-commerce in Sub-Saharan Africa: A theoretical model of infrastructure and culture for doing business using the Internet*. Unpublished PhD thesis, Louisiana State University, USA.

Olatokun, W., & Kebonye, M. (2010). e-Commerce technology adoption by SMEs in Botswana, International. *Journal of Emerging Technologies and Society, 8*(1), 42–56.

Oxley, J. E., & Yeung, B. (2001). E-commerce readiness: Institutional environment and international competitiveness. *Journal of International Business Studies, 32*(4), 705–723. doi:10.1057/palgrave.jibs.8490991

Pflughoeft, K., Ramamurthy, K., Soofi, E., Yasai-Ardekani, M., & Zahedi, F. (2003). Multiple conceptualizations of small Business web use and benefit. *Decision Sciences, 34*(3), 467–512. doi:10.1111/j.1540-5414.2003.02539.x

Podsakoff, P. M., MacKenzie, S. B., Lee, J. Y., & Podsakoff, N. P. (2003). Common method biases in behavioral research: A critical review of the literature and recommended remedies. *The Journal of Applied Psychology, 88*(5), 879–903. doi:10.1037/0021-9010.88.5.879

Poon, S., & Swatman, P. (1999). An exploratory study of small business Internet commerce issues. *Information & Management, 35*(1), 9–18. doi:10.1016/S0378-7206(98)00079-2

Premkumar, G., & Roberts, M. (1999). Adoption of new information technologies in rural small businesses, Omega: International. *Journal of Management Science, 27*(4), 467–484.

Ringle, C. M., Wende, S., & Will, A. (2005). *SmartPLS 2.0 (M3) beta, Hamburg*: Retrieved from: http://www.smartpls.de.

Rogers, E. M. (2003). *Diffusion of innovations* (5th ed.). New York: The Free Press.

Saffu, K., Walker, J. H., & Hinson, R. (2007). An empirical study of perceived strategic value and adoption constructs: the Ghanaian case. *Management Decision, 45*(7), 1083–1101. doi:10.1108/00251740710773925

Scupola, A. (2003). The adoption of Internet commerce by SMEs in the South of Italy: An environmental, technological and organizational perspective. *Journal of Global Information Technology Management*, *6*(1), 52–71.

Shih, C.-F., Dedrick, J., & Kraemer, K. L. (2005). Rule of law and the international diffusion of e-commerce. *Communications of the ACM*, *48*(11), 57–62. doi:10.1145/1096000.1096005

Tan, J., Tyler, K., & Manica, A. (2007). Business-to-business adoption of eCommerce in China. *Information & Management*, *44*, 332–351. doi:10.1016/j.im.2007.04.001

Teo, H. H., Tan, B. C. Y., & Wei, K. K. (1997). Organizational transformation using Electronic Data Interchange: The case of TradeNet in Singapore. *Journal of Management Information Systems*, *13*(4), 139–166.

Thong, J., & Yap, C. (1995). CEO characteristics, organisational, characteristics and information technology adoption in small business. *Omega: International Journal of Management Sciences*, *23*(4), 429–442. doi:10.1016/0305-0483(95)00017-I

Thong, J. Y. L., Yap, C. S., & Raman, K. S. (1996). Top management support, external expertise and information systems implementation in small business. *Information Systems Research*, *7*(2), 248–267. doi:10.1287/isre.7.2.248

Tornatzky, L. G., & Fleischer, M. (1990). *The processes of technological innovation*. Lexington, MA: Lexington Books.

Tornatzky, L. G., & Klein, R. J. (1982). Innovation characteristics and innovation adoption-implementation: A meta-analysis of findings. *IEEE Transactions on Engineering Management*, *29*(1), 28–45.

Turban, E., King, D., & Lang, J. (2010). *Introduction to electronic commerce. New York, NY*. NY: Prentice Hall.

UNCTAD. (2008). *Information Economy Report 2007-2008 Science and technology for development: The new paradigm of ICT*. Available at http://r0.unctad.org/ecommerce/ier07_en.htm. Accessed 12 Jan., 2011.

Uzoka, F-M. E., Seleka, G.G., & Khengere, J. (2007). E-commerce adoption in developing countries: a case analysis of environmental and organisational inhibitors, International *Journal of Information Systems and Change Management*, (3), 232-260.

Van der Deen, M. (2005). Measuring e-Business Adoption in SME. In During, W., Oakey, R., & Kauser, S. (Eds.), *New technology-based firms in the new millennium* (*Vol. 5*). Amsterdam, Holland: Elsevier.

WEF (World Economic Forum). (2011). *Global Competitiveness 2009-2010*. Available at http://www.weforum.org/reports.

## APPENDIX

*Table 5. The measurement items and scales*

| Relative Advantage |
|---|
| E-commerce solutions would allow our firm to manage its operations efficiently. |
| E-commerce solutions would improve the quality of our operations. |
| E-commerce solutions would enhance the effectiveness of our firm's operations. |
| E-commerce solutions would enable us to perform our operations more quickly. |
| E-commerce solutions would give us a greater control over our operations. |
| Compatibility |
| Use of E-commerce solutions would be compatible with all aspects of our business operations. |
| Use of E-commerce solutions would fit well with the way we operate. |
| Use E-commerce solutions would fit into our working style. |
| Use of E-commerce solutions would be completely compatible with our current business operations. |
| Complexity |
| Using E-commerce solutions would require a lot of mental effort |
| Using E-commerce solutions would be frustrating |
| Using E-commerce solutions would be too complex for our business operations |
| Management Support |
| Management is interested in the use of E-commerce solutions in our operations. |
| Management is supportive of the use of E-commerce solutions in our operations. |
| Our business has a clear vision regarding the use of E-commerce solutions. |
| Management communicates the need for E-commerce solutions usage in the firm. |
| Organizational Readiness |
| Our firm knows how IT can be used to support our operations. |
| Our firm has a good understanding of how E-commerce solutions can be used in our business. |
| We have the necessary technical, managerial and other skills to implement E-commerce solutions |
| Our business values and norms would not prevent us from adopting E-commerce solutions in our operations. |
| External pressure |
| Some of our competitors have already started using internet/e-business technologies. |
| Our competitors know the importance of E-commerce and are using them for operations. |
| We know our customers are ready to do business over the Internet. |
| Our customers are demanding the use of E-commerce in doing business with them. |
| Our partners are demanding the use of E-commerce in doing business with them. |
| We know our suppliers and partners are ready to do business over the Internet. |
| IS vendor support |

*continued on following page*

*Table 5. Continued*

| Relative Advantage |
|---|
| IS vendors in the region are actively promoting EC systems and other technologies by providing incentives for adoption. |
| IS vendors are encouraging our business to adopt EC systems by providing us with free training sessions. |
| We can obtain support easily from local IS vendors as we implement EC systems. |
| Adoption of EC |
| Our company makes use of EC systems, very often. |
| Our company uses EC systems, at all times, for its transactions. |
| Our company uses EC systems for its critical operations. |
| The number of business operations and activities in my company that requires EC systems is high. |

# Chapter 10
# An Empirical Evaluation of the Effects of Gender Differences and Self-Efficacy in the Adoption of E-Banking in Nigeria:
## A Modified Technology Acceptance Model

**Charles K. Ayo**
*Covenant University, Nigeria*

**Uyinomen O. Ekong**
*University of Uyo, Nigeria*

**Princely Ifinedo**
*Cape Breton University, Canada*

**Aderonke A. Oni**
*Covenant University, Nigeria*

## ABSTRACT

*The issues of gender disparity in the usage of information technology (IT), as well as self-efficacy, have received considerable interest and attention among researchers in recent times. Prior research has identified that gender differences and self-efficiency affect the attitude towards adoption and use of technology. In general, females are believed to be disadvantaged compared to their male counterparts with respect to IT usage and acceptance. The reasoning is that males are mostly more exposed to technology and tend to have more proficiency with such tools. Very little information exists in the extant literature regarding perceptions in developing parts of the world, including Africa. In this chapter, an empirical evaluation of the issues in the context of e-banking will be made in Lagos (Nigeria) and its environs. An extended Technology Acceptance Model (TAM) will be used as a conceptual framework to guide the discourse. Data analysis was done on SPSS 15.0. The study's results showed that gender differences moderated the acceptance of e-banking of users in the research context. Namely, computer self efficacy and perceived ease of use were of concerns to females, but less so for their male counterparts. Also, perceived usefulness of e-banking is discovered to be the most influencing factor for male users. The study's implications for research and practice are discussed in the chapter.*

DOI: 10.4018/978-1-4666-1637-0.ch010

## INTRODUCTION

The advent of electronic banking (e-banking) in Nigeria in the past few decades have greatly transformed the way banking activities are carried out and customers are reaping the benefits of such platforms (Chiemeke et al., 2006; Emordi, 2007; Adesina et al., 2008; Agbada, 2008). Some of the derived benefits to the customers in Nigeria include flexibility and convenience (Akpan, 2008; Gholami et al., 2010). The traditional system of banking in Nigeria is characterized with inconveniences that make banking a tedious task to customers (Ezeoha, 2005; Emordi, 2007; Akpan, 2008). It can be argued that banking is prone to errors and often times customers do spend long times in queues at banking halls in countries such as Nigeria (Emordi, 2007).

The term e-banking has been interchangeably used with online banking, internet banking and PC banking (Xu et al, 2006). However, for the purpose of this study, we will use the term e-banking to refer to all of the aforementioned examples. Pikkarainen et al. (2004) defined online banking as an Internet portal, through which customers can use different kinds of services ranging from bill payments to engraining in online investments. Here in this chapter, e-banking is defined as banking services such as transfer of funds, payment of bills, withdrawal, deposits, access to account information that are carried out on a bank's website through a personal computer (PC) connected to the Internet, WAP enabled mobile network, Automated Teller Machines Networks, automated telephone, web TV, SMS/FAX messaging and so forth. Without a doubt, the major goal of any large or small bank is to grow the number of their valuable customers through retention; in general, banks try to increase their offerings, product channels, and services (Xu et al, 2006).

Prior investigation of consumers' adoption of e-banking in Nigeria revealed that banks customers, who are active users of e-banking system tend to use it because of the convenience, ease of use, and the efficiency associated with the e-banking platforms (Akpan, 2008; Adesina et al., 2008; Gholami et al., 2010). The impact of e-banking in Nigeria banking system is evident in the increased speed; shorten processing periods, improved flexibility of business transactions and reduction in costs associated with having personnel serve customers physically (Chiemeke et al., 2006; Emordi, 2007; Adesina et al. 2008; Gholami et al., 2010). In brief, e-banking is an important platform for the country's economic development (Chiemeke et al., 2006; Emordi, 2007; Akpan, 2008).

Given the benefits of such a platform to users, it is important to investigate factors that influence the acceptance of e-banking platforms in Nigeria. Prior research has identified that gender differences and self-efficiency affect the attitude towards adoption and use of technology, in general. In short, females are believed to be disadvantaged compared to their male counterparts with respect to using IT innovations and applications. The reasoning is that males are mostly more exposed to technology and tend to have more proficiency with such tools (Venkatesh & Morris, 2000; Van Slyke et al., 2002; Ilie et al., 2005). Similarly, the literature suggests that self-efficacy has an effect on IT usage (Bandura, 1982; Compeau & Higgins, 1995).

These foregoing studies were carried out in the developed West. According to Hofstede (2001) perceptions regarding IT use, in differing parts of the world, vary significantly due to cultural underpinnings and conditioning. That being said, very little information exists in the extant literature regarding the effects of gender differences and self-efficacy on e-banking in developing countries, including Nigeria. The main objective of this paper is to investigate the impact of gender differences and computer self-efficacy on the adoption of e-banking in Nigeria.

## E-Banking in Nigeria

Nigeria banking system changed in 2004 after the Central Bank of Nigeria (CBN) introduced a reformation exercise that aimed to reduce the number of banks in the country; the essence of the exercise was to make emerging banks in the country stronger and reliable (Ezeoha, 2005; Adesina et al, 2008). One of the services that the CBN wants to promote is e-banking (Akpan, 2008; Emordi, 2007). Currently, e-banking in Nigeria has advanced to the point where almost all banks in the country are able to carry out sophisticated online services and transactions (Agbada, 2008). As a consequence, e-banking has gained wider acceptance among bank customers in Nigeria (Chiemeke et al., 2006; Akpan, 2008; Adesina et al., 2008). In fact, the trend is now moving toward mobile banking (m-banking) with customers able to perform banking services anytime, anywhere (Emordi, 2007; Adesina et al. 2008).

Several online banking services are now available in Nigeria. For example, the introduction of Magnetic Ink Character Recognition (MICR) cheques has revolutionized e-payment systems solutions in the country (Adesina et al. 2008). This was followed by the introduction of the Automated Teller Machines (ATMs) for dispensing of cash, checking for account balance, and paying utility bills in the early 1990s. By 1993 smart cards payment system was introduced by Central Bank of Nigeria (CBN) to deal with financial obligations (Agbada, 2008; Akpan, 2008). Debit cards (VISA, MasterCards, Euro cards, American Express, Valucard, EasyCash, and Smart pay) are used to make purchases and cash withdrawal in the country.

The first Credit Card was introduced in Nigeria in 2004 by Master Card in conjunction with Cards Technology Limited and Ecobank (one of the country's local banks). This enables the holder to make purchases or withdrawal of cash up to certain limits. By the end of 2007, the number of cards issued in Nigeria increased by 200% (i.e. from four million to twelve million cards) (Emordi, 2007). Today, other forms of e-banking such as ATM, mobile banking, Point of Sale (POS) and Web banking have become commonplace in the country. Table 1 shows the Economic Report of CBN for the first half of 2008 with a summary of the value and volume of electronic payment system as a percentage of total transactions in Nigeria (Emordi, 2007).

*Table 1. Percentage value and volume of e-payment in Nigeria*

| Channel of transaction | Volume in Percentage (%) | Value in Percentage (%) |
|---|---|---|
| ATM | 87 | 90.8 |
| Mobile | 7.3 | 0.10 |
| Web (Internet) | 3.2 | 4.8 |
| POS | 2.5 | 4.3 |

Despite the reported growth in the acceptance of e-banking and e-payment solutions in Nigeria, research studies (Ezeoha, 2005; Chiemeke et al, 2006; and Agbada, 2008; Adesina et al, 2008; Gholami et al., 2010) have shown that there are still problems facing the spread of e-banking in Nigeria. Examples of inhibiting factors noted in these studies include insecurity, fraud, lack of standardization of channels, illiteracy, age, and inadequate operational facilities such as telecommunication and electricity supply). This current research seeks to add to the discourse of factors affecting the acceptance of e-banking in Nigeria by investigating the influences of computer self-efficacy and gender differences in the context of the technology acceptance model (TAM), which prior research apparently did not consider. It is hoped that our contribution will provide new useful insights to both the practitioners' and researchers' communities.

## BACKGROUND THEORY: THE TECHOLOGY ACCEPTANCE MODEL (TAM)

The technology acceptance model (TAM) is regarded as the most widely used theoretical framework for assessing the acceptance of technologies in the literature (Legris et al., 2003). The TAM was developed by Davis (1989) who drew from Theory of Reasoned Action (TRA) proposed by Fishbein and Ajzen (1975). The TAM proposes that users' acceptance of a new IS can be predicted by the users' perceptions. These perceptions include the ease of use and usefulness of the IS (Davis, 1989). Constructs in the TAM include Perceived ease of use and Perceived usefulness. Researchers also tend to replace Usage in the original TAM with the Intention Use variable (Ifinedo, 2007; Lallmahamood, 2007).

The Perceived ease of use describes "The degree to which a person believes that using a particular system would be free of effort" (Davis, 1989, p. 320). Perceived usefulness describes the user's perceptions of the expected benefits derived from using a particular IS system (Davis, 1989). Intention to use Usage is theorized to be influenced by perceived usefulness and perceived ease of use. It is common for researchers to extend the TAM to include other relevant variables (Wang et al. 2003; Pikkarainen et al., 2004; Ifinedo, 2007; Lallmahamood, 2007; Hanudin 2007; Venkatesh and Bala, 2008).

### E-banking and the TAM

Previous research has used the TAM (or extended version of that framework) to investigate perceptions in the context of e-banking (Chau and Lai, 2003; Wang et al., 2003; Pikkarainen et al., 2004; Lai and Li, 2005; Ndubisi, 2007; Lallmahamood, 2007). For instance, Lallmahamood (2007) found Perceived ease of use and Perceived usefulness positively influence the Intention to Use e-banking in a developing country i.e. Malaysia. The same result was reported in other advanced countries as well (Chau & Lai, 2003; Wang et al., 2003). Riquelme and Rios (2010) showed that Perceived ease of use has a stronger influence on female respondents than male users of mobile banking. Similarly, Ndubisi's (2007) study found customers' perceptions and intention to adopt Internet banking was moderated by computer self-efficacy. Also, Hanudin (2007) found computer self-efficacy as a major influence on perceived ease of use in the context of Internet banking system. Davis (1989) had suggested that attitudes toward the use of technologies often positively influence the behavioral intention to use such systems.

### Gender Differences and the Acceptance of IT

The issue of gender difference and general attitude toward IT use has received considerable interest among researchers (Venkatesh and Morris, 2000; Van Slyke et al., 2002; Ilie et al., 2005; Nel & Raleting, 2010; Li and Kirkup, 2007; Rao & Troshani, 2007; Nysveen et al., 2005). For example, previous research has identified that gender difference affect the attitude towards adoption and use of technology. It was noted that females are often less advantaged compared to their male counterparts with regard to IT usage (Li and Kirkup, 2007). Likewise, Vankatesh and Morris (2000) argued that women are more likely to be influenced by social factors when it comes to adopting new technologies. Females also tend to have unequal access to technologies and exhibit more negative inclinations or attitudes toward IT (Van Slyke et al., 2002; Ilie et al., 2005; Nysveen et al., 2005; Nel & Raleting, 2010; Li & Kirkup, 2007).

## RESEARCH MODEL AND HYPOTHESES FORMULATION

The proposed research framework and the formulated hypotheses are highlighted in Figure

*Figure 1. Research Model and Hypothesis*

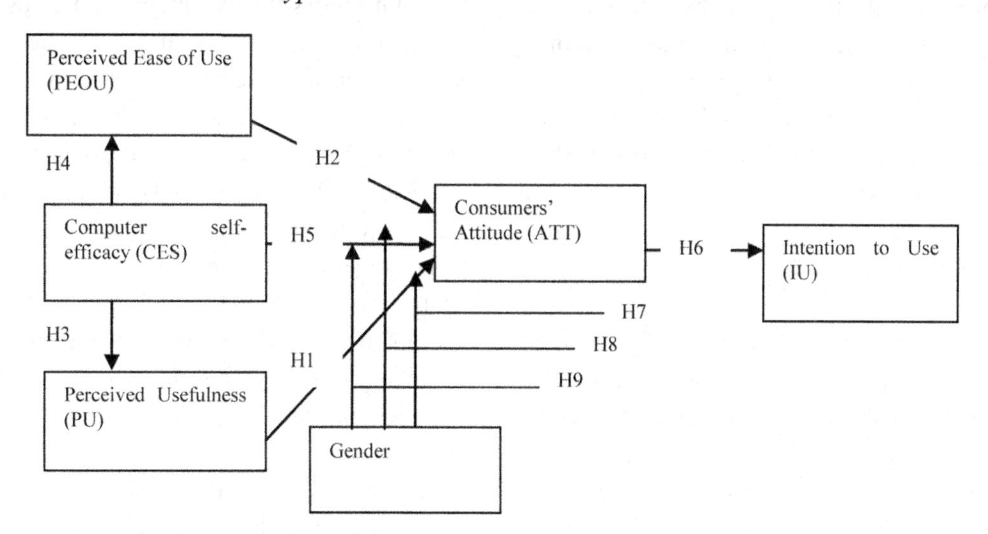


1. Discussions on each of the hypotheses are presented accordingly.

## Perceived Usefulness and Perceived Ease of Use

The TAM posits that PU is a significant factor affecting acceptance of an information system (Davis, 1989). That is, people tend to use an application to the extent they believe it will aid their performance. Similarly, according to the TAM perceived ease of use (PEOU) is a major factor affecting the acceptance of IS (Davis, 1989; Venkatesh & Bala, 2008). Several studies have provided support for this view in the context of e-banking (Wang et al., 2003; Pikkarainen et al., 2004; Lai & Li, 2005; Ndubisi, 2007; Lallmahamood, 2007). Thus, it is hypothesized that:

**H1:** Perceived usefulness (PU) will have a positive influence on customers' attitude toward e-banking acceptance in Nigeria.

**H2:** Perceived ease of use (PEOU) will have a positive influence on customers' attitude toward e-banking acceptance in Nigeria.

## Computer Self-Efficacy

Bandura (1982) defined self-efficacy as "judgments of how well one can execute courses of action required to deal with prospective situations." Self-efficacy beliefs are theorized to function as proximal determinants of behavior (Bandura, 1982; Compeau & Higgins, 1995). Indeed, Venkatesh and Davis (2000) provided evidence suggesting that self-efficacy is positively related to IS acceptance. Others such as Compeau and Higgins (1995) and Morris and Turner (2001) have also reported findings that affirm such a relationship. Furthermore, the relevance of computer self-efficacy to both perceived ease of use and perceived ease of use has been supported by prior studies (Venkatesh & Davis, 2000; Hanudin, 2007). Indeed, Hanudin (2007) found that computer self-efficacy has positive effects on both perceived usefulness and perceived ease of use of Internet banking in Malaysia. Thus, the following hypotheses are proposed:

**H3:** Computer self-efficacy will have a positive influence on perceived ease of use of e-banking systems in Nigeria.

**H4:** Computer self-efficacy will have a positive influence on perceived usefulness of the e-banking systems in Nigeria

**H5:** Computer self-efficacy will have a positive influence on customer's attitude toward the use of e-banking systems in Nigeria

## Customers' Attitudes

Davis (1989) and Karjaluoto et al. (2002) defined attitude as the users' desirability to use the system. Attitude is referred to as the driver of consumers' utility; it reveals the perceptions of usefulness, credibility and individual preferences to a phenomenon (Jahangir & Begum, 2007). It has been suggested that consumer's attitudes do have a strong, direct and positive effect on consumers' intention to actually use new information system (Jahangir & Begum, 2007). In fact, e-banking users' attitude varied in terms of perceptions regarding service offered, risk involved, personalization, visual appeal, navigation, and enjoyment. *Ceteris paribus*, when customers' attitudes of people who use e-banking in Nigeria is generally positive, it is to be expected that their Intention to use such platforms will be high as well. Thus, it is predicted that:

**H6:** Customers' attitude will have a positive influence on the Intention to use e-banking systems in Nigeria

## The Moderating Variable: Gender

Gender has been reported in the relevant literature to moderate the adoption of technology and related applications (Venkatesh & Morris, 2000; Li & Kirkup, 2007; Nysveen et al., 2005). Prior research revealed that men tend to exhibit task-oriented attitudes to indicate that they have a better understanding of the usefulness of technology than women (Venkatesh & Morris, 2000; Minton & Scheneider, 1980). Some of these previous studies also suggest that males tend to have more access to technologies than women; such disparities in use and access tend to cause a gap between the sexes when it comes to accepting technologies (Van Slyke et al., 2002; Ilie et al., 2005; Nel & Raleting, 2010). Bozionelos (1996) and Riquelme and Rios (2010) showed that perceived ease of use has a stronger influence on female respondents than male users of mobile banking. The literature on the moderating effects of gender on the other factors in this study is rare; nonetheless, the next set of hypotheses is formulated as follows to enhance our understanding in the area.

**H7:** Gender will moderate the relationship between Perceived usefulness and Customers' attitude toward e-banking systems acceptance in Nigeria

**H8:** Gender will moderate the relationship between Perceived Ease of Use and Customers' attitude toward e-banking systems acceptance in Nigeria

**H9:** Gender will moderate the relationship between Computer self-efficacy and Customers' attitude toward e-banking systems acceptance in Nigeria

# RESEARCH METHODOLOGY

The survey research strategy was used in this study as it affords the researchers an opportunity to understand the phenomenon under investigation with empirical data (Ifinedo, 2011).

## Data Collection

A survey was conducted to validate the proposed research model. The study' population included bank customers in Lagos and its environs that use e-banking platforms. A questionnaire survey was developed from previously validated scales. This was sent to respondents in order to obtain their views on the issues under focus. 200 questionnaires were distributed to the selected bank customers in the area. 172 responses were received of which 22 were deemed invalid as they were incomplete. The remaining 150 valid questionnaires were used for data analysis. The effective response rate is 75%. Of the respondents, 48.0% of them were females while 52.0% are males. The statistical package for social sciences (SPSS) version 15.0 was used for analysis.

### Research Instrument

The questionnaire was divided into two parts. The first part consists of demographic profile and information regarding Internet usage of the respondents. The second part consists of 23 questions i.e. 5 questions each for the Perceived ease of use and Perceived usefulness; these were obtained from Davis (1989) and Karjaluoto et al. (2002). Six (6) questions were used to operationalize Computer self-efficacy; these were adapted from Compeau and Higgins (1995) and Pikkarainen et al. (2004). Three (3) questions were used to represents Consumers' attitude; these were taken from Jahangir and Begum (2007). The four (4) used to represent Intention to use were modified from Lallmahamood (2007) and Ifinedo (2007). The participants were asked to indicate their choice on a Likert-type scales ranging from "strongly disagree" (1) to "strongly agree" (5). The questionnaire items were adopted from the following prior studies. A full list of the constructs and their measurement items are provided in the Appendix.

### Demographic Profile and Technology Usage of Respondents

Table 2 shows the demographic profile of the respondents. 82.6 percent of the respondents is between ages 21–50; 65.3 percent of them have B.Sc/HND qualifications. Table 3 shows the analysis of the technology usage for the respondents. Despite high level of computer and internet use at home and work place by the respondents, the data still indicates that 18.7% of the respondents conduct online banking transaction. However, 74 percent of them use ATM machines. A good number of the respondents use internet and the internet at work, home and Cybercafés. A small percentage use wireless phones for banking.

## DATA ANALYSIS

To test the formulated hypotheses, a multivariate analytical methodology involving path analysis was used to empirically examine the sets of relationships in the form of linear causal models (Hair et al., 1998). The use path analysis in this research is consistent with approaches used by others in similar studies (Dishaw & Strong, 1999; Lee et al., 2001, Klopping et al., 2004). To determine the effect of gender differences in the model, separate analyses were carried out for both sexes. The individual path analysis for the two groups showed that not all the constructs in the model have significant effects in the research conceptualization.

H1 is accepted at 0.01 significant level (Sig = .003). H2 is significant at 5% level with Sig = .005. H3 is also supported (Sig = .007) to indicate that computer self-efficacy has a positive effect on perceived usefulness. Similarly, the data supported H4 (Sig = .012) to indicate that computer self-efficacy has positive effects on perceived ease of use. H5 is not confirmed (Sig = 0.42). H6 is supported to show the costumers' attitude has significant effect on the intentions to use e-banking systems in Nigeria (Sig = .005).

A split data was used with the hope it will enable useful insight regarding the effects of gender differences in the research model to emerge. Table 4 highlights the key information in that respect. Namely, there was no significant difference between both groups regarding the effect of perceived usefulness on customers' attitude to e-banking. The data showed that the path coefficient of CSE to ATT for the female has negative coefficient with a significance value of $p < 0.010$

*Table 2. Demographic profile of the respondents*

| Gender | | | |
|---|---|---|---|
| | | Frequency | Percent |
| Valid | Male | 78 | 52.0 |
| | Female | 60 | 40.0 |
| | Total | 138 | 92.0 |
| Missing | System | 12 | 8.0 |
| Total | | 150 | 150 |
| **Educational Background** | | | |
| | | Frequency | Percent |
| Valid | Undergraduate | 8 | 5.0 |
| | HMD/B.Sc | 98 | 65.3 |
| | Post Graduate | 30 | 20 |
| | Total | 136 | 90.6 |
| Missing | System | 14 | 9.3 |
| Total | | 150 | 150 |
| **Age** | | | |
| | | Frequency | Percent |
| Valid | <20 | 16 | 10.6 |
| | 21-30 | 91 | 60.7 |
| | 31-40 | 28 | 18.7 |
| | 41-50 | 5 | 3.0 |
| | Total | 140 | 93.3 |
| Missing | System | 10 | 6.6 |
| Total | | 150 | 150 |

*Table 3. Technology usage by the respondents*

| | Perent |
|---|---|
| **I use a computer at home** | **84.0** |
| **Use a computer at work** | **66.7** |
| **I have internet connection at home** | **42.7** |
| **I have internet connection at working place** | **69.3** |
| **I use a computer at another location e.g. Cybercafe** | **81.3** |
| **My mobile phone has internet facility** | **46.7** |
| **I use automated teller machine of e-banking** | **74.0** |
| **I use WAP (mobile phone) for e-banking** | **12.0** |
| **I mostly conduct banking transactions online** | **18.7** |
| **I mostly conduct banking transactions at the bank** | **77.3** |
| **I use the internet several times a day** | **60.7** |

value. Similarly, the effect of perceived ease of use on costumers' attitude toward e-banking was significant for females and not so for the males in the collected data.

## DISCUSSIONS

This study aimed at presenting information regarding gender differences in acceptance of e-banking as well as the issue of technology–related self-efficacy in Nigeria. An extended technology acceptance model (TAM) that incorporated computer self-efficacy was used for this research. Furthermore, the research aimed at presenting information regarding the moderating influence of gender in the research context. To that end, the research's results supported previous studies suggesting that perceived ease of use has a stronger influence on female respondents than male users of online banking (e.g. Bozionelos, 1996; Riquelme & Rios, 2010). Also, the result showed that computer self-efficacy has a negative effect on the attitude of female users; the same result was seen for male users of e-banking in Nigeria.

### Implications of the Study for Practice and Research

This paper has provided information about the factors influencing the acceptance of e-banking in Nigeria, a developing country. Information on the study's theme from the emerging regions of the world are not readily available in the extant IS literature. By extending the TAM, the authors have added to the growing body of knowledge in the area. To that end, this study affirmed the view noting that perceived usefulness and perceives ease of use may not be sufficient to determine the consumer's behavioral intention to use of IS.

The results of the statistical analysis lend credence to viewpoints in the literature affirming the relevance of the TAM factors in the acceptance of e-banking. Other researchers could build upon the research model used in this chapter for future similar inquires. Management of banks that provide e-banking systems solutions can benefit from this study's findings. It is suggested herein that Internet banking sites or portal with easy to use features can be beneficial to customers. Men and women in Nigeria may have different perceptions and abilities when it comes to using innovations such as e-banking. Banks should endeavor to provide more assistance to their female users to ensure the widespread acceptance of such innovations in the country.

### Limitations and Future Research

Asking only one respondent to present a view on behalf of their organization may be problematic. The findings from this study cannot be generalized for the whole of Nigeria given that only one part of the country was sampled. Data from other parts of the country may be different from what is reported and discussed in this chapter. Accordingly, caution should be exercised in interpreting the results presented herein. The sample is not randomly selected and this might be limiting to the study. This study opens up avenues for future research. Whenever possible some of the aforementioned limitations could be addressed in subsequent studies. This research effort can be replicated in other parts of Nigeria. The data used in this study is cross-sectional in nature; future

*Table 4. Path coefficients and hypothesis testing: Moderating influences*

| | Male | | Female | |
|---|---|---|---|---|
| Hypotheses | Coefficient | p -value | Coefficient | p – value |
| H7: PU -> ATT | 0.574 | <.05 | 0.395 | <.05 |
| H8: PEOU -> ATT | 0.115 | n.s. | -0.139 | <.010 |
| H3: CSE -> ATT | 0.104 | n.s. | -0.031 | <.010 |

efforts could consider using longitudinal data to facilitate more insight. Such factors as perceived security risk and trust, not considered in this study should be explored in future research to increase knowledge in the area.

## CONCLUSION

This chapter focused on the factors affecting the intention to use e-banking in Nigeria. An extended TAM was used to guide the discourse. Issues related to gender differences and computer self-efficacy were given adequate consideration in this study. The research's results like several other similar works in the extant literature confirmed the pertinence of the TAM factors for the adoption of technological innovations such as e-banking. Importantly, both gender differences and computer self-efficacy were found to be issues deserving of attention to both researchers and practitioners in the research context and in comparable countries. Importantly, the literature benefits from the information provided in this study, and it is hoped that future research will build upon the findings reported herein as efforts are made to understand technology diffusion in developing countries such as Nigeria.

## REFERENCES

Adesina, A. A., Ayo, C. K., & Ekong, U. O. (2008). An empirical investigation of the level of users' acceptance of e-banking in Nigeria: based on technology acceptance model. In *Proc. of 1st Int'l Conf. on Mobile e-Services.* Ogbomosho, Nigeria: LAUTECH.

Agbada, A.O. (2008). E-banking in Nigeria, problems and prospects from customer's perspective. *CBN Bullion Magazine, 32*(4), October-December 2008 edition.

Akpan, N., (2008, February 27). E-payment solutions: are banks getting it right? *Business day Newspaper*

Ayo, C. K., Adebiyi, A., Fatudimu, I. T., & Ekong, U. O. (2008). A framework for e-commerce implementation: Nigeria a case study. *Journal of Internet Banking and Commerce, 13*(2), 1–12.

Bandura, A. (1982). Self-efficacy mechanism in human agency. *Journal of American Psychologist, 37*(2), 122–147. doi:10.1037/0003-066X.37.2.122

Bozionelos, N. (1996). Psychology of computer use: prevalence of computer anxiety in British managers and professionals. *Psychological Reports, 78*(3), 995–1002. doi:10.2466/pr0.1996.78.3.995

Chau, P. Y. K., & Lai, V. S. K. (2003). An empirical investigation of the determinants of user acceptance of Internet banking. *Journal of Organizational Computing and Electronic Commerce, 13*(2), 123–145. doi:10.1207/S15327744JOCE1302_3

Chiemeke, S. C., Evwiekpaefe, O., & Chete, F. (2006). The Adoption of Internet Banking in Nigeria: An Empirical Investigation, *Journal of Internet Banking and Commerce, 11*(3), Available: http://www.arraydev.com/commerce/jibc/

Compeau, D., & Higgins, C. A. (1995). Computer self-efficacy: development of a measure and initial test. *Management Information Systems Quarterly, 19*(2), 189–212. doi:10.2307/249688

Davis, F. D. (1989). Perceived usefulness, perceived ease of use, and user acceptance of information technology. *Management Information Systems Quarterly, 13*(3), 319–339. doi:10.2307/249008

Dishaw, M. T., & Strong, D. M. (1999). Extending the technology acceptance model with task–technology fit constructs. *Information & Management, 36*(1), 9–21. doi:10.1016/S0378-7206(98)00101-3

Emordi, C.N.O., (2007). Recent development in Nigeria's Payment System, *CBN Briefs*, Series No. 2006-2007/0323-30.

Ezeoha, A. E. (2005). *Regulating internet banking in Nigeria: problems and challenges – Part 1*. Retrieved October 13, 2010 from http://www.arraydev.com/commerce/jibc/.

Fishbein, M., & Ajzen, I. (1975) *Belief, attitude, intention, and behavior: an introduction to theory and research*. Reading, Mass: Addison-Wesley.

Gholami, R., Ogun, A., Koh, E., & Lim, J. (2010). Factors affecting e-payment adoption in Nigeria. *Journal of Electronic Commerce in Organizations, 8*(4), 51–67. doi:10.4018/jeco.2010100104

Hair, J. F. Jr, Anderson, R. E., Thatham, R. L., & Black, W. C. (1998). *Multivariate data analysis*. Upper Saddle River, NJ: Prentice-Hall International, Inc.

Hanudin, A. (2007). Internet banking adoption among young Intellectuals, *JIBC, 12*(3). Retrieved September 13, 2011, from http://www.arraydev.com/commerce/jibc/

Hofstede, G. (2001). *Culture's consequences: comparing values, behaviors, institutions, and organizations across nations* (2nd ed.). Thousand Oaks, CA: Sage Publications.

Ifinedo, P. (2007). Investigating the antecedents of continuance intention of course management systems use among Estonian undergraduates. *International Journal of Information and Communication Technology Education, 3*(4), 76–92. doi:10.4018/jicte.2007100107

Ilie, V., Van Slyke, C., Green, G., & Lou, H. (2005). Gender differences in perceptions and use of communication technologies: a diffusion of innovation approach. *Information Resources Management Journal, 18*(3), 16–31. doi:10.4018/irmj.2005070102

Jahangir, N., & Begum, N. (2007). The role of perceived usefulness, perceived ease of use, security and privacy, and customer attitude to engender customer adaptation in the context of e-banking. *African Journal of Business Management, 2*(1), 32–40.

Karjaluoto, H., Mattila, M., & Pento, T. (2002). Factors underlying attitude formation towards online banking in Finland. *International Journal of Bank Marketing, 20*(6), 261–272. doi:10.1108/02652320210446724

Klopping, I. M., & McKinney, E. I. (2004). Extending the technology acceptance model and the task-technology fit model to consumer e-commerce. *Information Technology, Learning and Performance Journal, 22*(1), 35–48.

Lai, S. V., & Li, H. (n.d). (200). Technology acceptance model for internet banking: an invariance analysis. *Information & Management, 42*(34), 373–386.

Lallmahamood, M. (2007). An examination of individual's perceived security and privacy of the internet in Malaysia and the influence of this on their intention to use e-commerce: using an extension of the Technology Acceptance Model. *Journal of Internet Banking and Commerce, 12*(3), 1–26.

Lee, D., Park, J., & Ahn, J. (2001). On the explanation of factors affecting e-commerce adoption, *Proceedings of the 22nd Int'l Conf. in Information Systems*, (pp. 109-120.)

Legris, P., Ingham, J., & Collerette, P. (2003). Why do people use information technology?: a critical review of the technology acceptance model. *Information & Management*, *40*(3), 191–204. doi:10.1016/S0378-7206(01)00143-4

Li, N., & Kirkup, G. (2007). Gender and cultural differences in Internet use: a study of China and the UK. *Computers & Education*, *48*(2), 301–317. doi:10.1016/j.compedu.2005.01.007

Minton, G. C., & Scheneider, F. W. (1980). *Differential Psychology*. Prospect Heights, IL: Waveland Press.

Morris, M. G., & Turner, J. M. (2001). Assessing users' subjective quality of experience with the World Wide Web: an exploratory examination of temporal changes in technology acceptance. *International Journal of Human-Computer Studies*, *54*(6), 877–901. doi:10.1006/ijhc.2001.0460

Ndubisi, N. O. (2007). Customers' perceptions and intention to adopt Internet banking: the moderation effect of computer self-efficacy. *AI & Society*, *21*(3), 315–327. doi:10.1007/s00146-006-0062-5

Nel, J., & Raleting, T. (2010). *Gender differences in non-users' attitude towards WIG-Cellphone banking*. Retrieved March 2011, from http://anzmac2010.org/proceedings/pdf/anzmac10Final00038.pdf.

Nysveen, H., Pedersen, P. E., & Thornbjørnsen, H. (2005). Explaining intention to use mobile chat services: moderating effects of gender. *Journal of Consumer Marketing*, *22*(5), 247–256. doi:10.1108/07363760510611671

Pikkarainen, T., Pikkarainen, K., Karjaluoto, H., & Pahnila, S. (2004). Consumer acceptance of online banking: an extension of the technology acceptance model. *Internet Research*, *14*(3), 224–235. doi:10.1108/10662240410542652

Rao, S., & Troshani, I. (2007). A conceptual framework and propositions for the acceptance of mobile services. *Journal of Theoretical Applied Electronic Commerce Research*, *2*(2), 61–73.

Riquelme, H. E., & Rios, R. E. (2010). The moderating effect of gender in the adoption of mobile banking. *International Journal of Bank Marketing*, *28*(5), 328–341. doi:10.1108/02652321011064872

Van Slyke, C., Comunale, C., & Belanger, F. (2002). Gender differences in perceptions of Web-based shopping. *Communications of the ACM*, *45*(8), 82–86. doi:10.1145/545151.545155

Venkatesh, V., & Bala, H. (2008). Technology acceptance model 3 and a research agenda on intervention. *Decision Sciences*, *39*(2), 273–315. doi:10.1111/j.1540-5915.2008.00192.x

Venkatesh, V., & Davis, F. D. (2000). A theoretical extension of the technology acceptance model: four longitudinal field studies. *Management Science*, *46*(2), 186–204. doi:10.1287/mnsc.46.2.186.11926

Venkatesh, V., & Morris, M. G. (2000). Why don't men ever stop to ask for directions? gender, social influence, and their role in technology acceptance and usage behavior. *Management Information Systems Quarterly*, *24*(1), 115–139. doi:10.2307/3250981

Venkatesh, V., Morris, M. G., Davis, G. B., & Davis, F. D. (2003). User acceptance of information technology: toward a unified view. *Management Information Systems Quarterly*, *27*(3), 425–478.

Wang, Y., Wang, Y., Lin, H., & Tang, T. (2003). Determinants of user acceptance of Internet banking: an empirical study. *International Journal of Service Industry Management*, *14*(5), 501–519. doi:10.1108/09564230310500192

Xu, M. X., Wilkes, S., & Shah, M. H. (2006). *e-banking Application and Issues in Abbey National PLC*, In M. Khosrow (eds.), (pp. 253-258), *Encyclopedia of e-commerce, e-government and Mobile Commerce*. Hershey PA: Idea Group Inc.

## KEY TERMS AND DEFINITIONS

**Gender Differences:** This refers to salient differences between genders with respect to technology use.

**Self-Efficacy:** This is the belief that one is capable of performing in a certain goal.

**Developing Countries:** This refers to countries having a low level of material or economic well-being.

**Technology Acceptance Model:** This is a widely used framework used in predicting technology usage.

**Customers' Attitudes:** This refers to the hypothetical construct representing an individual's degree of like or dislike for something

**Technology Usage:** This refers to the actual usage of technological products by individuals

**Perceived Usefulness:** This refers to the extent to which an individual believes that the use of technological systems would positively impact their job performance.

**Perceived Ease of Use:** This refers to the extent to which an individual believes that the use of technological systems would be free of effort.

## APPENDIX

### Survey Questions

Perceived ease of use

- My interaction with e-banking system is clear and understandable
- I find e-banking system flexible to interact with
- Learning to use e-banking system is easy
- It would be easy for me to become skillful at using the e-banking systems
- Using e-banking systems requires mental effort

Perceived usefulness

- Using e-banking services has increased my productivity
- Using e-banking enables me to utilize banking services more quickly
- Using e-banking improves my performance of utilizing banking services
- Using e-banking gives me control over my banking transactions
- Using e-banking makes my financial transaction to be more efficient

Costumers' attitude

- Using e-banking is a good idea
- E-banking makes banking transactions more interesting
- Using e-banking is fun

Computer Self-efficacy

- I would be confident in using e-banking: ….

o Even if there is no one around to show me how to use it
o Only if have prior knowledge of how to operate the system
o Only if I have seen someone else using it before I try it myself
o If someone will assist me to get started
o If I had first gone through a lesson on how to use it
o If I can call on someone to assist if I get struck

Intentions to use

- Intention to use e-banking solutions
- I am interested in using e-banking in the future
- I am committed to begin to use e-banking solution
- I will strongly recommend e-banking for all bank customers

# Chapter 11
# Enhancing Trust in E-Commerce in Developing IT Environments:
## A Feedback-Based Perspective

**Iwara I. Arikpo**
*University of Calabar, Nigeria*

**Adenike O. Osofisan**
*University of Ibadan, Nigeria*

**Idongesit E. Eteng**
*University of Calabar, Nigeria*

## ABSTRACT

*E-commerce has become the most common means of exchange of goods and services in the new world order, with the Internet as the driving force. E-commerce has also proven to be cheaper, faster, and more efficient over traditional methods. In spite of all these advantages, e-commerce is still not living up to its full potential, due, apparently, to lack of trust by end-users regarding these technology-enabled exchanges.*

*Most research in e-commerce and trust have assumed advanced information technology (IT) infrastructural environments, so results from these studies have little impact on Developing IT environments, where internet infrastructure is still at the developmental stage, and the people are used to traditional commercial methods. This situation affects the level of trust and participation of end-users in e-commerce. This paper presents a unique approach for enhancing trust in e-commerce in less-advanced IT environments, with a perspective on feedback mechanisms in e-commerce websites. Survey results support the importance of feedback in promoting and sustaining end-user trust in online market environments.*

DOI: 10.4018/978-1-4666-1637-0.ch011

## INTRODUCTION

Almost every research on trust in e-commerce typically views trust as an important condition of successful commercial exchange. Various researches on this area aim to identify relevant factors of trust and establish how these factors influence potential buyers' decisions to interact with vendors. The aim is to provide ways of increasing trust. E-commerce has dominated global economy in terms of the exchange of goods and services. E-commerce has become the most common means of exchange of goods and services in the new world order, with the Internet as the driving force; and as a result, research on trust in e-commerce has become a veritable industry. The reason for this interest is that, e-commerce, despite its many advantages, is still not living up to its full potential, more so, in emerging IT environments, where internet infrastructure is still at the developmental stage. This is apparently caused by the lack of trust that end-users have in technology and technology-enabled exchange of goods and services, and the attendant risks associated with these exchanges. Since lack of trust is a major obstacle for the success of e-commerce, most research concentrate on understanding trust and its components in order to facilitate the development of trust.

This paper aims to present a feedback-based perspective on how to enhance trust in e-commerce in developing IT environments. First, we provide a detailed background of trust and trust in e-commerce, including types of trust and trust-building in e-commerce, and then types of online feedback. We also discuss the survey results, and then, end with a conclusion of the paper.

## BACKGROUND

Trust is a catalyst for human cooperation. It allows people to interact spontaneously and helps the economy to operate smoothly. Lack of trust on the other hand is like sand in the social machinery. It makes us waste time and resources on protecting ourselves against possible harm and thereby clogs up the economy (Patton & Jøsang, 2004).

### Trust in E-Commerce

There is a wealth of literature on trust in general, and trust in e-commerce in particular, and so we cannot claim a comprehensive review herein. In the discussion of trust, our work will concentrate on trust in e-commerce, with a focus at trust in business-to-consumer (B2C) kind of business relationships. However, there are other potential online trust relationships such as managerial trust (Soule, 1998; Stanton & Stam, 2003), trust in virtual teams (Jones & Bowie, 1998; Gallivan, 2001; Brown et al., 2004; Pauleen, 2003); trust in supply chains (Welty & Becerra-Fernandez, 2001), and others that are not discussed in this paper. Besides, there are related areas such as trust in the economic system in general (Cantrell, 2000) or trust in e-government (Yee et al., 2005) that the paper cannot touch upon.

### Definition of Trust

Trust has become a most frequently used term in every economic exchange, of which e-commerce is a part; hence, there is no generally agreed upon definition of trust (Rousseau, 1998). One reason for this is that trust covers a range of issues and problems that are not necessarily identical. Trust can therefore mean different things to different people. In a most positive view, trust tends to be endowed with a purpose. This purpose is usually to facilitate interaction or exchange. This is usually the crucial point in research on trust in e-commerce (Hoffman, 1999; Cheskin, 1999).

One central issue about trust is that it is a psychological state of the trusting person, the trustor (Yee et al., 2005). Trust is an attitude (Alpern, 1997) that is typically based upon a belief (Egger, 2001), connected to an expectation (Mui et al.,

2002), and often accompanied by certain feelings (Solomon & Flores, 2001). All of these aspects of trust are only relevant in a relationship. Trust can only arise in a relationship between a trustor and a trustee (Reagle Jr., 1996) and possibly other entities (Viega et al., 2001). The trustee can be anything from a person or physical entity, to abstract notions such as software or a cryptographic key (Jøsang, 1996).

A trusting relationship can arise in situations where the trustor does not have complete control over the trustee. The trustor relies on the trustee (Jones et al., 2000), and so needs to accept a certain amount of vulnerability (Brenkert, 1998; Hosmeh, 1995). Consequently, the willingness to accept vulnerability has been suggested as a definition of trust (Mayer et al., 1995; (Gallivan & Depledge, 2003; Pennington et al., 2004). Customers are likely to accept vulnerability if they have the confidence that, the person to whom they make themselves vulnerable will be benevolent (Bhattacherjee, 2002). McKnight & Chervany (1996) define trust as the extent to which one party is willing to depend on something or somebody in a given situation with a feeling of relative security, even though negative consequences are possible.

A positive review of trust often emphasizes its functions. The possibly most important function is the reduction of uncertainty. Uncertainty in a situation of economic exchange is closely related to risk. Trust is therefore often described as relevant in risky situations (Mayer et al., 1995) or as a risk management approach. Trust seems to be most valuable in situations where control is lacking and future interactions are difficult to predict (like the Internet) (Lane & Bachmann, 1996). Accordingly, trust is of high relevance in e-commerce transactions because customers often have little knowledge of vendors and must deal with ambiguity, uncertainty and risks outside of their control. Higher levels of trust should thus lead to more transactions (Bhattacherjee, 2002). Trust can then also be seen as a form of social capital (Preece, 2002) or an asset of the firm that can attract economic exchange.

## Types of Trust

There are many different ways of classifying trust. Different schools of thought classify trust differently. For instance, Koehn (2003) distinguishes between goal-based, calculative, knowledge-based, and respect-based trust. Gefen, Karahanna & Straub (2003) identify knowledge-based, institution-based, calculative-based, cognition-based, and personality-based trust. This reflects a similar but shorter list by Berg & Kalish (1997), who distinguish between calculus-based, knowledge-based and identification-based trust. Lane & Bachmann (Lane & Bachmann, 1996), drawing on Zucker (1986), list process-based, characteristic-based and institutionally-based trust. According to Rousseau et al. (1998), definitions of trust can be distinguished according to the academic discipline in which they are used. For Dribben (2004), trust can be divided according to the "layer" in which it is active, helping him to distinguish dispositional trust, learnt trust, and situational trust.

Furthermore, there are different stages of trust, with initial trust clearly differing from trust that is well established (McKnight et al., 2002). The schema of trust development can be more complex, as for example, for Flores & Solomon (1998), Solomon & Flores (2001), who distinguish between simple trust, naive trust, trust as yet unchallenged, unquestioned (the faith of a well brought up child), blind trust, obstinate, possibly even self-deluding, basic trust, and authentic trust.

Trust is of varying degrees of importance. There seems to be a general agreement that trust in situations of economic exchange requires or is built upon reliable institutions (McKnight & Chervany, 2000; Pavlou & Gefen, 2004; Rousseau et al., 1998). The nature of economic interaction also implies rational economic actors who are able and willing to maximize their expected utility, which gives a central role to calculative trust (Ba & Pavlou, 2002; Lewicki & Stevenson, 1997).

## Building Trust in e-Commerce

We will present the stages of trust building in e-commerce using the extended Trust Transition Model by Jøsang et al. (2005) (adapted from Cheskin (1999)). Various technologies for use in building trust by e-commerce players (presented by Patton & Jøsang (2004)) fit into this extended model.

Jøsang et al. (2005) made a distinction between *extrinsic trust factors* which are information elements that are communicated between parties, and *intrinsic trust factors* which are information elements emerging from personal experience. These take precedence at different stages in the trust transition model of Figure 1. According to Cheskin (1999), an unaware (potential) customer first has to be attracted to, or made aware of a service provider, in order for that customer to be able to develop trust in that service provider. Let us assume that the principal is aware of several service providers with similar offerings regarding specified price and quality. Then in the initial phase, the extrinsic trust factors will determine the principal's choice of a service provider.

These extrinsic factors can be, for instance, that the service provider has a well-known brand with a good reputation, that the web site offers ease of navigation, that the service provider presents satisfactory privacy and complaint policies, and that the communication channel is encrypted. The customer then gets first hand experience with the chosen service provider. A good experience will improve trust, whereas a bad experience normally will cause the trust level to drop below the purchase threshold, as indicated by the dotted arrow in Figure 1. There are techniques for regaining lost trust. The provider must be able to determine when something has gone wrong and give the dissatisfied customer adequate apology and compensation. Studies show that a unsatisfied customer who receives compensation can end up having stronger trust than a satisfied customer. The obvious explanation is that receiving apology and compensation is evidence of good fulfillment, which in the end becomes a very strong positive intrinsic trust factor (Jøsang et al., 2005).

# TYPES OF FEEDBACK IN E-COMMERCE

There are two types of feedback in e-commerce as identified by Walczak and Gregg (2009). They propose direct feedback and open feedback. Direct feedback refers to qualitative comments left by customers about past transactions with an online business. It has been proposed to be a more reliable mechanism for communicating information about an online business than reputation systems; and so, many e-businesses take the development of direct feedback mechanisms as priority (Covert, 2007; Gogoi, 2007; Hudson & Gilbert, 2006). Direct feedback is very popular for web users that rely on the extrinsic motivator of external feedback for forming opinions.

Open feedback, on the other hand, provides qualitative information concerning either a business or its products (potentially from non-customers). It is becoming popular, as the new web-savvy population wants to see what others are saying about a business and/or product, and also wants to be heard (Gogoi, 2007; Kiplinger, 2007). Open feedback forums are highly sought after by information seekers, especially if the forum appears to be candid and unbiased. A good example is the blog postings by several Microsoft employees that describe interesting information about computing in general, but also occasionally describe problems with various Microsoft products and potential fixes that the bloggers have attempted (Walczak & Gregg (2009).

*Figure 1. E-Commerce Trust Transition Model (Adapted from Cheskin (1999) & Jøsang (2005)*

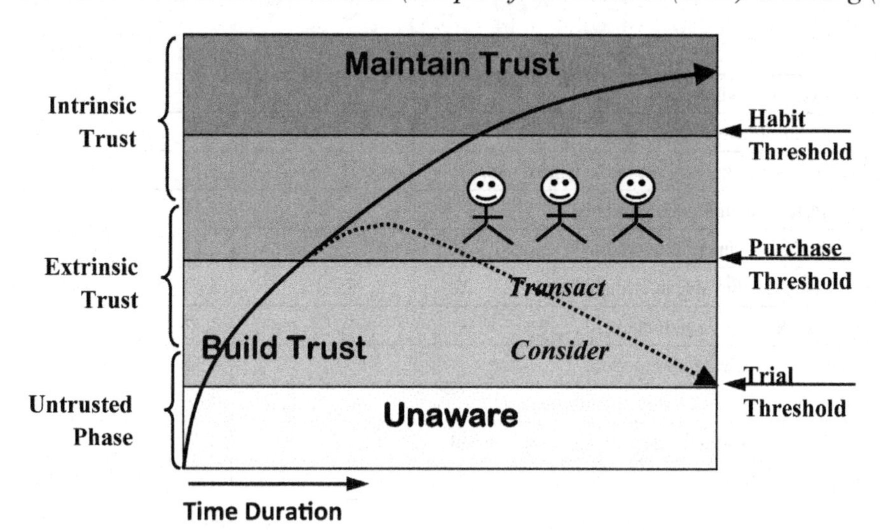


## RESEARCH METHODOLOGY

A survey was conducted to assess the general perception of respondents about e-commerce websites and what factors they consider important in enhancing their trust when making decisions about online businesses. The survey instrument is shown in Appendix A. Some of the survey questions are taken directly or with only slight modification from Walczak & Gregg (2009); Barnes & Vidgen (2001); and Barnes & Vidgen (2002). However, additional questions were added to address feedback factors not covered by these website quality instruments. The survey asked respondents to specify the importance of each factor using a 7-point Likert scale. We administered the survey in November 2009 to undergraduate students of Computer Science, Mathematics/Statistics, graduate students in both Faculties of Science and Social Sciences and some staff of a large-sized university in the southern part of Nigeria. A total of 68 surveys were returned. The majority of respondents indicated they spent an average of 6 or more hours a week online and had a high level of familiarity with both the Web (4+ years) and with making purchases online (5+ purchases). The use of the university community represents a convenience sample, and also fairly representative of the subpopulation of Internet users in Nigeria.

## EMPIRICAL DATA AND DISCUSSION

Table 1 summarizes the data collected from the survey on the factors that respondents felt were most important for enhancing their trust when making decisions about online exchange of goods and services. The table is a summary of the datasets from the 68 respondents. Three summary items are shown in the table for each question. They are mean, standard deviation and mode, respectively.

The results suggest that there are a number of priorities demanded from online businesses by (potential) users of e-commerce websites, as shown in the column for the mean. Particularly, customers are most concerned with provision of accurate information, provision of appropriate security measures, ease of site navigation, and provision of timely information. Intuitively, from the point of view of trust, these are the factors one would expect as critical to an online customer. Conversely, there seems to be much less emphasis on technical factors (e.g., question 3),

*Table 1. Survey responses evaluating factors that enhance trust in e-commerce*

| Q. No. | Description | Mean | Std. Dev. | Mode |
|---|---|---|---|---|
| 1 | The site is easy to navigate. | 5.72 | 0.93 | 5 |
| 2 | The site has an attractive appearance. | 5.06 | 1.09 | 5 |
| 3 | The site has a design appropriate to the type of site. | 3.79 | 1.37 | 2 |
| 4 | The site creates a memorable experience | 4.50 | 1.42 | 6 |
| 5 | The site provides accurate information. | **6.24** | 0.81 | 7 |
| 6 | The site provides believable information. | 5.69 | 0.82 | 5 |
| 7 | The site provides timely information. | 5.72 | 0.86 | 5 |
| 8 | The site provides relevant information. | 4.54 | 1.04 | 4 |
| 9 | The site provides easy to understand information. | 4.66 | 0.82 | 5 |
| 10 | The site provides information at the right level of detail. | 3.57 | 0.85 | 3 |
| 11 | The site presents the information in an appropriate format. | 4.06 | 0.86 | 4 |
| 12 | The site provides appropriate security measures. | **6.15** | 0.74 | 6 |
| 13 | The site provides a forum that allows users to discuss products and services. | 4.21 | 0.92 | 4 |
| 14 | The site has appropriate prices. | 5.15 | 1.01 | 6 |
| 15 | The site makes it easy and convenient to make purchases. | 5.04 | 0.72 | 5 |
| 16 | The site provides appropriate product information. | 4.59 | 0.50 | 5 |
| 17 | The site provides customer service information. | 4.68 | 0.91 | 4 |
| 18 | The site provides customer feedback about products. | 5.79 | 0.66 | 6 |
| 19 | The site provides appropriate company information including valid telephone numbers and postal address. | 5.94 | 0.67 | 6 |
| 20 | The company has a good reputation rating (provided by former customers). | 5.51 | 0.70 | 5 |
| 21 | The company responds promptly to email inquiries. | **6.10** | 0.74 | 6 |
| 22 | The company provides an easy-to-understand Contact Us form. | 5.59 | 0.74 | 5 |
| 23 | The company uses Forums to answer support questions publicly. | **6.03** | 0.62 | 6 |
| 24 | The company provides Live Chat for answering support queries. | 5.71 | 0.75 | 6 |
| 25 | The company provides an Instant Messaging address on their site. | 5.88 | 0.87 | 6 |

which appears to be a general trend (Barnes & Vidgen, 2002; Dutta, & Segev, 2001).

However, the results show a very interesting pattern for feedback-related factors (questions 18 to 25) as trust enhancing mechanisms, apart from the factors discussed above. This is apparently due to the fact that in less-advanced IT environments, people are more used to the traditional face-to-face transactions, and so moving to e-commerce settings, where they do not physically see the other party, can be very apprehensive. They would normally prefer a form of prompt feedback to assure that their transactions are successful. For example, in Nigeria today, where online banking is taking its roots, people rush to those banks that send them (customers) SMS alerts on their mobile phones once a transaction is completed in their (customer) accounts. Prompt response to email is the highest feedback factor (and 3$^{rd}$ highest overall), due probably to the fact that email remains the cheapest and most convenient means of online communication in Nigeria, as most people can now check and send mails with their mobile phones. Besides, in traditional environments, customers can get answers to product support questions directly from their vendors. This is not the case with e-commerce. This accounts for the high mean score of question 23, meaning that, respondents rate the use of forums to answer product support questions publicly as a very important trust factor.

There are some differences in the standard deviations for particular questions, although, overall, the patterns are quite similar. For example, respondents appear more certain about security, accurate information, ease of use/navigation and the bulk of the feedback factors, than most technical factors like, site design, memorable experience, and attractive appearance. This is shown in the values for standard deviation. Besides, the mode for most of the feedback factors is approximately 6, respectively, meaning that most respondents rate feedback factors as very important to trust.

## CONCLUSION

This chapter has presented a unique perspective on enhancing trust in e-commerce in developing IT environments. Empirical evidence supports the importance of a variety of factors that customers consider important before trusting an online business for a transaction. Consistent with earlier research on website quality (e.g., Walczak & Gregg, 2009; Barnes & Vidgen, 2001; Barnes & Vidgen, 2002), this work shows that traditional website quality attributes, like ease of use, security, and timely information are important to potential customers when assessing a company's trustworthiness. In addition to the foregoing factors, the results from this study has also shown other factors like quick response to email inquiries, use of forums to answer product support questions publicly, customer feedback about products, and other feedback factors (questions 18 to 25) as very strong trust-enhancing mechanisms in up-coming e-commerce environments, where traditional marketing is predominant.

## REFERENCES


Alpern, K. D. (1997). What Do We Want Trust to Be. *Business and Professional Ethics Journal*, 16(1–3), 29–46: Special Issue on Trust and Business: Barriers and Bridges. D. Koehn (Ed.).

Ba, S., & Pavlou, P. A. (2002). Evidence of the Effects of Trust Building Technology in Electronic Markets: Price Premiums and Buyer Behavior. *Management Information Systems Quarterly*, *26*(3), 243–268. doi:10.2307/4132332

Barnes, S. J., & Vidgen, R. T. (2001). Assessing the Quality of Auction Web Sites. *In Proceedings of the 34th Hawaii International Conference on Systems Sciences* (pp. 1–10). Los Alamitos, CA: IEEE Computer Society Press.

Barnes, S. J., & Vidgen, R. T. (2002). An Integrative Approach to the Assessment of E-Commerce Quality. *Journal of Electronic Commerce Research*, *3*(3), 114–127.

Berg, T. C., & Kalish, G. I. (1997). Trust and Ethics in Employee-Owned Companies. *Business and Professional Ethics Journal*, 16(1–3), Special Issue on Trust and Business: Barriers and Bridges, D. Koehn (Ed.), 211–224.

Bhattacherjee, A. (2002). Individual Trust in Online Firms: Scale Development and Initial Test. *Journal of Management Information Systems*, *19*(1), 211–241.

Brenkert, G. (1998). Trust, Business and Business Ethics: An Introduction. *Business Ethics Quarterly*, *8*(2), 195–203.

Brown, H. G., Scott, M. P., & Rodgers, T. L. (2004). Interpersonal Traits, Complementarities, and Trust in Virtual Collaboration. *Journal of Management Information Systems*, *20*(4), 115–137.

Cantrell, S. (2000). E-Market Trust Mechanisms. *Accenture Research Note: E-Commerce Networks, 11*, 1 – 3.

Cheskin Research and Studio Archetype/Sapient. (1999). *eCommerce Trust Study*. Retrieved May 23, 2010, from http://www.cheskin.com/cms/files/i/articles//17__report-eComm%20Trust1999.pdf

Covert, J. (2007). Online Clothes Reviews Give 'Love That Dress' New Clout. *Wall Street Journal – Eastern Edition*, 248, pp. B1– B4.

Dribben, M. R. (2004). Exploring the Processual Nature of Trust and Cooperation in Organisations: A Whiteheadian Analysis. *Philosophy of Management*, 4(1), Special Issue on Organization and Decision Processes. Leonard Minkes and Tony Gear (Ed.), 25–39.

Dutta, S., & Segev, A. (2001). Business Transformation on the Internet. In Barnes, S., & Hunt, B. (Eds.), *Electronic Commerce and Virtual Business*. Oxford: Butterworth-Heinemann.

Egger, F. N. (2001). Affective Design of E-Commerce User Interfaces: How to Maximize Perceived Trustworthiness. In Helander, Khalid & Tham (Ed.), *Proceedings of The International Conference on Affective Human Factors Design* (pp. 317–324). London: Asean Academic Press.

Flores, F., & Solomon, R. C. (1998). Creating Trust. *Business Ethics Quarterly*, *8*(2), 205–232. doi:10.2307/3857326

Gallivan, M. J. (2001). Striking a balance between trust and control in a virtual organization: A content analysis of open source software case studies. *Information Systems Journal, 11*(4), 277–304. doi:10.1046/j.1365-2575.2001.00108.x

Gallivan, M. J., & Depledge, G. (2003). Trust, Control and the Role of Interorganizational Systems in Electronic Partnerships. *Information Systems Journal, 13*(2), 159–190. doi:10.1046/j.1365-2575.2003.00146.x

Gefen, D., Karahanna, E., & Straub, D. W. (2003). Trust and TAM in Online Shopping: An Integrated Model. *Management Information Systems Quarterly, 27*(1), 51–90.

Gogoi, P. (2007). Retailers Take a Tip from MySpace. *Business Week Online*. Retrieved May 23, 2010, from http://www.businessweek.com/bwdaily/dnflash/content/feb2007/db20070213_626293.htm.

Hoffman, D. L., Novak, T. P., & Peralta, M. (1999). Building Consumer Trust Online. *Communications of the ACM, 42*(4), 80–85. doi:10.1145/299157.299175

Hosmeh, L. T. (1995). Trust: The Connecting Link between Organizational Theory and Philosophical Ethics. *Academy of Management Review*, *20*(2), 379–403.

Hudson, S., & Gilbert, D. (2006). The Internet and Small Hospitality Businesses: B&B Marketing in Canada. *Journal of Hospitality & Leisure Marketing, 14*(1), 99–116. doi:10.1300/J150v14n01_06

Jones, S., Wilikens, M., Morris, P., & Masera, M. (2000). Trust Requirements in E-Business - A conceptual framework for understanding the needs and concerns of different stakeholders. *Communications of the ACM, 43*(12), 80–87.

Jones, T. M., & Bowie, N. E. (1998). Moral Hazards on the Road to the "Virtual" Corporation. *Business Ethics Quarterly*, *8*(2), 273–292. doi:10.2307/3857329

Jøsang, A. (1996). The right type of trust for distributed systems. In C. Meadows (Ed.), *Proceedings of the 1996 New Security Paradigms Workshop, ACM.* New York, NY: ACM Press

Jøsang, A., Keser, C., & Dimitrakos, T. (2005). Can We Manage Trust? *Proceedings of the 3rd International Conference on Trust Management, (iTrust),* Paris.

Kiplinger's Staff. (2007). Walk-in Critics. *Kiplinger's Personal Finance, 61*(1), 24.

Koehn, D. (2003). The Nature of and Conditions for Online Trust. *Journal of Business Ethics, 43*(1-2), 3–19. doi:10.1023/A:1022950813386

Lane, C., & Bachmann, R. (1996). The Social Construction of Trust: Supplier Relations in Britain and Germany. *Organization Studies, 17*(3), 365–395. doi:10.1177/017084069601700302

Lewicki, R. J., & Stevenson, M. A. (1997). Trust Development in Negotiation: Proposed Actions and Research Agenda. *Business and Professional Ethics Journal*, 16(1–3), Special Issue on Trust and Business: Barriers and Bridges. D. Koehn (Ed.), 99–132.

Mayer, R. C., Davis, J. H., & Schoorman, F. D. (1995). An Integrative Model of Organizational Trust. *Academy of Management Review, 20*(3), 709–734.

McKnight, D., & Chervany, N. (1996). *The Meanings of Trust, Technical Report MISRC 96-04. Management Information Systems Research Center*. University of Minnesota.

McKnight, D. H., & Chervany, N. L. (2000). What is Trust? A Conceptual Analysis and an Interdisciplinary Model. *Proceedings of the Americas Conference on Information Systems*, (pp. 827–833.)

McKnight, D. H., Choudhury, V., & Kacmar, C. (2002). Developing and Validating Trust Measures for e- Commerce: An Integrative Typology. *Information Systems Research, 13*(3), 334–359. doi:10.1287/isre.13.3.334.81

Mui, L., Mohtashemi, M., & Halberstadt, A. (2002). A Computational Model of Trust and Reputation. *In Proceedings of the 35th Annual Hawaii International Conference on Systems Sciences*, Hawaii.

Patton, M. A., & Jøsang, A. (2004). *Technologies for Trust in e-Commerce*. Netherlands: Kluwer Academic Publishers.

Pauleen, D. J. (2003). An Inductively Derived Model of Leader-Initiated Relationship Building with Virtual Team Members. *Journal of Management Information Systems, 20*(3), 227–256.

Pavlou, P., & Gefen, D. (2004). Building Effective Online Marketplaces with Institution-Based Trust. *Information Systems Research, 15*(1), 37–59. doi:10.1287/isre.1040.0015

Pennington, R., Wilcox, H. D., & Grover, V. (2004). The Role of System Trust in Business-to-Consumer Transactions. *Journal of Management Information Systems, 20*(3), 197–226.

Preece, J. (2002). Supporting Community and Building Social Capital. *Communications of the ACM, 45*(4), 37–39. doi:10.1145/505248.505269

Reagle, J. M. Jr. (1996). Trust in Electronic Markets. *First Monday, 1*(2).

Rousseau, D. M., Sitkin, S. B., Burt, R. S., & Camerer, C. (1998). Not so Different After All: A Cross-Discipline View of Trust. *Academy of Management Review, 23*(3), 393–404. doi:10.5465/AMR.1998.926617

Solomon, R. C., & Flores, F. (2001). *Building Trust in Business, Politics, Relationships, and Life*. Oxford: Oxford University Press.

Soule, E. (1998). Trust and Managerial Responsibility. *Business Ethics Quarterly, 8*(2), 249–272. doi:10.2307/3857328

Stanton, J. M., & Stam, K. R. (2003). Information Technology, Privacy, and Power within Organizations: a view from Boundary Theory and Social Exchange perspectives. *Surveillance & Society, 1*(2), 152–190.

Viega, J., Kohno, T., & Potter, B. (2001). Trust (and Mistrust) in Secure Applications. *Communications of the ACM, 44*(2), 31–36. doi:10.1145/359205.359223

Walczak, S., & Gregg, D. G. (2009). Factors Influencing Corporate Online Identity: A New Paradigm. *Journal of Theoretical and Applied Electronic Commerce Research, 4*(3), 17–29. doi:10.4067/S0718-18762009000300003

Welty, B., & Becerra-Fernandez, I. (2001). Managing Trust and Commitment in Collaborative Supply Chain Relationships. *Communications of the ACM, 44*(6), 67–73. doi:10.1145/376134.376170

Yee, G., El-Khatib, K., Korba, L., Patrick, A. S., Song, R., & Xu, Y. (2005). Privacy and Trust in E- Government. In Huang, W., Siau, K., & Wei, K. K. (Eds.), *Electronic Government Strategies and Implementation* (pp. 145–189). Hershey, PA: Idea Group Publishing.

Zucker, L. G. (1986). Production of trust: Institutional sources of economic structure, 1840-1920. *Research in Organizational Behavior, 8*(1), 53–111.

# APPENDIX

## E-Commerce Survey

**Problem Situation:** You are considering making a major purchase from an online company, and are trying to select which company or vendor to buy from. Respondents are asked to rate each of the following factors from 1 – 7 (using the 7-point Likert Scale), with 1 representing not important, and 7 representing extremely important that can enhance their trust on a potential vendor or online business.

1. The site is easy to navigate.
2. The site has an attractive appearance.
3. The site has a design appropriate to the type of site.
4. The site creates a memorable experience.
5. The site provides accurate information.
6. The site provides believable information.
7. The site provides timely information.
8. The site provides relevant information.
9. The site provides easy to understand information.
10. The site provides information at the right level of detail.
11. The site presents the information in an appropriate format.
12. The site provides appropriate security measures.
13. The site provides a forum that allows users to discuss products and services.
14. The site has appropriate prices.
15. The site makes it easy and convenient to make purchases.
16. The site provides appropriate product information.
17. The site provides customer service information.
18. The site provides customer feedback about products.
19. The site provides appropriate company information including valid telephone numbers and postal address.
20. The company has a good reputation rating (provided by former customers).
21. The company responds promptly to email inquiries.
22. The company provides an easy-to-understand Contact Us form.
23. The company uses Forums to answer support questions publicly.
24. The company provides Live Chat for answering support queries.

# Chapter 12
# Building a Conceptual Model of Factors affecting Personal Credit and Insolvency in China based on the Methodologies used in Western Economies

**Grzegorz Majewski**
*University of the West of Scotland, UK*

**Abel Usoro**
*University of the West of Scotland, UK*

**Pattarin Chumnumpan**
*Bangkok University, Thailand*

## ABSTRACT

*Chinese economy is developing at an unprecedented pace. This expansion is prominent not only in the external aspect (increased export), but also internally in the increase in the demand for goods and services by common Chinese families. This demand cannot always be met by the monthly salary and therefore the need for personal credit. Because of the substantial risk involved in lending, there is need for robust and reliable credit evaluation procedures, strategies, policies, and systems. Lessons learned from the subprime mortgage crisis in U.S. are that lending can be a very risky activity that can lead to recession for a whole economy. Banks and other financial institutions in China are in need of appropriate procedures and systems should a barrier to further economic development be avoided. Besides, existing models and systems that are prevalent in the West may not fully match Chinese banking environment or the society itself. An appropriate personal credit rating methodology should take into account the differences between the Western and Chinese society and culture. There apparently does not exist such a methodology in literature that takes into consideration the unique Chinese situation. The aim of this chapter is to begin to fill this gap in knowledge by building a conceptual model of factors influencing demand for consumer credit and insolvency (bad debts) in China, based on the available methodologies used in the Western societies.*

DOI: 10.4018/978-1-4666-1637-0.ch012

## BACKGROUND

Unprecedented growth in recent years may be an indication ofChinese success in all regards, including finance. It may be a sign of an improvement in the Chinese banking system. Simultaneously, demand for the personal credit in China has continued to increase at a very high rate (Alicia et al., 2006). This increase has benefited both indigenous and Western financial organisations that have gained from the entry of China into the World Trade Organisation (WTO) in November 2001. This entry was crucial for the development of China as it beckoned a new era of consumer choice with the lifting of all restrictions to foreign trade from 2007. For transitional economies as China the Western financial interest is mainly in the credit card business that tries to fill the credit needs of the citizens (Zhao et al, 2010). It is however difficult for the Western banks to enter and compete in the Chinese financial services market under the numerous administrative and legal restrictions as well as the impediments of the historical, cultural and structural differences that make the Chinese financial market unique. In order to maintain a high economic growth and its commitment to fully open up its banking system to foreign competition, China urgently requires a more comprehensive strategy, with a long-term vision of the desired structure of the Chinese banking system (Steve, 2005). A very early attempt to achieve this objective is the model developed by this chapter for assessing demand for credit as well as bad debts.

The rest of this chapter will present (a) factors affecting demand for personal credit in China, (b) credit rating methodologies used in the Western societies, (c) construction of a theoretical model and (d) summary, implications and areas for further investigations.

## DEMAND FOR PERSONAL CREDIT IN CHINA

With the increased capitalization of housing and urbanization in China, personal assets have much increased but also has demand for personal credit risen (Smith, 2009). However, most of the borrowers have poor credit history including late payments, high debt levels, low incomes and inconsistent employment history, which lead to their low credit ratings. Though the lenders' profits are rising, the lenders are taking increased risk in "overlending" to customers with unstable income and low ability to repay the loans (Whale, C. 2005).

Durvasula & Lysonski (2010) compared personal credit markets in China and the U.S.A. They noted that China is "undergoing an unprecedented metamorphosis as it evolves from a Communist society with government planning to one that is more market driven and consumer oriented" (Durvasala & Lyonski, 2010). This change in the economy has a profound effect in the psyche of Chinese consumers as well. Money, its possession and its pursuit has taken on a more important role. Almost 50 percent of Chinese think that money is either as important as or more important than friendship or ideas (Rosen, 2004). These changes were also noticed by the press (Fan, 2007). New extremely rich Chinese upper class with a high income can buy anything from expensive cars to posh apartments. Attitude to money of other Chinese who observe the rich is also changing. It may be observed that money has become an important topic in China; people are being encouraged to seek it, acquire it and flaunt it. Wang (2005) notes that in the modern China it is true that "you are what you consume – for those situated lower on the hierarchy, there is no faster way of acquiring social prestige than emulating the lifestyle of those higher up on the pecking order" (2005). Author noted the so-called "bobo" subculture – very rich individuals, who demand

*Table 1. Chinese card, ATM and POS (point-of-sale) data*

| Year | 2004 | 2005 | 2006 | 2007 | 2008 | 2009 | Mar 2010 |
|---|---|---|---|---|---|---|---|
| Number of cards (millions) | 783 | 960 | 1000 | 1200 | 1620 | 2080 | 2169 |
| Number of credit cards (millions) | 29 | 38 | 45 | 74 | 122 | 175 | 183 |
| ATM (units) | 69800 | 82000 | 96000 | 123,000 | 192,000 | 221,600 | 237,000 |
| POS (units) | 451,850 | 610,000 | 806,200 | 1,000,000 | 1,845,100 | 2,408,300 | 2,587,000 |

*Source:* Guangli et al. (2010)

the best from life and look for luxurious products of finest taste and quality.

In a report published by Chunlin (2004) it is possible to find crucial statistics on the Chinese middle class and changes occurring to it. The author applies four criteria to assess whether one belongs to the middle class: income, professional status, patterns of lifestyle consumption and subjective cognition. The data was collected by a research team at the Chinese Academy of Social Sciences engaged in a study titled "Structural Changes of Contemporary Chinese Society". The conclusion was that although the three first conditions were not met, a significant number of people believed they belonged to the middle class. These aspirations indicate changes in the traditional Chinese society and a potential demand for personal credits.

In order to manage increased demand for personal credit and potential risks associated with insolvent borrowers, a robust and reliable lending system is required and currently banks and other financial institutions in China are in a grave need for such systems (Allen and Snyder 2009).

Currently, the prevalent form of personal lending that has also attracted American banking majors like Citibank is the credit card business. As visible on Table 1, there was a significant increase in the number of credit cards from only 29 million in 2004 to 183 million in March 2010. This increased availability of credit cards has significantly contributed to the huge increase in the use of ATMs (from 69,800 in 2004 to 237,000 in March 2010) and POS (from 451,850 in 2004 to 2,587,000 in March 2010) systems. These figures may be an indication of a great potential in this form of lending. This may still be an underestimation as all these huge figures represent only a little fraction of the country's 1.3 million people who have credit cards. In order to be able to turn these potentials into profits, banks and other financial organizations need some unified and reliable credit system which would overcome the current regulatory and administrative burdens (Aldas-Manzano et al., 2009, Allen and Snyder, 2009; Evans, 2008). In the case of the Western banks there may be a need to adapt their current models and practices in order to overcome cultural and other barriers (Liu, 2009).

## Credit Rating Methodologies

The credit rating system was firstly introduced in China in 1987 (Arner et al, 2010). The goal of a good credit scoring model is to classify credit applicants into two classes: the 'good credit' class that is able to reimburse the financial obligation and the 'bad credit' class that should be denied credit due to the high probability of defaulting on their financial obligations. This classification is contingent on the borrower's socio-demographic characteristics (such as age, education level, occupation and income), the repayment performance on previous loans and the type of loan requested. There have been various quantitative methods proposed in the literature in the last few decades to evaluate consumer loans and improve the credit scoring accuracy (Crook et al., 2007). The main methods are decision tree model, logistic regression model and artificial neural network model.

## Decision Tree Model

The decision tree model has been available since the 1980's and has been applied to the development of credit scoring models (Frydman et al., 1985; Davis et al., 1992). In general this model provides a simple way to select appropriate choices from a pool of available options. Let us consider that a lending institution has a database of several credit applications described by n attributes or characteristics: $x_1, x_2 \ldots\ldots x_n$. A decision tree based on this pool of applicants would consist of a set of sequential binary splits of the data. Its goal would be to select which applicants belong to two classes which can be denoted by 'good credits' and 'bad credits'.

The decision tree algorithm begins with a root node containing a sample of good and bad credit applicants. Figure 1 consists of a set of sequential binary splits of the data through which the algorithm loops over all possible binary splits in order to find the attribute x and the corresponding cut-off value c, which gives the best separation into one side having mostly good credits and the other mostly bad credits. Decision trees are a powerful and flexible classifier. On the disadvantages side a well known limitation of decision tree model is their instability, since small fluctuations in the data sample may result in large variations in the classifications assigned to the instances (Bastos, 2008).

## Logistic Regression Model

One of the most popular statistical tools for classification problems is the logistic regression model. It is also suitable for the credit scoring problems (Press & Wilson, 1978). There have been several methods or variations to the traditional binary logistic regression model in order to increase its accuracy and flexibility. Multinomial logistic regression model (Agresti, 1990, Aldrich & Nelson, 1984, DeMaris, 1992, Knoke & Burke, 1980, Liao, 1994) or logistic regression model for ordered categories (McCullagh, 1980) are examples of them. Therefore, the generalized logistic regression model is the general form of both the binary logistic regression model and the multinomial logistic regression model. Let a p-dimensional explanatory variables $x = (x_1, x_2, \ldots, x_p)$ and Y be the response variable with categories 1, 2, …, r. Then the multinomial logistic regression model is given by the equation

$$\text{logistic}(\pi) = \ln\left[\frac{P(Y = j|x)}{P(Y = k|x)}\right] = x'\beta_j, \quad 0 \le j \le r, \quad j \ne k \tag{1}$$

Where $\beta_j$ is a (p+1) vector of the regression coefficients for the $j^{th}$ variable. Let the last response level be the reference level and then the response probabilities $\pi_1, \pi_2, \ldots, \pi_r$ can be calculated by the equations

$$\pi_r \equiv P(Y = r|x) = \frac{e^{x'\beta_r}}{\sum_{l=1}^{r} e^{x'\beta_1}} = \frac{e^{x'\beta_r}}{e^{x'\beta_r} + \sum_{l=1}^{r-1} e^{x'\beta_1}} = \frac{1}{1 + \sum_{l=1}^{r-1} e^{x'\beta}} \tag{2}$$

$$\pi_j \equiv P(Y = j|x) = \pi_r e^{x'\beta_j}, \quad 1 \le j \le r - 1 \tag{3}$$

where *l* is a response level, and

$$l = l(\beta_j, 1 \le j \le r, j \ne k) = \sum_{i=1}^{n} \ln(P(Y = y_i|x_i)), \quad l \in [1, 2, \ldots, r] \tag{4}$$

*Figure 1. Illustration of decision tree. (Source: Bastos, 2008.)*

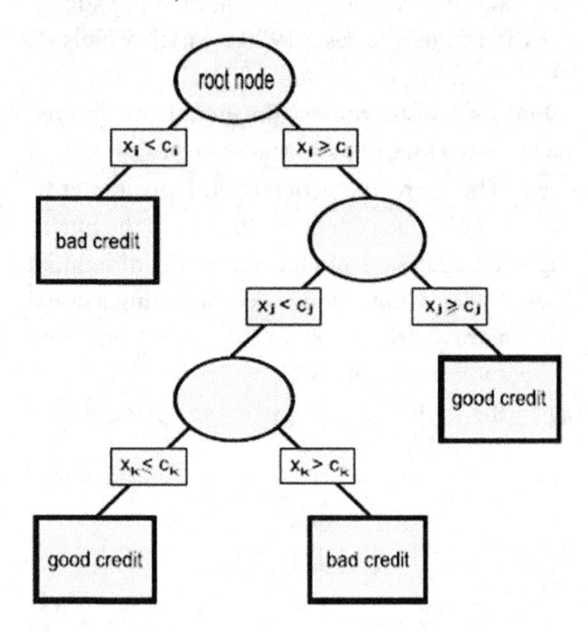


These equations are the logarithmic (ln) probability for the multinomial logistic regression model and $\{(y_i,x_i), 1 \leq i \leq n\}$ denotes the sample of n objects. When the category is equal to two, the multinomial logistic regression model reduces to a binary logistic regression model. Logistic regression model can perform well in many applications; however when the relationships of the system are non-linear, the accuracy of logistic regression decreases and Artificial Neural Networks may be a better choice to deal with this problem (Ong et al., 2005).

## Artifical Neural Network Model (ANN)

Artificial neural network was developed to mimic the neurophysiology of the human brain to be a type of flexible non-linear regression, discriminant, and clustering models. The architecture of ANN can usually be represented as a three-layer system, named input, hidden, and output layers. The input layer first processes the input features to the hidden layer. After that the hidden layer calculates the adequate weights by using the transfer function such as hyperbolic tangent, softmax, or logistic function before sending to the output layer (Ong et al., 2005). The strength of ANN lies in combining many computing neurons into a highly interconnected system. We can detect the complex non-linear relationship in the data. The simple three-layer perception, which is most used in credit scoring problems, can be depicted as shown in Figure 2.

## Factors determining demand for consumer credit in China

This study hypothesizes five independent variables that either directly or indirectly influence the level of outstanding consumer credit in China. These are:

1. Unemployment rate
2. Disposable personal income
3. Government financial policy (Interest Rate)
4. Consumer propensity to save (or Borrow)
5. Methodology

There are also two variables that are dependent on others:

1. Demand for consumer credit
2. Bad debts

Demand for Consumer Credit also influences the amount of Bad Debts as can be seen in Figure 3. Seven hypotheses reflect relationships between independent and dependent variables and these hypotheses are discussed in this section.

**$H_1$:** Unemployment rate has a negative impact on the demand for personal credit.

Unemployment rate measures the percentage of the labour force that is looking for employment in the period. Unemployment takes away income and thus may result in a decreased demand for personal credit. In the opposite situation when unemployment rate decreases, consumers be-

*Figure 2. Three-layer neural network*

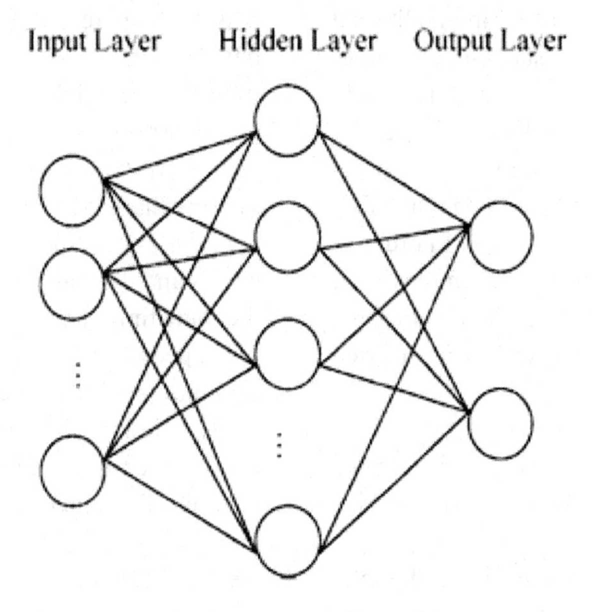


*Figure 3. Research model*

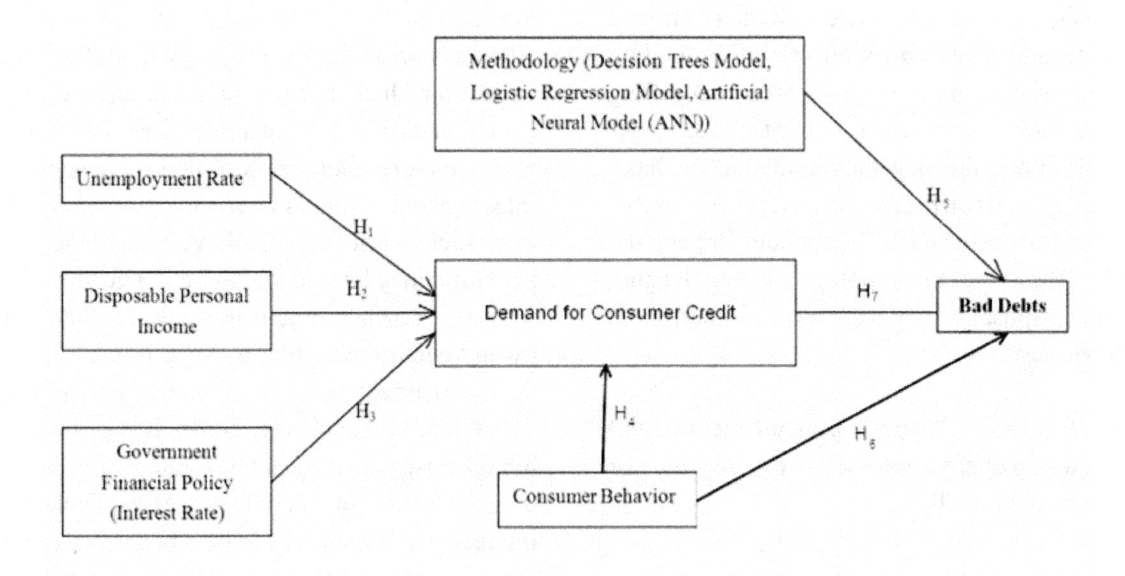

come more optimistic about the future. This can make them be less mindful of taking additional debt thus increasing their outstanding consumer credits. Hence, the sign of the unemployment rate coefficient will be negative. This is especially true in China, where the model for consumption is much more traditional and based on "save first and spend later" (Wang et al., 2011). In order to save it is necessary to earn first. Unemployment affects the demand for credit much the same as it affects the rate of delinquency in a society (Grieb at al., 2001).

**$H_2$:** Disposable personal income has a negative impact on the demand for personal credit.

Disposable personal income measures the level of income after taxes. It is used for both consumption and savings. In this case it is hypothesised that as disposable personal income increases, consumers' need to borrow funds to finance current spending habits decreases. This results in lower demand for consumer credit. Also, although low-income households in general can be granted loan, it requires much more effort from the lending institutions and more sophisticated counselling (Hartarska & Gonzales-Vega, 2006). Zhu & Meeks (1994) support the view that family income has a negative impact on the amount of debt. Amount of debt is in turn affected by the demand for personal credit. Therefore, the hypothesis is that the sign on the disposable personal income coefficient will be negative.

**$H_3$:** Government financial policy (interest rate) has a negative impact on the demand for personal credit.

Interest rate is the percent charged, or paid, for the use of money. It is charged when the money is being borrowed, and paid when it is being loaned. Banks use money for loan as their merchandise to generate profit. In general banks are financially intermediating by buying money from surplus economic units (e.g. a rich businessman with spare cash) and selling the money to deficit economies units. Bank will have to repay interest to its lender(s) (surplus economic units) and therefore it has to charge interest from the borrower(s) (deficit economic units). Usually the interest charged to the bank's borrowers is higher than the interest paid to the lenders. This way a bank can cover all its costs and make profits at the same time. Thus, when interest rates are high, fewer people and businesses can afford to borrow. This may slow down the economy (Adedej, 2002).

The view that interest rates affect cost of capital is supported by Ramirez (2004). Cost of capital in turn affects demand for personal credit. This view is generally regarded as obvious as far as western economies are concerned. In the Chinese economy interest rates are not as important due to the fact that "Chinese authorities have traditionally relied mainly on administrative and quantitative measures in conducting monetary policy" (Koivu 2009). This situation, however, has been changing in the past few years though there is a long way to go to match the Western standards. One of the major changes in the Chinese economy that affects the situation with interest rates and demand for credit is that lending and deposit rates are now allowed to move more freely around state set benchmark rates. Apart from that, some administrative regulations such as price controls have been reduced. In general it may be said that there is a general shift from state owned enterprises towards privately owned enterprises (ibid, p. 456). Interest rate is an independent variable to partially determine the demand for consumer credit. It is possible to hypothesise that as the interest rate increases, the demand for consumer credit decreases. Therefore, interest rate is expected to be a negative sign on the demand for consumer credit. As a result, the growing demand for consumer credit leads to more bad debts. It is possible to state therefore that interest rate is negatively related to the amount of bad debts.

**$H_4$:** Consumer propensity to save (or borrow) has a negative impact on the demand for personal credit.

In general consumer behaviour has a relationship with the demand for consumer credit and also the amount of unpaid debts. In China the situation is influenced by the Chinese history, tradition and culture. These factors dampen the effect of foreign investment (Liu, 2006). This optimistic picture, however, may change if we consider the extremely high level of domestic savings. In fact, for an average 40 percent domestic investment to GDP (fully financed by domestic savings), an 8 to10 percent growth is not such a high return to investment. This may be a very rough indicator of potential misallocation of resources, namely, domestic savings, which has been a common feature of the finally closed economies, and even more so of the centrally-planned ones (Alicia et al., 2006).

China's culture makes its population to be strongly predisposed to saving income rather than spending it. The culture of "buy now, pay later" promoted by the Western banks attempting to enter the Chinese market may be contradictory to the deeply rooted Chinese values. For instance, American Express, Citigroup and HSBC all launched their first credit-card programs in mainland China. These companies are salivating at the prospect of introducing the joys of borrowing to what MasterCard reckons as an emerging market of 45 million to 60 million increasingly affluent Chinese households. So far their stake on the market was minute: of the 668 million cards circulating in the mainland today, only 5 million are true revolving credit cards, the kind that allows consumers to pay off purchases over time. The rest are essentially ATM cards. The most intimidating challenge to China's consumer credit development is neither the lack of infrastructure nor the legal or accounting systems, but the potential customer base (Huang, 2005).

It is necessary therefore to consider consumer behaviour and his or her propensity to save (or borrow) as one of the most important factors influencing amount of bad debts. The hypothesis is that as the consumer saving increases, the demand for consumer credit decreases. Consumer behaviour may affect both the demand for consumer credit as well as the amount of the bad debts. It is hypothesised that this relation is negative – i.e. the demand for consumer credit increase bad debts.

**$H_5$:** Efficiency of methodology used by the lender has a negative impact on the amount of bad debt.

As presented previously a variety of lending methodologies can be applied by banks and other financial institutions in order to minimise unpaid debts (bad debts) in their portfolio. Efficiency of the methodology applied can decide banks' solvency. There are numerous cases in the recent history where even powerful financial institutions became insolvent because of their bad lending decisions. The most recent cases are the Lehmann Brothers (Joe, 2007), Northern Rock (Franco and David, 2009, pp. 196) and Bank of Scotland (Louise, 2010). Therefore the methodology applied by the lender turns to be one of the crucial factors affecting the amount of bad debts. In general the better the methodology the lower should be the amount of the bad debts.

Artificial neural network model (ANN) is composed of artificial neurons that mimic the behavior of brain. Each of the artificial neurons receives input, processes them and delivers a single output. Thus, an artificial neural network model is a collection of artificial neurons that are grouped in layers, mainly the input layer, the hidden layer, and the output layer. The input variables can be attributes such as the applicant's income, debt, and the monthly payments out of the applicant's income. The outcome can be a decision whether it is a good loan or a bad loan. In order to calculate output, an artificial neural network uses weights. A weight is a representation of a connection between two neurons. The weights express the relative importance of each input to a processing element. For example, an input is the person whose income is GBP 2,000 per month. A low weight to this income level could cause the loan to be denied whereas a high weight to an income of GBP 2,500 or more per month could produce a positive output that would enable the granting of the loan to the lender.

According to the above analysis, usage of methodologies such as decision tree models, logistic regression models and models based on artificial neural network are all negatively correlated to bad debts. Thus, it is possible to formulate the fifth hypothesis that efficiency of methodology applied is negatively correlated with the amount of bad debts.

**$H_6$:** Consumer propensity to save (or borrow) has a negative impact on the amount of bad debt.

As it was presented in previous sections, Chinese consumers tend to be more eager to save and are rather reluctant to buy on credit. This tendency results in a smaller total debt. The less credit is granted, the less debts repayments are defaulted and as a result the amount of bad debts decreases. This view is also present in the research by Tam & Dholakia (2011). Therefore it is possible to formulate the hypothesis that consumer's propensity to save has a negative impact on the amount of bad debt.

**$H_7$:** Demand on the consumer credit has a positive impact on the amount of bad debt.

With regards to growing indebtedness in Western societies, Kamleitner and Kirchler (2007) noted that "indebtedness and bankruptcy in private households as a result of growing consumer credit use are rapidly increasing in Western societies" (2007). Therefore the link between demand for consumer credit and bad debts is clearly established in Western societies such that there is a conscious effort to dampen the demand by discouraging irresponsible lending in Western Societies like the Unied States (Zinman, 2010).

Kamleitner and Kirchler (2007) have also observed that the growth of outstanding consumer credit in the new member states of the European Union is in some cases exceeding that of old European states (such as France). These countries share some common characteristics with Chinese economy (transition from the centrally planned into market regulated economy as well as longing for Western living standards). Therefore it is possible to predict that in the Chinese society similar patterns may follow and this hypothesis is still valid as well.

## SUMMARY, IMPLICATIONS AND AREAS FOR FURTHER INVESTIGATIONS

This paper has described most common credit rating methodologies present in the Western world. It has also described the potential for personal credit business in the fast growing economy of China. This growing potential is already evidenced in the increase of credit card possession and use at ATMs and point-of-sales (POS). The huge Chinese population is also a sign of much potential that has attracted foreign financial investors. However, problems come by way of an inadequate sound credit rating system and the unique administrative and cultural history of China that necessitates the adaptation of any Western methodologies that is intended to be applied to the Chinese market.

As a very early stage of conceptualising a sound credit rating system, this chapter has attempted to build a research model that expresses the demand for consumer credit and bad debts as a function of five factors. Five statistical models commonly used in the West for credit decision making were discussed in detail to show their potential of being used in China.

As indicated in the paper, any Western methodology has to be carefully adapted to the Chinese environment. This adaptation and incorporation into a sound credit system for China is a subject for further investigation. The statistical models have been specifically chosen because they are within the control of banks and other lending financial institutions to which this study principally is directed. Also, it could be interesting to investigate how the methodologies presented can be computerised to provide an automated lending decision system. In the first place, it would be useful to test the research model of this chapter with empirical data and analysis. An empirically validated model will be a first step towards building a sound credit system for China. Hopefully, such a system should also be applicable to developing or transition economies which typify China.

## REFERENCES

Adedej, A. (2002). *Why Firms in the UK Use Interest Rate Derivatives.*, *28*(11), 53–74.

Agresti, A. (1990). *Categorical Data Analysis*. New York: Wiley.

Aldas-Manzano, J., Lassala-Navarre, C., Ruiz-Mafe, C., & Sanz-Blas, S. (2009). The role of consumer innovativeness and perceived risk in online banking usage. *International Journal of Bank Marketing*, *27*(1), 53–75. doi:10.1108/02652320910928245

Aldrich, J. H., & Nelson, F. D. (1984). *Linear Probability, Logit, and Probit Models*. Beverly Hills, CA: Sage.

Alicia, G. H., Sergio, G., & Daniel, S. (2006). 'China's Banking Reform: An Assessment of its Evolution and Possible Impact.'. *CESifo Economic Studies*, *52*(2), 304–363. doi:10.1093/cesifo/ifl006

Allen, R. E., & Snyder, D. (2009). New thinking on the financial crisis. *Critical Perspectives on International Business*, *5*(1/2), 36–55. doi:10.1108/17422040910938677

Andreeva, G. (2005). *European generic scoring models using logistic regression and survial analysis.* Bath: Young OR Conference.

Arner, D. W., Hsu, B. F. C., & Lifen, P. (2010). *Credit Rating in China Chinese Law & Government*, *43*(3), 3–7. doi:10.2753/CLG0009-4609430300

Bastos, J. (2008). Credit scoring with boosted decision. *Munich Personal RePEc Archive Paper*, *8156*, 2–4.

Chen, M. C., & Huang, S. H. (2007). 'Credit scoring and rejected instances reassigning through evolutionary computation techniques'. *Expert Systems with Applications*, *24*(4), 433–441. doi:10.1016/S0957-4174(02)00191-4

Chunlin, L. (2004). Zhongchan jieceng Zhongguo shehui zhide guanzhu de rengun, [The Middle Class: A Chinese Social Group Worthy of Our Attention] In Ru Xin, Lu Xueyi, and Li Peilin (Eds.), 2004: Zhongguo shehui xingshi fenxi yu yuce [*2004: Analysis and Forecast on China's Social Development*] (pp. 51-63)BeijingL Sheke wenxian chuban she, 2004.

Crook, J. N., Edelman, D. B., & Thomas, L. C. (2007). Recent developments in consumer credit risk assessment. *European Journal of Operational Research*, *183*, 1447–1465. doi:10.1016/j.ejor.2006.09.100

Davis, R. H., Edelamn, D. B., & Gammerman, A. J. (1992). Machine learning algorithms for credit-card applications. *IMA Journal of Management Mathematics*, *4*, 43–51. doi:10.1093/imaman/4.1.43

DeMaris, A. (1992). *Logit Modeling*. Beverly Hills, CA: Sage.

Durvasula, S., & Lysonski, S. (2010). Money, money, money – how do attitudes toward money impact vanity and materialism? – The case of young Chinese consumers. *Journal of Consumer Marketing*, *27*(2), 169–179. doi:10.1108/07363761011027268

Evans, J. W. (2008). Challenging Confucius: Western banks in the Chinese credit card market. *Business Horizons*, (n.d)., 519–527. doi:10.1016/j.bushor.2008.07.004

Fan, M. (2007). Confucius making a comeback in moneydriven modern China. *Washington Post*. Retrieved January 6, 2011 from http://www.washingtonpost.com/wp-dyn/content/article/2007/07/23/AR2007072301859.html.

Fensterstock, F. (2005). Credit scoring and the next step: business credit. New York: National *Association ofCredit Management, 107*(3), 46-49.

Franco, B., and David T. L., (2009). The Failure of Northern Rock: A Multi-dimensional Case Study. *SUERF-The European Money and Finance Forum*, 196.

Frydman, H. E., Altman, E. I., & Kao, D.-L. (1985). Introducing recursive partitioning for financial classification: the case of financial distress. *The Journal of Finance*, *40*(1), 269–291. doi:10.2307/2328060

Grieb, T., Hegji, C., & Jones, S. T. (2001). Macroeconomic factors, consumer behavior, and bankcard default rates. *Journal of Economics and Finance*, *25*(3), 316–327. doi:10.1007/BF02745892

Guangli, N., Yibing, C., Lingling, Z., & Yuhong, G. (2010). Credit card customer analysis based on panel data clutering. *International Conference on Computational Science, ICCS 2010*, (pp. 2483-2491)ICCS

Hartarska, V., & Gonzales-Vega, C. (2006). Evidence on the effect of credit counselling on mortgage loan default by low-income households. *Journal of Housing Economics*, *15*, 63–79. doi:10.1016/j.jhe.2006.02.002

Huang, N. (2005). China on credit: The iron rice bowl goes plastic. *Time Asia*, Available: http://www.time.com/time/asia/covers/501050516/china_debt.html

Joe, B. B. (2007). Lehman Brothers 1Q Profit Up 5.6 Pct. *The Associated Press*.89.

Kamleitner, B. & Kirchler, E., (2007). Crédit à la consommation: modèle de processus et revue de literature. [Consumer credit use: a process model and literature review]. *Revue européenne de psychologie appliquée*, 57, 267-283.

Knoke, D., & Burke, P. J. (1980). *Log-linear Models*. Beverly Hills, CA: Sage.

Koivu, T. (2009). Has the Chinese economy become more sensitive to interest rates? Studying credit demand in China. *China Economic Review*, *20*, 455–470. doi:10.1016/j.chieco.2008.03.001

Liao, T. F. (1994). *Interpreting Probability Model: Logit, Probit, and Other Generalized Linear Models*. Beverly Hills, CA: Sage.

Liu, M. T. (2009). Do credit card redemption reward programs work in China? An empirical study. *Journal of Consumer Marketing*, *26*(6), 403–414. doi:10.1108/07363760910988229

Liu, T. (2006). The entry of foreign banks into the Chinese banking sector. *Bank for International Settlements*. Available: http://www.bis.org/publ/bppdf/bispap04c.pdf

Louise, S. (2010). Competition and the banking crisis. *Business and Transport Section, SN/BT/5272*, pp. 8.

McCullagh, P. (1980). Regression Model for Ordinal Data. *Journal of the Royal Statistical Society. Series B. Methodological*, *42*(2), 109–142.

Ong, C. S., Huang, J. J., & Tzeng, G. H. (2005). Building Credit Scoring Models Using Genetic Programming. *Expert Systems with Applications*, (n.d)., 41–47. doi:10.1016/j.eswa.2005.01.003

Press, S. J., & Wilson, S. (1978). Choosing between logistic regression and discriminant analysis. *Journal of the American Statistical Association*, *73*(4), 699–705. doi:10.2307/2286261

Ramirez, C. D. (2004). Monetary policy and the credit channel in an open economy. *International Review of Economics & Finance*, *13*, 363–369. doi:10.1016/S1059-0560(03)00038-8

Rosen, S. (2004). The victory of materialism: aspirations to join China's urban moneyed classes and the commercialization of education. *China Journal (Canberra, A.C.T.)*, *51*, 27–51. doi:10.2307/3182145

Smith, A. D. (2009). Internet retail banking: A competitive analysis in an increasingly financially troubled environment. *Information Management & Computer Security*, *17*(2), 127–150. doi:10.1108/09685220910964009

Tam, L., & Dholakia, U. M. (2011). Delay and duration effects of time frames on personal savings estimates and behavior. *Organizational Behavior and Human Decision Processes*, *114*, 142–152. doi:10.1016/j.obhdp.2010.10.009

Wang, J. (2005). Bourgeois bohemians in China? Neo-tribes and the urban imagery. *The China Quarterly*, *183*, 532–548. doi:10.1017/S0305741005000342

Wang, L., Lu, W., & Malhotra, N. K. (2011). Demographics, attitude, personality and credit card features correlate with credit card debt: A view from China. *Journal of Economic Psychology*, *32*, 179–193. doi:10.1016/j.joep.2010.11.006

Whalen, C. (2005). The next great pyramid game. *Inter Economics*, *19*(4), 22–56.

Worthington, S. (2005). Entering the market for financial services in transitional economies; a case study of creidt cards in China. *International Journal of Bank Marketing*, *25*(5), 381–396. doi:10.1108/02652320510612465

Zhao, A. L., Koenig-Lewis, N., Hanmer-Lloyd, S., & Ward, P. (2010). Adoption of internet banking services in China: is it all about trust? *International Journal of Bank Marketing*, *28*(1), 7–26. doi:10.1108/02652321011013562

Zhu, Y. L., & Meeks, B. C. (1994). Effect of low-income families ability and willingness to use consumer-credit on subsequent outstanding credit balance. *The Journal of Consumer Affairs*, *28*(2), 403–422. doi:10.1111/j.1745-6606.1994.tb00859.x

Zinman, J. (2010). Restricting consumer credit access: Household survey evidence on effects around the Oregon rate cap. *Journal of Banking & Finance*, *34*, 546–556. doi:10.1016/j.jbankfin.2009.08.024

# Section 4

# Using Information Technology to Support Education in Developing Economies:

## Investing e-Library and e-Learning

# Chapter 13
# Integrating Information Communication Technologies (ICT) with Information Literacy and Library-Use-Instructions in Nigerian Universities

**Aniebiet I. Ntui**
*University of Calabar, Nigeria*

**Eno J. Ottong**
*University of Calabar, Nigeria*

**Abel Usoro**
*University of the West of Scotland, UK*

## ABSTRACT

*Curriculum contents in developing economies like Nigeria has the objectives of developing students' higher order thinking skills, ability to acquire and utilize learning sources in the library, develop adequate competence in the use of needed information among others. It should aim as developing technological capability for handling information that would achieve these objectives. This study evaluates the information literacy and library-use programmes introduced in Nigerian universities to achieve the aforementioned objectives. An empirical work done on three Nigerian Universities, as a sample, compares their curriculum contents and explores ways that information technology can be integrated into them. Among the study findings is inadequate attention paid to information and technology literacy. One of the study's recommendations is to give adequate attention to information and technology literacy without loading the students with unnecessary library technicalities, as the study found out. The study also presented curriculum structures that can improve the situation.*

DOI: 10.4018/978-1-4666-1637-0.ch013

## INTRODUCTION

The ultimate goal of education has been argued to be the leading of "individuals to understand how the world functions and help them find new ways to make the world" Konidari (2011). The National policy on education (2004) localizes this goal by specifying that the philosophy and goal of education in Nigeria is functional education, for the promotion of a progressive united Nigeria. To this end, school programmes need to be relevant, purposive and comprehensive. Accordingly, life long education is ensured as the basis of the nation's educational policy. The major goal of Nigeria University system is to teach, research and determine the content of courses. Libraries are becoming ever more important partners for research and teaching, with both print and non-print resources. Nigerian universities are also trying to offer their communities not only hard copies of books and journals but also their electronic forms sometimes organized in databases that are assessable to the readers.

The National University commission recommended that library-use-instruction should be taught under the general studies programme, to ensure that students make use of the enormous resources in the library. In response, Nigerian Universities have introduced and implemented library-use-instruction programme (LUIP) as stipulated by NUC. It is a formally structured programme of activities designed to transmit knowledge and skills about acquisition and utilization of learning resources in the library. Undergraduate students who pass through LUIP, apart from acquiring the knowledge to use library resources should be able to acquire skills that enable them to develop adequate competence in the use of information and become information literate. Association of College and Research Library, ACRL (2000) puts information literacy as a key component of, and contributor to life long learning. Information literacy is generally defined as having the ability to recognize when information is needed, and then to be able to locate and evaluate appropriate information and use (American Library Association, 1989).

The concern to get undergraduate students in Nigerian Universities properly educated in the utilization of library resources and to acquire information literacy competence has made the university librarians to develop curriculum contents for information literacy and LUI programme. This instruction is taught under the course Use of English/Communication Skills in the General Studies programme in most Nigerian Universities. The focus of the instruction is on 100/200 level (first and second year) undergraduates. The information literacy (IL) and library-use-instructions (LUI) curriculum content is to enable the student utilize the library resources, and have the ability to locate, access, analyse, and evaluate the needed information. A study by Lwehabura (1999) reveals that the course contents of the programme pose problems to users especially freshpersons, with too much technicalities of the library profession which may hinder good assimilation of knowledge. Sanni and Idiodu (2004) study reveals that IL and LUI curriculum contents in Nigerian Universities does not involve the whole information and communication processes, critical thinking skills and ICT concepts. It is against this background that this study sets out to examine the curriculum contents of library-use-instruction and information literacy in Nigeria Universities. The study will also identify the constraints of the programme and suggest measures of integrating ICT into the curriculum.

## LITERATURE REVIEW

Bruce (2011) emphasized the necessity for information literacy in library studies. Eisenberg and Berkowitz (1990) and Eisenberg and Brown (1992) researched on the nature and scope, value, impact and effective methods of information literacy skills instructions. They focused on the value of an integrated approach. But Bernard Long (2005), in UNESCO publication analysis on ICT and higher education in developing countries was trying to bridge the digital divide. Higher education instructions are challenged to integrate technologies into their strategies, organization and educational processes. ICT is a major tool both for on-campus students and for reaching out towards new target groups engaged in lifelong processes or on professional markets. The Australian and New Zealand information literacy framework (2004) postulated that curriculum integration is the best approach for developing information literacy and that curriculum, classed and activities should be developed jointly by faculty and librarians to achieve course objectives and outcomes.

These activities should be incorporated into subject based assignments and should form part of an effective information literacy curriculum that requires collaboration at many levels. Curriculum must be aligned both horizontally and vertically to ensure that knowledge and skills are introduced, reinforced and mastered across content areas and grade levels. The Quest R III, school library system (2006) constructed a regional information literacy curriculum to enable them address four fundamental paradigm shifts: information problem–solving, current to emerging technologies, a redirection in the optimal development of literacy and conscious development of social responsibility in the digital age. This curriculum collaboration should boost student's achievement and maturity as well as develop higher order thinking and life-long learning habits. Furthermore, it would promote a school culture of collaboration and enhanced knowledge in content areas.

Orr and Wallin (2001), in central Queensland University (CQU), developed a framework on information literacy philosophy and flexible delivery. In this model the students from variety of background are central to all teaching and learning. The model identifies the need to integrate information literacy and library-use-instruction across the subject background, link the undergraduate students to the ever changing world of information resources, understand and utilize the traditional catalogue, and the online catalogues, Opac, databases, prepare a search strategy, keywords, use sophisticated searching technologies on CD-ROM and learn appropriate forms of citation. As reported by Hosein Sharida (2006), the working group on the teaching of information literacy at the University of the West Indies in Triinidad developed seven modules in the course contents. They are as follows: basic computer literacy, basic research skills; use of the Online Public Access catalogue (OPAC), the internet as a research tool, the West Indiana and special collections, online databases and managing references. Each module has its own objectives; it also includes an important section on information ethics where topics such as copyright and plagiarism are covered. Studies on ICT literacy assessment by the Education Training Services (2006) reveal that most students were not able to demonstrate ICT skills, construct presentation slide, and some were not able to organize large amounts of information nor sort information to clarify related material after passing through the curriculum contents because ICT was not integrated into their curriculum.

The American Library Association (1989) examined, defined, and analyzed the information literacy curriculum and posits that the curriculum should contain elements on the ability to locate, interpret, analyzed, synthesize, evaluate and communicate needed information, although they have not integrated ICT with information literacy curriculum. Eisenberg/Berkowitz (1990) on information problem-solving (the Big 6 skills) in New South Wales, United Kingdom examined and compared the information skills process models. Bruce (1995) reported seven key characteristics of an information literate person using the framework for Higher Education in the Australian Library Journals. But they did not examine the curriculum on the teaching of IL skills and how ICT can be integrated. Department of information studies from the Ontario School Library Association explore information literacy curriculum, studied the expectation and scope/sequence. But none of the studies has been able to compare the curriculum of each University or library. But according to Etim and Nssien (2007), information literacy can be facilitated by e-learning. New technologies can enable information literate person organized to differentiate their needs and target the strategies. According to her, education institutions should integrate technologies into their curriculum and become more skilled and successful in accessing and using digitized information. The purpose of this present study is therefore to:

1. Analyse the curriculum of information literacy (IL) and library-use-instructions (LUI) in Nigerian Universities;
2. Identify the constraints of the curriculum;
3. Suggest measures of integrating ICT into IL and LUI curriculum.

The study will also seek to look beyond the examination of the curriculum on information literacy (IL) and library-use-instruction (LUI) programme and review issues and practices associated with the General Studies (GSS) programme that may relate to IL and LUI curriculum. The paper provides insight into the level, issues and challenges associated with IL and LUI curriculum in Nigerian Universities and it concludes with recommendations that require continued exploration.

## METHOD

The study is an empirical case study covering three of the Federal Universities in Nigeria, namely University of Abuja, (Unibuja) University of Ibadan (UI) and University of Calabar (Unical). The choice of the three Nigerian Universities was based on having well developed libraries, geographical spread and they are also offering the information Literacy (IL) and library-use-instruction (LUI) programmes. The programme is offered under the course code General (GSS) 101 or 1101, Use of English. Prior to visiting the three Nigerian Universities, the researchers who are also lecturers of the IL and LUI programme conducted interviews with other lecturers and coordinators of the programme in these Universities. This enabled them to understand better the curriculum contents of other Universities.

The following research strategies guided the site visits.

- Comparison of the curriculum contents of Information Literacy (IL) and Library-Use-Instruction (LUI) programme in the three Nigerian Universities;
- Examination of the weaknesses and defects of the curriculum; and
- Determination of the ways of integrating ICT into information literacy and library-use-instruction curriculum in Nigerian Universities.

The data for this work were gathered through a questionnaire. The choice of the questionnaire as the appropriate instrument for the study is based on objective oriented rating in measuring curriculum contents. Hosein (2006) used similar questionnaire with rewarding success during IL curriculum development at the University of the West Indies in Trinidad. The questionnaire was tested and had twenty seven (27) items. The first part of the questionnaire consisted of information on length of time as lecturer on LUI programme. Before the questionnaire was introduced to a respondent, the researchers sought to know if she had adequate experience as an instructor in the LUI programme before the questionnaire was introduced. The second part elicited data on curriculum contents of LUI programme and constraints/weaknesses affecting the IL and LUI curriculum.

*Table 1. Curriculum contents of IL and LUI programme in three Nigerian Universities*

| Curriculum contents Responses by Universities | | | | | | | | |
|---|---|---|---|---|---|---|---|---|
| | Uniabuja | | Unical | | Unibadan | | Total | |
| | N | % | N | % | N | % | N | % |
| Concept of the Library | 9 | 100 | 20 | 100 | 11 | 100 | 40 | 100 |
| Types of libraries | 8 | 88.8 | 17 | 85.0 | 9 | 81.8 | 34 | 85.0 |
| Information Resources/source | 9 | 100 | 15 | 85.0 | 7 | 63.6 | 31 | 77.5 |
| The catalogue (organization information) | 8 | 88.8 | 16 | 80.0 | 10 | 90.9 | 34 | 85.0 |
| **Classification** | | | | | | | | |
| Retrieval of information materials | 5 | 55.56 | 10 | 50.0 | 7 | 63.6 | 22 | 55.0 |
| Reference sources/services | 4 | 44.4 | 15 | 85.0 | 6 | 54.5 | 25 | 62.5 |
| How to locate a book | 3 | 33.3 | 10 | 50.0 | 5 | 45.5 | 18 | 45.0 |
| How to use the catalog | 8 | 88.8 | 17 | 85.0 | 8 | 72.7 | 33 | 82.5 |
| How to retrieve information from data bases e.g. CD-ROM, OPAC etc | 5 | 55.5 | 6 | 30.0 | 9 | 81.8 | 20 | 50.0 |
| Tour of the university library | 7 | 77.8 | 16 | 80.0 | 10 | 90.9 | 33 | 82.5 |
| How to access, evaluate analyze needed information etc | 4 | 44.4 | 5 | 15.0 | 2 | 18.2 | 11 | 27.5 |

## RESULTS

A total of 43 copies of the questionnaire were administered in the three Nigerian Universities. Forty usable copies were returned which represent a response rate of 93.0%. Frequency and percentages distribution were the descriptive analytical tools adopted.

## FINDINGS

Table 1, summarizes the frequency of curriculum contents of IL and LUI and topics taught by the three Universities. The most widely reported topic in the curriculum is concept of the library that has 100% for the total of the three universities and for each of the Universities. Other topics included types of libraries 85%, organization of information resources, cataloging and classification 85%, how to use the catalogue 82.5% and tours of the university libraries 82.5% and the topic on tours of the library are also highly rated in UI 91.9%.

The findings reveal that a topic like how to locate books from the shelf is generally rated low (45%) and very low in the University of Abuja (33.3%). How to retrieve information from data bases e.g. CD-ROM is rated very low in the University of Calabar (30%). The findings show that only 27.5% of the respondents in the three Nigerian Universities says that they know how to access, analyze and evaluate needed information in their curriculum, that is 15% in Unical and 18.2% in Unibadan. Interviewed respondents overwhelmingly indicated that the curriculum contents of IL and LUI in the three Universities is not related to the undergraduate's subject background. A lecturer from the University of Abuja says and I quote "we are yet to understand this information literacy, all we understand is to teach the students how to find their ways around the library". In another interview a faculty member from University of Calabar indicated that, there seem to be too much technicalities of the library profession in the IL and LUI curriculum instead of incorporating the skill on how to become information competent.

In order to establish the problems, weaknesses and defects of the curriculum in the three Nigerian University, the 40 lecturers/coordinators of the programme were given the list of constraints/weaknesses to indicate the constraint affecting IL and LUI curriculum.

The data on Table 2 show the percentage of respondents indicating various types of constraints affecting IL and LUI curriculum. Overwhelmingly the constraints indicated by the highest percentage of respondents are that of having the course as a unit under Use-of-English 97.5%. Others include no information literacy tutorials 97.5%, followed by curriculum not integrated into students' subject background 90.0%, inadequate time to cover the curriculum 85.0% and attitude of students towards the programme 80.0%, ICT not integrated into the curriculum 70.0% and in Unical 90.0% but Unibadan differs with a low rate of response on ICT integration 27.2%. On the other hand, standards and/guidelines for IL and LUI curriculum is 25.0%, incorporate online search strategy into the curriculum 25.0%, bibliographic data search 37.5%. While Unibadan is rated high with 63.6%, Uniabuja is rated low with 33.3%. The respondents indicated too much technicalities of the library and information science core courses as a constraint (72.5%), and also no pre-planned curriculum for IL and LUI (50.0%) especially in the University of Abuja 33.3%.

## KEY FINDINGS AND DISCUSSION

### Curriculum Contents

The result reveals that IL and LUI curriculum focuses much on library and information science core technical areas, as shown on Table 1. However, a close observation reveals inadequate courses to help students acquire the skills on how to use the large volume of complex learning resource in the University libraries. But the librarians in these universities have not come together to assess the influence of the curriculum on the students. Some respondents complain of being bugged with library science technicality, instead of teaching them how to use the library resources. The findings have also confirm Oyesola's study (2008) that curriculum contents of IL and LUI in Nigerian Universities possess problem to users, with too much technicalities of library profession. Information literacy concepts are not fully integrated into the curriculum. Findings also show that the curriculum contents are not related to the students' background of the study. Students also complain of lack of practicals or demonstration on how to locate, evaluate, access or analyse information materials for assignment/class work. This is contrary to the Australian and New Zealand information literacy framework (2004) which postulated that curriculum integration is the best approach for developing students' information literacy competences. A similar situation was reported by Flaming (2004) that an effective information literacy curriculum requires collaboration at many levels, and that the curriculum must be aligned both horizontally and vertically to ensure that knowledge and skills are introduced, re-enforced and mastered across content areas and grade levels.

### Constraints of IL and LUI Curriculum

It was evident from the investigation from the three Nigerian Universities that the government does not have a pre-planned, or standards and guidelines of IL and LUI curriculum. Although 65.0% of the respondents from Unical say their IL and LUI curriculum is pre-planned this, Unical attestation could be due to the fact that the librarians meet and discuss the curriculum. Interview with the lecturers reveal that the instructional programme should be well planned by experts and not just an "organized" programme by the university authority. This is not contrary to the

*Table 2. Constraint of IL and LUI Curriculum*

| | Proportion of Respondents by Universities | | | | | | | |
|---|---|---|---|---|---|---|---|---|
| | **9 Uniabuja** | | **20 Unical** | | **11 Unibadan** | | **40 Total** | |
| | N | % Yes | N | % Yes | N | % Yes | N | %Yes |
| Pre-planed Curriculum for IL and LUI | 3 | 33.3 | 13 | 65.0 | 4 | 36.3 | 20 | 50.0 |
| Standard/guidelines for IL and LUI | 2 | 22.2 | 5 | 25.0 | 3 | 27.2 | 10 | 25.0 |
| No proper framework | 3 | 33.3 | 10 | 50.0 | 3 | 27.2 | 16 | 40.0 |
| The course as a unit under Use-of-English | 8 | 88.9 | 20 | 100.0 | 11 | 100.0 | 39 | 97.5 |
| Inadequate time to cover the curriculum | 7 | 77.8 | 18 | 90.0 | 9 | 81.8 | 34 | 85.0 |
| No cooperation between libraries and faculty | 8 | 88.9 | 13 | 65.0 | 9 | 81.8 | 30 | 75.0 |
| Too much technicalities of the library and information science core courses | 7 | 77.8 | 14 | 70.0 | 8 | 72.7 | 29 | 72.5 |
| Lack of information literacy concepts/ elements | 6 | 66.6 | 12 | 60.0 | 7 | 63.6 | 25 | 62.5 |
| Curriculum not integrated into students subject background. | 9 | 100.0 | 17 | 85.0 | 10 | 90.9 | 36 | 90.0 |
| No information literacy tutorials | 8 | 88.9 | 20 | 100.0 | 11 | 100.0 | 39 | 97.5 |
| ICT not integrated into the curriculum | 7 | 77.7 | 18 | 90.0 | 3 | 27.3 | 28 | 70.0 |
| Incorporate online search strategy for into the curriculum | 2 | 22.2 | 5 | 25.0 | 3 | 27.2 | 10 | 25.0 |
| Bibliography database | 3 | 33.3 | 5 | 25.0 | 7 | 63.6 | 15 | 37.5 |
| Poor search attitude of students towards the programme | 8 | 88.8 | 18 | 90.0 | 6 | 54.5 | 32 | 80.0 |

Association of College and Research Libraries (2000) who published the information literacy competency standards for Higher Education and specified that each institution must be guided by this standard. There is no proper framework or model in the teaching of IL and LUI in these Nigerian Universities. The curriculum does not support a variety of disciplines, nor promote the collaboration between libraries and Faculty members, as it is being stipulated by Orr and Wallin (2001) and Sharida (2006).

The findings also reveal that the course is offered as a unit under Use-of-English, and that the time allocated to it is inadequate to cover the curriculum. These universities include IL and LUI on the timetable as an afterthought after several circulars might have come from the librarian stressing the need to have this programme for the students. The result of the interview with some lecturers reveals that the university itself does not attach great importance to the curriculum being covered in terms of time, and space allocation in the overall timetable and that the marks allocated for the course is too low. For example, in the University of Calabar, Use of English takes 80% whereas IL and LUI course takes only 20%. Most of the time, lecturers of the Use of English take over the teaching of the IL and LUI course. The faculties do not share information with librarians and neither do they see librarians as partners in the teaching process.

Too much technicalities of the library and information science core courses, lack of information literacy concepts and the curriculum not being integrated into students' subject background are great constraints to the IL and LUI curriculum contents. The curriculum does not integrate LUI and IL courses into faculty core courses to enable the course to have an impact on the undergraduate students. Therefore, it does not provide a framework for instructional partnership linking librarians, faculty members and students in an active learning situation. This is not in line with ACRL (2000) and the Quest R II School Library System (2006) recommendations.

In recent times librarians are developing digital libraries in which they make available vast amounts of information – primary and secondary. An average university library nowadays offers its patrons hundreds of databases, thousand of electronic journals, e-books being on their way up. But the three Nigerian Universities do not integrate technologies, incorporate online search nor bibliography database into IL and LUI curriculum. Thus, the students may not be able to acquire skills to use their needed information. This is not in line with the Seven modules in IL and LUI curriculum contents developed by Sharid (2006) to include: basic computer skills, use of the online access public catalogue (OPAC), the internet as a research tool, special collections, on line data bases and managing reference. Another constraint and finding of the study is the poor attitude of students towards the curriculum contents of IL and LUI in the three Nigerian Universities. Students' attitude problem is also attributed to lack of computers, non incorporation of ICT skills, into the curriculum and the inability to deliver the instructions on the Web as it is being done in Canada and USA. These have contributed to students lacking interest and looking at the classroom lectures, demonstrations and tours as old fashioned and boring.

## RECOMMENDATIONS

Based on the observation of this study concerning the defects in the operation of the current information literacy and library use instruction curriculum in the three Nigerian Universities, it is observed that there is need to reposition information literacy concept and integrate ICT skills into the curriculum for effective delivery. Looking at what other libraries are doing in the area of Information Literacy Curriculum in the international world, the paper recommends as follows:

- National University Commission (NUC) and Nigerian Library Association (NLA) should plan, set up standard and articulate the philosophy of IL and LUI curriculum. The guidelines should govern all Universities in Nigeria participating in the teaching of IL and LUI;
- The course should be offered as a lone course under General Studies (GSS), but not as a unit under "Use of English" with only 20 marks allocated to it, as it is applicable in the University of Calabar;
- The instructions should be given on the Web as it is being done in Canada and the USA, to develop students' interest in the programme;
- The faculty and librarian should jointly develop classes or activities to achieve course objectives outcomes. These activities should be incorporated into subject based assignment and form part of the course assessment.

### Information Literacy and LUI Curriculum Contents:

- It is also recommended that the IL and LUI curriculum contents should be organized under three segments, namely: library instructions, ICT and Information literacy skills.

- Library-Use-Instructions
  - The concept of the Library/ Information
  - Information Resources and services
  - How to use the catalogue
  - How to find a book using author, title, subject and call number
  - How to borrow a book.
  - Tour of the University library.
- Information Literacy Skills
  - Determine, identify needed information
  - Select information sources
  - Implement search strategies
  - Locate Information Resources
  - Organize and use information Resources
- ICT Skills
  - Define problem and identify the types of amount of information needed, using e-mail, online discussion, local networks or idea generating software.
  - Assess the value of various types of electronic resources for data gathering, including databases, CD-ROM resources, internet online resources, on-line discussion, e-mail,
  - Locate and Access, Online Catalogue (OPAC) full text sources, online services, electronic reference materials, current literature in relative to Nigerian University Homepage.
  - Use, connect and operate the computer technology needed, use software and hardware.
  - Synthesise, classify and group information using database, create information and use projector, properly cite and credit electronic sources.
  - Evaluate electronic presentation in terms of contents and format.

## CONCLUSION

Integrating the current emerging technologies into information literacy and Library-Use-Instructions curriculum will boost the students' achievement and motivation. As observed in this paper, there are no standards or guidelines by NUC or NLA to build curriculum contents. The course is offered as a unit under Use-of English with only 20 marks allocated to it, which makes it impossible for the existing curriculum to be completed. It is appropriate for Faculties and Librarians to jointly work together and re-assess the existing IL and LUI curriculum using the recommended curriculum in this study as a guideline. In this way the curriculum contents will develop the students' higher order thinking skills, ability to acquire and utilized learning resources in the library, develop adequate competence in the use of needed information and lifelong learning with productive habit of mind.

Integrating technologies into their curriculum will enable the students to become more successful in using digitized information and help an information literate person to be organized to differentiate their needs and target the strategies. The framework should also eliminate much of the library core courses as shown on table I in the traditional bibliographic instruction curriculum content since ICT and Information Literacy are well integrated. Although the framework has standardized content they can be customized through incorporating into subject base assignments, exercises and information resources and tools. Faculties should be encouraged to integrate specific parts of this curriculum in some of their taught courses. This will ensure that students actually follow the curriculum to improve their information literacy skills. In the three Nigerian Universities, the IL and LUI courses is already made compulsory for all students. Therefore strongly suggest that the course should be run as a general course.

## REFERENCES

American Library Association (ALA). (1989). American Library Association Committee on Information Literacy Final Report, *Eric clearing on Information Technology ED315074*, Chicago.

Association of College and Research Libraries. (2000). *Information Literacy Competency Standards for higher education*. Association of College and Research Libraries, Chicago, IL. Available at *http://www.alaorg/acrl/ilcomstan.htnl.*

Belcher, G., & Rosenberg, D. (2006). ICT Training: INASP Workshops for African University Library Staff. *Information Development.*, *22*(2), 116–122. doi:10.1177/0266666906065574

Bruce, C. (1995). Information Literacy: A Framework for Higher Education. *The Australian Library Journal*, *44*, 158–159.

Bruce, E. M. (2011). Information literacy instruction in the library: now more than ever. *New Library World*, *112*(5-6), 274–277.

Eisenberg, B. (1990). *Information Problem Solving, The Big Six Skills Approach to Library and Information Skills, Instruction*. Norwood, New York: Ablex.

Eisenberg, M. E., & Brown, M. K. (1992). Current Themes regarding and information in skill instruction research supporting and research lacking. *School Library Media. Quarter*, *2*, 103–107.

Etim, F. E., & Nssien, F. U. (2007). *Information Literacy for Library Search*. Nigeria: Abaams.

Federal Republic of Nigeria. (2004). *National Policy on Education* (4th ed.) Lagos: Federal Government Press

Hosein, S (2006). Teaching Information Literacy at the University of the West Indies *Trindad, Information Development 22* (2).

Information Literacy for Academics – IL Projects/ Learning Services. (2009). *The University of Auckland Library.* http://www.library.auckland.ac.nz/instruct/ll/integrating.html.

Konidari, V. (2011). Education in a complex world: a political question to be answered. *Horizon*, *19*(2), 75–84. doi:10.1108/10748121111138272

Lwehabura, M. J. (1999). User Education and Information Skills: A need for a systematic programme in African University Libraries. *African Journal of Library Archives and Information Science*, *9*(2), 129–141.

Orr, A., & Wallin, A. (2001). Information Literacy and Flexible Delivery: Creating a conceptual Framework and model. *Journal of Academic Librarianship*, *27*(6), 457–463. doi:10.1016/S0099-1333(01)00263-4

Quest, R. School Library System. (2006). Information Literacy Curriculum. *NOVELNY, New York: Online Virtual Electronic Library*. https//www.questar.org/library/curriculum.httml.

# APPENDIX

## Questionnaire on Information Literacy (IL) and Library-Use-Instruction (LUI) programme in Nigerian Universities.

Name of university:

How long have you been teaching the LUI course:

Please indicate the curriculum contents of LUI in your university.

Please indicate the constraints/weakness affecting LUI curriculum in your university.

| CURRICULUM CONTENTS | RESPONSE | |
|---|---|---|
| | YES | NO |
| Concept of the Library | | |
| Types of libraries | | |
| Information Resources/source | | |
| The catalogue (organization information) | | |
| Retrieval of information materials | | |
| Reference sources/services | | |
| How to locate a book | | |
| How to use the catalog | | |
| How to retrieve information from data bases e.g. CD-ROM, OPAC etc | | |
| Tour of the university library | | |
| How to access, evaluate analyze needed information etc | | |

Please indicate the constraints/weakness affecting LUI curriculum in your university.

| Constraint of LUI curriculum | | |
|---|---|---|
| | YES | NO |
| Pre-planed Curriculum for IL and LUI | | |
| Standard/guidelines for IL and LUI | | |
| No proper framework | | |
| The course as a unit under Use-of-English | | |
| Inadequate time to cover the curriculum | | |
| No cooperation between libraries and faculty | | |
| Too much technicalities of the library and information science core courses | | |
| Lack of information literacy concepts/elements | | |
| Curriculum not integrated into students subject background. | | |
| No information literacy tutorials | | |
| ICT not integrated into the curriculum | | |
| Incorporate online search strategy for into the curriculum | | |
| Bibliography database | | |
| Poor search attitude of students towards the programme | | |

# Chapter 14
# E-Learning in Higher Education:
## The Nigerian Universities' Experience

**Abel Usoro**
*University of the West of Scotland, UK*

**Rosemary C. Akuchie**
*University of Abuja, Nigeria*

## ABSTRACT

*Technological innovations have enhanced performance in all sectors of economic and social activities including education. The purpose of the educational system is to achieve efficient communication, which involves transmission of information, knowledge, skills, values, and attitudes to the learner. This study therefore seeks to survey the extent to which e-learning is applied in Nigerian Universities for effective teaching and learning processes. The sample comprised four government universities in the north central geopolitical zone of Nigeria. Twenty five lecturers and 25 students (from second year level and above) totaling 100 in each case were randomly selected. Six research questions guided the study. The findings of the work showed that lecturers are better exposed to Information and Communication Technology (ICT) than students, most e-learning facilities though available in the universities are not entirely functional and adequate. Also lecturers and students do not employ most ICT facilities for teaching and learning respectively.*

## INTRODUCTION

E-learning has been a hot topic since the late 1990s with the dramatic developments in communication and information technology. These developments continue with the introduction of Web 2.0 and its social networking. While developing countries are quick at absorbing these technologies to develop their e-learning, the adoption of e-learning in developing economies like Nigeria has not been in the same pace. However, there is sufficient interest in e-learning in Nigeria, beginning from the Universities, to warrant periodic reviews of its development. Therefore this study conducted

DOI: 10.4018/978-1-4666-1637-0.ch014

in early part of 2011 endeavours to review the situation using four universities as the sample. The rest of this chapter will present (a) e-learning background, (b) e-learning in Nigeria, (c) research questions, (d) method, (e) results, (f) discussion, (g) conclusion and recommendations, and (d) limitations and areas for further studies.

## E-LEARNING BACKGROUND

The Internet had its explosion in the late 1990s when it was possible not only to browse but to place contents that users can easily access. This explosion was accompanied with interest from both practitioners and academics in e-learning which can be regarded as "the delivery of training, education and collaboration using various electronic media, but predominantly the Internet" (Usoro and Abiagam, 2009). This definition essentially includes every learning with the use of ICT to be e-learning since the "e" stands for electronic. Thus, it does not need to be distant though in practice most e-learning is done in distance and asynchronously. Unlike the US that is prominently succeessful with pure e-learning with no human interaction in the delivery, the UK is typified with use of the mixed (face-to-face and ICT-utilised) e-learning, sometimes termed "blended learning." For example, the delivery of courses by University of the West of Scotland at TEI Piraeus University in Greece was done by Blackboard as an e-learning platform but at the same time, lecturers would fly once a month to Athens to perform eye-ball-to-eye-ball deliveries. The blended approach recognizes that it is very difficult for information technology to fully replace the physical human interaction between lecturers and students as well as among the students themselves.

It has to be accepted though that modern technology is pushing the boundaries of human-interaction in the delivery of learning. The increasing ease of producing and distributing electronic videos and animations makes possible the production of engaging electronic games and the same technology is also applied to e-learning. It can be reasoned that if most game players do not need human teachers, e-learning materials that are fashioned in the same way should do without much human teachers; thus, the great interest in games-based learning. Perhaps at last the problem of student motivation as a result of absence of the teacher will be removed from the list of e-learning drawbacks and problems as listed by Connolly and Stansfield (2007) and Carr (2000).

Another significant development in e-learning is in the incorporation of Web 2.0 technology which allows for social networking and ease of participants to contribute content on the Internet. Even outside learning, electronic social networking has been significantly accepted by both the young and even the not-so-young as evidenced in the use of Facebook, Twitter and other popular tools. Incorporation of this technology into e-learning means a chance is given to make the learning active and participatory; moreover, student's management and speed of feedback is enhanced (Rath, 2011; Loving and Ochoa, 2011). It is also significant that this technology is available in most modern mobile devices like internet phones and tablets (iPads). The consequence is not only the delivery but engagement in learning while the learner is on the move with his telephone for instance. Thus, e-learning is expanded to the concept of m-learning. Kim et al (2011) in their research, for instance found various ways that m-learning could be utilized in hospitality industry.

Even before the wide uptake of these high level e-learning, many researchers had started to offer evidence of superior outcomes of e-learning: removal of obstacles of time, cost, socio-economic status and distance but at the same time allowing individuals to take more responsibility for their learning which now can continue throughout their lives (cf Usoro and Abiagam, 2009; Larson and Bruning, 1996; Alexander, 2001; Stansfield et al, 2004). The benefits of e-learning are derived not only by educational institutions but also by private companies who use e-learning to increase the 'corporate IQ' (Cross, 2004) and to enhance their knowledge management efforts especially when they incorporate social networking (Wang, 2011). The advantages of e-learning follow the penetration of e-learning which is more significantly in developed economies.

## E-LEARNING IN NIGERIA

Though largely less technologically advanced, Nigeria, like other developing economies, has already been recognized as standing to benefit from the e-learning for various reasons (Yusuf, M, 2005). The need for education is more felt in developing economies because with the present number of teachers, millions of inhabitants stand no chance of getting any form of education if a significant supplementary effort is not put. Inhabitants of these economies, like Nigeria, also share the same obstacle of time-release from full time employments to attend full-time education. Thus e-learning has the time and place flexibility that would suit employees (and employers) in Nigeria.

Nigeria is listed in literature as one of the countries with low income per capita (Ballantyne, 2011). This level of income is a strong barrier to full-time education in terms of fees, relocation and upkeep. On the other hand, e-learning uses Internet technology which is relatively low in price more so as much economies of scales are achieve through significant replication of the effort of a few professors who may be producing the learning materials. With a combination of computer animation and other dynamic aspects of information technology, the learning can be made interesting while drastically reducing the unit cost with the wide audience. Moreover, there are a few international efforts at funding e-learning in developing regions like Africa. Such efforts make the learning facilities free on the Internet so that it can reach the developing economies.

Another major reason that developing economies, including Nigeria, are interested in e-learning is that it connects them with the rest of the world. They can "sing from the same hymn book" because the Internet can deliver materials and instructions from across the world without any feel of distance. Nigeria can benefit from initiatives such as the University of the People (http://www.uopeople.org/) - the first tuition-free University launched in 2009 to access the worldwide presence of the Internet and the decreasing cost of education delivered on it. Thus, human resources capable of meeting the challenges of the new world economy can be produced from any corner of the world or Nigeria.

Ajadi et al. (2008) traced the history of e-learning in Nigeria to the development of telecommunication in 1886 when e-cable connection was establish between Lagos and London for colonial business. Though that ancient, he notes that because of inadequate electricity, the digital divide and other developmental hindrances, e-learning in Nigeria is still at infancy compared to developed economies. Despite these difficulties, institutions such as University of Ibadan, Obafemi Awolowo University, University of Benin, University of Abuja, University of Lagos, Niational Open University of Nigeria among others have the facilities for e-learning even if they are only large internet cafes like AfriHUB eg at the University of Calabar.

This increasing adoption of e-learning as noted by researchers like Ajadi et al (2008) warrants evaluation of its effectiveness from time to time. Thus, a few researchers have attempted to evaluate e-learning in Nigeria. These studies are centered at university level. Sharma (2006) performed an exploratory study of the critical factors affecting the acceptability of e-learning in Nigerian universities. Her results indicated mass unawareness, low computer literacy level and cost as critical factors that hindered the acceptance of e-learning in Nigeria. Also Eteng and Ntui (2009) examined University of Calabar as a case study of access to e-learning in the Nigerian university system

(NUS). The study sought to find out how both teachers and students were fairing on e-learning and it found the two groups of participants okay though it was noted that the ICT facilities provided by AfriHUB was not adequate. This study shows the importance of e-learning literacy not only for students but also for teachers in the first place.

Since the adoption of e-learning is improving with time in Nigeria, it is appropriate to repeat evaluations of its impact in Nigerian universities. This study attempts to do this.

## RESEARCH QUESTIONS

To perform the evaluation of e-learning in Nigerian universities, the following research questions were used:

A. To what extent are university lecturers literate in ICT?
B. To what extent are university students literate in ICT?
C. To what level are e-learning facilities available in the universities?
D. How functional are the available e-learning facilities in the universities?
E. What is the extent of lecturers' involvement in employing ICT facilities in teaching?
F. What is the extent of students' involvement in employing ICT facilities in learning?

## METHOD

The research was structured as explained in the rest of this section.

### Design and Population

This study is a survey research design carried out on universities in the north central geo-political zone of Nigeria. The population is made up of all the seven government universities in the geopolitical zone under study.

### Sample

Four government universities in the north central geopolitical zone were randomly selected. From each of these universities, 25 lecturers and 25 students (from 200 level and above) were randomly sampled. This gave a total of 100 lecturers and 100 students.

### Instrument

Seventeen-item questionnaire was designed for both lecturers and students covering: level of literacy in ICT, availability and functionality of e-learning facilities, lecturers and students involvement in using ICT for teaching and learning respectively.

The rating was based on a four point scale of Strongly Agree (SA) Agree (A), Disagree (D), Strongly Disagree (SD).

### Validity and Reliability of Instrument

The instrument was face and content validated by experts. The internal consistency reliability estimate using the Cronbach Alpha method yielded 0.85.

### Data Collection Technique and Analysis

On the spot administration and collection of the questionnaires to both lecturers and students was adopted giving a 100% return. Mean scores were used for the analyses. A mean score of 2.50 to 4.00 shows agreement while a mean score of 1.00 to 2.49 shows disagreement.

## RESULTS

**Research Question 1:** To what extent are University lecturers literate in ICT?

Table 1 shows that lecturers in the universities studied have computers for their use and are conversant with word processing and use of email and databases. These have mean ratings ranging from 2.65 to 2.79. However, they did not undergo intensive computer training and do not use spreadsheets and projectors in lecture delivery. The mean ratings of these items are below 2.55.

**Research Question 2:** To what extent are university students literate in ICT?

In Table 2, the result shows that the students have not undergone computer training, no computer for their use and are not literate in word processing and use of spreadsheets. Their mean scores are below 2.50. The students use e-mail and databases with mean ratings 2.62 and 2.85 respectively.

**Research Question 3:** To what level are e-learning facilities available in the universities?

Table 3 shows that the universities have ICT centres with internet facilities and generator. These have mean scores between 2.87 and 3.14. However, electronic gadgets are not used to deliver lectures, no virtual library and inadequate number of computers for staff and students. Their mean scores fall below 2.50.

**Research Question 4:** How functional are the available e-learning facilities in the universities

*Table 1. The extent of University lecturers' literacy in ICT*

| S/No | Level of Literacy in ICT | Mean Scores | Standard Deviation (SD) | Interpretation |
|---|---|---|---|---|
| 1 | I have undergone an intensive computer training | 2.15 | 0.57 | Disagreed |
| 2 | I have a computer for my use | 2.65 | 0.91 | Agreed |
| 3 | I have learnt how to use the following packages<br>Word processing<br>i) e-mail<br>ii) Internet search<br>iii) Engines/databases<br>iv) Spreadsheets<br>v) Multimedia/overhead projectors in lecture delivery | 2.57<br>2.66<br>2.79<br>1.75<br>2.34 | 0.94<br>0.65<br>0.71<br>0.98<br>0.80 | Agreed<br>Agreed<br>Agreed<br>Disagreed<br>Disagreed |

*Table 2. The level of university students' literacy in ICT*

| SN | Level of literacy in ICT | Mean scores | SD | Interpretation |
|---|---|---|---|---|
| 1 | I have undergone an intensive computer training | 2.19 | 0.80 | Disagreed |
| 2 | I have a computer for my use | 1.51 | 0.84 | Disagreed |
| 3 | I have learnt how to use the following packages<br>i) word processing<br>ii) e-mail<br>iii) Internet search engines/Databases<br>iv) Spreadsheets | 2.27<br>2.62<br>2.85<br>1.64 | 0.85<br>0.85<br>0.93<br>0.99 | Disagreed<br>Agreed<br>Agreed<br>Disagreed |

Table 4 reveals that the computers in the ICT are workable and the assistants in these centres capable. Their mean scores are2.72 and 2.50 respectively. It is also shown that the generator is not reliable when there is power failure and the internet service is not regular and not effective. Their mean scores are below 2.50.

**Research Question 5:** What is the extent of lecturers' involvement in employing ICT facilities in teaching?

Table 5 shows that university lecturers make use of databases for their lecture materials with mean score of 2.73. On the other hand, electronic gadgets, e-mail and conferencing are not employed by lecturers in teaching. These have mean scores of between 1.25 and 1.47.

**Research Question 6:** What is the extent of students' involvement in employing ICT facilities in learning?

The result from Table 6 shows that, the students make use of internet databases to get their study materials. The mean score is 2.68. However, they do not use other electronic gadgets, e-mail and conferencing in learning. The mean ratings of these items range from 1.25 to 2.01.

## DISCUSSION

The findings of the study showed that although university did not undergo intensive computer training, they can use word processing and internet search engines. This result is in line with Eteng and Ntui's (2009) that basic computer literacy appears not to be a problem. This literacy could be promoted by the proliferation of Internet cafes which many Nigerians are increasingly using. The knowledge and experience there can easily be transferred to using e-learning platforms to deliver instructional materials.

However, the lecturers were not using projectors, e-mail, and conferencing in lecture delivery. This could be account for by low availability of these materials and the cost of providing them in Nigerian universities.

On the part of students, they used e-mail and internet search engines but are not conversant with word processing and spreadsheets. As already pointed out, emails and internet search engines are easily available at Internet cafes even outside the universities. Word processing and spreadsheets are not so often used at Internet cafes. Much work especially with word processing are often delegated to typists and secretaries whose services are not as expensive as in developed economies. In general, some e-learning facilities available in the universities are not always functional. A key problem is the epileptic nature of electricity supply in Nigeria. Whereas South African electric power consumption was put at 3882 Kwh per capita but Nigerian at 85KwH per capita while the OECD recommended 85000 Kwh per capita (Raji et al, 2006, p 5). There is great dependence on generators but their services do not go round in most universities in Nigeria.

The findings in this research of non-constant functioning and availability of ICT facilities is better than the findings of the studies by Akudolu (1988 and 2002) that reported lack of ICT facilities in Nigerian education system and therefore giving teachers and students no opportunity to use them. The difference in this study is that there are some facilities but their services are not always available. There is still room for improvement here.

Nwaboku (1997) also had the same view when he stated that the use of new technologies has not been fully implemented in sub-Saharan Africa where there are problems of finance, training and appropriate operational skills.

*Table 3. The level of availability of e-learning facilities in the universities*

| S/N | E-learning facilities | Mean Scores | SD | Interpretation |
|---|---|---|---|---|
| 1 | My university has an Information and Communication Centre (ICT) | 3.14 | 0.88 | Agreed |
| 2 | The ICT Centre has Internet facilities | 2.87 | 0.87 | Agreed |
| 3 | Electronic gadgets are used for lecture delivery | 2.13 | 0.91 | Disagreed |
| 4 | There is a generator attached to the ICT centre | 3.07 | 0.67 | Agreed |
| 5 | The university has a virtual library (electronic library) | 2.27 | 0.81 | Disagreed |
| 6 | There is adequate number of computers for staff and students' use | 2.05 | 0.54 | Disagreed |

*Table 4. Functionality of e-learning facilities in the universities*

| S/N | Level of functionality of e-learning facilities | Mean scores | SD | Interpretation |
|---|---|---|---|---|
| 1 | The computer in the ICT centre are workable | 2.72 | 0.92 | Agreed |
| 2 | The generator is always reliable during power failure | 1.92 | 0.81 | Disagreed |
| 3 | There is regular and effective internet service | 1.95 | 0.59 | Disagreed |
| 4 | There are capable assistants in the ICT centre | 2.50 | 0.95 | Agreed |

*Table 5. The extent university lectures employ ICT facilities in teaching*

| S/No | Extent of employing ICT facilities in teaching | Mean Scores | SD | Interpretation |
|---|---|---|---|---|
| 1 | I get my teaching materials also from the internet search engines/ databases | 2.73 | 0.85 | Agreed |
| 2 | I use electronics gadgets in delivering my lectures | 1.47 | 0.98 | Disagreed |
| 3 | I use the e-mail to communicate with my students | 1.30 | 0.71 | Disagreed |
| 4 | I employ conferencing method in lecturing | 1.25 | 0.35 | Disagreed |

*Table 6. The extent University students employ ICT facilities in learning*

| S/N | Extent of employing ICT facilities in learning | Mean scores | SD | Interpretation |
|---|---|---|---|---|
| 1 | I get my study materials also from internet search engines /databases | 2.68 | 0.97 | Agreed |
| 2 | I use different electronic gadgets in carrying out my school work | 2.01 | 0.54 | Disagreed |
| 3 | I communicate with my lecturers using the e-mail | 1.39 | 1.21 | Disagreed |
| 4 | I employ conferencing method with lecturers and students in learning | 1.25 | 0.52 | Disagreed |

## CONCLUSION AND RECOMMENDATIONS

This study has endeavoured to update earlier studies on Nigerian Universities as it relates to e-learning. This calls for urgent action to make the universities Information Age Compliant in order to compete favourably with the international communities bearing in mind that the world today is a global village. A positive response to remedy this situation will no doubt lead to the production of individuals who have achieved self development and can thus contribute meaningfully to the development of the Nigerian nation and beyond.

For specifically, it can be recommended that the government and university management should ensure that training on ICT forms a major aspect of lecturers' capacity building. The trained lecturers in turn will be in a position to produce computer literate students. In addition, continued attention should be paid to provision of facilities including infrastructure. In particular, electricity provision should be a major goal of the government because as shown by Luiz (2010) this infrastructure can significantly affect the cost of doing business as well as operating information technology. As a temporary measure, the government should provide each university with sophisticated and reliable generators and provisions made for their maintenance and running costs. Another form of infrastructure is the internet backbone preferably by fiber optics so that the spread of data transfer over the internet will be much faster than the satellite dishes which smaller broad bands which are common. This will help the facilities provided to be maximally utilized.

Apart from seeking foreign aid, the government should provide for e-learning in its annual budgets and the money allocated should transparently and accountably be used. With regards to the computer training given to students, it should be made more practical than it is now, so as to remove the current lack of skills in skills like word processing and use of spreadsheet. Such training should be made available to all students.

Finally on recommendations, the development and implementation of virtual libraries should be pursued so that both students and teachers can gain access to international materials from the libraries (Vandi and Djebbari, 2011). Paying attention to ICT provision in the library will also address the problem of internet connectivity in them as reported by Baro and Asaba (2010)

## LIMITATIONS AND AREAS FOR FURTHER STUDIES

Primary study was conducted in only four universities and only in the north central part of Nigeria. It would be interesting to replicate the study in other universities and other locations of the country. Also, since the increase in mobile phone use in Nigeria is significantly increasing (Aker, 2010), a further study could investigate this cheaper and more available device can be used as a platform for e-learning or m-learning (Weaver, 2011). This study examined the perspective of students and teachers. A further study can examine the perspective of administrators and the technical support staff for e-learning.

### Contributions

Dr Rosemary Akuchie designed, carried out and wrote the findings of the primary study; while Dr Abel Usoro performed the desk research and its write-up. He also wrote the limitations and areas for further studies as well as contributed to the writing of the discussion and conclusion and recommendations.

## REFERENCES


Ajadi, T O, Salawu, I. O. & Adeoye, F. A. (2008). E-Learning and distance education in Nigeria. *The Turkish Online Journal of Educational Technology – TOJET, 7*(4), 7, 1303-6521.

Aker, J., Jenny, C., & Mbiti, I. M. (2010). Mobile phones and economic development in Africa. *The Journal of Economic Perspectives, 24*(3), 207–232. doi:10.1257/jep.24.3.207

Akudolu, L. R. (1988). Computer literacy among primary school pupils as an effective platform for technological education. *Paper presented at the international conference on information and education*. Nsukka, University of Nigeria.

Akudolu, L. R. (2002). Restructuring Nigerian secondary education system through Information and Communication Technology-Driven Curriculum. *Journal of the World Council for Curriculum and Instruction, 3*(1), 8–17.

Alexander, S. (2001). E-learning developments and experiences. *Education + Training, 43*, 240–248. doi:10.1108/00400910110399247

Ballantyne, J., Curry, A., & Sumner, A. (2011). Africa 2010-2020: poverty reduction beyond the global crisis. *Foresight, 13*(3), 24–37. doi:10.1108/14636681111138749

Baro, E. E., & Asaba, J. O. (2010). Internet connectivity in university libraries in Nigeria: the present state. *Library Hi Tech News, 27*(9/10), 13–19. doi:10.1108/07419051011110603

Berg, Z., & Collins, M. (1995). *Computer mediated communication and the online classroom*. Cresskill, NJ: Hampton Press.

Carr, S. (2000). As distance education comes of age, the challenge is keeping the students. *The Chronicle of Higher Education, 46*(23), A39–A41.

Connolly, T. M. & Stransfield, M. (2007). From e-learning to games- based e-learning: Using interactive technologies in teaching an IS Course. *Int. J. Information Technology and Management. 6*(2-3-4), 188-195.

Cross, J., O'Driscoil, T. & Trondsen, E. (2007). Another life: virtual worlds as tools for learning. *eLearn Magazine, 3*(2).

Eteng, U., & Ntui, A. (2009). Access to E-Learning in the Nigerian university system (NUS): a case study of University of Calabar. *The Information Technologist*, 6(2), Retrieved from: http://www.ajol.info/index.php/ict/article/view/52694 accessed 25 July 2011.

Kim, J., & Kizildag, M. (2011). M-learning: next generation hotel training system. *Journal of Hospitality and Tourism Technology, 2*(1), 6–33. doi:10.1108/17579881111112395

Larson, M. R., & Bruning, R. (1996). Participant perceptions of a collaborative satellite-based mathematics course. *American Journal of Distance Education, 10*(1), 6–22. doi:10.1080/08923649609526906

Loving, M., & Ochoa, M. (2011). Facebook as a classroom management solution. *New Library World, 112*(3/4), 121–130. doi:10.1108/03074801111117023

Luiz, J. (2010). Infrastructure investment and its performance in Africa over the course of the twentieth century. *International Journal of Social Economics, 37*(7), 512–536. doi:10.1108/03068291011055450

Nwaboku, N. C. (1997). New information technologies in education and new roles for potential teachers. *UNESCO – Africa, 15*(15), 30-37.

Raji, M. O., Ayoade, O. B., & Usoro, A. (2006). The prospects and problems of adopting ICT for poverty eradication in Nigeria. *The Electronic Journal of Information Systems in Developing Countries*, *28*(8), 1–9.

Rath, L. (2011). The effects of Twitter in online learning environment. *eLearn Magazine*, Retrieved from: http://elearnmag.acm.org/featured.cfm?aid=1944486 accessed 24 July, 2011.

Sharma, S. K. (2006). An exploratory study of the critical factors affecting the acceptability of e-learning in Nigerian universities. *Information Management & Computer Security*, *14*(5), 494–505.

Stansfield, M., McLellan, E., & Connoly, T. (2004). Enhancing student performance in online learning and traditional face-to-face class delivery. *Journal of Information Technology Education*, *3*, 173–188.

Usoro, A. & Abiagam, B. (2009). "Providing operational definitions to quality constructs for e-learning in higher education." *e-Learning, 6*(2), 172-186.

Vandi, C., & Djebbari, E. (2011). How to create new services between library resources, museum exhibitions and virtual collections. *Library Hi Tech News*, *28*(2), 15–19. doi:10.1108/07419051111135236

Wang, M. (2011). Integrating organizational, social, and individual perspectives in Web 2.0-based workplace e-learning. *Information Systems Frontiers*, *13*(2), 191–205. doi:10.1007/s10796-009-9191-y

Weaver, J. (2011). M-libraries 2: A Virtual Library in Everyone's Pocket. *Library Management*, *32*(3), 230–231.

Yusuf, M. (2005). Information and communication technology and education, analyzing the Nigerian national policy for information technology. *International Education Journal*, *6*(3), 316–321.

# Chapter 15
# The Issues of Digital Natives and Tourists:
## Empirical Investigation of the Level of IT/IS Usage between University Students and Faculty Members in a Developing Economy

**Nwachukwu Prince Ololube**
*University of Education, Nigeria*

**Samuel Amaele**
*University of Education, Nigeria*

**Peter James Kpolovie**
*University of Port Harcourt, Nigeria*

**Daniel Elemchukwu Egbezor**
*University of Port Harcourt, Nigeria*

## ABSTRACT

*Frequently it is presumed that Nigerian students and faculties have been unable to find effective ways to use technology in the classroom and other aspects of their teaching and learning. Yet, considerable debate remains over the most efficient techniques and procedures to measure students and faculties IT/IS use. In most developing countries, the challenges associated with carrying out IT/IS measurements are different from those in developed countries, as are the methods for selecting appropriate IT/IS contents. The thrust of this chapter is to examine IT/S contents with a view to analyse their meaning and impact on educational offerings. This study gathered data using a five item demographic variable and a fifty item questionnaire to measure student and faculty academic IT/IS use in two universities in Nigeria. This study is based on the 191 responses received to the questionnaire. The results reveal significant differences between the academic use of IT/IS by students and faculty members. This groundbreaking study recommends that universities become valuable and proactive actors in the provision of technology based learning, teaching and research for students and academic staff so as to foster an effective academic environment aimed at meeting MDG education goals. This scholarly discourse has implication for researchers, education practitioners, planners, policy makers and government.*

DOI: 10.4018/978-1-4666-1637-0.ch015

## INTRODUCTION

Studies of inequality in access to and use of information and communication technology (ICT) among students and faculties (lecturers) have over the years attracted significant attention by researchers, policy makers and the global community at large (Toledo, 2007; Margaryan & Littlejohn, 2008; Waycott et al., 2010; Bennett & Maton, 2010; Feeney, 2010; Anne, Seppo & Shoji, 2010; Margaryan, Littlejohn & Vojt, 2011; Nwokeocha, 2011; Ololube, 2011). IT/IS have become key educational tools and have had a revolutionary impact on how we see and live in the world (Kaba et al., 2008; Ololube, 2009). Globally, IT/IS is having a revolutionary impact on educational methodology (Ifinedo, 2006; Fan, 2010). However, this revolution is not universal and needs to be reinforced to reach a larger share of the world's population (Akdogan, 2009; Anne, Seppo & Shoji, 2010).

In Nigeria, the academic landscape includes the teaching and learning process, along with educational programs and courses and the pedagogy or methodology of teaching; the research process, including dissemination and publication; and libraries and information services, including higher education administration and management (Beebe, 2004; Ololube, 2006b). There is no doubt that the best way to enhance excellent instruction in schools is through quality information technology (IT) and information system (IS) usage and integration, which is the key in understanding the knowledge and skills required in teaching and learning today (Ololube, Ubogu & Egbezor, 2007; Afari-Kumah & Tanye, 2009).

Education is one of the most important institutions needed to ensure the well-being of a society. Because of its importance, education is a powerful instrument of social progress without which neither an individual nor a nation can grow professionally (Ololube, 2006a). To this end, UNESCO's strategic objectives in education include improving the quality of education through the diversification of contents and methods, and promoting experimentation, innovation, and the diffusion and sharing of information and best practices as well as policy dialogue (UNESCO, 2002). In a complex society like Nigeria, many factors affect IT/IS usage and integration, making the use of an interdisciplinary and integrated approach necessary to ensure the successful development of Nigeria's economy and society (Moja, 2000; Mac-Ikemenjima, 2005). Of particular note, however, is the fact that the development of IT and IS, its penetration and use in higher education programs, and its diffusion into education in general remain dependant on governmental policies (Ololube, 2006b).

Evidence (Tuomi, 2000) seems to suggest that in some countries and regions the digital divide is closing rapidly. Over the course of the last decade, especially in developed countries, millions of people have gained access to computers each year. The term digital divide is used to explain the divergences between people who have and people who do not have the skills, knowledge and abilities, in addition to access and resources, to use new IT/IS tools. This divide can exist between the educated and uneducated, privileged and underprivileged, developed and developing nations, and those living in rural and urban areas (Ololube, 2009).

Owing to the shrinking divide, never in human history has there been so many people with access to computers, digital networks, and electronic communication technologies (Margaryan et al., 2011; Waycott et al., 2010). At any given moment millions of university students are online whether at home, at school, at friends houses, or - if they have Internet access on their handheld devices or cell phones - almost anywhere. This pervasive use of technology tends to render students digital natives rather than digital tourists (Awake, 2008).

Information technologies are not without problems. Paramount among these is Internet safety as the Web has been exploited by all manner of unscrupulous individuals. Many websites feature explicit pornography and are relatively easy for the unwary to stumble upon. In the United States, 90 percent of youth said that they have had unintentionally encountered pornography online, in most cases while doing assignments. The web also provides easy access to sites that promote teen gambling. In Canada, nearly one in four males surveyed admitted to having visited such sites (Awake, 2008).

Arguably, today's students are no longer the people our educational system was designed to teach. From kindergarten through college, they represent the first generation to grow up with many of these new technologies. They have spent their entire lives surrounded by and using computers, videogames, digital music players, video cameras, cell phones, and the many other toys and tools of the digital age. Most college graduates today have spent less than 5,000 hours reading, but more than 10,000 hours playing video games (not to mention 20,000 hours watching TV). Computer games, email, the Internet, cell phones and instant messaging are integral parts of their lives (Prensky, 2001). In Canada nearly half of all youths with cell phones can use them to access the Internet. Likewise, in India, the sharp rise in the number of Internet users, increasing to 54 percent in just one year, is largely attributed to the youth. In the United Kingdom, 57 percent of youth between the ages of 9 and 19 use the Internet weekly while in the United States this jumps to 93 percent for youth aged 12 to 17 (Awake, 2008). The same is true in Turkey where young people are the largest group using new ICT, especially mobile technology. Their dynamism, new ideas, performance and effort expectancy are of immense value in the ICT policy making processes (Akdogan, 2009).

Much like the use of ICTs by individuals, the use of ICTs by education institutions around the globe has increased over the last decade (Fan, 2010). Higher education institutions have been adopting IT/IS teaching and learning technologies in an effort to create an environment that enables both students and their instructors to engage in collaborative learning and to gain access to information (Ifinedo, 2006).

Despite the revolutionary impact of IT/IS on education globally, many Nigerian students and faculty members have been unable to find effective ways to use technology in their classrooms or other aspects of teaching and learning (Ololube, 2011). For students, the fear or tension surrounding contact with a computer may be inconsistent with the actual danger posed and so cause them to neglect the use of IT/IS tools. Such fears have been associated with decreased use and growing avoidance/anxiety (if left untreated) that can seriously affect academic achievement (Ololube, 2009; Ololube & Ubogu, 2009). While the outcomes of a study by Margaryan and Littlejohn (2008) suggests that the calls for radical transformations in educational approaches may be legitimate, it would be misleading to ground the arguments for such change solely in students' shifting expectations as well as patterns of learning and technology use.

Notwithstanding specifications in the National Policy of Education of the Federal Government of Nigeria (FRN, 2004), Nigeria as a nation came late and slowly to the use of ICT in all sectors, especially higher education. This is largely a result of the limitations caused by chronic economic strife and detrimental government policies. These factors in turn have direct consequences on the nation's educational development (Ololube, Ubogu & Egbezor, 2007). At the same time, while we recognize the insensitive academic environment in Nigeria that researchers (Ifinedo & Ololube, 2007) have posited as being responsible for slow growth rates in the use and integration of IT/IS, the use of IT/IS in teaching and learning is gradually taking hold in university education in Nigeria, particularly in private universities (Ololube, 2011).

Internet searches confirm that very little has been written about this domain of study in Nigeria. The few studies that do exist include the ones by Nwokeocha (2011); Nweze (2010 and Tiemo et al. (2010). The enthusiasm to write this article arose from a desire to examine student and faculty members' software use and application, perceived performance and effort expectancy, social influence, compatibility, facilitating conditions, computer anxiety, self-efficacy, attitudes towards computer systems, behavioural intentions, and computer use in learning, teaching, research and socialization methodologies (technology-based materials). It also arose from a desire to assess students' and faculties' readiness and role in employing technology-based education as a way of attaining teaching and learning effectiveness and, finally, to determine success so far in terms of academic achievements.

To address the above objectives, two research hypotheses were formulated. The hypothesis statements are based on the notion that perceived use of learning is strongly correlated with ease in student academic use of IT/IS. The same seems to be true for faculty members' use of learning methodologies (technology-based materials) to present content in the teaching and learning processes. Indeed, results in Prensky (2001), Ifinedo (2006, 2007), Nwokeocha (2011) and Ololube (2011) show that students and faculty members who have no difficulty finding and understanding useful information, view IT/IS as easy to use, and may have higher regard for such systems' usefulness. Thus it is hypothesized that:

**$HO_1$:** Students and faculties differ significantly in their perceived use and application IT/IS in their academic activities

**$HO_2$:** The perception of students and faculty members are significantly different in terms of their use of IT/IS in academic activities

## CONTEXTUALIZATION

Universities are dedicated to excellence in teaching. In an educational context, excellence can be taken to mean effectively providing learning experiences that prepare students for the challenges of today's multifaceted, ever varying, and diverse workplace (Ololube, 2009). The guiding philosophy of university education is to produce scholars with sharp intellectual minds capable of further critical intellectual inquiry (Ololube, 2011). Universities are one of several institutions in Nigeria that offer educational services. They are composed of several faculties/colleges, which can include Natural and Applied Sciences, Health Sciences, Management and Social Sciences, Education, Arts, Humanities, Environmental Sciences, Information and Communication, and Agriculture.

Introduction to computer science is a central course for all Nigerian students either as part of their program or as a part of a major in some faculties/colleges. The teaching of computer science is ideally executed in a general and applied fashion aimed at producing graduates who are scientifically and technically skilled in information processing, data collection and analyses, and communication. All of these are set in a problem-solving context where students learn about the planning and management processes involved in using computers. Introduction to computer science also involves teaching about the information needs of computers, the design of information management, and the principles and practices of system usage and design.

The successful completion of an introductory course in computer science is a critical accomplishment for undergraduate students who may one day be at the helm of decision making in their workplace and looking to keep pace with the demands of a globalized economy. This course is equally important for students who are planning to further their studies in the future and who, as graduates, will need to make informed professional development decisions using IT/IS. Consequently, introduction to computer courses are an essential requirement of undergraduate programs in Nigerian universities.

Introduction to computer courses are challenging classes to teach because the technical complexity of the course material is quite high while student interest in this material can, unfortunately, be quite low. In most cases, take home assignments are given to students with basic instructions and sources for materials on the Internet. In some cases, assignments are submitted to faculty members via e-mail and feedback is provided to students days after the deadline for submission.

## Students as Digital Natives/Tourists

The term digital native has gained popularity in recent years as a means of describing a generation of technology-driven young people who are immersed in digital technologies and for whom the education system has a hard time keeping pace (Bennett & Maton, 2010). While some prefer to refer to today's students the N-[for Net]-gen or D-[for digital]-gen, digital native remains the most useful as almost all young people today are "native speakers" of the digital language of computers, video games and the Internet (Prensky, 2001). The appropriateness of this label is confirmed by a recent study (Waycott et al., 2010) that investigated Australian university staff and students' perceptions and use of current and emerging technologies both in their daily lives and in teaching and learning contexts. It concluded that students are digital natives while teaching staff remain digital immigrants, suggesting the need for a more sophisticated understanding of the role technologies play in the lives of both students and staff.

Studies by Margaryan and Littlejohn (2008) and Margaryan, Littlejohn and Vojt (2011), investigating the nature of Glasgow university students' use of digital technologies for learning and socializing, found that students use a limited range of the more well established technologies. Use of collaborative knowledge creation tools, virtual worlds, and social networking sites was low. They also found that students in technical disciplines (e.g., Engineering) tended to use more technology tools compared to those in non-technical disciplines (e.g., Social Work). These findings were mediated by the fact that engineering courses, for example, often required more intensive and extensive access to technology than non-technical courses. The authors concluded that student attitudes towards learning and technology were most influenced by teaching approaches that conformed to traditional pedagogies but that included some incorporation of technology tools for delivering content.

According to Prensky (2001), age-related differences in technology use and skill have created a digital differentiation between generations. Margaryan and Littlejohn (2008) likewise found evidence of this with younger engineering students making somewhat more active, though limited, use of technology tools than older ones. Endorsing the findings of these studies, Waycott et al. (2010) contend that young people who have grown up with computers and the Internet have a natural attraction to technology and are ready and able to effortlessly adopt and adapt to changes in the digital landscape. Older users of technology, who have encountered digital technology later in life, are thought to be more challenged by this technology and show less affinity and literacy than their younger counterparts. The notion of paradigm shift (e.g., Kennedy et al., 2007; Philip, 2007; Barnes, Marateo & Ferris, 2007; Oblinger & Oblinger, 2005) suggests that this student familiarity with digital technology has shaped their preferences and skills in key areas relating to education. Students as digital natives increasingly demand instant access to information, have low tolerance for lectures, including passive forms of learning, and expect technology to be an integral part of the educational process.

Interestingly, Open Education (2011a) revealed that as of late some commentators are pointing out that being young or born during the digital period does not necessarily mean that one has the aptitude for or an interest in computers. Tucker (2010), Rosen (2010), Toledo (2007) and Feeney (2010) likewise believe that relationships to the digital world are based not on age but on attitudes and the implementation of digital technologies. A study by Siragusa and Dixon (2008) confirmed that students' use of technologies was greatly motivated by factors such as compatibility, social influence, attitudes and/or planned behaviour (behavioural intentions). They found a high level of participation/use by undergraduate students who described ICT activities as pleasant, helpful and easy. These observations that undermine the young-old technology dichotomy allow for more informed decisions about the implementation of educational technologies in higher education institutions (Waycott et al., 2010).

## Faculties as Digital Natives/Tourists

Information communication technology (ICT) has been the single most important vehicle in the emergence of the global information society. Information technology (IT) includes the acquisition, processing, storage and dissemination of vocal, pictorial, textual and numeric information via the microelectronic-based combination of computer and telecommunication (Ololube, 2008, 2011). Individuals, groups or nations that lack the access or training to effectively use ICT are largely shut out from meaningful participation in the global society (Nwokeocha, 2011).

The word "faculties" is used in this chapter generically to include all levels of academic staff to cover teachers, lecturers, tutors, professors, etc., engaged in the teaching and learning processes in higher education. Most teachers in Nigerian colleges and universities do not possess sufficient experience or competence in the use of computers for educational or industrial purposes (Yusuf, 2005a, 2005b). Consequently, most Nigerian teachers overlook critical opportunities to use technology in their classrooms or other aspects of their teaching (Ololube, 2006b). Possible explanations for this failure to successfully integrate technology include that the use of technology in the classroom has not been sufficiently encouraged and that teaching staff are not well trained in the educational use of ICT (Ololube, 2011).

Pedagogical reflections on ICT must focus on how these resources can benefit students, what they represent in terms of the curriculum, and what learning, competencies, and attitudes they can foster in students, without losing sight of the kind of citizens and professionals that our present society demands. Students seem to learn best when they are excited and engaged. Even those who have not been exposed to technology and high levels of sensory input respond very well to classrooms that are stimulating for learners. Ultimately, we expect that teachers should look for every opportunity to produce a classroom that inspires children and technology is one of the best ways to create such a classroom (Open Education, 2011b). In order to successfully move towards the greater use of technology in the classroom, it is first necessary to satisfy the training demands of the lecturers (García-Valcárcel & Tejedor, 2009). The competencies required by faculty members, so as to ensure ICT application in education, include the ability to make personal use of ICT, the ability to make professional use of ICT as a teaching tool, mastering the range of educational paradigms that make use of ICT, mastering the range of assessment paradigms that make use of ICT, use of ICT as an intelligence tool, and competencies in understanding the policy dimensions of the use of ICT for teaching and learning (Kirschner & Davis, 2003).

# METHODOLOGY

## Research Design

The methodology adopted in this study is linguistic, empirical, and contextual. For the most part, the research design of this study follows a logical sequence that connects empirical data to the study's hypotheses and ultimately to its conclusions. This study has included specific design features from broad empirical and theoretical perspectives to help address the research hypotheses at hand - the quality of student and faculty members' software application and computer usage. Quantitative assessment design was employed as a questionnaire was used to measure software application and computer use and perceptions of software application and computer use. This study ultimately measured the need to ascertain and redesign central education programmes and offers an approach that may be useful for IT/IS education planners, administrators and policy makers as they come to terms with new realities in university administration and management.

This study used a combination of text-based materials and questionnaires for gathering data. Simple random sampling was chosen over other sampling methods. Simple random sampling is by far the easiest and most basic probability sampling technique in terms of conceptualization and application. It does not necessarily require knowledge of the exact composition of the population. This sampling technique allowed for the inclusion of the acuity of the description, performance and experiences that would facilitate broad understanding of the population.

Researchers, with the assistance of heads of departments, distributed 200 questionnaires to students and 80 to faculties of the two universities. The sample excluded students and lecturers in computer science and related programmes, because by the nature of their programmes and field they are considerably engaged in the use of computers. The number of student questionnaires successfully completed and returned was 121 for a 60.5% return rate. It was 70 (88.9% return rate) for faculty members. The overall return rate was 68.2%.

## Research Instrument (Questionnaire)

For the purpose of gathering data, the researchers designed a questionnaire on computer usage with the help of relevant literature, and IT/IS experts and colleagues to suit the present research framework. Reflections on the quality of a good questionnaire by Fink (2008), Fowler (2008), Dillman, Smyth and Christian (2008) also guided the design.

Participants from two universities (one private and one public) responded to a three section questionnaire that employed six and seven-point Likert-type scales. Section 'A' included questions about respondents' demographic information: gender, age, status, faculty and department. Section 'B' pertained to respondents' perception of their software application competence based on a six-point Likert-type scale where 0 = no skill at all; 1 = minimal skill; 2 = below average skill; 3 = average skill; 4 = above average skill; and 5 = very competent. Section 'C' focused more specifically on the dimensions of computer use and questions involved a seven-point Likert-type scale where 1 = strongly disagree (SD), 2 = disagree (D), 3 = partly disagree (PD), 4 = neutral, 5 = partly agree (PA), 6 = agree (A), 7 = strongly agree (SA). These rating scales, which participants responded to indicate their perceptions and how these perceptions affected teaching and learning development (Fink, 2008), were considered to be of approximately equal attitudinal value.

## Validity of Instrument

The items included in this study's questionnaire were drawn from literature, ICT experts, and senior faculty colleagues. The instrument was thereafter pre-tested on a group outside of the study sample and responses were used to improve on the items and to ensure that both students and lecturers had no difficulty understanding the precise meaning of the constructs and grammar used. In this research questionnaire, we used terms in a fairly straightforward or commonsense manner. We believe that this commonsense use of terms is consistent with the way they are generally used by researchers and does not pose any serious philosophical problems (Ololube, 2006b).

## Data Analysis Procedure

In satisfying our investigation, a number of statistical analyses were conducted using SPSS Version 18. These include descriptive statistics (percentages, mean point value, standard deviation), t-test and one-way-analysis of variance (ANOVA). *T*-test was used to find statistically significant differences between students and faculty members on all the variables. ANOVA was employed to test if differences exist between and within the means of the opinions of students and faculty members on the variables. The statistical significance of this study was set at $p < 0.05$ to measure if the level of confidence observed in the sample also existed in the general population (Kpolovie, 2010).

Statistically evaluating the reliability of questionnaire responses was regarded as appropriate given that students and faculty members may have answered the questions randomly or to give a certain perception to researchers because they were not interested in the study or because negative results may have infringed on their current teaching and learning preferences. The research instrument was quantitatively analyzed and received a cumulative Cronbach alpha coefficient of .933 (see Table 2). The research instrument was thus accepted as very reliable as it was able to elicit the required information concerning the theme of this study and certified the consistency or repeatability of what the researchers set out to measure (Okeke & Kpolovie, 2006; Kpolovie, 2011).

Based on the reliability theory by Cronbach et al. (1972), an instrument reliability test was conducted. This test was used to determine the percentages of variance in the distribution of scores obtained from test that can be attributed to the true scores, and to determine the standard error of measurement in the full range of scores (Render, Stair & Hannan, 2005; Kpolovie, 2010, 2011). The means and standard deviations of each of the dimensions of the dependent variables were also examined and their relationships were compared with other variables in the dimensions under investigation. Thus, the internal consistency of group dimensions was investigated by estimating scale reliabilities and Cronbach's alpha coefficients. No group dimensions were below .750, except facilitating conditions which was .583.

## RESULTS

Descriptive statistics for respondents demographic variable indicates that 110 (57.6%) of the respondents were male, while 81 (42.4%) were female. Information on age showed that 15 (7.9%) of the respondents were less than 20 years, 107 (56.0%) were between 21 and 30 years old, 28 (14.7%) were 31 to 40 years old, 24 (12.6%) were 41 to 50 years old, and 17 (8.9%) were 51 years of age or older. The majority of respondents, 121 (63.4%), were students, while 70 (36.6%) were faculty members. Their software use and is presented in Figure 1. Information on the three faculties from which data was collected revealed that 63 (33.0%) respondents were from Management and Social Sciences, 69 (36.1%) were from Humanities and 59 (30.9%) were from Education. In terms of department, 43 (22. 5%) were from Business Administration and Management, 44 (23.0%) were from Marketing, 33 (17.3%) were from Religion, 40 (20.9%) were from History, and 31 (16.2%) were from Educational Foundations and Management.

Table 1 highlights the essence of the research hypotheses in this study which are collectively aimed at testing the degree to which students and faculties differ in their use of IT/IS in academic activities. These hypotheses were tested using the responses to items 1-50 on sections "B and C" of the research questionnaire. Analyses using the two basic statistical indicators, means and standard deviation, were carried out. The overall means and standard deviations of the responses from students were significantly different from those

*Figure 1. Bar Chart Presentation by Status of Respondents*

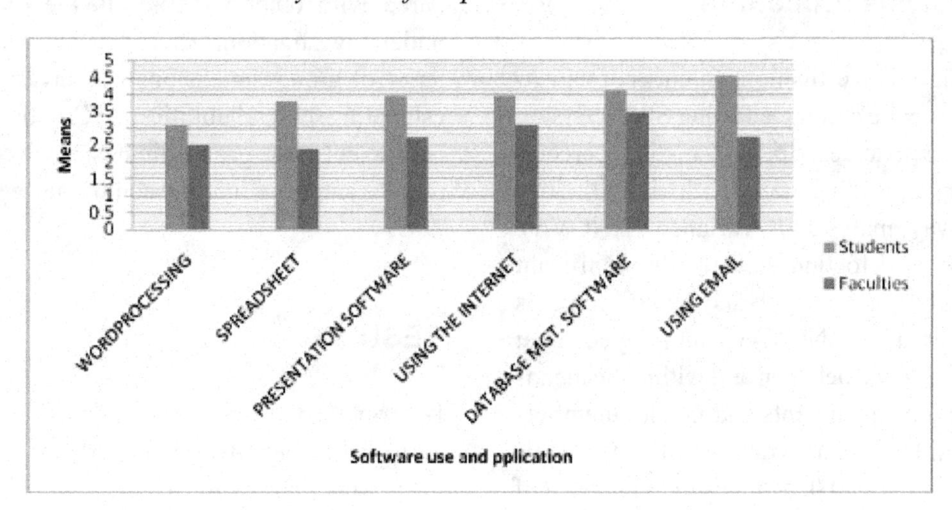


of faculties. Students appear to perform better than faculty members in the use of computer systems and in general have a more positive attitude towards the use of IT/IS in their academic activities. Consequently, hypothesis one accepted.

To verify our analytical information further, a *t*-test analysis of paired samples was conducted. The *t*-test analysis was aimed at determining if significant differences existed between student and faculty means. The result revealed significant differences between students and faculty members on all the dimensions (variables) measured. SPSS Version 18 displayed it at significance levels of .000 - .008. Table 2 shows the highest *t*-value as 10.079 and the lowest *t*-value as 2.733, meaning that students tend to use computers more frequently than lecturers (faculties). This provided sufficient cause for accepting hypothesis one which state that students and faculty members differ significantly in their use and application of IT/IS in academic activities.

One-way analysis of variance (ANOVA), set at $p. < 0.05$, was used to test if the perception of students and faculty members are significantly different (hypothesis 2) in terms of their academic use of IT/IS. In this context the independent variables include gender, age, status, faculty and department. The data obtained was computed and the results showed that mixed significant difference existed in the respondents' opinions. The analysis of variance with gender as an independent variable and items 1 to 50 in sections B and C of the research questionnaire as dependent variables, showed significant gender differences with an F-ratio of 4.776 and F-probability of .040. The perceptions of respondents towards IT/IS use also revealed age significant differences. In Table 6 it can be seen that the F-ratio of 7.113 and F-probability of .021 both depict significant age differences. There were two possible status categories for respondents: student or faculty member. The results indicated no significant differences in their opinions at an F-ratio of 1.249 and an F-probability of .292. Opinions based on faculty of study and teaching also showed no significant differences in opinion given the F-ratio of .778 and the F-probability of .541. The different categories of respondents based on faculties all hold the use of IT/IS in academic activities in high esteem. The demographic information on department likewise revealed no significant differences in opinion at an F-ratio of 2.106 and an F-probability of .082, this confirmed the lack of differences.

*Table 1. Descriptive Statistics of all the Dimensions on the Use of Computer Systems*

| s/n | Dimensions (Variables) | Students (n = 121) | | Faculties (lecturers) (n = 70) | |
|---|---|---|---|---|---|
| | | M | SD | M | SD |
| 1 | Software use and application | 4.3998 | .82382 | 2.4168 | .50442 |
| 2 | Peformance expectancy | 4.6283 | .95786 | 2.3764 | .60987 |
| 3 | Effort expectancy | 4.8586 | .99981 | 2.5760 | .54658 |
| 4 | Social influence | 5.7696 | .73817 | 1.9982 | .64728 |
| 5 | Compatibility in computer usage | 4.8939 | .79901 | 2.2361 | .58200 |
| 6 | Facilitating conditions | 4.6073 | .93256 | 2.4114 | .60452 |
| 7 | Computer anxiety | 3.6283 | .95786 | 2.2232 | .58442 |
| 8 | Self-efficacy in the use of computer | 6.8586 | .69987 | 1.9444 | .74728 |
| 9 | Attitudes towards computer | 5.7696 | .68824 | 2.2263 | .82002 |
| 10 | Behavioural intentions | 4.8730 | .77451 | 2.3554 | .70452 |
| 11 | Computer system use | 4.6674 | .91359 | 2.2309 | .54422 |

*Table 2. T-test Analysis of Students and Faculties Perception of their Software Application and Computer Usage*

| | Dimensions (Variables) | t | df | Sig. (2-tailed) |
|---|---|---|---|---|
| 1 | Software use and application | 7.807 | 190 | .000 |
| 2 | Peformance expectancy | 2.733 | 190 | .007 |
| 3 | Effort expectancy | 7.651 | 190 | .000 |
| 4 | Social influence | 2.804 | 190 | .008 |
| 5 | Compatibility in computer usage | 3.803 | 190 | .001 |
| 6 | Facilitating conditions | 3.430 | 190 | .001 |
| 7 | Computer anxiety | 6.748 | 190 | .000 |
| 8 | Self-efficacy in the use of computer | 6.241 | 190 | .000 |
| 9 | Attitudes towards computer | 6.306 | 190 | .000 |
| 10 | Behavioural intentions | 5.111 | 190 | .003 |
| 11 | Computer system use | 10.079 | 190 | .000 |

Df = N-1
Significant level set at $p < .05$

## DISCUSSION

Internet searches confirm that there have been no investigations of student and faculties perceptions of IT/IS based on the eleven dimensions employed in this research which measure inequalities in access and integration. Likewise, no study, to the best of our knowledge, has scrutinized learning interventions using IT/IS benchmarks. Thus, no unique attention has been paid to the development of student and faculty member capabilities in the use of IT/IS to foster educational achievement in Nigeria. The present study aimed to add to the lead author's previous research (Ololube, 2011) by examining the extent to which students and faculty members are at risk in their IT/IS developmental delays. The organization of this study adhered to a simple framework for conceptualizing whether students are indeed native while faculties are tourists in the use of IT/IS in educational activities. Overall, the study found that students and faculty members in private universities are more grounded in their use of IT/IS compared to their counterparts at public universities. Consequently, the latter group requires greater support to reach an acceptable level of IT/IS skill and use.

In terms of perceived software use and application by students and faculty members, a significant difference ($t=7.807, p<.000$) was detected. Both student competencies in the use of computer applications and software to tackle academic problems, and the quality and skills of students in completing assignments were high. This can be compared to the marginal competencies of faculty members in their use of software and computers in teaching and research activities. Levels of comfort with and integration of IT/IS materials such as computers, software (MS Words, PowerPoint, MS Excel, MS Access, E-mails) slides, overhead projectors, and video equipment confirm that students are indeed technological natives relative to faculty members who appear to be tourists in their use of these tools. One possible reason for such disparities may be the relatively younger age of the students (Margaryan & Littlejohn, 2008, Jegede; 2009). In general, the youth, who have grown up immersed in technology, tend to be "native speakers" of the digital language of computers, video games and the Internet (c.f., Prensky, 2001). This study thus finds that Digital Natives (c.f., Bennett & Maton, 2010) is indeed a useful designation of today's students.

Significant differences ($t = 2.733, p < .007$) were also detected with regards to perceived performance expectancy of students and faculties. The majority of students found computer systems useful in their studies, which they presume will increase their chances of securing a good job. Likewise, they also feel that computer systems enable them to accomplish assignments more quickly, and increase their learning ability and academic growth (Ifinedo, 2006; Ololube, 2011).

Scores were also generated based on the t-test analysis for the differences in the perceived effort expectancy of students and faculties. This analysis revealed significant differences between students and faculties ($t=7.651, p<.000$). Students generally found computer systems easy to use, found interactions with computer systems to be clear and understandable, and became skilful in their computer use. A contrasting pattern prevailed for faculty members. Nwokeocha (2011) reported similar findings – that computer technology was helpful and easy to use for students. Again, one possible reason for these differences may be that younger people tend to embrace technology more than their older counterparts. According to Waycott et al. (2010), young people who have grown up with computers and the Internet have a natural attraction to technology and are ready and able to effortlessly adopt and adapt to changes in the digital landscape.

Perceived social influence was shown to have a significant effect on student than on faculty IT/IS development. This is arguable because university programmes support the use of computers by students and because students are more likely than teachers to come from families of higher socio-economic standing and consequently own computers, laptops and/or cell phones that enable them have access to the Internet on daily basis. Students also receive more assistance from their peers which tends to reinforce their love for information technologies. Kaba et al. (2008), in studying the factors that influence attitudes toward and the use of mobile technologies in developing countries, found that social influence and the possession of technology resources are indeed major factors when considering the impact of IT in education. Siragusa and Dixon (c.f., 2008) likewise found that student participation in the use of technologies was greatly motivated by several factors including social influence. This study's data, as displayed in Table 5, confirms that students tend to be more influenced by social factors than faculty members ($t = 2.804$, $p < .008$).

Perceived compatibility in the use of computers by students and faculties also revealed significant differences ($t = 3.803$, $p < .001$). Kaba et al. (2008), Siragusa and Dixon (2008), and Nwokeacha (2011) all likewise found that there is a relationship between perceptions of compatibility and the use of computers as students (more than faculty members) tend to believe that computer system use is compatible with their learning style and their study plan.

One of the most important issues in IT/IS use is the facilitating conditions that make the use of computers easier and more useful. In this study, we discovered significant differences ($t = 3.430$, $p < .001$) in access to resources that would enable students to use computer systems at school. According to Pelgrum and Law (2003) and Afari-Kumah and Tanye (2009), access to and the availability of computers in the university community can influence the use of electronic resources. In turn, computer technology offers a way to advance more responsive educational environments, which provide students with the opportunity to access available experts, the best resources and the most up- to-date information (Ololube, 2011).

Evidence from this study concerning perceived computer anxiety revealed a digital divide, although it is slowly closing, between students and faculty members. Over the last decade, millions of Nigerians have gained access to computers, digital networks, and electronic communication technologies. Nevertheless, we found that faculty members continue to express greater fear or tension around imminent contact with computer technologies than students do ($t = 6.748$, $p < .000$). This imbalance has students rather than faculty members poised to reap the benefits of the information age (Ololube, 2009). Similarly, Nwokeocha (2011) found that while both students and lecturers had access to ICT, students were more likely than the lecturers to use it as they have less anxiety towards computers.

In this study, the majority of faculty members and a small number of students felt indecisive, demoralized, nervous, scared, panicky and/or uneasy around computers, in part, for fear of losing vital information or making mistakes that they cannot correct. Consequently, faculty members are not able to find valuable ways to make use of technology in their classrooms or other aspects of their teaching and learning life (c.f., Ololube, 2006b). In an attempt to bridge the digital gap between students and faculty members, and to facilitate the use of ICT in teaching and learning among both students and lecturers in Nigeria universities, the Nigeria Communication Commission (NCC) organized a workshop to train lecturers in ICT skills and knowledge. The workshop was broadly welcomed and attended since most lecturers do indeed find it difficult to integrate ICT in their academic work (Tiemo et al., 2010).

Significant differences ($t = 6.241$, $p < .000$) were detected in the perceived computer use self-efficacy of students and faculties. While the majority of students were able to call someone or consult the built-in help facility for assistance if they got stuck, only a few faculty members were able to do so. Most students were also able to modestly complete a job or task using a computer on their own. Some of the factors that likely lead to this ability among students and in turn this student-faculty divergence include the availability of free time, the need/desire for social networking through use of ICT, and the various basic level and university entry examinations undertaken by students over the years which have become compulsory online components (Nwokeocha, 2011). Increasingly as well, students are encountering a post-secondary emphasis on self-direction and responsibility in/for the learning process, which often requires self-directed learning on a computer either on campus or at home (Pelgrum & Law, 2003).

The predisposition of a person to respond positively or negatively towards computers was used in scale form to test significant differences. A person's predisposition affects everything a person does with a computer and often reflects past computer experiences, and hence is a determining factor in a user's present behaviour and attitudes towards computers. The user's predisposition provides the user with a framework within which to interpret the effect and the integration of computers in the user's life (Ololube, 2009). The t-test statistical analysis for perceived attitudes towards computer systems exposed the fact that students' attitudes towards computers were more positive than those of faculty members ($t = 6.306$, $p < .000$). Respondents were asked to reflect on three core issues (interest, good idea as well as fun and exciting) in relation to their attitudes and beliefs about teaching, learning and conducting research using computer related devices. A greater percentage of students believed that using a computer to learn was a good idea, interesting, and fun and exciting. Thus, the majority of students go beyond competence and skill, and posses the positive attitudes and stamina needed to carry action (even) through difficult circumstances (Sam, Othman & Nordin, 2005; Husu, 2006; Ololube, 2009). Faculty members must be further and continuously encouraged to develop the needed skills in the use of ICTs and to develop positive attitudes towards their possibilities for teaching and research (Yusuf & Onasanya, 2004). Of importance here, as Margaryan and Littlejohn (2008) contend, is the fact that students' attitudes towards learning appear to be influenced by the approaches adopted by their lecturers. Thus, if lecturers fail to adopt and integrate contemporary technology in the classroom, there is a chance that students may inherit some of their technological reluctance.

In the present study, the perceived behavioural intentions of students and faculty members also showed significant differences ($t = 5.111$, $p < .003$). Students' expectations, intentions and planned use of computers were found to be greater than that of faculty members. Siragusa and Dixon (c.f., 2008) see planned behaviour (behavioural intentions) and high levels of participation by undergraduates in the use of ICT as related to their view of ICT as pleasant, helpful and easy to use, though some student did experience feelings of anxiety and intimidation in the course of their use of ICT tools. Interestingly, while both the students and faculty members were convinced of the need to use university's computer systems in the future, faculty members seemed to be more aware of the critical role of ICT.

Four reference scales (items) (frequency in the use of computers, the use of computers to understand problems, the use of computers to find answers to problems and the frequency of computer use in academic work) were employed to test the perceived use of computers by students and faculties. Students were found to be more frequent users of computers at universities and at home ($t = 10.079$, $p < .000$) than faculty members. Students were also found to use computer systems to understand and to answer problems more frequently than faculty members. Overall, this study was able to determine that students use computer related devices for academic purposes more often than faculty members.

Based on the results of this study, it is possible to conclude that the role of faculties in the adoption and implementation of ICT in education is problematic. The knowledge, skills and experiences needed for effective implementation of ICT in education remain a major obstacle. Faculties must accept new roles and responsibilities as the use of technology in the classroom increasingly becomes non-negotiable. Faculties must be given opportunities to regularly update their ICT knowledge and skills (Pelgrum & Law, 2003) and ICT integration should be included as a core instructional delivery competency in all teacher training programs/workshops (Yusuf & Onasanya, 2004). Ultimately, the use of ICT in teaching, learning and research, and the resulting free flow of information will facilitate both individual and national development (Nweze, 2010).

## CONCLUDING REMARKS

This research study has focused on the perceived use, usefulness, ease of understanding, self-efficacy, facilitating conditions, behavioural intentions, and attitudes and anxieties towards computer use among higher education students and faculty members in a developing economy. It is believed that IT/IS constitute an important force in efforts to build an information technology society and to join the international community in meeting the Millennium Development Goals. Higher education institutions are enduring entities that must ensure and create the diffusion of knowledge for national development. Society depends on these institutions for its growth and for the production of new knowledge, its transmission through education and training, and its dissemination through information communication technologies (Ololube, 2009).

Development is essentially about proper knowledge use and application in developing countries such as Nigeria (Nweze, 2010). To keep pace with global developments it is imperative that students, lecturers, educational institutions and Nigerian society at large adopt and become proficient in the use of ICT as ICT stands to significantly change the speed and depth of information available and the distribution of knowledge in what is increasingly a knowledge society. A knowledge society in this paradigm refers to an association of people that have similar interests, be they social, economic, political or cultural, who by making effective use of their collective knowledge in their areas of interest contribute to further knowledge that will lead to national progress and global development (Ololube, 2009).

This study focused on the digital divide between digital natives (students) and digital immigrants (faculty members) in higher education in Nigeria. The findings suggest that we need to develop a more sophisticated understanding of the role technologies play in the lives of both students and staff. Bennett and Maton (2010) argue that we must in fact move beyond simple dichotomies (natives-tourists) towards a more nuanced analysis of experiences with technology. An enhanced understanding of student and faculty member perspectives on ICT use will allow for more informed decisions about the implementation of educational technologies in today's higher education institutions (Waycott et al., 2010). For Nigeria and other developing countries, promoting ICT literacy agendas is central to realizing the role of higher education in national/regional social, technological, economic and educational development.

This academic discourse has implication for researchers, education practitioners, planners, policy makers and government who, in turn, have much to do to ensure a critical review of the theme of this study. Thus, further studies are recommended because this study is not an end in itself but a means for actualizing the MDG 2015 education goals.

The main purpose of this paragraph is to show the rigorous investigative effort of the researchers in conducting this investigation. It was the researchers' desire to contribute to knowledge through a comprehensive description regarding students and faculties use of IT/IS in educational achievement. This study was able to provide insights into the themes and state of this study. The investigators contributed to the conceptualization of natives and tourists in IT/IS education offerings. To make this study more elaborate, we looked into other relevant issues that may perhaps influence students and faculties' performance and their relationship to the teaching and learning process. This study has particular implications for the intended readers. Empirically, the need to consider the social and facilitating conditions and its influence on educational achievement was proven. The findings from this investigation, if put into effect, might go a long way toward the standardization of education in Nigeria and can be applied to similar situations in other parts of the world. The basis of this study could guide the Ministry of Education on their management origination move in order to analyze the entire educational structure to determine what areas need urgent attention. In all, IT/IS management is made appealing to higher education institutions and will assist them in reaping their objectives. It could also help educational institutions save both human and material resources. This is where the contribution of this investigation could play a significant role if adequately utilized.

## REFERENCES


Afari-Kumah, E., & Tanye, H. A. (2009). Tertiary Students' View on Information and Communications Technology Usage in Ghana. *Journal of Information Technology Impact*, *9*(2), 81–90.

Akdogan, I. (2009). Evaluating and Improving e-Paticipation in Istanbul. In T. Janoswski and J. Davis (Eds.), *Proceedings of the 3rd International Conference on the Theory and Practice of Electronic Governance,* (pp. 103-108) Bogota Colombia.

Anne, N., Seppo, T., & Shoji, N. (2010). University teachers' approaches to teaching and their pedagogical use of ICTs: A comparative case study of Finland, Japan and India. *US-China Education Review*, *7*(7), 1–14.

Awake (2008). Your Child and the Internet. *Awake, 89*(10), 3-9.

Barnes, K., Marateo, R., & Ferris, S. (2007). Teaching and learning with the net generation. *Innovate* 3(4), Retrieved May 23 2011, from http://innovateonline.info/pdf/vol3_issue4/Teaching_and_Learning_with_the_Net_Generation.pdf

Beebe, M. A. (2004). Impact of ICT Revolution on the African Academic Landscape. In *CODESRIA Conference on Electronic Publishing and Dissemination*, Retrieved March 29, 2011, from http://www.codesria.org/Links/conferences/el_publ/beebe.pdf

Bennett, S., & Maton, K. (2010). Original article: Beyond the "digital natives" debate: Towards a more nuanced understanding of students' technology experiences. *Journal of Computer Assisted Learning, 26*(5), 321–331. doi:10.1111/j.1365-2729.2010.00360.x

Bullen, M. (2011). *Key Trends: Mobile, Online and Blended Learning and E-books*. Retrieved April 30, 2011, from http://www.markbullen.ca/

Fan, A. (2010). The readiness of schools of Macao to integrate IT in education and the extent of actual IT integration. *International Journal of Education and Development using Information and Communication Technology* *6*(4), 52-63.

Federal Reublic of Nigeria. (2004). *Natial Policy on Education (4th edition).* Lagos: NERDC Press.

Feeney, L. (2010). Digital denizens. In *Instructional technology resources: In the spotlight.* Retrieved June 12 2011, from http://loki.stockton.edu/~intech/spotlight-digital-denizens.htm

García-Valcárcel, A., & Tejedor, F. J. (2009). Training demands of the lecturers related to the use of ICT. *World Conference on Educational Sciences, Nicosia, North Cyprus, 4-7 February 2009, 1*(1), 178-183.

Ifinedo, P. (2006). Acceptance and Continuance Intention of Web-Based Learning Technologies (WLT) among University Students in a Baltic Country. *The Journal of Information Systems in Developing Countries*, *23*(6), 1–20.

Jegede, P. O. (2009). Age and ICT-Related Behaviours of Higher Education Teachers in Nigeria. *Issues in Informing Science and Information Technology*, *6*, 771–777.

Kaba, B., N'Da, K., & Mbarika, V. (2008). Understanding the Factors Influencing the Attitude Toward and Use of Mobile Technology in Developing Countries: A Model of Cellular Phone Use in Guinea. *Proceedings of the 41st Hawaii International Conference on System Sciences*, (pp. 1-12).Washington, DC: IEEE Press

Kennedy, G., Dalgarno, B., Gray, K., Judd, T., Waycott, J., Bennett, S., et al. (2007). The net generation are not big users of Web 2.0 technologies: Preliminary findings. In *ICT: Providing choices for learners and learning. Proceedings ascilite Singapore 2007*. Retrieved May 23 2011, from http://www.ascilite.org.au/conferences/singapore07/procs/kennedy.pdf

Kirschner, P. A., & Davis, N. E. (2003). Pedagogic benchmarks for information and communication technology in teacher education. *Technology, Pedagogy and Education*, *12*(1), 127–149.

Kpolovie, P. J. (2010). *Advanced Research Methods. Owerri*. Springfield Publishers.

Kpolovie, P. J. (2011). *Statistical Techniques for Advanced Research. Owerri*. Springfield Publishers.

Mac-Ikemenjima, D. (2005). e-Education in Nigeria: Challenges and Prospects*". Paper presentation at the 8th UN ICT Task Force Meeting* Dublin, Ireland.

Margaryan, A., & Littlejohn, A. (2008). *Are digital natives a myth or reality?: Students' use of technologies for learning*. Retrieved March, 29, 2011, from http://www.academy.gcal.ac.uk/anoush/documents/DigitalNativesMythOrReality-MargaryanAndLittlejohn-draft-111208.pdf

Margaryan, A., Littlejohn, A., & Vojt, G. (2011). Are digital natives a myth or reality? University students' use of digital technologies. *Computers & Education*, *56*(2), 429–440. doi:10.1016/j.compedu.2010.09.004

Moja, T. (2000). *Nigeria Education Sector Analysis: An Analytical Synthesis of Performance and Main Issues*. WORLD BANK Report

Nweze, C. M. T. (2010). The Use of ICT in Nigerian Universities: A Case Study of Obafemi Awolowo University, Ile-Ife. *College & Research Libraries*, *65*(4), 276–286.

Nwokeocha, S. (2011). *The Digital Divide between Students and Lecturers: A Case study of Access and Attitudes towards Information Communication Technology (ICT) in Selected Nigerian Universities*. Retrieved March 21, 2011 from http://www.iiis.org/CDs2010/CD2010IMC/ICSIT_2010/PapersPdf/HB369QL.pdf

Oblonger, D., & Oblinger, J. (2005). *Is It Age or IT: First Steps Toward Understanding the Net Generation*. Retrieved May 23 2011, from http://net.educause.edu/ir/library/pdf/pub7101.pdf

Ololube, N. P. (2006a). The Impact of Professional and Non-professional Teachers' ICT Competencies in Secondary Schools in Nigeria. *Journal of Information Technology Impact*, *6*(2), 101–118.

Ololube, N. P. (2006b). Appraising the Relationship Between ICT Usage and Integration and the Standard of Teacher Education Programs in a Developing Economy. *International Journal of Education and Development Using ICT*, *2*(3), 70–85.

Ololube, N. P. (2007). The Relationship between Funding, ICT, Selection Processes, Administration and Planning and the Standard of Science Teacher Education in Nigeria. *Asia-Pacific Forum on Science Learning and Teaching*, *8*(1), Article 4.

Ololube, N. P. (2008). Computer Communication and ICT Attitude and Anxiety Among Higher Education Students. In Cartelli, A. (Ed.), *Encyclopedia of Information and Communication Technology* (pp. 100–105). Hershey, PA: Idea Group Publishing. doi:10.4018/978-1-59904-845-1.ch014

Ololube, N. P. (2009). Computer Communication and ICT Attitude and Anxiety Among Higher Education Students. In Cartelli, A., & Palma, M. (Eds.), *Encyclopedia of Information and Communication Technology* (pp. 100–105). Hershey, PA: Information Science Reference. doi:10.4018/978-1-59904-845-1.ch014

Ololube, N. P. (2011). Blended Learning in Nigeria: Determining Students' Readiness and Faculty Role in Advancing Technology in a Globalize Educational Development. In Kitchenham, A. (Ed.), *Blended Learning Across Disciplines: Models for Implementation* (pp. 190–207). Hershey, PA: IGI Publishing. doi:10.4018/978-1-60960-479-0.ch011

Ololube, N. P., & Ubogu, A. E. (2009). ICTs and Distance Education: The Nigerian Experience. In Cartelli, A., & Palma, M. (Eds.), *Encyclopedia of Information and Communication Technology* (pp. 396–400). Hershey, PA: IGI Global.

Ololube, N. P., Ubogu, A. E., & Egbezor, D. E. (2007). ICT and Distance Education Programs in a Sub-Saharan African Country: A Theoretical Perspective. *Journal of Information Technology Impact*, *7*(3), 181–194.

Open education. (2011a). *Of Digital Immigrants and Digital Natives Teaching the Net Generation*. Retrieved April 30, 2011, from http://www.openeducation.net/2011/03/01/digital-immigrants-and-digital-natives-teaching-the-net-generation/

Open Educaton. (2011b). *Though Net Generation Concerns Over-hyped, Integrating Technology the Right Step*. Retrieved Aripl 30, 2011, from http://www.openeducation.net/2008/09/26/though-net-generation-concerns-overhyped-integrating-technology-the-right-step/

Pelgrum and Law. (2003). *ICT in Education Around the World: Trends, Problems and Prospects*. Paris: UNSCO, International Institute for Educational Planning.

Philip, D. (2007). The Knowledge Building Paradigm: A Model of Learning for Net Generation Students. *Innovate, 3*(5). Retrieved May 23 2011, from www.personal.psu.edu/...blog/.../human-capital-theory-and-criti.html

Prensky, M. (2001). Digital Natives, Digital Immigrants. *MCB University Press*, *9*(5), 1–6.

Rosen, L. (2010). *Rewired: Understanding the iGeneration and the Way They Learn*. New York: Palgrave Macmillan.

Sam, H. K., Othman, A. E. A., & Nordin, Z. S. (2005). Computer self-efficacy, computer anxiety, and attitudes toward the Internet: A study among undergraduates in UNIMAS. *Journal of Educational Technology & Society*, *8*(4), 205–219.

Siragusa, L., & Dixon, K. C. (2008). Planned Behaviour: Student Attitudes Towards the Use of ICT Interactions in Higher Education. *Proceedings of ASCILITE*, (pp. 942-953)Melbourne, Australia

Tiemo, P. A., Emiri, O. T., & Tiemo, A. J. (2010). Information and Communication Technology (ICT) Training among Lecturers in the South-South Zone in Nigeria by the Nigeria Communication Commission (NCC). *International Journal of Information and Communication Technology Education*, *6*(1), 55–66. doi:10.4018/jicte.2010091105

Toledo, C. A. (2007). Digital Culture: Immigrants and Tourists Responding to the Natives' Drumbeat. *International Journal of Teaching and Learning in Higher Education*, *19*(1), 84–92.

Tucker, H. (2010). *Digital Natives and Digital Immigrants*. Retrieved June 32011, from http://ccnmtl.columbia.edu/enhanced/primers/digital_natives.html

Tuomi, I. (2000). *Beyond the digital divide*. Retrieved March 13, 2011, from http://www.cs.berkeley.edu/~jfc/hcc/retreat3/Divide.pdf

UNESCO. (2002). *Information and Communication Technologies in Teacher education: A Planning Guide*. Paris: UNESCO.

UNESCO. (2003). *Manual for Pilot Testing the Use of Indicators to Assess Impact of ICT Use in Education*. Retrieved March 10, 2011, from http://www.unescobkk.org/education/ict/resource

UNESCO. (2005). "United Nations Decade of education for Sustainable development 2005-2014. Retrieved on the March 20, 2011, from http://portal.unesco.org/education/en/ev.php-URL_ID=27234&URL_DO=DO_TOPIC&URL_SECTION=201.html

Waycott, J., Bennett, S., Kennedy, G., Dalgarno, B., & Gray, K. (2010). Digital divides? Student and staff perceptions of information and communication technologies. *Computers & Education*, *54*(4), 1202–1211. doi:10.1016/j.compedu.2009.11.006

Yusuf, M. O. (2005a). An Investigation into Teachers' Self-Efficacy in Implementing Computer Education in Nigerian Secondary Schools. *Meridian: A Middle School Computer Technologies Journal* *8*(2).

Yusuf, M. O. (2005b). Information and Communication Technologies and Education: Analyzing the Nigerian National Policy for Information Technology. *International Education Journal*, *6*(3), 316–321.

Yusuf, M. O. & Onasanya, S. A. (2004). Information and Communication technology (ict) and teaching in tertiary institutions. *Teaching in Tertiary Intitutions* 67-76.

## KEY TERMS AND DEFINITIONS

**Faculties:** Is used to include all levels of academic staff to cover teachers, lecturers, tutors, and professors engaged in the teaching and learning processes in higher education.

**Technology:** The application of scientific knowledge for practical purposes, which involves the usage, knowledge, skill and competence in solving problem or perform specific function

**Computer Systems:** These include the computer along with its softwares and other devices that are necessary to make a computer function.

**Academic Activities:** The degree of academic activities and competitions designed to enhance and extend classroom instruction and provide students and faculty members the opportunity to use their academic skills for educational purposes

**Digital Natives:** Digital native: Digital natives' belief in the use technology for numerous tasks no matter the circumstance, they adapt to the changing techniques and methods.

**Digital Tourists:** Digital toursts: sometimes referred to as digital immigrant, use technology but are not familiar to all of its potential, with the belief that technology can be used successfully for some tasks and not for the others.

**Developing Economy:** This is often used to refer to countries that are backward in terms of economic, social, political, and technological growth and development as compared to developed countries.

# Compilation of References


Abiagam, B. (2009). *The use of the Internet in arranging travels in the United Kingdom with some implication for Nigerian Tourism*. Thesis Project, University of the West of Scotland.

Acemoglu, D. (2009). *Introduction to Modern Economic Growth*. Princeton, NJ: Princeton University Press.

Adedej, A. (2002)... *Why Firms in the UK Use Interest Rate Derivatives.*, *28*(11), 53–74.

Adesina, A. A., Ayo, C. K., & Ekong, U. O. (2008). An empirical investigation of the level of users' acceptance of e-banking in Nigeria: based on technology acceptance model. In *Proc. of 1st Int'l Conf. on Mobile e-Services.* Ogbomosho, Nigeria: LAUTECH.

Afari-Kumah, E., & Tanye, H. A. (2009). Tertiary Students' View on Information and Communications Technology Usage in Ghana. *Journal of Information Technology Impact*, *9*(2), 81–90.

Agbada, A.O. (2008). E-banking in Nigeria, problems and prospects from customer's perspective. *CBN Bullion Magazine, 32*(4), October-December 2008 edition.

Aghaunor, L., & Fotoh, X. (2006). *Factors affecting e-commerce adoption in Nigerian Banks*. Sweden: Jonkoping University.

Agresti, A. (1990). *Categorical Data Analysis*. New York: Wiley.

Aitken, B. J., & Harrison, A. E. (1999). Do Domestic Firms bene□t from Direct Foreign Investment?: Evidence from Venezuela. *The American Economic Review*, *89*(3), 605–618. doi:10.1257/aer.89.3.605

Ajadi, T O, Salawu, I. O. & Adeoye, F. A. (2008). E-Learning and distance education in Nigeria. *The Turkish Online Journal of Educational Technology – TOJET,* 7(4), 7, 1303-6521.

Ajayi, G. O. (2003). *NITDA and ICT in Nigeria. Developing Countries Access to Digital Knowledge*. Trieste, Italy: ICTP.

Ajzen, I., & Fishbein, M. (1975). *Belief, attitude, intention and behaviour*. Reading, UK: Addison-Wesley.

Akdogan, I. (2009). Evaluating and Improving e-Paticipation in Istanbul. In T. Janoswski and J. Davis (Eds.), *Proceedings of the 3rd International Conference on the Theory and Practice of Electronic Governance,* (pp. 103-108) Bogota Colombia.

Aker, J., Jenny, C., & Mbiti, I. M. (2010). Mobile phones and economic development in Africa. *The Journal of Economic Perspectives*, *24*(3), 207–232. doi:10.1257/jep.24.3.207

Akinwale, E. J. (1999) *Human Resources Management.* (An overview). (2nd Edition) Lagos: Concept Publications.

Akpan, N., (2008, February 27). E-payment solutions: are banks getting it right? *Business day Newspaper*

Akudolu, L. R. (1988). Computer literacy among primary school pupils as an effective platform for technological education. *Paper presented at the international conference on information and education*. Nsukka, University of Nigeria.

Akudolu, L. R. (2002). Restructuring Nigerian secondary education system through Information and Communication Technology-Driven Curriculum. *Journal of the World Council for Curriculum and Instruction*, *3*(1), 8–17.

Aldas-Manzano, J., Lassala-Navarre, C., Ruiz-Mafe, C., & Sanz-Blas, S. (2009). The role of consumer innovativeness and perceived risk in online banking usage. *International Journal of Bank Marketing*, *27*(1), 53–75. doi:10.1108/02652320910928245

Aldehayyat, J. S., Al Khattab, A. A., & Anchor, J. R. (2011). The use of strategic planning tools and techniques by hotels in Jordan. *Management Research Review*, *34*(Iss: 4), 477–490. doi:10.1108/01409171111117898

Aldrich, J. H., & Nelson, F. D. (1984). *Linear Probability, Logit, and Probit Models*. Beverly Hills, CA: Sage.

Alexander, S. (2001). E-learning developments and experiences. *Education + Training*, *43*, 240–248. doi:10.1108/00400910110399247

Alicia, G. H., Sergio, G., & Daniel, S. (2006). 'China's Banking Reform: An Assessment of its Evolution and Possible Impact.'. *CESifo Economic Studies*, *52*(2), 304–363. doi:10.1093/cesifo/ifl006

Allan, G. M., Allan, N. D., Kadirkamanathan, V., & Fleming, P. J. (2007). Risk Mining For Strategic Decision Making. In Wegrzyn-Wolska, K. M., & Szczepaniak, P. S. (Eds.), *Adv. In Intel. Web, ASC 43* (pp. 21–28). Berlin Heidelberg., Germany: Springer-Verlag.

Allen, R. E., & Snyder, D. (2009). New thinking on the financial crisis. *Critical Perspectives on International Business*, *5*(1/2), 36–55. doi:10.1108/17422040910938677

Alonso, A., & Oiarzabal, P. (2010). *Diasporas in the New Media Age: Identity, Politics, and Community*. Reno: University of Nevada Press.

Alpern, K. D. (1997). What Do We Want Trust to Be. *Business and Professional Ethics Journal*, 16(1–3), 29–46: Special Issue on Trust and Business: Barriers and Bridges. D. Koehn (Ed.).

Al-Qirim, N. (2007). The adoption of ecommerce communications and applications technologies in small businesses *in New Zealand. Electronic Commerce Research and Applications*, *6*(4), 462–473. doi:10.1016/j.elerap.2007.02.012

Alrifai, M., & Risse, T. (2009). Combining Global Optimization with Local Selection for Efficient QoS-aware Service Composition. In *International World Wide Web Conference*, (pp. 881–890) New York, NY: ACM Press

American Library Association (ALA). (1989). American Library Association Committee on Information Literacy Final Report, *Eric clearing on Information Technology ED315074*, Chicago.

Amjad, U. (2004). Mobile Computing and Wireless Communications. University of Pennsylvania: NGE Solutions, Inc.

Anandarajan, M., Igbaria, M., & Anakwe, U. (2002). IT acceptance in a less-developed country: a motivational factor perspective. *International Journal of Information Management*, *22*(1), 47–65. doi:10.1016/S0268-4012(01)00040-8

Andreeva, G. (2005). *European generic scoring models using logistic regression and survial analysis.* Bath: Young OR Conference.

Anne, N., Seppo, T., & Shoji, N. (2010). University teachers' approaches to teaching and their pedagogical use of ICTs: A comparative case study of Finland, Japan and India. *US-China Education Review*, *7*(7), 1–14.

Anonymous. (2010). E-Epiheirein. Retrieved November 28, 2010, from http://www.go-online.gr/ebusiness/specials/article.html?article_id=1561&PHPSESSID=ada989def1b7181b263c589c35cf4aec

Antle, J. (1983). Infrastructure and Aggregate Agricultural Productivity: International Evidence. *Economic Development and Cultural Change*, *31*(3), 609–619. doi:10.1086/451344

Ardagna, D., & Pernici, B. (2007). Adaptive service composition in flexible processes. *IEEE Transactions on Software Engineering*, *33*(6), 369–384. doi:10.1109/TSE.2007.1011

Argyris, C. (1957). The individual and organization: some problems of mutual adjustment. *Administrative Science Quarterly*, *2*, 1–24. doi:10.2307/2390587

Arikpo, I. I., Osofisan, A., & Usoro, A. (2009). Bridging the digital divide: the Nigerian journey so far. *International Journal of Global Business, 2*(1)181-204, available at: http://gsmi-ijgb.com/Documents/V2%20N1%20IJGB%20-P08%20-Arikpo%20%20Bridging%20the%20Digital%20Divide%20-June%202009.pdf, retrieved on12/2/2011.

Armstrong, M. (2004). *A Hand Book of Human Resources management practice* (9th ed.). India: Kogan Page Publishers.

Arner, D. W., Hsu, B. F. C., & Lifen, P. (2010)... *Credit Rating in China Chinese Law & Government, 43*(3), 3–7. doi:10.2753/CLG0009-4609430300

Aschauer, D. A. (1989). Is Public Expenditure Productive? *Journal of Monetary Economics*, (n.d). 177–200. doi:10.1016/0304-3932(89)90047-0

Association of College and Research Libraries. (2000). *Information Literacy Competency Standards for higher education*. Association of College and Research Libraries, Chicago, IL. Available at *http://www.alaorg/acrl/ilcomstan.htnl.*

Attewell, P. (1992). Technology diffusion and organizational learning: The case of business computing. *Organization Science, 3*(1), 1–19. doi:10.1287/orsc.3.1.1

Aversano, L., Pent, M., & Taneja, K. (2006). A genetic programming approach to support the design of service compositions. *International Journal of Computer Systems Science and Engineering, 4*, 247–254.

Awake (2008). Your Child and the Internet. *Awake, 89*(10), 3-9.

Ayo, C. K., Adebiyi, A., Fatudimu, I. T., & Ekong, U. O. (2008). A framework for e-commerce implementation: Nigeria a Case Study. *Journal of Internet Banking and Commerce, 13*(2), 1–12.

Bagchi, K., Udo, G., & Kirs, P. (2006). Global diffusion of the Internet XII: the Internet growth in Africa: some empirical results. *Communications of the Association for Information Systems, 19*(16), 323–351.

Baguma, R., Bommel, P., Wanyama, T., & Ogao, P. (2007). Web Accessibility in Uganda: a study of Webmaster Perceptions. In *proceedings of the Third Annual International Conference on Computing & ICT Research (ICCIR 2007)*, Kampala: Uganda.

Baldwin, E. (2006). Hilton Highlights link between staff loyalty and e-learning. *Human Resource Management International Digest, 14*(1), 36–38. doi:10.1108/09670730610643990

Ballantyne, J., Curry, A., & Sumner, A. (2011). Africa 2010-2020: poverty reduction beyond the global crisis. *Foresight, 13*(3), 24–37. doi:10.1108/14636681111138749

Bandura, A. (1982). Self-efficacy mechanism in human agency. *Journal of American Psychologist, 37*(2), 122–147. doi:10.1037/0003-066X.37.2.122

Bandwidth Consortium. (2011). Retrieved from http://www.foundation-partnership.org/

Banks, K. (2008). *Mobile Phones and the Digital Divide*. Retrieved November 28, 2010, from http://www.pcworld.com/article/149075/mobile_phones_and_the_digital_divide.html

Barnes, K., Marateo, R., & Ferris, S. (2007). Teaching and learning with the net generation. *Innovate* 3(4), Retrieved May 23 2011, from http://innovateonline.info/pdf/vol3_issue4/Teaching_and_Learning_with_the_Net_Generation.pdf

Barnes, S. J., & Vidgen, R. T. (2001). Assessing the Quality of Auction Web Sites. *In Proceedings of the 34th Hawaii International Conference on Systems Sciences* (pp. 1–10). Los Alamitos, CA: IEEE Computer Society Press.

Barnes, S. J., & Vidgen, R. T. (2002). An Integrative Approach to the Assessment of E-Commerce Quality. *Journal of Electronic Commerce Research, 3*(3), 114–127.

Baro, E. E., & Asaba, J. O. (2010). Internet connectivity in university libraries in Nigeria: the present state. *Library Hi Tech News, 27*(9/10), 13–19. doi:10.1108/07419051011110603

Baroudi, J. J. (1985). The impact of role variables on IS personnel work attitudes and intentions. *Management Information Systems Quarterly, 9*(4), 341–356. doi:10.2307/249234

Baroudi, J. J., & Ginzberg, M. J. (1992). Career Orientation of IS Personnel. *Computer Personnel, 14*(2), 15–29. doi:10.1145/147114.147118

Barquin, R. C. (2001). What is Knowledge Management? In Barquin, R. C., Bennet, A., & Remez, S. G. (Eds.), *Knowledge Management: the Catalyst for Electronic Government* (pp. 3–24). Vienna, Virginia: Management Concepts.

Barro, R. J., & Lee, J.-W. (2010). A New Data Set of Educational Attainment in the World, 1950–2010. *The national bureau for economic research (NBER)*, working paper no. 15902.

Bartol, K. M., & Martin, D. C. (1998). *Management* (3rd ed.). New York, NY: McGraw-Hill, Inc.

Ba, S., & Pavlou, P. A. (2002). Evidence of the Effects of Trust Building Technology in Electronic Markets: Price Premiums and Buyer Behavior. *Management Information Systems Quarterly*, *26*(3), 243–268. doi:10.2307/4132332

Bastos, J. (2008). Credit scoring with boosted decision. *Munich Personal RePEc Archive Paper, 8156*, 2–4.

Bateman, T. S., & Snell, A. S. (2002). *Management: Competing in the New Era* (5th ed.). New York, NY: McGraw-Hill, Inc.

Bebensee, T., Helms, R., & Spruit, M. (2011). Exploring Web 2.0 Applications as a Means of Bolstering up Knowledge Management. *Electronic Journal of Knowledge Management*, *9*(1), 1–9.

Becerra-Fernandez, I., Gonzalez, A., & Sabherwal, R. (2004). *Knowledge Management: Challenges, Solutions and Technologies*. Upper Saddle River, NJ: Prentice Hall.

Beebe, M. A. (2004). Impact of ICT Revolution on the African Academic Landscape. In *CODESRIA Conference on Electronic Publishing and Dissemination*, Retrieved March 29, 2011, from http://www.codesria.org/Links/conferences/el_publ/beebe.pdf

Beecham, S., Baddoo, N., Hall, T., Robinson, H., & Sharp, H. (2007). *Motivation in Software Engineering: A Systematic Literature Review.* Retrieved October 30, 2008 from https://uhra.herts.ac.uk/dspace/bitstream/2299/989/1/S70.pdf

Belcher, G., & Rosenberg, D. (2006). ICT Training: INASP Workshops for African University Library Staff. *Information Development.*, *22*(2), 116–122. doi:10.1177/0266666906065574

Bellinger, G., Durval, C., & Mills, A. (1997). Data, Information, Knowledge, and Wisdom, available at: http://www.outsightscom/systems/dikw/dikw.htm, retrieved on 18/10/2010.

Bell, M. (1980). Rural-Urban Movement among Botswana's Skilled Manpower: Some Observations on the Two Sector Model. *Africa: Journal of the International African Institute*, *50*(4), 404–421. doi:10.2307/1158431

Benatallah, B. B., & Rachid, H. R. (2003). A Petri net-based model for web service composition. *Proceedings of the 14th Australasian database Conference, Australian Computer Society, Inc. Darlinghurst,* Australia. Retrieved July 13th 2011, from http://arxiv.org/PS_cache/cs/pdf/0406/0406055v1.pdf.

Bennett, S., & Maton, K. (2010). Original article: Beyond the "digital natives" debate: Towards a more nuanced understanding of students' technology experiences. *Journal of Computer Assisted Learning*, *26*(5), 321–331. doi:10.1111/j.1365-2729.2010.00360.x

Benson, G. S. (2006). Employee development, commitment and intention to turnover: a test of 'employability' policies in action. *Human Resource Management Journal*, *16*(2), 173–192. doi:10.1111/j.1748-8583.2006.00011.x

Berg, T. C., & Kalish, G. I. (1997). Trust and Ethics in Employee-Owned Companies. *Business and Professional Ethics Journal*, 16(1–3), Special Issue on Trust and Business: Barriers and Bridges, D. Koehn (Ed.), 211–224.

Berg, Z., & Collins, M. (1995). *Computer mediated communication and the online classroom*. Cresskill, NJ: Hampton Press.

Bertino, E., Squicciarini, A., Martino, L., & Paci, F. (2010). An adaptive access control model for Web services *International Journal of Web Services Research, 3*(3), 27–60. doi:10.4018/jwsr.2006070102

Bhattacherjee, A. (2002). Individual Trust in Online Firms: Scale Development and Initial Test. *Journal of Management Information Systems*, *19*(1), 211–241.

Bird, D. R. (2005). *Personnel management concepts and application* (10th ed.). New Jersey: Irwin McGraw Hill.

Bodley, J. H. (1994). *Cultural anthropology: tribes, states, and the global system*. Mountain View, CA: Mayfield Publishing.

Boone, L. E., & Kurtz, D. L. (1987). *Contemporary Business* (5th ed.). Chicago: The Dryden Press.

Boscov-Ellen, D. (2009). *Mobile Internet Narrows the Digital Divide Domestically*. Retrieved November, 28, 2010 from http://www.newpolicyinstitute.org/2009/09/mobile-internet-narrows-the-digital-divide-domestically/

Bouaka, N., & Amos, D. (2004). A Proposal of a Decision Maker Problem for a Better Understanding of Information Needs. *IEEE Explore*, (pp 551 - 552) http://ieeexplore.ieee.org/iel5/9145/29024/01307879.pdf

Bouncken, R. (2002). Knowledge management for quality improvements in hotels. *Journal of Quality Assurance in Hospitality & Tourism*, *3*(3-4), 25–59. doi:10.1300/J162v03n03_03

Bozionelos, N. (1996). Psychology of computer use: prevalence of computer anxiety in British managers and professionals. *Psychological Reports*, *78*(3), 995–1002. doi:10.2466/pr0.1996.78.3.995

Brenkert, G. (1998). Trust, Business and Business Ethics: An Introduction. *Business Ethics Quarterly*, *8*(2), 195–203.

Brian, A. W. (1994). *Increasing returns and path dependence in the economy*. Ann Arbor, MI: University of Michigan Press.

Bridges Organization. (2001), *Comparison of e-readiness assessment models*. Retrieved October 5, 2007, from http://www.bridges.org/ereadiness/tools.html.

Brown, B. B. (1983). The Impact of Male Labor Migration on Women in Botswana. *African Affairs*, *82*(328), 367–388.

Brown, H. G., Scott, M. P., & Rodgers, T. L. (2004). Interpersonal Traits, Complementarities, and Trust in Virtual Collaboration. *Journal of Management Information Systems*, *20*(4), 115–137.

Bruce, C. (1995). Information Literacy: A Framework for Higher Education. *The Australian Library Journal*, *44*, 158–159.

Buhalis, D. (2003). *eTourism: information technology for strategic tourism management*. London: Pearson Education.

Buhalis, D., & Schertler, W. (1999). *Information and communication technologies in tourism 1999*. Vienna: Springer. doi:10.1007/978-3-7091-6373-3

Bui, T. X., Sankaran, S., & Sebastian, I. M. (2003). A framework for measuring national e-readiness. *International Journal of Electronic Business*, *1*(1), 3–22. doi:10.1504/IJEB.2003.002162

Bullen, M. (2011). *Key Trends: Mobile, Online and Blended Learning and E-books*. Retrieved April 30, 2011, from http://www.markbullen.ca/

Business Process Execution Language for Web Services. (n.d.) *BEA Systems, Microsoft, and IBM.* ftp://www6.software.ibm.com/software/developer/library/ws-bpel.pdf, 2002.32

Butler, P. (2006). *Well connected: releasing power and restoring hope through kingdom partnerships*. Springs, CO: Biblica.

Buttle, F. (1986). *Hotel and food service marketing: A Managerial Approach*. England: Continuum International Publishing.

BV2016C (Botswana Vision 2016 Council) (2004). *Towards Prosperity for All*. Retrieved January 18, 2008 from http://www.vision2016.co.bw

Byrne, Z. S., & Cropanzano, R. (2001). The history of organizational justice: The founders speak. In Cropanzano, R. (Ed.), *Justice in the workplace: From theory to practice (2)*. Mahwah, NJ: Lawrence Erlbaum Associates, Inc.

Caldeira, M. M., & Ward, J. M. (2002). Understanding the successful adoption and use of IS/IT in SMEs: An explanation from Portuguese manufacturing industries. *Information Systems Journal*, *12*(2), 121–152. doi:10.1046/j.1365-2575.2002.00119.x

Campbell, E. K. (2003). Attitudes of Botswana Citizens towards Immigrants: Signs of Xenophobia. *International Migration (Geneva, Switzerland)*, *41*(4), 11–71. doi:10.1111/1468-2435.00253

Canfora, G., Penta, M. D., Esposito, R., & Villani, M. L. (2005). An Approach for QoS-aware Service Composition based on Genetic Algorithms. *Proceedings of the Genetic and Computation Conference (GECCO'05),* Washington DC, USA: ACM Press.

Canning, D. (1994). Infrastructure and Growth. In Baldassarri, M., Paganetto, L., & Phelps, E. (Eds.), *International Differences in Growth Rates* (pp. 113–147). New York, NY: Macmillan Press.

Canning, D. (1999). A Database of World Stocks of Infrastructure, 1950-95. *The World Bank Economic Review*, *12*(3), 529–547.

Cantrell, S. (2000). E-Market Trust Mechanisms. *Accenture Research Note: E-Commerce Networks, 11*, 1 – 3.

Carmichael, C., Turgoose, C., Gary, M. O., & Todd, C. (2000). Innovation and SMEs the case of Yorkshire, UK. *Journal of Industry and Higher Education*, *14*(4), 244–248. doi:10.5367/000000000101295147

Carr, S. (2000). As distance education comes of age, the challenge is keeping the students. *The Chronicle of Higher Education*, *46*(23), A39–A41.

Caselli, F., & Coleman, W. (2001). Cross-country technology diffusion: the case of computers. *The American Economic Review*, *91*(2), 328–335. doi:10.1257/aer.91.2.328

Catherine, M Gustafson. (2002). Staff turnover: Retention. *International Journal of Contemporary Hospitality Management*, *14*(3), 106–110.

Ceriello, V. R., & Freeman, C. (1991). *Human Resources Management Systems: Strategies, Tactics and Techniques. San Fransisco*. Jossey-Bass Publisher.

Chadwick, A. (2009). *Routledge handbook of Internet politics*. New York: Taylor & Francis.

Chau, P. Y. K., & Lai, V. S. K. (2003). An empirical investigation of the determinants of user acceptance of Internet banking. *Journal of Organizational Computing and Electronic Commerce*, *13*(2), 123–145. doi:10.1207/S15327744JOCE1302_3

Chen, M. C., & Huang, S. H. (2007). 'Credit scoring and rejected instances reassigning through evolutionary computation techniques'. *Expert Systems with Applications*, *24*(4), 433–441. doi:10.1016/S0957-4174(02)00191-4

Cheskin Research and Studio Archetype/Sapient. (1999). *eCommerce Trust Study*. Retrieved May 23, 2010, from http://www.cheskin.com/cms/files/i/articles//17__report-eComm%20Trust1999.pdf

Chiemeke, S. C., Evwiekpaefe, O., & Chete, F. (2006). The Adoption of Internet Banking in Nigeria: An Empirical Investigation, *Journal of Internet Banking and Commerce, 11*(3), Available: http://www.arraydev.com/commerce/jibc/

Chinn, M. D., & Fairlie, R. W. (2004). *The determinants of the global digital divide: a cross-country analysis of computer and Internet penetration*. Retrieved October 8, 2008 from http://ssrn.com/abstract=519082.

Chin, W. (1998). Issues and opinion on structural equation modeling. *Management Information Systems Quarterly*, *22*(1), vii–xvi.

Chircu, A. M., & Kauffman, R. J. (2000). Limits to value in electronic commerce-related IT investments. *Journal of Management Information Systems*, *17*(2), 59–80.

Chong, S., & Pervan, G. (2007). Factors influencing the extent of deployment of electronic commerce for small and medium-sized enterprises. *Journal of Electronic Commerce in Organizations*, *5*(1), 1–29. doi:10.4018/jeco.2007010101

Choo, C. W. (2002). *The strategic management of intellectual capital and organisational knowledge*. Oxford: University Press.

Chui, C.-M., Wang, C., Eric, T. G., Shih, F.-J., & Fan, Y.-W. (2011). Understanding knowledge sharing in virtual communities: An integration of expectancy disconfirmation and justice theories. *Online Information Review*, *35*(1), 134–153. doi:10.1108/14684521111113623

Chunlin, L. (2004). Zhongchan jieceng Zhongguo shehui zhide guanzhu de rengun, [The Middle Class: A Chinese Social Group Worthy of Our Attention] In Ru Xin, Lu Xueyi, and Li Peilin (Eds.), 2004: Zhongguo shehui xingshi fenxi yu yuce [*2004: Analysis and Forecast on China's Social Development*] (pp. 51-63)BeijingL Sheke wenxian chuban she, 2004.

CIA WorldFact. (2011). *Country reports*. Retrieved October 8, 2011 from https://www.cia.gov/.

CIA WorldFact. (2011). *Nigeria Reports*. Available at https://www.cia.gov/library/publications/the-world-factbook/geos/ni.html. Accessed April 3, 2011.

Clinton, R. J., Williamson, S. & Bethke, A. L. (1994). Implementing Total Quality Management: The Role of Human Resource Management. *SAM Advanced Management Journal, 59*.

Coello, C. A. (2002). Theoretical and numerical constraint-handling techniques used with evolutionary algorithms: A survey of the state of the art. *Computer Methods in Applied Mechanics and Engineering*, (191): 11–12.

Comin, D., & Hobijn, B. (2004). Cross-country technology adoption: making the theories face the facts. *Journal of Monetary Economics*, *51*(1), 39–83. doi:10.1016/j.jmoneco.2003.07.003

Compeau, D., & Higgins, C. A. (1995). Computer self-efficacy: development of a measure and initial test. *Management Information Systems Quarterly*, *19*(2), 189–212. doi:10.2307/249688

Cone, E. (1998). Managing that churning sensation. *InformationWeek*, *680*, 50.

Connolly, T. M. & Stransfield, M. (2007). From e-learning to games- based e-learning: Using interactive technologies in teaching an IS Course. *Int. J. Information Technology and Management*. *6*(2-3-4), 188-195.

Consumers spend almost half of their waking hours using media and communications (2010). *Ofcom. Independent regulator and competition authority for the UK communications industries*, Retrieved November 28, 2010, from http://media.ofcom.org.uk/2010/08/19/consumers-spend-almost-half-of-their-waking-hours-using-media-and-communications

Cooper, C. (2006). Knowledge Management and Tourism. *Annals of Tourism Research*, *33*(1), 47–64. doi:10.1016/j.annals.2005.04.005

CORAS -. *A platform for risk analysis of security critical systems*. (2000). Retrieved from: http://coras.sourceforge.net.

Council of Europe. (2009). *Parliamentary Assembly Working Papers - 2008 Ordinary Session*, Fourth Part, 29 September-3-october 2008 - 2009, Volume 7. Retrieved from http://www.coe.int/

Covert, J. (2007). Online Clothes Reviews Give 'Love That Dress' New Clout. *Wall Street Journal – Eastern Edition*, 248, pp. B1– B4.

Cragg, P., & King, M. (1993). Small-firm computing: Motivators and inhibitors. *Management Information Systems Quarterly*, *17*(1), 47–60. doi:10.2307/249509

Crepeau, R. G., Crook, C. W., Goslar, M. D., & McMurtrey, M. E. (1992). Career Anchors of Information Systems Personnel. *Journal of Management Information Systems*, *9*(2), 145–160.

Crook, J. N., Edelman, D. B., & Thomas, L. C. (2007). Recent developments in consumer credit risk assessment. *European Journal of Operational Research*, *183*, 1447–1465. doi:10.1016/j.ejor.2006.09.100

Cross, J., O'Driscoil, T. & Trondsen, E. (2007). Another life: virtual worlds as tools for learning. *eLearn Magazine*, *3*(2).

Cultural Capital. (2010) *Wikipedia, the Free Encyclopedia* Retrieved November 28, 2010, from http://en.wikipedia.org/wiki/Cultural_capital

Curran, J. M., Meuter, M. L., & Surprenant, C. F. (2003). Intentions to use self-service technologies: a confluence of multiple attitudes. *Journal of Service Research*, *5*(3), 209–224. doi:10.1177/1094670502238916

Curwen, P., & Whalley, J. (2011). The restructuring of African mobile telecommunications provision and the prospects for economic development. *Info*, *13*(2), 53–71. doi:10.1108/14636691111121638

Danziger, N., & Valency, R. (2006). Career anchors: distribution and impact on job satisfaction: The Israeli case. *Career Development International*, *11*(4), 293–303. doi:10.1108/13620430610672513

Darley, W. K. (2001). The internet and emerging e-commerce: challenges and implications for management in Sub-Saharan Africa. *Journal of Global Information Technology Management*, *4*(4), 4–18.

Dasgupta, S., Lall, S., & Wheeler, D. (2001). Policy reform, economic growth, and the digital divide: an econometric analysis. *Development Research Group, World Bank*. Retrieved October 8, 2008, from http://econ.worldbank.org/external/default/main?pagePK=64165259&piPK=64165421&theSitePK=469372&menuPK=64216926&entityID=000094946_01032705352348

David, A., & Odile, T. (2004). *Prise en Compte du Profil de l'Utilisateur dans un Système d'Information Strategique*. [Taking into Account in the User Profile of a strategic information system] Vandœuvre-lès-Nancy, France: Publications Loria

David, B., & David, A. (2001). METIORE: A Personalized Information Retrieval System. *Proceedings of the 8th International Conference on user modeling*, (pp 168 – 177) New York, NY: Springer

Davis, F. D. (1989). Perceived usefulness, perceived ease of use, and user acceptance of information technology. *Management Information Systems Quarterly*, *13*(3), 319–339. doi:10.2307/249008

Davis, F. D. (1993). User acceptance of information technology: system characteristics, user perceptions and behavioral impacts. *International Journal of Man-Machine Studies*, *38*, 475–487. doi:10.1006/imms.1993.1022

Davis, R. H., Edelamn, D. B., & Gammerman, A. J. (1992). Machine learning algorithms for credit-card applications. *IMA Journal of Management Mathematics*, *4*, 43–51. doi:10.1093/imaman/4.1.43

DBI. (2011). Digital Bridge Institute. Retrieved from http://www.dbieducation.org/

DeConinck, J. B., & Johnson, J. T. (2009). The Effects of Perceived Supervisor Support, Perceived Organizational Support, and Organizational Justice on Turnover Among Salespeople. *Journal of Personal Selling & Sales Management*, *29*(4), 333–351. doi:10.2753/PSS0885-3134290403

Dedrick, J., Gurbaxani, V., & Kraemer, K. L. (2003). Information technology and economic performance: a critical review of the empirical evidence. *ACM Computing Surveys*, *35*(1), 1–28. doi:10.1145/641865.641866

Delgado-Hernandez, D. J., Wong, K. Y., De-La-Torre-Rivera, S., Rigaud-Tellez, N., Velarde, J. I. S., Gaxiola, D. M., et al. (2009). *Computer Science and Information Technology (IACSITSC)* - Spring Conference,(pp. 313 – 316.) Washington, DC: IEEE Press

DeMaris, A. (1992). *Logit Modeling*. Beverly Hills, CA: Sage.

Derr, C. B. (1986). *Managing the New Careerists*. San Francisco, CA: Jossey Bass.

Devine, F. (1997). *Social class in America and Britain*. Edinburgh, Scotland: Edinburgh University Press.

Dewan, S., Ganley, D., & Kraemer, K. L. (2004). *Across the digital divide: a cross-country analysis of the determinants of IT penetration.* Retrieved October 8, 2008, from http://unpan1.un.org/intradoc/groups/public/documents/APCITY/UNPAN022642.pdf.

Digital Divide. (2010) *Wikipedia, the Free Encyclopedia*. Retrieved November 28, 2010, from http://en.wikipedia.org/wiki/Digital_divide

Ding, L., & Haynes, K. (2006). The role of telecommunications infrastructure in regional economic growth in China. *Australasian Journal of Regional Studies*, *12*(3), 281–302.

DiPietro, R. B., & Wang, Y. R. (2010). Key issues for ICT applications: impacts and implications for hospitality operations. *Worldwide Hospitality and Tourism Themes*, *2*(1), 49–67. doi:10.1108/17554211011012595

Disabled people a growing tourism market - Caribbean360. (2010). Caribbean news - Caribbean360, news around the Caribbean.Retrieved November 28, 2010, from http://www.caribbean360.com/index.php/travel/25982.html

Dishaw, M. T., & Strong, D. M. (1999). Extending the technology acceptance model with task–technology fit constructs. *Information & Management*, *36*(1), 9–21. doi:10.1016/S0378-7206(98)00101-3

Dribben, M. R. (2004). Exploring the Processual Nature of Trust and Cooperation in Organisations: A Whiteheadian Analysis. *Philosophy of Management*, 4(1), Special Issue on Organization and Decision Processes. Leonard Minkes and Tony Gear (Ed.), 25–39.

Drucker, P. (1981). *Managing in Turbulent Times*, London: Pan.

Duffing, G. David, A., & Thiery, A. (2005). *Contribution de la Gestion du Risqué a la Démarché d'Intelligence Economique*.[Contribution of the Risk Management to the economic intelligence approach] Vandœuvre-lès-Nancy, France: Publications Loria

Durvasula, S., & Lysonski, S. (2010). Money, money, money – how do attitudes toward money impact vanity and materialism? – The case of young Chinese consumers. *Journal of Consumer Marketing*, *27*(2), 169–179. doi:10.1108/07363761011027268

Dutta, S., & Segev, A. (2001). Business Transformation on the Internet. In Barnes, S., & Hunt, B. (Eds.), *Electronic Commerce and Virtual Business*. Oxford: Butterworth-Heinemann.

Dutton, W. (2005). *Transforming enterprise: the economic and social implications of information technology*. Massachusetts: MIT Press.

Easterly, W., & Rebelo, S. (1993). Fiscal Policy and Economic Growth: An Empirical Investigation. *Journal of Monetary Economics*, *32*, 417–458. doi:10.1016/0304-3932(93)90025-B

ECA (Economic Commission for Africa). (2000). *The ECA/IDRC: Pan-African Initiative on e-Commerce*. Available at http://www.uneca.org/codi/documents/pdf/doc30en.pdf

Eddie Kilkelly, (2011). Using training and development to recover failing projects. *Human Resource Management International Digest, 19* (4).3 – 6.

Edgell, D. (2006). *Managing sustainable tourism: a legacy for the future*. New York, NY: Routledge.

Egger, F. N. (2001). Affective Design of E-Commerce User Interfaces: How to Maximize Perceived Trustworthiness. In Helander, Khalid & Tham (Ed.), *Proceedings of The International Conference on Affective Human Factors Design* (pp. 317–324). London: Asean Academic Press.

Eisenberg, B. (1990). *Information Problem Solving, The Big Six Skills Approach to Library and Information Skills, Instruction*. Norwood, New York: Ablex.

Eisenberg, M. E., & Brown, M. K. (1992). Current Themes regarding and information in skill instruction research supporting and research lacking. *School Library Media. Quarter*, *2*, 103–107.

EIU (Economic Intelligence Unit). (2011). *Global intelligence and analysis.* Available at http://www.eiu.com/public/.

Elliott, R., & Boshoff, C. (2005). The Influence of Organisational Factors in Small Tourism Businesses on The Success of Internet marketing. *Management Dynamics*, *14*(3), 44–58.

Elwell, C. K., Labonte, M., & Wayne, M. M. (2007). *Is China a Threat to the U.S. Economy?* Retrieved July 13th 2011, from http://www.fas.org/sgp/crs/row/RL33604.pdf.

Emordi, C.N.O., (2007). Recent development in Nigeria's Payment System, *CBN Briefs*, Series No. 2006-2007/0323-30.

Erl, T. (2009). *Service Oriented Architecture: Concepts, Technology and Design*. Crawfordsville, IN: Pearson Education Inc.

Erumbam, A. A., & de Jong, S. B. (2006). Cross-country differences in ICT adoption: a consequence of culture? *Journal of World Business*, *41*(4), 302–314. doi:10.1016/j.jwb.2006.08.005

Eteng, U., & Ntui, A. (2009). Access to E-Learning in the Nigerian university system (NUS): a case study of University of Calabar. *The Information Technologist*, 6(2), Retrieved from: http://www.ajol.info/index.php/ict/article/view/52694 accessed 25 July 2011.

Etim, F. E., & Nssien, F. U. (2007). *Information Literacy for Library Search*. Nigeria: Abaams.

Etro, F. (2009) *The Economic Impact of Cloud Computing on Business Creation, Employment and Output in Europe*. Retrieved on 14th July, 2011, from http://www.intertic.org/Policy%20Papers/CC.pdf

Evans, J. W. (2008). Challenging Confucius: Western banks in the Chinese credit card market. *Business Horizons*, (n.d)., 519–527. doi:10.1016/j.bushor.2008.07.004

Ezeoha, A. E. (2005). *Regulating internet banking in Nigeria: problems and challenges – Part 1*. Retrieved October 13, 2010 from http://www.arraydev.com/commerce/jibc/.

Eze, U. C. (2008). E-business deployment in Nigerian financial firms: An empirical analysis of key factors. *International Journal of E-Business Research*, *4*(2), 29–47. doi:10.4018/jebr.2008040103

Fan, A. (2010). The readiness of schools of Macao to integrate IT in education and the extent of actual IT integration. *International Journal of Education and Development using Information and Communication Technology* *6*(4), 52-63.

Fan, M. (2007). Confucius making a comeback in money-driven modern China. *Washington Post*. Retrieved January 6, 2011 from http://www.washingtonpost.com/wp-dyn/content/article/2007/07/23/AR2007072301859.html.

Farhoomand, A. F., Tuunainen, V. K., & Yee, L. W. (2000). Barriers to global electronic commerce: A cross-country study of Hong Kong and Finland. *Journal of Organizational Computing and Electronic Commerce*, *10*(1), 23–48. doi:10.1207/S15327744JOCE100102

Federal Republic of Nigeria. (2004). *National Policy on Education* (4th ed.) Lagos: Federal Government Press

Feeney, L. (2010). Digital denizens. In *Instructional technology resources: In the spotlight.* Retrieved June 12 2011, from http://loki.stockton.edu/~intech/spotlight-digital-denizens.htm

Fensterstock, F. (2005). Credit scoring and the next step: business credit. New York: National *Association of Credit Management, 107*(3), 46-49.

Fishbein, M., & Ajzen, I. (1975) *Belief, attitude, intention, and behavior: an introduction to theory and research.* Reading, Mass: Addison-Wesley.

Fishbein, M., & Ajzen, I. (1975). *Belief, Attitude, Intention and Behaviour: An Introduction to Theory and Research.* Reading, MA: Addison-Wesley.

Flores, F., & Solomon, R. C. (1998). Creating Trust. *Business Ethics Quarterly*, *8*(2), 205–232. doi:10.2307/3857326

Ford, D. P., Conelly, C. E., & Meister, D. B. (2003). Information systems research and Hofstede's culture consequences: an uneasy and incomplete partnership. *IEEE Transactions on Engineering Management*, *50*(1), 8–25. doi:10.1109/TEM.2002.808265

Fornell, C., & Larcker, D. F. (1981). Evaluating structural equations models with unobservable variables and measurement error. *JMR, Journal of Marketing Research*, 1*8*(1), 39–50. doi:10.2307/3151312

Franco, B., and David T. L., (2009). The Failure of Northern Rock: A Multi-dimensional Case Study. *SUERF-The European Money and Finance Forum*, 196.

Friesl, M, Sackmann, S. A. & Kremser, S. (2011). Knowledge sharing in new organizational entities: The impact of hierarchy, organizational context, micro-politics and suspicion in *Cross Cultural Management: an international Journal, 18*(1) 71-86.

Frydman, H. E., Altman, E. I., & Kao, D.-L. (1985). Introducing recursive partitioning for financial classification: the case of financial distress. *The Journal of Finance*, *40*(1), 269–291. doi:10.2307/2328060

G8 DOT Force. (2001). *Issue objectives for the Genoa summit meeting 2001: DOT force.* Retrieved December 12, 2005 from http://www.g8.utoronto.ca/.

Gackowski, Z. J. (2004). Logical Interdependence of Data/Information Quality Dimensions: A Purpose-Focused View on IQ. *In Proceedings of the Ninth International Conference on Information Quality. ICIQ – 04*, (pp 126 – 140)Washington, DC: IEEE Press

Gackowski, Z. J. (2005). Informing Systems in Business Environments: A Purpose-Focused View on IQ. *In Informing Science Journal, 8*, 101-122.

Gackowski, Z. J. (2005). Operations Quality of Data and Information: Teleological Operations Research-Based Approach, Call for Discussion. *In Proceedings of the International Conference on Information Quality*. ICIQ – 05, Boston, MA: IEEE Press

Gackowski, Z. J. (2006). Redefining Information Quality and Its Measurement: The Operation Management Approach. *In Proceedings of the International Conference on Information Quality. ICIQ – 06*, Boston, MA: IEEE Press.

Gackowski, Z. J. (2006a). Quality of Informing: Credibility Provisional model of Functional Dependencies. *Proceedings of 2006 Informing Science and IT Education Joint Conference*. (pp 99 – 114) Salford, UK: University of Salford

Gackowski, Z. J. (2006b). Quality of Informing: Bias and Disinformation Philosophical Background and Roots. *In Issues in Informing Science and Information Technology, 3*. 731 - 744.

Gallivan, M. J. (2001). Striking a balance between trust and control in a virtual organization: A content analysis of open source software case studies. *Information Systems Journal*, *11*(4), 277–304. doi:10.1046/j.1365-2575.2001.00108.x

Gallivan, M. J., & Depledge, G. (2003). Trust, Control and the Role of Interorganizational Systems in Electronic Partnerships. *Information Systems Journal, 13*(2), 159–190. doi:10.1046/j.1365-2575.2003.00146.x

García-Valcárcel, A., & Tejedor, F. J. (2009). Training demands of the lecturers related to the use of ICT. *World Conference on Educational Sciences, Nicosia, North Cyprus, 4-7 February 2009, 1*(1), 178-183.

Gatignon, H., & Robertson, T. S. (1989). Technology diffusion: An empirical test of competitive effects. *Journal of Marketing, 53*(1), 35–49. doi:10.2307/1251523

Gbaje, E. S. (2007). Implementing a National Virtual Library for Higher Institutions in Nigeria. *Library and Information Science Research Electronic Journal, 17*(2), 1–15.

Ge, M., & Helfert, M. (2006). A Framework to Assess Decision Quality Using Information Quality Dimensions. *In Proceedings of the International Conference on Information Quality. ICIQ – 06*, Boston, MA: IEEE

Geertz, C. (1973). *The interpretation of cultures*. New York, NY: Basic Books.

Gefen, D., Karahanna, E., & Straub, D. W. (2003). Trust and TAM in Online Shopping: An Integrated Model. *Management Information Systems Quarterly, 27*(1), 51–90.

Gefen, D., & Straub, D. W. (2004). Consumer trust in B2C e-commerce and the importance of social presence: experiments in e-products and e-services. *Omega*, (n.d). 32407–32424.

Gholami, R., Ogun, A., Koh, E., & Lim, J. (2010). Factors affecting e-payment adoption in Nigeria. *Journal of Electronic Commerce in Organizations, 8*(4), 51–67. doi:10.4018/jeco.2010100104

Gibbs, J. L., & Kraemer, K. L. (2004). A cross-country investigation of the determinants of scope of e-commerce use: An institutional approach. *Electronic Markets, 14*(2), 124–137. doi:10.1080/10196780410001675077

Gibbs, J. L., Kraemer, K. L., & Dedrick, J. (2003). Environment and policy factors shaping global e-commerce diffusion: a cross-country comparison. *The Information Society, 19*(1), 5–18. doi:10.1080/01972240309472

Giddens, A. (1991). *Modernity and self-identity: self and society in the late modern age*. Cambridge, England: Polity Press.

Gillin, P. (2009). *Mobile Social Networking: The New Ecosystem*. Retrieved November 28, 2010, from http://www.virtualizationadmin.com/

Gillwald, A. (2008). *International Encyclopaedia of Communication* available at: http://www.communicationencyclopedia.com/public/tocnode?id=g9781405131995_yr2011_chunk_g97814051319958_ss78-1, retrieved on 21/3/2011.

Ginzberg, M., & Baroudi, J. J. (1992), Career orientations of IS personnel, *Proceedings of the ACM SIGCPR Conference, April 5-7*, (pp.41-55.) New York, NY: ACM Press.

GISW. (2007). Global Information Society Watch. Retrieved from: www.giswatch.org/

Gogoi, P. (2007). Retailers Take a Tip from MySpace. *Business Week Online*. Retrieved May 23, 2010, from http://www.businessweek.com/bwdaily/dnflash/content/feb2007/db20070213_626293.htm.

Goldberg, D. E. (1989). *Genetic Algorithms in Search Optimization and Machine Learning*. Reading, MA: Addison Wesley.

Goldstein, D. K., & Rockart, J. F. (1984). An Examination of Work-Related Correlates of Job Satisfaction in Programmer/Analysts. *Management Information Systems Quarterly, 8*(2), 103–115. doi:10.2307/249347

Gomez-Mejia, & Balkin (2001). *Managing Human Resources*. (3rd Ed). New Jersey: Prentice Hall Incorporation.

Grandon, E. E., & Pearson, J. (2004). Electronic commerce adoption: An empirical study of small and medium US Businesses. *Information & Management, 42*(1), 197–216. doi:10.1016/j.im.2003.12.010

Granovetter, M. (2005). The Impact of Social Structure on Economic Outcomes. *The Journal of Economic Perspectives, 19*(1), 33–50. doi:10.1257/0895330053147958

Grau. J. (2008). *Canada B2C e-Commerce: A work in progress*. Available at http://www.emarketer.com/Reports/All/Emarketer_2000547.aspx.

Gregorio, D. D., Kassicieh, S. K., & Neto, R. D. (2005). Drivers of e-business activity in developed and emerging markets. *IEEE Transactions on Engineering Management*, *52*(2), 155–166. doi:10.1109/TEM.2005.844464

Grieb, T., Hegji, C., & Jones, S. T. (2001). Macroeconomic factors, consumer behavior, and bankcard default rates. *Journal of Economics and Finance*, *25*(3), 316–327. doi:10.1007/BF02745892

Grizeli, F. (2003). Collaborative Knowledge Management in Virtual Service Companies-Approach for Tourism Destinations. *Journal of Tourism*, *51*(4), 371–385.

Guangli, N., Yibing, C., Lingling, Z., & Yuhong, G. (2010). Credit card customer analysis based on panel data cluter-ing. *International Conference on Computational Science, ICCS 2010*, (pp. 2483-2491)ICCS

Gupta, B., Iyer, L. S., & Aronson, E. J. (2000). Knowledge management: practices and challenges. *Industrial Management & Data Systems*, *100*(1), 17–21. doi:10.1108/02635570010273018

Gust, C., & Marquez, J. (2004). International comparisons of productivity growth: the role of information technologies and regulatory practices. *Labour Economics*, *11*(1), 33–58. doi:10.1016/S0927-5371(03)00055-1

Hackman, J. R., & Oldham, G. R. (1976). Motivation through the design of work: Test of a theory. *Organizational Behavior and Human Performance*, *16*(2), 250–279. doi:10.1016/0030-5073(76)90016-7

Hadidi, R. (2003). The status of e-finance in developing countries. *Electronic Journal of Information Systems in Developing Countries*, *11*(5), 1–5.

Hair, J. F. Jr, Anderson, R. E., Thatham, R. L., & Black, W. C. (1998). *Multivariate data analysis*. Upper Saddle River, NJ: Prentice-Hall International, Inc.

Hallin, C. A., & Marnburga, E. (2008). Knowledge management in the hospitality industry: a review of empirical research. *Tourism Management*, *29*, 366–381. doi:10.1016/j.tourman.2007.02.019

Hanudin, A. (2007). Internet banking adoption among young Intellectuals, *JIBC, 12*(3). Retrieved September 13, 2011, from http://www.arraydev.com/commerce/jibc/

Hanushek, E. A., & Wößmann, L. (2007a). *The role of School Improvement in Economic Development*, NBER Working paper No. 12832.

Hanushek, E. A., & Wößmann, L. (2007b). *Education Quality and economic growth.* Washington, DC: The World Bank. doi:10.1596/1813-9450-4122

Harrington, G. D., & Lipschutz, R. P. (2011).*Creating and Consuming web services* retrieved on 14th July, 2011, from http://www.blueopal.com/pdf/WebServices_tuto-rial_parts_1-2-3.pdf.

Harrison, L. E., & Huntington, S. P. (2000). *Culture matters: how values shape human progress*. USA: Basic books.

Hartarska, V., & Gonzales-Vega, C. (2006). Evidence on the effect of credit counselling on mortgage loan default by low-income households. *Journal of Housing Economics*, *15*, 63–79. doi:10.1016/j.jhe.2006.02.002

Hart, P. J., & Saunders, C. S. (1998). Emerging electronic partnerships: Antecedents and dimensions of EDI use from the supplier's perspective. *Journal of Management Information Systems*, *14*(4), 87–111.

Heijden, H. V., Verhagen, T., & Creemer, M. (2003). Understanding online purchase intentions: contributions from technology and trust perspectives. *European Journal of Information Systems*, *12*, 41–48. doi:10.1057/palgrave.ejis.3000445

Herzberg, F. (1968). One more time: how do you motivate employees? *Harvard Business Review*, *46*(1), 53–62.

Hierschman, A. O. (1958). *The Strategy of Economic Development*. New Haven, CT: Yale University Press.

Hilari, M. O. (2009).Quality of Service (QoS) in SOA Systems.*A Systematic Review.Masters' Degree Thesis* retrieved on 14th July, 2011, from http://upcommons.upc.edu/pfc/bitstream/2099.1/7714/1/Master%20thesis%20-%20Marc%20Oriol.pdf

Hoffman, D. L., Novak, T. P., & Peralta, M. (1999). Building Consumer Trust Online. *Communications of the ACM*, *42*(4), 80–85. doi:10.1145/299157.299175

Hofstede, G. (1980). *Culture's Consequences*. Beverly Hills, CA: Sage Publications.

Hofstede, G. (1983). Dimensions of National Cultures in Fifty Countries and Three Regions. In Deregowski, J. B., Dziurawiec, S., & Annis, R. C. (Eds.), *Expiscations in Cross-Cultural Psychology* (pp. 335–355). Lisse: Swets and Zeitlinger.

Hofstede, G. (1984). *Culture's consequences: International differences in work-related values*. Beverly Hills, CA: Sage Publications.

Hofstede, G. (2001). *Culture's consequences: comparing values, behaviors, institutions, and organizations across nations* (2nd ed.). Thousand Oaks, CA: Sage Publications.

Hofstede, G. (2005). Cultural constrains in management theories. In Redding, G., & Stening, B. (Eds.), *Cross-cultural management* (*Vol. II*, pp. 61–74). Cheltenham: Edward Elgar Publishing Limited.

Hogan, J. J. (1992). Turnover and what to do about it. *The Cornell HRA Quarterly.*, *33*(1), 40–45.

Honeycutt, J. (2000). *Knowledge Management strategies*. Canada: Microsoft press.

Horrigan, J. (2009). Mobile internet use increases sharply in 2009 as more than half of all Americans have gotten online by some wireless means. *Pew Internet and American Life Project*. Retrieved November 28, 2010, from http://www.pewinternet.org/Press-Releases/2009/Mobile-internet-use.aspx

Ho, S.-C., Kaufmann, R. J., & Liang, T.-P. (2007). A growth theory perspective on B2C E-commerce growth in Europe: An exploratory study. *Electronic Commerce Research and Applications*, *6*(3), 237–259. doi:10.1016/j.elerap.2006.06.003

Hosein, S (2006). Teaching Information Literacy at the University of the West Indies *Trindad, Information Development 22* (2).

Hosmeh, L. T. (1995). Trust: The Connecting Link between Organizational Theory and Philosophical Ethics. *Academy of Management Review*, *20*(2), 379–403.

Hox, J. J., & de Leeuw, E. D. (1994). A comparison of nonresponse in mail, telephone, and face-to-face surveys. Applying multilevel modeling to meta-analysis. *Quality & Quantity*, *28*, 329–344. doi:10.1007/BF01097014

Hsu, M. K., Chen, H. G., Jiang, J., & Klein, G. (2003). Career Satisfaction for Managerial and Technical Anchored IS Personnel in Later Career Stages. *ACM SIGMIS Database*, *34*(4), 64–72. doi:10.1145/957758.957766

Hsu, W. H. (2003). Control of Inductive Bias in Supervised Learning using EvolutionaryComputation: A Wrapper-Based Approach. In Wang, J. (Ed.), *Data Mining: Opportunities and Challenges*. Hershey, PA: Idea Group Publishing. doi:10.4018/978-1-59140-051-6.ch002

Huang, N. (2005). China on credit: The iron rice bowl goes plastic. *Time Asia*, Available: http://www.time.com/time/asia/covers/501050516/china_debt.html

Hudson, S., & Gilbert, D. (2006). The Internet and Small Hospitality Businesses: B&B Marketing in Canada. *Journal of Hospitality & Leisure Marketing*, *14*(1), 99–116. doi:10.1300/J150v14n01_06

Huntington, S. (1996). *The clash of civilizations: remaking of world order*. New York, NY: Simon and Schuster.

Iacobucci, D., & Churchill, G. A. (2009). *Marketing research: Methodological foundations (with Qualtrics Card)* (10th ed.). Cincinnati, OH: South-Western College Publishing.

Iacovou, C. L., Benbasat, I., & Dexter, A. S. (1995). Electronic data interchange and small organizations: adoption and impact of technolog. *Management Information Systems Quarterly*, *19*(4), 465–485. doi:10.2307/249629

Ibrahim, A. (2004). *NUNet topology and connectivity.* Abuja,Nigeria: National Universities Commission Internet World Stats. (2011). Retrieved from http://www.internetworldstats.com/af/ng.htm

Ifinedo (2005b). E-government initiative in a developing country: strategies and implementation in Nigeria, *In Proceedings of 6th. World Congress on Electronic Business*,(pp. 1-11) Hamilton, Ontario, Canada.

Ifinedo, (2006). Factors affecting e-business Adoption by SMEs in Sub-Saharan Africa: An exploratory study from Nigeria. In N. Al-Qirim (Ed.), *Global Electronic Business Research: Opportunities and Directions*, (pp. 319 – 346) Hershey, PA: Idea Group Publishing,

Ifinedo, P. (2003). *Employee Motivation and Job Satisfaction in Finnish Organizations: A Study of Employees in the Oulu Region, Finland.* Master of Business Administration Thesis, University of London.

Ifinedo, P. (2004). Motivation and Job Satisfaction among Information Systems Developers-Perspectives from Finland, Nigeria and Estonia: A Preliminary Study. In Vasilecas, O., Caplinskas, A., Wojtkowski, W., Wojtkowski, W. G., Zupancic, J. and Wryczw, S. (Eds.), *Proceedings of the 13th. International Conference on Information Systems Development: Advances in Theory, Practice Methods, and Education* (pp. 161 -172)).

Ifinedo, P. (2005).Measuring the e-readiness of five Sub-Saharan African (SSA) countries: An assessment of SSA'S preparedness for the global networked economy, In Palvia P. and Pinjani, P. (Eds.), *Proceedings of the 6th. Global Information Technology Management Conference (GITM '05), Anchorage, Alaska*, (pp. 5 – 8)

Ifinedo, P. (2005a). Measuring Africa's e-readiness in the global networked economy: a nine-country data analysis. *The International Journal of Education and Development using Information and Communication Technology, 1*(1), 53-71.

Ifinedo, P. (2008). Internet commerce and SMEs in Sub-Saharan Africa: Perspectives from Nigeria, *Conference on Information Technology and Economic Development (CITED2008)*, (pp. 1- 8)

Ifinedo, P., & Usoro, A. (2009). Study of the relationships between economic and cultural factors and network readiness: a focus on African's regions, in *International Journal of Global Business, 2* (1)101-123, available at: http://gsmi-ijgb.com/Documents/V2%20N1%20 IJGB%20-P04%20- Ifenedo%20%20Economic%20 and%20Cultural%20-June%202009.pdf.

Ifinedo, P. (2006). Acceptance and Continuance Intention of Web-Based Learning Technologies (WLT) among University Students in a Baltic Country. *The Journal of Information Systems in Developing Countries, 23*(6), 1–20.

Ifinedo, P. (2006). Towards e-government in a Sub-Saharan African country: impediments and initiatives in Nigeria. *Journal of E-Government, 3*(1), 4–28. doi:10.1300/J399v03n01_02

Ifinedo, P. (2007). A Study of the relationships between economic climates, national culture and E-government e-readiness: A global perspective. In Kurihara, Y., Takaya, S., Harui, H., & Kamae, H. (Eds.), *Information Technology and Economic Development* (pp. 234–247). Hershey, PA: IGI Global. doi:10.4018/978-1-59904-579-5.ch017

Ifinedo, P. (2007). Investigating the antecedents of continuance intention of course management systems use among Estonian undergraduates. *International Journal of Information and Communication Technology Education, 3*(4), 76–92. doi:10.4018/jicte.2007100107

Ifinedo, P. (2009). The Internet and SMEs in Sub-Saharan Africa. In Mehdi, K. (Ed.), *Encyclopedia of Information Science and Technology* (2nd ed., pp. 2183–2188). Hershey, PA: Idea Group Publishing. doi:10.4018/978-1-60566-026-4.ch344

Ifinedo, P. (2011). (Forthcoming). Internet/e-business technologies acceptance in Canada's SMEs: An exploratory investigation. *Internet Research.* doi:10.1108/10662241111139309

Igbaria, M. & Baroudi J.J. (1993). A short-form measure of career orientations: A psychometric evaluation, *Journal of Management Information Systems*, Fall, *10*(2), 132-145.

Igbaria, M., & Greenhaus, J. H. (1991). Career orientations of MIS employees: An empirical analysis. *Management Information Systems Quarterly, 15*(2), 151–170. doi:10.2307/249376

Igbaria, M., & Greenhaus, J. H. (1992). Determinants of MIS Employees' Turnover Intentions: A Structural Equation Model. *Communications of the ACM, 35*(2), 35–49. doi:10.1145/129630.129631

Igbaria, M., Greenhaus, J. H., & Parasuraman, S. (1991). Career orientations of MIS employees: an empirical analysis. *Management Information Systems Quarterly, 15*(2), 151–169. doi:10.2307/249376

Igbaria, M., & Guimaraes, T. (1999). Exploring differences in employee turnover intentions and its determinants among telecommuters and non-telecommuters. *Journal of Management Information Systems, 16*(1), 147–164.

Igbaria, M., & McCloskey, D. W. (1996). Career orientations of MIS employees in Taiwan. *Computer Personnel, 17*(2), 3–24. doi:10.1145/227728.227729

Igbaria, M., Meredith, G., & Smith, D. (1995). Career orientations of information-systems employees in South-Africa. *International Journal of Strategic Systems*, *4*(4), 319–340. doi:10.1016/0963-8687(95)80002-8

Ilie, V., Van Slyke, C., Green, G., & Lou, H. (2005). Gender differences in perceptions and use of communication technologies: a diffusion of innovation approach. *Information Resources Management Journal*, *18*(3), 16–31. doi:10.4018/irmj.2005070102

ILO. (2000). *The International Labour Organization (ILO) – Activities*. Retrieved August 7, 2010, from http://www.nationsencyclopedia.com/United-Nations-Related-Agencies/The-International-Labour-Organization-ILO-ACTIVITIES.html.

InfoDev (2007). *The information for development program*. Retrieved December 12, 2010, www.infodev.org/.

Information Literacy for Academics – IL Projects/Learning Services. (2009). *The University of Auckland Library.* http://www.library.auckland.ac.nz/instruct/ll/integrating.html.

Information Society in Greece. (2010) Information Society: the Official Greek Portal for I.S... Retrieved November 28, 2010, from http://www.infosoc.gr/infosoc/en-UK/default.htm

Internet Usage in Asia. (2010). *Miniwatts Marketing Group*. Retrieved November 28, 2010, from http://www.internetworldstats.com/stats3.htm

Internet World Stats. (2008). *Botswana Internet Usage and Marketing Report*. Retrieved October 23, 2008 from http://www.internetworldstats.com/af/bw.htm

Internetworldstats (2011). *Country Reports*. Available at http://www.internetworldstats.com/

Isaacs, S. (2007). ICT in Education in Botswana, *Survey of ICT and Education in Africa*. Retrieved October 21, 2008 from http://www.infodev.org/en/Publication.387.html

Iskander, M., Kapila, V., & Karim, M. (2010). *Technological Developments in Education and Automation*. The Netherlands: Springer. doi:10.1007/978-90-481-3656-8

ISO. (1991). *ISO 9126/ISO*, IEC (Hrsg.): International Standard ISO/IEC 9126, Information

ISO. (2002). *UNI EN ISO 8402* Quality Vocabulary. *Part of the ISO*, *9000*, 2002.

ITIM. (2011). *Geert Hofstede cultural dimensions*. Retrieved September, 6, 2006 from http://www.geert-hofstede.com/hofstede_dimensions.php.

ITU International Telecommunication Union. (2011*). Weekly Update*. Available at http://www.itu.int/en/pages/default.aspx.

ITU. (2010). *Measuring the Information Society*. Geneva, Switzerland: International Telecommunication Union
NCC (2011). Quarterly summary of Telecom Subscribers in Nigeria. Retrieved from http://www.ncc.gov.ng/industrystatistics/subscriberdata_files/Subscriber_Quarterly_Summary_201006-201103.pdf

Ituma, A. (2006). The internal career: an explorative study of the career anchors of information technology workers in Nigeria, *SIGMIS CPR '06*: *Proceedings of the 2006 ACM SIGMIS CPR conference on computer personnel research: Forty four years of computer personnel research: achievements, challenges & the future.* New York, NY: ACM Press

Ituma, A., & Simpson, R. (2007). Moving Beyond Schein's Typology: Individual Career Anchors in the Context of Nigeria. *Personnel Review*, *36*(6), 978–005. doi:10.1108/00483480710822463

Jackson, S. E., & Schuler, R. S. (1985). A meta-analysis and conceptual critique of research on role ambiguity and role conflict in work settings. *Organizational Behavior and Human Decision Processes*, *36*, 16–78. doi:10.1016/0749-5978(85)90020-2

Jahangir, N., & Begum, N. (2007). The role of perceived usefulness, perceived ease of use, security and privacy, and customer attitude to engender customer adaptation in the context of e-banking. *African Journal of Business Management*, *2*(1), 32–40.

Janczewski, L. J. (1992). Relationships between nformation Technology and Competitive advantage in New Zealand Businesses, *In Proceedings of 1992 Information Resources Management Association Charleston*, (pp. 347-364.) Hershey, PA: Idea Group Publishing

Jegede, P. O. (2009). Age and ICT-Related Behaviours of Higher Education Teachers in Nigeria. *Issues in Informing Science and Information Technology*, *6*, 771–777.

Jeyaraj, A., Rottman, J. W., & Lacity, M. C. (2006). A review of the predictors, linkages, and biases in IT innovation adoption research. *Journal of Information Technology*, *21*(1), 1–23. doi:10.1057/palgrave.jit.2000056

Jiang, J.J. (2000). Supervisor Support and Career Anchor Impact on the Career Satisfaction of the Entry-Level Information Systems Professional, *Journal of Management Information Systems*, Winter, *16*(3), 219-241.

Jiang, J. J., & Klein, G. (2000). Software development risks to project effectiveness. *Journal of Systems and Software*, *52*, 3–10. doi:10.1016/S0164-1212(99)00128-4

Jiang, J. J., & Klein, G. (2002). A discrepancy model of information system personnel turnover. *Journal of Management Information Systems*, *19*(2), 249–272.

Joe, B. B. (2007). Lehman Brothers 1Q Profit Up 5.6 Pct. *The Associated Press*.89.

Johnson, S. M. (1990). *Teachers at work*. New York: Basic Books.

Jones, G. R., & George, J. M. (2003). *Contemporary Management* (3rd ed.). New York: McGraw-Hill, Inc.

Jones, S., Wilikens, M., Morris, P., & Masera, M. (2000). Trust Requirements in E-Business - A conceptual framework for understanding the needs and concerns of different stakeholders. *Communications of the ACM*, *43*(12), 80–87.

Jones, T. M., & Bowie, N. E. (1998). Moral Hazards on the Road to the "Virtual" Corporation. *Business Ethics Quarterly*, *8*(2), 273–292. doi:10.2307/3857329

Jorgenson, D. W. (2001). Information technology and economy. *The American Economic Review*, *9*(1), 1–32. doi:10.1257/aer.91.1.1

Jøsang, A. (1996). The right type of trust for distributed systems. In C. Meadows (Ed.), *Proceedings of the 1996 New Security Paradigms Workshop, ACM*. New York, NY: ACM Press

Jøsang, A., Keser, C., & Dimitrakos, T. (2005). Can We Manage Trust? *Proceedings of the 3rd International Conference on Trust Management, (iTrust)*, Paris.

Joseph, D., Ng, K., & Koh, C., &, S. (2007). Turnover of Information technology Professionals: A narrative review, meta-analytic structural equation modelling, and Model development. *Management Information Systems Quarterly*, *31*(3), 547–577.

Jung, W. (2004). A Review of Research: An Investigation of the Impact of Data Quality on Decision Performance.: *International Symposium on Information & Communication Technologies (ISITC '04)*, (pp166 – 171) Washington, DC: IEEE Press

Kaba, B., N'Da, K., & Mbarika, V. (2008). Understanding the Factors Influencing the Attitude Toward and Use of Mobile Technology in Developing Countries: A Model of Cellular Phone Use in Guinea. *Proceedings of the 41st Hawaii International Conference on System Sciences*, (pp. 1-12). Washington, DC: IEEE Press

Kalargyrou, V., & Woods, R. H. (2011). Wanted: training competencies for the twenty-first century. *International Journal of Contemporary Hospitality Management*, *23*(3), 361–376. doi:10.1108/09596111111122532

Kamleitner, B. & Kirchler, E., (2007). Crédit à la consommation: modèle de processus et revue de literature. [Consumer credit use: a process model and literature review]. *Revue européenne de psychologie appliquée*, 57, 267-283.

Kanungo, R. N., & Jaeger, A. M. (1990). Introduction: the need for indigenous management in developing countries. In Jaeger, A. M., & Kanungo, R. N. (Eds.), *Management in Developing Countries*. London: Routledge.

Karjaluoto, H., Mattila, M., & Pento, T. (2002). Factors underlying attitude formation towards online banking in Finland. *International Journal of Bank Marketing*, *20*(6), 261–272. doi:10.1108/02652320210446724

Kasavana, M., Nusair, K., & Teodosic, K. (2010). Online social networking: Redefining the human web. *Journal of Hospitality and Tourism Technology*, *1*(1), 68–82. doi:10.1108/17579881011023025

Kautto-Koivula, K. (1993). *Degree-Oriented Professional Adult Education in the Work Environment. A Case Study of the Mian Determinants in the management of a Long-term Technology Education Process*. Published PhD dissertation, University of Tampere, Finland.

Kautto-Koivula, K. (1996). Degree-Oriented Adult Education in the Work Environment. In Ruohotie, P., & Grimmett, P. P. (Eds.), *Professional Growth and Development: Direction, Delivery and Dilemmas* (pp. 149–188). Canada and Finland: Career Education Books.

Kemeny, J. (2011). Are international technology gaps growing or shrinking in the age of globalization? *Journal of Economic Geography*, *11*(1), 1–35. doi:10.1093/jeg/lbp062

Kendall, J. D., Tung, L. L., Chua, K. H., Hong, C., Ng, D., & Tan, S. M. (2001). Receptivity of Singapore's SMEs to electronic commerce adoption. *The Journal of Strategic Information Systems*, *10*(3), 223–242. doi:10.1016/S0963-8687(01)00048-8

Kennedy, G., Dalgarno, B., Gray, K., Judd, T., Waycott, J., Bennett, S., et al. (2007). The net generation are not big users of Web 2.0 technologies: Preliminary findings. In *ICT: Providing choices for learners and learning. Proceedings ascilite Singapore 2007*. Retrieved May 23 2011, from http://www.ascilite.org.au/conferences/singapore07/procs/kennedy.pdf

Kennedy, P. (1998). *A guide to econometrics*. Cambridge, MA: The MIT Press.

Khosrow-Pour, M. (2003). *Information technology and organizations: trends, issues, challenges & solutions*, Volume 1. London: Idea Group Inc (IGI).

Kiiski, S., & Pohjola, M. (2002). Cross country diffusion of the internet. *Information Economics and Policy*, *14*(2), 297–310. doi:10.1016/S0167-6245(01)00071-3

Kim, W. (2001). The human society and the Internet: Internet-related socio-economic issues. *Proceedings of the First International Conference Human. Society @ Internet 2001*, Seoul,South Korea

Kim, J., & Kizildag, M. (2011). M-learning: next generation hotel training system. *Journal of Hospitality and Tourism Technology*, *2*(1), 6–33. doi:10.1108/17579881111112395

Kiplinger's Staff. (2007). Walk-in Critics. *Kiplinger's Personal Finance*, *61*(1), 24.

Kirschner, P. A., & Thijssen, J. (2005). Competency Development and Employability. *LL in E Longlife Learning in Europe, 10* (2). 70-75.

Kirschner, P. A., & Davis, N. E. (2003). Pedagogic benchmarks for information and communication technology in teacher education. *Technology, Pedagogy and Education*, *12*(1), 127–149.

Klopping, I. M., & McKinney, E. I. (2004). Extending the technology acceptance model and the task-technology fit model to consumer e-commerce. *Information Technology, Learning and Performance Journal*, *22*(1), 35–48.

Klusch, M., & Gerber, A. (2006).Fast composition planning of owl-s services and application. *In ECOWS '06: Proceedings of the European Conference on Web Services* Washington, DC, USA: IEEE Computer Society.

Knoke, D., & Burke, P. J. (1980). *Log-linear Models*. Beverly Hills, CA: Sage.

Koehn, D. (2003). The Nature of and Conditions for Online Trust. *Journal of Business Ethics*, *43*(1-2), 3–19. doi:10.1023/A:1022950813386

Koivu, T. (2009). Has the Chinese economy become more sensitive to interest rates? Studying credit demand in China. *China Economic Review*, *20*, 455–470. doi:10.1016/j.chieco.2008.03.001

Konidari, V. (2011). Education in a complex world: a political question to be answered. *Horizon*, *19*(2), 75–84. doi:10.1108/10748121111138272

Kovačić, Z. J. (2005). The impact of national culture on worldwide e-government readiness. *Informing Science: International Journal of an Emerging Discipline*, *8*, 143–158.

Kpolovie, P. J. (2010). *Advanced Research Methods. Owerri*. Springfield Publishers.

Kpolovie, P. J. (2011). *Statistical Techniques for Advanced Research. Owerri*. Springfield Publishers.

Krishnan, S. K., & Singh, M. (2010). Outcomes of intention to quit of Indian IT professionals. *Human Resource Management*, *49*(3), 419–435. doi:10.1002/hrm.20357

Kula, V., & Tatoglu, E. (2003). An exploratory study of Internet adoption by SMEs in an emerging market economy. *European Business Review*, *15*(5), 324–333. doi:10.1108/09555340310493045

Lacity, R. P., & Iyer, V. (2008), Understanding turnover among Indian IS Professionals, in Lacity & Rottman (eds.)*Offshore Outsourcing of IT Work* (pp. 209-244), Palgrave, London.

Lai, S. V., & Li, H. (n.d). (200). Technology acceptance model for internet banking: an invariance analysis. *Information & Management*, *42*(34), 373–386.

Lallmahamood, M. (2007). An examination of individual's perceived security and privacy of the internet in Malaysia and the influence of this on their intention to use e-commerce: using an extension of the Technology Acceptance Model. *Journal of Internet Banking and Commerce*, *12*(3), 1–26.

Lane, C., & Bachmann, R. (1996). The Social Construction of Trust: Supplier Relations in Britain and Germany. *Organization Studies*, *17*(3), 365–395. doi:10.1177/017084069601700302

Langan, M. (1998). *Welfare: needs, rights, and risks*. New York, NY: Routledge.

Langer, A. (2002). *Applied ecommerce: analysis and engineering for ecommerce systems*. West Sussex, UK: Wiley.

Langmia, K. (2005). The role of ICT in the economic development of Africa: the case of South Africa. *International Journal of Education and Development using Information and Communication Technology*, *2*(4), 144-156.

Larson, M. R., & Bruning, R. (1996). Participant perceptions of a collaborative satellite-based mathematics course. *American Journal of Distance Education*, *10*(1), 6–22. doi:10.1080/08923649609526906

Law, R., & Bai, B. (2008). How do the preferences of online buyers and browser different on the design and content of travel websites. *International Journal of Contemporary Hospitality Management*, *20*(4), 388–400. doi:10.1108/09596110810873507

Leadpile, (2010). *United States E-commerce Sales to Top 120 Billion, says Leadpile*. Available at http://www.leadpile.com/press/2006-10-24_press1.html.

Lee, D., Park, J., & Ahn, J. (2001). On the explanation of factors affecting e-commerce adoption, *Proceedings of the 22nd Int'l Conf. in Information Systems*, (pp. 109-120.)

Lee, K.-S., & Anas, A. (1992). *The Impact of Infrastructure Deficiencies on Nigerian Manufacturing, Infrastructure Department working Paper, No INU 98*. Washington, DC: World Bank.

Lee, P. C. B. (2002). Career Goals and Career Management Strategy among Information Technology Professionals. *Career Development International*, *7*(1), 6–13. doi:10.1108/13620430210414829

Legris, P., Ingham, J., & Collerette, P. (2003). Why do people use information technology?: A critical review of the technology acceptance model. *Information & Management*, *40*(3), 191–204. doi:10.1016/S0378-7206(01)00143-4

Leidner, D. E., & Kayworth, T. (2006). A review of culture in information systems research: toward a theory of information technology culture conflict. *Management Information Systems Quarterly*, *30*(2), 357–399.

Leino, J. (1996). Developing and Evaluation of Professional Competence. In Ruohotie, P., & Grimmett, P. P. (Eds.), *Professional Growth and Development: Direction, Delivery and Dilemmas* (pp. 71–90). Canada and Finland: Career Education Books.

Levin, H. M., & Lockheed, M. E. (1993). *Effective schools in developing countries*. London, UK: Routledge.

Lewicki, R. J., & Stevenson, M. A. (1997). Trust Development in Negotiation: Proposed Actions and Research Agenda. *Business and Professional Ethics Journal*, 16(1–3), Special Issue on Trust and Business: Barriers and Bridges. D. Koehn (Ed.), 99–132.

Lewis, P. S., Goodman, S. H., & Fandt, P. M. (1995). *Management: Challenges in the 21st Century*. New York: West Publishing Company.

Liao, T. F. (1994). *Interpreting Probability Model: Logit, Probit, and Other Generalized Linear Models*. Beverly Hills, CA: Sage.

Li, C., & Li, L. (2007). Utility-based QoSoptimization strategy for multi-criteria scheduling on the grid. *Journal of Parallel and Distributed Computing*, *67*(2), 142–153. doi:10.1016/j.jpdc.2006.09.003

Li, N., & Kirkup, G. (2007). Gender and cultural differences in Internet use: a study of China and the UK. *Computers & Education, 48*(2), 301–317. doi:10.1016/j.compedu.2005.01.007

Lipset, S. M. (1959). Some Social Requisites of Democracy: Economic Development and Political Legitimacy. *The American Political Science Review, 53*(1), 69–105. doi:10.2307/1951731

Liu, T. (2006). The entry of foreign banks into the Chinese banking sector. *Bank for International Settlements*. Available: http://www.bis.org/publ/bppdf/bispap04c.pdf

Liu, M. T. (2009). Do credit card redemption reward programs work in China? An empirical study. *Journal of Consumer Marketing, 26*(6), 403–414. doi:10.1108/07363760910988229

Liu, X. N., & Baras, S. J. (2004). Modeling multidimensional QoS: some fundamental constraints: *Research Articles. International Journal of Communication Systems, 17*, 193–215. doi:10.1002/dac.652

Livi, E. (2008). Information Technology and New Business Models in the Tourism Industry. *8th Global Conference on Business and Economics*. Florence: Italy.

Li, W., Jiang, X., Li, K., Moser, L., Guo, Z., & Du, L. (2005). A robust hybrid between genetic algorithm and support vector machine for extracting an optimal feature gene subset. *Genomics, 85*(1), 16–23. doi:10.1016/j.ygeno.2004.09.007

Lochhead, C., & Stephens, A. (2004). Employee retention, labour turnover and knowledge transfer: A case study from the Canadian plastic sector, *Canadian Labour and Business Centre*. Downloaded on August 30, 2010 from http://www.cpsc-ccsp.ca/PDFS/CPSC%20Final%20Report%20June28%20-%207%20case%20studies2%20oct%207%2004.pdf

Looi, H. C. (2005). E-commerce adoption in Brunei Darussalam: A quantitative analysis of factors influencing its adoption. *Communications of the Association for Information Systems, 15*(3), 61–81.

Louise, S. (2010). Competition and the banking crisis. *Business and Transport Section, SN/BT/5272*, pp. 8.

Love, P. E. D., & Irani, Z. (2004). An exploratory study of information technology evaluation and benefits management practices of SMEs in the construction industry. *Information & Management, 42*, 227–242. doi:10.1016/j.im.2003.12.011

Loving, M., & Ochoa, M. (2011). Facebook as a classroom management solution. *New Library World, 112*(3/4), 121–130. doi:10.1108/03074801111117023

Luiz, J. (2010). Infrastructure investment and its performance in Africa over the course of the twentieth century. *International Journal of Social Economics, 37*(7), 512–536. doi:10.1108/03068291011055450

Lwehabura, M. J. (1999). User Education and Information Skills: A need for a systematic programme in African University Libraries. *African Journal of Library Archives and Information Science, 9*(2), 129–141.

Macharia, J. (2009). Factors affecting the adoption of e-commerce in SMEs in Kenya, International. *Journal of Technology Intelligence and Planning, 5*(4), 386–401. doi:10.1504/IJTIP.2009.029377

Mac-Ikemenjima, D. (2005). e-Education in Nigeria: Challenges and Prospects". *Paper presentation at the 8th UN ICT Task Force Meeting* Dublin, Ireland.

Mani, A., & Nagarajan, A. (2002). *Understanding Quality of Services for Web Services*. Retrieved Nov. 1,2010, from: www.ibm.com/developerworks/library/wsquality.html.

Mannathoko, C. (1999). What does it mean to be a middle class woman in Botswana? In Zmroczek, C., & Mahony, P. (Eds.), *Women and Social Class: International Feminist Perspectives*. London: UCL Press Ltd.

Mapesa, M. (2009). Uganda takes tourism trade into cyberspace. *The Observer*. Retrieved November 28, 2010, from http://www.observer.ug/index.php?option=com_content&view=article&id=3219:uganda-takes-tourism-trade-into-cyberspace

Margaryan, A., & Littlejohn, A. (2008). *Are digital natives a myth or reality?: Students' use of technologies for learning.* Retrieved March, 29, 2011, from http://www.academy.gcal.ac.uk/anoush/documents/DigitalNativesMythOrReality-MargaryanAndLittlejohn-draft-111208.pdf

Margaryan, A., Littlejohn, A., & Vojt, G. (2011). Are digital natives a myth or reality? University students' use of digital technologies. *Computers & Education*, *56*(2), 429–440. doi:10.1016/j.compedu.2010.09.004

Martin, D. C., & Bartol, K. M. (2003). Factors influencing expatriate performance appraisal system success: an organizational perspective. *Journal of International Management*, *9*(2), 115–132. doi:10.1016/S1075-4253(03)00030-9

Martin, T. N. (1979). A contextual model of employee turnover intentions. *Academy of Management Journal*, *22*(2), 313–324. doi:10.2307/255592

Mayer, S. E., (2003). *What is a disadvantaged group?* Minneapolis, MN: Effective Communities Project

Mayer, R. C., Davis, J. H., & Schoorman, F. D. (1995). An Integrative Model of Organizational Trust. *Academy of Management Review*, *20*(3), 709–734.

Mbarika, V. W., Okoli, C., Byrd, T. A., & Datta, P. (2005). The neglected continent of IS research: A research agenda for Sub-Saharan Africa. *Journal of the Association for Information Systems*, *6*(5), 130–170.

McClelland, D. C. (1961). *The Achieving Society*. Princeton, NJ: Van Nostrand.

McCullagh, P. (1980). Regression Model for Ordinal Data. *Journal of the Royal Statistical Society. Series B. Methodological*, *42*(2), 109–142.

McKnight, D. H., & Chervany, N. L. (2000). What is Trust? A Conceptual Analysis and an Interdisciplinary Model. *Proceedings of the Americas Conference on Information Systems*, (pp. 827–833.)

McKnight, D. H., Choudhury, V., & Kacmar, C. (2002). Developing and Validating Trust Measures for e- Commerce: An Integrative Typology. *Information Systems Research*, *13*(3), 334–359. doi:10.1287/isre.13.3.334.81

McKnight, D., & Chervany, N. (1996). *The Meanings of Trust, Technical Report MISRC 96-04. Management Information Systems Research Center*. University of Minnesota.

Medlik, S. (1990). *The Business of Hotels*. Oxford: Heinemann.

Mehrtens, J., Cragg, P. B., & Mills, A. M. (2001). A Model of internet adoption by SMEs. *Information & Management*, *39*(3), 165–176. doi:10.1016/S0378-7206(01)00086-6

Mendonca, M., & Kanungo, R. N. (1996). Impact of culture on performance management in developing countries. *International Journal of Manpower*, *17*(4-5), 65–75. doi:10.1108/01437729610127640

Meso, P., Checchi, P. M., Sevcik, G. R., Loch, K. D., & Straub, D. W. (2006). Knowledge spheres and the diffusion of national IT policies. *The Electronic Journal of Information Systems in Developing Countries*, *23*, 1–16.

Mgaya, K. V., Shemi, A. P., & Kitindi, E. (2005). Gender inequality in the information systems workforce: challenges and implications for management in Botswana, *World Review of Science. Technology and Sustainable Development*, *2*(2), 126–138.

Michaels, C. E., & Spector, P. E. (1982). Causes of employee turnover: A test of the Mobley, Griffeth, Hand, and Meglino Model. *The Journal of Applied Psychology*, *67*(1), 53–59. doi:10.1037/0021-9010.67.1.53

Minghetti, V., & Buhalis, D. (2009). Digital Divide and Tourism: Bridging the gap between markets and destinations. *Journal of Travel Research*, ▪▪▪, 1–15.

Minton, G. C., & Scheneider, F. W. (1980). *Differential Psychology*. Prospect Heights, IL: Waveland Press.

Mirchandani, A. A., & Motwani, J. (2001). Understanding small business electronic adoption: An empirical analysis. *Journal of Computer Information Systems*, *41*(3), 70–73.

Mobile Computing. (2010) *Wikipedia, the Free Encyclopedia*. Retrieved November 28, 2010, from http://en.wikipedia.org/wiki/Mobile_computing

Mobley, W., Horner, S., & Hollingsworth, A. (1978). An evaluation of precursors of hospital employee turnover. *The Journal of Applied Psychology*, *63*, 408–424. doi:10.1037/0021-9010.63.4.408

Moja, T. (2000). *Nigeria Education Sector Analysis: An Analytical Synthesis of Performance and Main Issues*. WORLD BANK Report

Molla, A. (2000). Downloading or uploading? the information economy and Africa current status. *Information Technology for Development, 9*(3-4), 205–221. doi:10.1080/02681102.2000.9525333

Molla, A., & Licker, P. S. (2005). eCommerce adoption in developing countries: a model and instrument. *Information & Management, 42*, 877–899. doi:10.1016/j.im.2004.09.002

Moon, J. W., & Kim, Y. G. (2001). Extending the TAM for a World Wide Web Context. *Information & Management, 38*(4), 217–237. doi:10.1016/S0378-7206(00)00061-6

Morawczynski, O., Ngwenyama, O., Andoh-Baidoo, F. K., & Bollou, F. (2006). Is there a relationship between ICT, health, education And Development? an empirical analysis of five West African Countries from 1997-2003. *The Electronic Journal on Information Systems in Developing Countries, 23*(5), 1–15.

Morris, M. G., & Turner, J. M. (2001). Assessing users' subjective quality of experience with the World Wide Web: an exploratory examination of temporal changes in technology acceptance. *International Journal of Human-Computer Studies, 54*(6), 877–901. doi:10.1006/ijhc.2001.0460

Mui, L., Mohtashemi, M., & Halberstadt, A. (2002). A Computational Model ofTrust and Reputation. *In Proceedings of the 35th Annual Hawaii International Conference on Systems Sciences*, Hawaii.

Muliawan, A. D., Green, P. F., & Robb, D. A. (2009). The Turnover Intentions of Information Systems Auditors. *International Journal of Accounting Information Systems, 10*(3), 117–136. doi:10.1016/j.accinf.2009.03.001

Mutahi, K., & Kagwe, H. (2008*). Kenya's First E Tourism Conference Stresses the Need to Stay Competitive Online*, Retrieved November 28, 2010, from http://www.balancingact-africa.com/news/en/issue-no-333/computing/kenya-s-first-e-tourism-conference-stresses-the-need-to-stay-competit

Mutula, S. M., & van Brakel, P. (2006). E-readiness of SMEs in the ICT sector in Botswana with respect to information access. *The Electronic Library, 24*(3), 402–417. doi:10.1108/02640470610671240

Myers, M. D., & Tan, F. B. (2002). Beyond models of national culture in information systems research. *Journal of Global Information Management, 10*(1), 24–32. doi:10.4018/jgim.2002010103

Myerson, R. B. (1981). Utilitarianism, Egalitarianism, and the Timing Effect in Social Choice Problems. *Econometrica. Econometric Society, 49*(4), 883–897. doi:10.2307/1912508

Nath, R., & Murthy, V. N. R. (2004). A study of the relationship between internet diffusion and culture. *Journal of International Technology and Information Management, 13*(2), 123–132.

National Restaurant Association. (2011). Available at: www.restaurant.org/forecast, retrieved on 20/2/2011.

Nau, D., Au, T.-C., Ilghami, O., Kuter, U., Murdock, W., Wu, D., & Yaman, F. (2003). SHOP2: an HTN planning system. *Journal of Artificial Intelligence Research, 20*(4), 379–404.

Naylor, J. (1999). *Management*. Harlow: Prentice Hall.

NCC. (2011). Subscriber Data 2001 - 2010. Retrieved from http://www.ncc.gov.ng/subscriberdata.htm

Ndubisi, N. O. (2007). Customers' perceptions and intention to adopt Internet banking: the moderation effect of computer self-efficacy. *AI & Society, 21*(3), 315–327. doi:10.1007/s00146-006-0062-5

Ndubuisi, N. O., & Jantan, M. (2003). Evaluating IS usage in Malaysia small and medium-sized firms using the technology acceptance model. *Logistics Information Management, 16*(6), 440–450. doi:10.1108/09576050310503411

Nel, J., & Raleting, T. (2010). *Gender differences in non-users' attitude towards WIG-Cellphone banking*. Retrieved March 2011, from http://anzmac2010.org/proceedings/pdf/anzmac10Final00038.pdf.

Niederman, F., Sumner, M., & Maertz, C. P. (2006). An analysis and synthesis of research related to turnover among IT personnel', *Proceedings of ACM SIGMIS-CPR*, Claremont, CA, (pp.130–136.) New York, NY: ACM Press

Niederman, F., Brancheau, J. C., & Wetherbe, J. C. (1991). Information systems management issues for the 1990s. *Management Information Systems Quarterly, 15*(4), 475–495. doi:10.2307/249452

Nigeria Daily News. (2011). Retrieved from http://www.nigeriadailynews.com/latest-additions/23879-nigeria%E2%80%99s-population-to-hit-166-million-by-october,-says-npc.html

NITDA. (2011). National Information Technology Development Agency. Retrieved from http://www.nitda.gov.ng/

Nonaka, I., & Takeuchi, H. (1995). *The Knowledge-Creating Company: How Japanese Companies create the dynamics of Innovation*. Oxford: University Press.

Norris, P. (2001). *Digital divide: civic engagement, information poverty, and the Internet worldwide*. Cambridge, UK: Cambridge University Press.

NUC. (2008). National Universities Commission. Retrieved from: http://www.nuc.edu.ng

NUC. (2011). National Universities Commission Data Base. Retrieved from http://www.nucdb.com/

Nunnally, J. C. (1967). *Psychometric Theory* (1st ed.). New York, NY: McGraw-Hill.

Nunnaly, J. C. (1978). *Psychometric theory*. New York, NY: McGraw-Hill.

Nusair, K. K., Hua, N., & Li, X. (2010). A conceptual framework of relationship commitment: e-travel agencies. *Journal of Hospitality and Tourism Technology*, *1*(2), 106–120. doi:10.1108/17579881011065029

Nwaboku, N. C. (1997). New information technologies in education and new roles for potential teachers. *UNESCO – Africa, 15*(15), 30-37.

Nweze, C. M. T. (2010). The Use of ICT in Nigerian Universities: A Case Study of Obafemi Awolowo University, Ile-Ife. *College & Research Libraries*, *65*(4), 276–286.

Nwokeocha, S. (2011). *The Digital Divide between Students and Lecturers: A Case study of Access and Attitudes towards Information Communication Technology (ICT) in Selected Nigerian Universities.* Retrieved March 21, 2011 from http://www.iiis.org/CDs2010/CD2010IMC/ICSIT_2010/PapersPdf/HB369QL.pdf

Nworgu, B. G. (1991). *Educational Research: Basic Issues and Methodology*. Ibadan: Wisdom Publishers.

Nysveen, H., Pedersen, P. E., & Thornbjørnsen, H. (2005). Explaining intention to use mobile chat services: moderating effects of gender. *Journal of Consumer Marketing*, *22*(5), 247–256. doi:10.1108/07363760510611671

Oblonger, D., & Oblinger, J. (2005). *Is It Age or IT: First Steps Toward Understanding the Net Generation.* Retrieved May 23 2011, from http://net.educause.edu/ir/library/pdf/pub7101.pdf

Odedra, M., Lawrie, M., Bennett, M., & Goodman, S. E. (1993). Sub-Saharan Africa: a technological desert. *Communications of the ACM*, *36*(2), 25–29. doi:10.1145/151220.151222

Odueyungbo, F. (2006). *Business Management: A Practical Approach*. Lagos: Nolachid Associates.

Odufuwa, Fola (2006). *Nigeria ICT Outlook and Forecasts. Lagos, Nigeria:* eShekels Limited.

Oh, H., & Pizam, A. (2008). *Handbook of Hospitality marketing management*. London, UK: Butter-Heinemann.

Oh, S. C., Lee, D., & Kumara, S. R. T. (2008). Effective web service composition in diverse and large-scale service networks. *IEEE Trans ServComput*, *1*(1), 15–32.

Okeke, E. C., & Kpolovie, P. J. (2006). *Basic Research Methods and Statistics. Owerri.* Springfield Publishers.

Okoli, C. (2003). *Expert assessments of e-commerce in Sub-Saharan Africa: A theoretical model of infrastructure and culture for doing business using the Internet*. Unpublished PhD thesis, Louisiana State University, USA.

Okotoni, O., & Erero, J. (2005). Manpower Training and Development in the Nigerian Public Service. *African Journal of Public Administration and Management*, *16*(1), 1–13.

Olatokun, W., & Kebonye, M. (2010). e-Commerce technology adoption by SMEs in Botswana, International. *Journal of Emerging Technologies and Society*, *8*(1), 42–56.

Ololube, N. P. (2007). The Relationship between Funding, ICT, Selection Processes, Administration and Planning and the Standard of Science Teacher Education in Nigeria. *Asia-Pacific Forum on Science Learning and Teaching*, *8*(1), Article 4.

Ololube, N. P. (2006a). The Impact of Professional and Non-professional Teachers' ICT Competencies in Secondary Schools in Nigeria. *Journal of Information Technology Impact*, *6*(2), 101–118.

Ololube, N. P. (2006b). Appraising the Relationship Between ICT Usage and Integration and the Standard of Teacher Education Programs in a Developing Economy. *International Journal of Education and Development Using ICT*, *2*(3), 70–85.

Ololube, N. P. (2007). Professionalism, Demographics, and Motivation: Predictors of Job Satisfaction Among Nigerian Teachers *International Journal of Education Policy and Leadership*, *2*(7).

Ololube, N. P. (2009). Computer Communication and ICT Attitude and Anxiety Among Higher Education Students. In Cartelli, A., & Palma, M. (Eds.), *Encyclopedia of Information and Communication Technology* (pp. 100–105). Hershey, PA: Information Science Reference. doi:10.4018/978-1-59904-845-1.ch014

Ololube, N. P. (2011). Blended Learning in Nigeria: Determining Students' Readiness and Faculty Role in Advancing Technology in a Globalize Educational Development. In Kitchenham, A. (Ed.), *Blended Learning Across Disciplines: Models for Implementation* (pp. 190–207). Hershey, PA: IGI Publishing. doi:10.4018/978-1-60960-479-0.ch011

Ololube, N. P., & Ubogu, A. E. (2009). ICTs and Distance Education: The Nigerian Experience. In Cartelli, A., & Palma, M. (Eds.), *Encyclopedia of Information and Communication Technology* (pp. 396–400). Hershey, PA: IGI Global.

Ololube, N. P., Ubogu, A. E., & Egbezor, D. E. (2007). ICT and Distance Education Programs in a Sub-Saharan African Country: A Theoretical Perspective. *Journal of Information Technology Impact*, *7*(3), 181–194.

Ong, C. S., Huang, J. J., & Tzeng, G. H. (2005). Building Credit Scoring Models Using Genetic Programming. *Expert Systems with Applications*, (n.d.)., 41–47. doi:10.1016/j.eswa.2005.01.003

Onifade, O. F. W. (2008). Cognitive Based Risk Factor Model for Strategic Decision Making in Economic Intelligence Process. *GDR-IE Workshop*Retrieved from: http://s244543015.onlinehome.fr/ciworldwide/wp-content/uploads/2008/06/nancy_onifadeofw.pdf

Open education. (2011a). *Of Digital Immigrants and Digital Natives Teaching the Net Generation.* Retrieved April 30, 2011, from http://www.openeducation.net/2011/03/01/digital-immigrants-and-digital-natives-teaching-the-net-generation/

Open Educaton. (2011b). *Though Net Generation Concerns Over-hyped, Integrating Technology the Right Step.* Retrieved Aripl 30, 2011, from http://www.openeducation.net/2008/09/26/though-net-generation-concerns-overhyped-integrating-technology-the-right-step/

Orr, A., & Wallin, A. (2001). Information Literacy and Flexible Delivery: Creating a conceptual Framework and model. *Journal of Academic Librarianship*, *27*(6), 457–463. doi:10.1016/S0099-1333(01)00263-4

Osofisan, A. O., Onifade, O. F. W., Longe, O. B., & Lala, G. O. (2007). Towards a Risk Assessment and Evaluation Model for Economic Intelligent Systems. *Proceedings of the International Conference on Applied Business & Economics*. Available online at www.icabeconference.org

Osotimehin, K. O., Akinkoye, E. Y., & Olasanmi, O. O. (2010). *The Effects of Investment in Telecommunication Infrastructure on Economic Growth in Nigeria (1992-2007),* Paper for the Oxford Business and Economic Conference.

Otong, J. G. (1993). *Notes on Social Research Basic Issues.* (3rd Ed). Calabar: University of Calabar press.

Ouzzani, M. (2004). *Efficient Delivery of Web Services.* Unpublished doctoral dissertation, Virginia Polytechnic Institute and State University.

Oxford Economics for the British Hospitality Association. (2010). Available at: http://www.baha- uk.org/OxfordEconomics.pdf, retrieved on 3/3/2011.

Oxley, J. E., & Yeung, B. (2001). E-commerce readiness: Institutional environment and international competitiveness. *Journal of International Business Studies*, *32*(4), 705–723. doi:10.1057/palgrave.jibs.8490991

Ozturk, S. G. (2007). *Classifying and predicting country types through development factors that influence economic, social, educational and health environments of countries*, SWDI Proceedings paper S759, (p 665-674), JEL classification: N01, N70, O15, O19.

Panagiotakopoulos, A. (2011) What drives training in industrial micro-firms? Evidence from Greece, *Industrial and Commercial Training43* (2).113 – 120.

Patton, M. A., & Jøsang, A. (2004). *Technologies for Trust in e-Commerce*. Netherlands: Kluwer Academic Publishers.

Pauleen, D. J. (2003). An Inductively Derived Model of Leader-Initiated Relationship Building with Virtual Team Members. *Journal of Management Information Systems*, *20*(3), 227–256.

Pavlou, P., & Gefen, D. (2004). Building Effective Online Marketplaces with Institution-Based Trust. *Information Systems Research*, *15*(1), 37–59. doi:10.1287/isre.1040.0015

Pelgrum and Law. (2003). *ICT in Education Around the World: Trends, Problems and Prospects*. Paris: UNSCO, International Institute for Educational Planning.

Pennington, R., Wilcox, H. D., & Grover, V. (•••). (204). The Role of System Trust in Business-to-Consumer Transactions. *Journal of Management Information Systems*, *20*(3), 197–226.

Perez, M. P., Sanchez, A. M., Carnicer, P. L., & Jimenez, A. I. (2004). A Technology Acceptance Model of Innovation Adoption: The Case of Teleworking. *Journal of Innovation Management*, *7*(4), 280–390. doi:10.1108/14601060410565038

Peters, P. (1983). Gender, Developmental Cycles and Historical Processes: A Critique of Recent Research on Women in Botswana. *Journal of Southern African Studies*, *10*(1), 100–122. doi:10.1080/03057078308708070

Pflughoeft, K., Ramamurthy, K., Soofi, E., Yasai-Ardekani, M., & Zahedi, F. (2003). Multiple conceptualizations of small Business web use and benefit. *Decision Sciences*, *34*(3), 467–512. doi:10.1111/j.1540-5414.2003.02539.x

Philip, D. (2007). The Knowledge Building Paradigm: A Model of Learning for Net Generation Students. *Innovate*, *3*(5). Retrieved May 23 2011, from www.personal.psu.edu/...blog/.../human-capital-theory-and-criti.html

Philips, L. A., Rodger, C., & Ming-Tong, L. (1994). International Technology Adoption: Behaviour Structure, Demand Certainty and Culture. *Journal of Business and Industrial Marketing*, *9*(4), 347–362.

Pikkarainen, T., Pikkarainen, K., Karjaluoto, H., & Pahnila, S. (2004). Consumer acceptance of online banking: an extension of the technology acceptance model. *Internet Research*, *14*(3), 224–235. doi:10.1108/10662240410542652

Pineda-Herrero, P; Belvis, E; Moreno, V; Duran-Bellonch, M. M. & Úcar, X (2011) Evaluation of training effectiveness in the Spanish health sector, *Journal of Workplace Learning,.23* (5).315 – 330.

Pisinger, D. (1995). *Algorithms for Knapsack Problems*. PhD thesis, Dept. of Computer Science.University of Copenhagen

Pizam, A. (2005). *International encyclopedia of hospitality management*. London, UK: Butterworth-Heinemann.

Platzer, C., Rosenberg, F., & Dustdar, S. (2009). Web Service Clustering using Multi-Dimensional Angles as Proximity Measures. *ACM Transactions on Internet Technology*, *9*(3), 1–26. doi:10.1145/1552291.1552294

Png, I. P. L., Tan, B. C. Y., & Wee, K.-L. (2001). Dimensions of national culture and corporate adoption of IT infrastructure. *IEEE Transactions on Engineering Management*, *48*(1), 36–45. doi:10.1109/17.913164

Podsakoff, P. M., MacKenzie, S. B., Lee, J. Y., & Podsakoff, N. P. (2003). Common method biases in behavioral research: A critical review of the literature and recommended remedies. *The Journal of Applied Psychology*, *88*(5), 879–903. doi:10.1037/0021-9010.88.5.879

Pohjola, M. (2002). The new economy: facts, impacts and policies. *Information Economics and Policy*, *14*(2), 133–144. doi:10.1016/S0167-6245(01)00063-4

Pohjola, M. (2003). The adoption and diffusion of ICT across countries: patterns and determinants. In Jones, D. C. (Ed.), *The New Economy Handbook* (pp. 77–100). New York, NY: Academic Press.

Poon, S., & Swatman, P. (1999). An exploratory study of small business Internet commerce issues. *Information & Management, 35*(1), 9–18. doi:10.1016/S0378-7206(98)00079-2

Powers, T., & Barrows, C. W. (2006). *Introduction to Management in the Hospitality Industry*. London, UK: John Wiley.

Preece, J. (2002). Supporting Community and Building Social Capital. *Communications of the ACM, 45*(4), 37–39. doi:10.1145/505248.505269

Premkumar, G., & Roberts, M. (1999). Adoption of new information technologies in rural small businesses, Omega: International. *Journal of Management Science, 27*(4), 467–484.

Prensky, M. (2001). Digital Natives, Digital Immigrants. *MCB University Press, 9*(5), 1–6.

Press, S. J., & Wilson, S. (1978). Choosing between logistic regression and discriminant analysis. *Journal of the American Statistical Association, 73*(4), 699–705. doi:10.2307/2286261

Pringle, J. K., & Mallon, M. (2003). Challenges for the boundaryless career odyssey. *International Journal of Human Resource Management, 14*(5), 839–853. doi:10.1080/0958519032000080839

Process of Personal Change. (2010) *Businessballs free online learning for careers, work, management, business training and education* Retrieved April 4, 2011, from http://www.businessballs.com/personalchangeprocess.htm

Punch, K. F. (1998). *Introduction to Social Research: Quantitative and Qualitative Approaches*. Thousand Oaks, CA: Sage.

Quest, R. School Library System. (2006). Information Literacy Curriculum. *NOVELNY, New York: Online Virtual Electronic Library*. https//www.questar.org/library/curriculum.httml.

Rainer, R., & Cegielski, C. (2009). *Introduction to Information Systems: Enabling and Transforming Business*. West Sussex, UK: John Wiley and Sons.

Raji, M. O., Ayoade, O. B., & Usoro, A. (2006). The prospects and problems of adopting ICT for poverty eradication in Nigeria. *The Electronic Journal of Information Systems in Developing Countries, 28*(8), 1–9.

Ramirez, C. D. (2004). Monetary policy and the credit channel in an open economy. *International Review of Economics & Finance, 13*, 363–369. doi:10.1016/S1059-0560(03)00038-8

Ran, S.A Model for Web Services Discovery with QoS. (2003). *ACM Inc., 4*(1), 1-1.

Ranjan, J. (2011). Study of sharing knowledge resources in business schools. *The Learning Organization, 18*(2), 102–114. doi:10.1108/09696471111103713

Ranjan, J., & Bhatnagar, V. (2011). Role of knowledge management and analytical CRM in business: data mining based framework. *The Learning Organization, 18*(2), 131–148. doi:10.1108/09696471111103731

Rao, J., Kungas, P., & Matskin, M. (2006). Composition of semantic web services using linear logic theorem proving. *Information Systems, 31*(4-5), 340–360. doi:10.1016/j.is.2005.02.005

Rao, S., & Troshani, I. (2007). A conceptual framework and propositions for the acceptance of mobile services. *Journal of Theoretical Applied Electronic Commerce Research, 2*(2), 61–73.

Rashid, A. T., & Elder, L. (2009). mobile phones and development: an analysis of IDRC-supported projects. *The Electronic Journal on Information Systems in Developing Countries, 2*, 1–16.

Rath, L. (2011). The effects of Twitter in online learning environment. *eLearn Magazine*, Retrieved from: http://elearnmag.acm.org/featured.cfm?aid=1944486 accessed 24 July, 2011.

Razmerita, L., Kirchner, K., & Sudzina, F. (2009). Personal knowledge management: The role of Web 2.0 tools for managing knowledge at individual and organisational levels. *Online Information Review, 33*(6), 1021–1039. doi:10.1108/14684520911010981

Reagle, J. M. Jr. (1996). Trust in Electronic Markets. *First Monday, 1*(2).

Redman, T. C. (1998). The Impact of poor Data Quality on the Typical Enterprise. *Communications of the ACM*, *41*(2), 79–82. doi:10.1145/269012.269025

Reza, F. (2005). *Mobile computing principles: designing and developing mobile applications with UML and XML*. Cambridge, UK: Cambridge University Press.

Ringle, C. M., Wende, S., & Will, A. (2005). *SmartPLS 2.0 (M3) beta, Hamburg*: Retrieved from: http://www.smartpls.de.

Riquelme, H. E., & Rios, R. E. (2010). The moderating effect of gender in the adoption of mobile banking. *International Journal of Bank Marketing*, *28*(5), 328–341. doi:10.1108/02652321011064872

Rodriguez-Mier, P., Mucientes, M., Lama, M., & Couto, M. I. (2010). Composition of web services through genetic programming. *Evol.Intel.*, *3*, 171–186. doi:10.1007/s12065-010-0042-z

Rogers, A. (2006). ICT will ultimately bridge the digital and poverty Divides, UNCDF, available at:http://www.uncdf.org/english/local_development/uploads/thematic/2006-11-ICT%20will%20ultimately%20bridge%20the%20digital%20and%20poverty.pdf, accessed on 14/5/11.

Rogers, E. M. (2003). *Diffusion of innovations* (5th ed.). New York: The Free Press.

Roller, L. H. & Wavernman, L. (2001). Telecommunications Infrastructure and Economic Development: A Simultaneous Approach. *American Economic Review Journal, 91* (4).

Root, F. (1994). *Entry strategies for international markets* New York, NY: Lexington.

Rosen, L. (2010). *Rewired: Understanding the iGeneration and the Way They Learn*. New York: Palgrave Macmillan.

Rosen, S. (2004). The victory of materialism: aspirations to join China's urban moneyed classes and the commercialization of education. *China Journal (Canberra, A.C.T.)*, *51*, 27–51. doi:10.2307/3182145

Rouse, P. (2001). Voluntary turnover related to information technology professionals: A review of rational and instinctual models. *The International Journal of Organizational Analysis*, *9*(3), 281–291. doi:10.1108/eb028937

Rousseau, D. M., Sitkin, S. B., Burt, R. S., & Camerer, C. (1998). Not so Different After All: A Cross-Discipline View of Trust. *Academy of Management Review*, *23*(3), 393–404. doi:10.5465/AMR.1998.926617

Roycroft, T. R., & Anantho, A. (2003). Internet subscription in Africa: policy for a dual digital divide. *Telecommunications Policy*, *27*(1/2), 61–74. doi:10.1016/S0308-5961(02)00091-5

Ruhanen, L., & Cooper, C. (2004). Applying a knowledge management framework to tourism research. *Tourism Recreation Research*, *29*(1), 83–88.

Rutledge, P. (2008). *The Truth about Profiting from Social Networking*. New Jersey: FT Press.

Rutner, P. S., Hardgrave, B. C., & McKnight, D. H. (2008). Emotional Dissonance and the Information Technology Professional. *Management Information Systems Quarterly*, *32*(3), 635–652.

Saffu, K., Walker, J. H., & Hinson, R. (2007). An empirical study of perceived strategic value and adoption constructs: the Ghanaian case. *Management Decision*, *45*(7), 1083–1101. doi:10.1108/00251740710773925

Sallis, E., & Jones, G. (2002). *Knowledge management in education: enhancing learning & education*. London, UK: Routledge.

Sam, H. K., Othman, A. E. A., & Nordin, Z. S. (2005). Computer self-efficacy, computer anxiety, and attitudes toward the Internet: A study among undergraduates in UNIMAS. *Journal of Educational Technology & Society*, *8*(4), 205–219.

Saunders, M., Lewis, P., & Thornhill, A. (2000). *Research Methods for Business Studies* (2nd ed.). Harlow: Prentice Hall.

Schein, E. H. (1984). Coming to a New Awareness of Organizational Culture. *MIT Sloan Management Review*, (25), 3–16.

Schein, E. H. (1978). *Career dynamics: Matching individual and organizational needs*. Reading, MA: Addison –Wesley.

Schein, E. H. (1985). *Career Anchors: Discovering Your Real Values*. San Diego, CA: University Associates.

Schein, E. H. (1987). Individuals and careers. In Lorsch, J. W. (Ed.), *Handbook of Organizational Behavior* (pp. 155–171). Englewood Cliffs, NJ: Prentice-Hall.

Schein, E. H. (1996). Career Anchors Revisited: Implications for Career Development in the 21st Century. *The Academy of Management Executive*, *10*(4), 80–88. doi:10.5465/AME.1996.3145321

Schiller, J. (2003). *Mobile communications*. Essex, UK: Pearson Education.

Schoderbek, P. P., Cosier, R. A., & Aplin, J. C. (1988). *Management*. San Diego: Harcourt Brace Jovenovick Publisher.

Scupola, A. (2003). The adoption of Internet commerce by SMEs in the South of Italy: An environmental, technological and organizational perspective. *Journal of Global Information Technology Management*, *6*(1), 52–71.

Servon, L. (2002). *Bridging the digital divide: technology, community, and public policy*. Oxford, UK: Wiley-Blackwell. doi:10.1002/9780470773529

Shane, S. A. (1993). Cultural influences on national rates of innovation. *Journal of Business Venturing*, *8*(1), 59–73. doi:10.1016/0883-9026(93)90011-S

Sharma, S. K. (2006). An exploratory study of the critical factors affecting the acceptability of e-learning in Nigerian universities. *Information Management & Computer Security*, *14*(5), 494–505.

Shih, C.-F., Dedrick, J., & Kraemer, K. L. (2002). *Determinants of IT spending at the country level*. Irvine, CA: University of California.

Shih, C.-F., Dedrick, J., & Kraemer, K. L. (2005). Rule of law and the international diffusion of e-commerce. *Communications of the ACM*, *48*(11), 57–62. doi:10.1145/1096000.1096005

Shore, B., & Venkatachalam, A. R. (1996). Role of national culture in the transfer of information technology. *The Journal of Strategic Information Systems*, *5*(1), 19–35. doi:10.1016/S0963-8687(96)80021-7

Siphambe, H. K. (2003). Understanding unemployment in Botswana. *The South African Journal of Economics*, *71*(3), 480–495. doi:10.1111/j.1813-6982.2003.tb00082.x

Siragusa, L., & Dixon, K. C. (2008). Planned Behaviour: Student Attitudes Towards the Use of ICT Interactions in Higher Education. *Proceedings of ASCILITE*, (pp. 942-953)Melbourne, Australia

Sirin, E., Parsia, B., Wu, D., Hendler, J., & Nau, D. (2004). Htn planning for web service composition using shop2. *Journal of Web Semantics*, *1*(4), 377–396. doi:10.1016/j.websem.2004.06.005

Smith, A. D. (2009). Internet retail banking: A competitive analysis in an increasingly financially troubled environment. *Information Management & Computer Security*, *17*(2), 127–150. doi:10.1108/09685220910964009

Social Mobility. (2010) Sociology subject index and sociological subfields. Retrieved November 28, 2010, from www.sociologyindex.com

Solomon, R. C., & Flores, F. (2001). *Building Trust in Business, Politics, Relationships, and Life*. Oxford: Oxford University Press.

Song, C. (2011*). The Regional Macroeconomic effects of public infrastructure in China*, PhD Thesis George Masion University, USA.

Soule, E. (1998). Trust and Managerial Responsibility. *Business Ethics Quarterly*, *8*(2), 249–272. doi:10.2307/3857328

Spaniol, O., Linnhoff-Popien, C., & Meyer, B. (2004). (Eds.) *Lecture Notes in Computer Science*, (pp. 94-107) Springer-Verlag. 1161.

Stansfield, M., McLellan, E., & Connoly, T. (2004). Enhancing student performance in online learning and traditional face-to-face class delivery. *Journal of Information Technology Education*, *3*, 173–188.

Stanton, J. M., & Stam, K. R. (2003). Information Technology, Privacy, and Power within Organizations: a view from Boundary Theory and Social Exchange perspectives. *Surveillance & Society*, *1*(2), 152–190.

Steers, R. M., Meyer, A. D., & Sanchez-Runde, C. J. (2008). National culture and the adoption of new technologies. *Journal of World Business*, *43*(3), 255–260. doi:10.1016/j.jwb.2008.03.007

Stone, M. H. (2002). *Management of human resources* (6th ed.). Chicago: Prentice Hall.

Straub, D. W., Loch, K. D., & Hill, C. E. (2001). Transfer of information technology to developing countries: a test of cultural influence modeling in the Arab world. *Journal of Global Information Management, 9*(4), 6–28. doi:10.4018/jgim.2001100101

Sussman, D. (2006). *Public sector training: Training and development in the public sector varies among states and cities. American Society for Training & Development, Inc.* Retrieved 16th December 2009, from http://www.faqs.org/abstracts/Human-resources-and-labor-relations/Public-sector-training-Training-and-development-in-the-public-sector-varies-among-states-and-cities.html

Suutari, V., & Taka, M. (2004). Career anchors of managers with global careers. *Journal of Management Development, 23*(9), 833–847. doi:10.1108/02621710410558440

Swarbrooke, J., & Horner, S. (1999). *Consumer Behavior in Tourism*. Oxford, UK: Butterworth-Heinemann Publishing.

Tam, L., & Dholakia, U. M. (2011). Delay and duration effects of time frames on personal savings estimates and behavior. *Organizational Behavior and Human Decision Processes, 114*, 142–152. doi:10.1016/j.obhdp.2010.10.009

Tan, J., Tyler, K., & Manica, A. (2007). Business-to-business adoption of eCommerce in China. *Information & Management, 44*, 332–351. doi:10.1016/j.im.2007.04.001

Taylor, C. (2011). Web 2.0 Knowledge technologies and the enterprise. *Library Review, 60*(2), 168–169.

Teidemann, N, Birgele, M. & Semeijn, J. (2009), Increasing hotel responsiveness to customers through information sharing in *Tourism Review, 64*(4) 12-26.

Teo, H. H., Tan, B. C. Y., & Wei, K. K. (1997). Organizational transformation using Electronic Data Interchange: The case of TradeNet in Singapore. *Journal of Management Information Systems, 13*(4), 139–166.

Thatcher, J. B., McKnight, D. H., Baker, E. W., Arsal, R. E., & Roberts, N. H. (2011). The Role of Trust in Postadoption IT Exploration: An Empirical Examination of Knowledge Management Systems. *IEEE Technology Management Council, 58*(1), 56–70.

The Heritage Foundation. (2008). *Index of economic freedom*. Retrieved January 17, 2007 from http://www.heritage.org/Index/

Thong, J. Y. L., Yap, C. S., & Raman, K. S. (1996). Top management support, external expertise and information systems implementation in small business. *Information Systems Research, 7*(2), 248–267. doi:10.1287/isre.7.2.248

Thong, J., & Yap, C. (1995). CEO characteristics, organisational, characteristics and information technology adoption in small business. *Omega: International Journal of Management Sciences, 23*(4), 429–442. doi:10.1016/0305-0483(95)00017-I

Tiedemann, J., Taylor, S., Fiorile, R., & Sciarappa, W. (2006). *Vulnerable Wetlands and Associated Riparian Areas in the Shark River Estuary Watershed. US EPA Wetlands Protection Project Grant Final Report Monmouth University Centre for Coastal Watershed Management*. N.J: W. Long Branch.

Tiemo, P. A., Emiri, O. T., & Tiemo, A. J. (2010). Information and Communication Technology (ICT) Training among Lecturers in the South-South Zone in Nigeria by the Nigeria Communication Commission (NCC). *International Journal of Information and Communication Technology Education, 6*(1), 55–66. doi:10.4018/jicte.2010091105

Toledo, C. A. (2007). Digital Culture: Immigrants and Tourists Responding to the Natives' Drumbeat. *International Journal of Teaching and Learning in Higher Education, 19*(1), 84–92.

Tornatzky, L. G., & Fleischer, M. (1990). *The processes of technological innovation*. Lexington, MA: Lexington Books.

Tornatzky, L. G., & Klein, R. J. (1982). Innovation characteristics and innovation adoption-implementation: A meta-analysis of findings. *IEEE Transactions on Engineering Management, 29*(1), 28–45.

Transparency International. (2007). *Corruption perception index – 2007*. Retrieved January 27, 2007 from http://www.transparency.org/news_room/in_focus/2007/cpi2007/cpi_2007_table

Tregaskis, C. (2004). *Constructions of disability: researching the interface between disabled and non-disabled people*. New York, NY: Routledge. doi:10.4324/9780203299517

Tseng, S.-M. (2011). The effects of hierarchical culture on knowledge management processes. *Management Research Review*, *34*(5), 595–608. doi:10.1108/01409171111128742

Tucker, H. (2010). *Digital Natives and Digital Immigrants*. Retrieved June 32011, from http://ccnmtl.columbia.edu/enhanced/primers/digital_natives.html

Tuomi, I. (2000). *Beyond the digital divide*. Retrieved March 13, 2011, from http://www.cs.berkeley.edu/~jfc/hcc/retreat3/Divide.pdf

Turban, E., King, D., & Lang, J. (2010). *Introduction to electronic commerce. New York, NY*. NY: Prentice Hall.

Turmusani, M. (2003). *Disabled people and economic needs in the developing world: a political perspective from Jordan*. Hampshire, UK: Ashgate Publishing, Ltd.

UN ICT TASK Force. (2004). *The history of the United Nations information and communication technologies task force*. Retrieved January 17, 2007 from http://www.unicttaskforce.org/index.html.

UNCTAD. (2005). *Information Economy Report*. New York, NY: United Nations Conference on Trade and Development.

UNCTAD. (2008). *Information Economy Report 2007-2008 Science and technology for development: The new paradigm of ICT*. Available at http://r0.unctad.org/ecommerce/ier07_en.htm. Accessed 12 Jan., 2011.

UNDP. (2010). Human Development Report, The *Real Wealth of Nations: Pathways to Human Development* available at: http://www.hdr.undp.org/en/reports/global/hdr2010/, retrieved on 20/12/2010.

UNECA. (2007). *National information and communications strategies*. Retrieved January 10, 2008 from http://www.uneca.org/aisi/nici/nici_country_pages.htm

UNESCO. (2002). *Information and Communication Technologies in Teacher education: A Planning Guide*. Paris: UNESCO.

UNESCO. (2003). *Manual for Pilot Testing the Use of Indicators to Assess Impact of ICT Use in Education*. Retrieved March 10, 2011, from http://www.unescobkk.org/education/ict/resource

UNESCO. (2005). "United Nations Decade of education for Sustainable development 2005-2014. Retrieved on the March 20, 2011, from http://portal.unesco.org/education/en/ev.php-URL_ID=27234&URL_DO=DO_TOPIC&URL_SECTION=201.html

Usoro, A & Majewski, G. (2011). Intensive knowledge sharing: Finnish Laurea lab case study in *Journal of Information and Knowledge Management Systems, 41*(1) 7-25.

Usoro, A. & Abiagam, B. (2009). "Providing operational definitions to quality constructs for e-learning in higher education." *e-Learning, 6*(2), 172-186.

Usoro, A., & Shoyelu, S. (2010). Task-technology fit and technology acceptance models applicability to e-tourism in *Journal of Economic Development, Management, IT, Finance and Marketing*, Volume 2, No 1, pp 1-32, available at: http://gsmi-jedmitfm.com/Documents/N2%20V1%20JEDMITFM%20-P01%20-Usoro%20-Task%20Technology%20Fit.pdf, accessed 2/2/2011.

Usoro, A., & Kuofie, M. (2008). Conceptualization of cultural dimensions as a major influence on knowledge-sharing. In Jennex, M. E. (Ed.), *Current Issues in Knowledge Management* (pp. 119–130). San Diego, CA: Information Science Reference. doi:10.4018/978-1-59904-916-8.ch009

Usoro, A., & Kuofie, M. H. S. (2006). Conceptualisation of Cultural Dimensions as a Major Influence on Knowledge-Sharing. *International Journal of Knowledge Management*, *2*(2), 16–25. doi:10.4018/jkm.2006040102

Uzoka, F-M. E., Seleka, G.G., & Khengere, J. (2007). E-commerce adoption in developing countries: a case analysis of environmental and organisational inhibitors, International *Journal of Information Systems and Change Management,* (3), 232-260.

Uzoka, F. M. E., & Akinyokun, O. C. (2005). Factor Analytic Model for Evaluating the Effects of HR Profile on Organizational Productivity: Case Study of University Academic Staff. *South African Journal of Higher Education, 19*(3), 527–538. doi:10.4314/sajhe.v19i3.25508

Van der Deen, M. (2005). Measuring e-Business Adoption in SME. In During, W., Oakey, R., & Kauser, S. (Eds.), *New technology-based firms in the new millennium* (*Vol. 5*). Amsterdam, Holland: Elsevier.

Van Sell, M., Brief, A. P., & Schuler, R. S. (1981). Role Conflict and Role Ambiguity: Integration of the Literature and Directions for Future Research. *Human Relations*, *34*(1), 43–71. doi:10.1177/001872678103400104

Van Slyke, C., Comunale, C., & Belanger, F. (2002). Gender differences in perceptions of Web-based shopping. *Communications of the ACM*, *45*(8), 82–86. doi:10.1145/545151.545155

Vandi, C., & Djebbari, E. (2011). How to create new services between library resources, museum exhibitions and virtual collections. *Library Hi Tech News*, *28*(2), 15–19. doi:10.1108/07419051111135236

Venkatesh, V. (2000). Determinants of perceived ease of use: integrating control, intrinsic motivation, and emotion into the technology acceptance model. *Information Systems Research*, *46*, 342–365. doi:10.1287/isre.11.4.342.11872

Venkatesh, V., & Bala, H. (2008). Technology acceptance model 3 and a research agenda on intervention. *Decision Sciences*, *39*(2), 273–315. doi:10.1111/j.1540-5915.2008.00192.x

Venkatesh, V., & Davis, F. D. (2000). A Theoretical Extension of the Technology Acceptance Model: For Longitudinal Field Studies. *International Journal of Management Science*, *46*(2), 186–204.

Venkatesh, V., & Morris, M. G. (2000). Why don't men ever stop to ask for directions? gender, social influence, and their role in technology acceptance and usage behavior. *Management Information Systems Quarterly*, *24*(1), 115–139. doi:10.2307/3250981

Venkatesh, V., Morris, M. G., Davis, G. B., & Davis, F. D. (2003). User acceptance of information technology: toward a unified view. *Management Information Systems Quarterly*, *27*(3), 425–478.

Viega, J., Kohno, T., & Potter, B. (2001). Trust (and Mistrust) in Secure Applications. *Communications of the ACM*, *44*(2), 31–36. doi:10.1145/359205.359223

W3C Recommendation (10 February 2004), (pp. 181–190) Washington, DC, USA: IEEE Computer Society.

Waarts, E., & van Everdingen, Y. (2005). The influence of national culture on the adoption status of innovations: an empirical study of firms across Europe. *European Management Journal*, *25*(6), 601–610. doi:10.1016/j.emj.2005.10.007

Walczak, S., & Gregg, D. G. (2009). Factors Influencing Corporate Online Identity: A New Paradigm. *Journal of Theoretical and Applied Electronic Commerce Research*, *4*(3), 17–29. doi:10.4067/S0718-18762009000300003

Walker, J. R., & Miller, J. E. (2008). *Supervising in the hospitality industry: Leading Human Resource*. London: John Wiley.

Walle, A. H. (1996). Tourism and the Internet. Opportunities for Direct Marketing. *Journal of Travel Research*, *35*(1), 72–77. doi:10.1177/004728759603500111

Wallsten, S. J. (2001). An econometric analysis of telecom competition, privatization, and regulation in Africa and Latin America. *The Journal of Industrial Economics*, *49*(1), 1–19. doi:10.1111/1467-6451.00135

Walsham, G. (2002). Cross-cultural software production and use: a structurational analysis. *Management Information Systems Quarterly*, *26*(4), 359–380. doi:10.2307/4132313

Wang, J. (2005). Bourgeois bohemians in China? Neo-tribes and the urban imagery. *The China Quarterly*, *183*, 532–548. doi:10.1017/S0305741005000342

Wang, L., Lu, W., & Malhotra, N. K. (2011). Demographics, attitude, personality and credit card features correlate with credit card debt: A view from China. *Journal of Economic Psychology*, *32*, 179–193. doi:10.1016/j.joep.2010.11.006

Wang, M. (2011). Integrating organizational, social, and individual perspectives in Web 2.0-based workplace e-learning. *Information Systems Frontiers*, *13*(2), 191–205. doi:10.1007/s10796-009-9191-y

Wang, Y., Wang, Y., Lin, H., & Tang, T. (2003). Determinants of User Acceptance of Internet Banking: An Empirical Study. *International Journal of Service Industry Management*, *14*(5), 501–505. doi:10.1108/09564230310500192

Warren, C. (2010). *Mobile Social Networking Usage Soars*. Retrieved November 28, 2010, from http://mashable.com/2010/03/03/comscore-mobile-stats

Waycott, J., Bennett, S., Kennedy, G., Dalgarno, B., & Gray, K. (2010). Digital divides? Student and staff perceptions of information and communication technologies. *Computers & Education*, *54*(4), 1202–1211. doi:10.1016/j.compedu.2009.11.006

Weaver, J. (2011). M-libraries 2: A Virtual Library in Everyone's Pocket. *Library Management*, *32*(3), 230–231.

Web Ontology Language Reference, O. W. L. W3C Recommendation (10 February, 2004). Retrieved on 4th June, 2011, from http://www.w3.org/TR/2004/REC-owl-ref-20040210/.

Webber, D., & Kauffman, R. J. (2011). *What drives global ICT adoption? Analysis and research directions, Electronic Commerce Research and Applications, Article still in press*. London, UK: Elsevier

WEF (World Economic Forum). (2011). *Global Competitiveness 2009-2010*. Available at http://www.weforum.org/reports.

Weise, T., & Geihs, K. (2006). Genetic Programming Techniques For Sensor Networks. In Marron, P. J. (Ed.), *Proceedings of 5. GI/ITG KuVSFach gesprach Drahtlose Sensornetze* (pp. 21–25).

Welty, B., & Becerra-Fernandez, I. (2001). Managing Trust and Commitment in Collaborative Supply Chain Relationships. *Communications of the ACM*, *44*(6), 67–73. doi:10.1145/376134.376170

Werthner, H., & Klein, S. (1999). *Information technology and tourism: a challenging relationship*. Vienna: Springer-Verlag. doi:10.1007/978-3-7091-6363-4

Whalen, C. (2005). The next great pyramid game. *Inter Economics*, *19*(4), 22–56.

What We are All About (2009). *E-Tourism Frontiers* Retrieved November 28, 2010, from http://www.e-tourismfrontiers.com/

Women use Mobile more than Men (2010) *Nielsen Research Group. For Social Networking*, Retrieved November 28, 2010, from http://blog.nielsen.com/nielsenwire/online_mobile/for-social-networking-women-use-mobile-more-than-men

Wong, K. Y. (2008). An exploratory study on Knowledge management adoption in the Malaysian Industry. *International Journal of Business Information Systems*, *3*(3), 272–283. doi:10.1504/IJBIS.2008.017285

World Bank Report. (1991). *The Challenge of Development*. New York, NY: World Bank Group.

World Bank. (2006). *Information and Communications for Development: Global Trends and Policies*. New York, NY: The World Bank Group.

World Bank. (2007). *Development data and statistics*. Retrieved December, 10, 2007 from http://web.worldbank.org/.

World Development Report, (1998). *Knowledge for Development*, London, UK: Oxford Press.

World Development Report. (1991). *Infrastructure for Development*. Washington, DC: The World Bank.

Worthington, S. (2005). Entering the market for financial services in transitional economies; a case study of creidt cards in China. *International Journal of Bank Marketing*, *25*(5), 381–396. doi:10.1108/02652320510612465

WSIS. (2007). *World summit on the information society*. Retrieved April 2, 2011 from http://www.itu.int/wsis/basic/about.html

Wu, Z., Gomadam, K., Ranabahu, A., Sheth, A. P., & Miller, J. A. (2007). Automatic composition of semantic web services using process and data mediation. *In Proceedings of the 9th international conference on enterprise information systems (ICEIS'07)*. (pp., 453–461) Funchal, Portugal: Gabler.

Wynne, L. A., Ferratt, T. W., & Biros, D. P. (2002). Career anchors of United States Air Force information systems workers: a turnover predictor? *In Proceedings of SIGCPR'2002*. 79-89

Xiaoming, H., & Chow, S. K. (2004). *Factors affecting Internet development: An Asian survey*. Retrieved November, 28 2010, from http://firstmonday.org/issues/issue9_2/hao/

Xu, M. X., Wilkes, S., & Shah, M. H. (2006). *e-banking Application and Issues in Abbey National PLC*, In M. Khosrow (eds.), (pp. 253-258), *Encyclopedia of e-commerce, e-government and Mobile Commerce*. Hershey PA: Idea Group Inc.

Yarnall, J. (1998). Career anchors results of an organizational study in the UK. *Career Development International*, *3*(2), 3. doi:10.1108/13620439810207536

Yee, G., El-Khatib, K., Korba, L., Patrick, A. S., Song, R., & Xu, Y. (2005). Privacy and Trust in E- Government. In Huang, W., Siau, K., & Wei, K. K. (Eds.), *Electronic Government Strategies and Implementation* (pp. 145–189). Hershey, PA: Idea Group Publishing.

Yufeng, K., Chang-Tien, L., & Sirwongwattana, S. (2011). *Survey of Fraud Detection Techniques* (p. 1045). Taiwan.

Yusuf, M. O. & Onasanya, S. A. (2004). Information and Communication technology (ict) and teaching in tertiary institutions. *Teaching in Tertiary Intitutions* 67-76.

Yusuf, M. O. (2005a). An Investigation into Teachers' Self-Efficacy in Implementing Computer Education in Nigerian Secondary Schools. *Meridian: A Middle School Computer Technologies Journal* *8*(2).

Yusuf, M. (2005). Information and communication technology and education, analyzing the Nigerian national policy for information technology. *International Education Journal*, *6*(3), 316–321.

Yusuf, M. O. (2005b). Information and Communication Technologies and Education: Analyzing the Nigerian National Policy for Information Technology. *International Education Journal*, *6*(3), 316–321.

Zaqqa, N. (2006). *Economic development and export of human capital - a contradiction?: the impact of human capital migration on the economy of sending countries; a case study of Jordan*. Kassel: University Press, GmbH.

Zeng, L., Benatallah, B., Dumas, M., Kalagnanam, J., & Sheng, Q. Z. (2003). Quality driven web services composition.In *Proceedings of the International World Wide Web Conference*,(pp. 411–421)

Zeng, L., Benatallah, B., Ngu, A. H. H., Dumas, M., Kalagnanam, J., & Chang, H. (2004). Qos-aware middleware for web services composition. *IEEE Transactions on Software Engineering*, *30*(5), 311–327. doi:10.1109/TSE.2004.11

Zhao, A. L., Koenig-Lewis, N., Hanmer-Lloyd, S., & Ward, P. (2010). Adoption of internet banking services in China: is it all about trust? *International Journal of Bank Marketing*, *28*(1), 7–26. doi:10.1108/02652321011013562

Zhu, Y. L., & Meeks, B. C. (1994). Effect of low-income families ability and willingness to use consumer-credit on subsequent outstanding credit balance. *The Journal of Consumer Affairs*, *28*(2), 403–422. doi:10.1111/j.1745-6606.1994.tb00859.x

Zinman, J. (2010). Restricting consumer credit access: Household survey evidence on effects around the Oregon rate cap. *Journal of Banking & Finance*, *34*, 546–556. doi:10.1016/j.jbankfin.2009.08.024

Zucker, L. G. (1986). Production of trust: Institutional sources of economic structure, 1840-1920. *Research in Organizational Behavior*, *8*(1), 53–111.

# About the Contributors

**Abel Usoro** lectures in the School of Computing, University of the West of Scotland, UK. His current research interests are information systems which include knowledge management, e-learning and tourism. He has published book chapters, in refereed international conferences and journals (such as International Journal of Global Information Management and International Journal of Knowledge Management). His academic work and research have taken him to countries in Africa, Europe, Asia, North and South America. He is Editor-in-Chief of Computing and Information Systems Journal, Associate Editor of JEDMIFM, and member of editorial boards of other international journals. He is a member of scientific committees of many international conferences and chairs one of them (Conference on Information Technology and Economic Development). He is also a member of the British Computing Society and the lead editor of Leveraging Developing Economies with the Use of Information Technology published by IGI Global. Contact: abel.usoro@uws.ac.uk or Web: http://cis.uws.ac.uk/abel.usoro/index.htm

**Grzegorz Majewski** holds an MSc degree awarded by the Warsaw School of Economics and another by the University of the West of Scotland. He has worked for the telecommunication and finance industry. He is active in the research field presenting his papers at international conferences and publishing in refereed journals. His current research focuses on Knowledge Management, Innovation, Social Networks, e-Learning and Immersive Virtual Worlds.

**Princely Ifinedo** is an Associate Professor in the Shannon School of Business at Cape Breton University, Canada. He holds a doctoral degree in Information Systems from the University of Jyväskylä (Eximia Cum Laude Approbatur) and master's degrees from the University of London and Tallinn University of Technology. He has presented research at various international IS conferences (including a Best Track Paper at the 2008 AMCIS), contributed chapters to several books/encyclopedias, and published in several reputable peer-reviewed journal including JCIS, DATABASE, JSS, CHB, JOCEC, JITM, IMDS, EIS, IJITDM, JITD, JITM, JGTIM, EG, JISP, and Internet Research. He has authored (and co-authored) more than 80 publications. Dr. Ifinedo's current research interests include ERP system success measurement, global IT management, IT adoption in SMEs and healthcare, cross-cultural issues in IS, IS security and privacy issues, and the diffusion of IS in transiting and developing economies. He is affiliated with AIS, ISACA, and DSI.

**Iwara I Arikpo** teaches Computer Science at the University of Calabar, Nigeria. His current research interests are software engineering which includes software project management, agile software development and software process improvement. He also researches in computer information systems, computer architecture, health informatics, among others. He has published papers, in refereed international conferences and journals (such as Global Journal of Mathematical Sciences, Computing Information System Journal, Scientia Africana, International Journal of Natural and Applied Sciences, International Journal of Global Business). His academic work has taken him to a number of African countries and some parts of Europe. He is a Local Chair of the international Conference on Information Technology & Economic Development (CITED); a member of professional bodies such as Computer Professionals Registration Council of Nigeria, Nigeria Computer Society; and an editor of Leveraging Developing Economies with the Use of Information Technology: Trends and tools published by IGI Global. Contact: iiarikpo@gmail.com

* * *

**Bridget Abiagam** obtained her BA(Ed) an MSc in Management. She is currently one of Dr Abel Usoro's final year PhD research students. Her current research interest is in e-hospitality and e-tourism. She has also acted as a research assistant and co-authored journal and conference publications in areas that include e-learning quality in higher education (you can find her name among co-author at http://cis.uws.ac.uk/abel.usoro/Papers). With 3 years' practical experience in the tourism and hospitality she is very enthusiastic in knowledge contribution to these industries in developing economies. She has been funded by South Scotland Business Solutions, UK, through University of the West of Scotland to assist Dr Usoro in various e-tourism consultancies in Scotland. She co-authors a book chapter in *Leveraging Developing Economies with the Use of Information Technology* published by IGI Global. Contact: bridget.abiagam@uws.ac.uk

**Oluwatosin Akinyede Ajayi** graduated from the Department of Business Administration College of Management and Social Sciences NOVENA University, Ogume, Nigeria. He has published with major contributions in human resources management and ICT in the public sector domain.

**Boluwaji Akinnuwesi** obtained a BSc (Computer Science) in 1998 and M.Tech in Computer Science in 2003 and PhD (Computer Science) in 2011. He is the Director of Computer Centre of the Bells University of Technology, Ota, Nigeria. He was a visiting Research Scholar in ICITD, Southern University, Baton Rouge, Louisiana in 2010. He has published in a number of reputable journals and conferences. His research interests include: user involvement issues, simulation and performance evaluation, expert systems, and software engineering.

**Rosemary Chiaka Akuchie** is a lecturer at the University of Abuja, Nigeria. She is currently the Head of Department of Educational Management of the University. She has published articles in reputable journals, book chapter and proceeding in the area of educational administration and planning. She is a member of international and national professional bodies such as: Commonwealth Council for Education Administration and Management, National Association of Educational Administration and Planning, Teachers' Registration Council of Nigeria. She is a member of the Editorial Boards of Journals like:

The Federal Capital Territory Journal of Curriculum and Instruction, Abuja Journal of Education and the Capital Journal for Educational Studies. She has also made tremendous contributions in the training of both primary and secondary school teachers towards attaining the Millennium Development Goal in education. Generally, Dr Rosemary Akuchie is highly reliable in activities towards the improvement of education in Nigeria.

**Samuel Amaele** earned his Ph.D. in Philosophy of Education. He is currently a Senior Lecturer in the Department of Educational Foundations and Management, Faculty of Education, University of Education, Port Harcourt, Nigeria. Dr. Amaele's research effort focuses on epistomological issues, school effectiveness, teacher effectiveness, ICT in education and method courses. Amaele have published widely in different international journals, chapters in books and conference proceedings.

**Charles K Ayo** holds a B.Sc. M.Sc. and Ph.D in Computer Science. He is a Professor of Computer Science and the Director of Academic Planning Unit of Covenant University, Nigeria. His research interests include: Mobile computing, Internet programming, eBusiness, eGovernment and Software Engineering. He is a member of the Nigerian Computer Society (NCS) and Computer Professionals (Registration Council) of Nigeria (CPN). He is a member of such international research bodies as the Centre for Business Information, Organization and Process Management (BIOPoM). He is on the Editorial Boards of Journal of Information and communication Technology for Human Development (IJICTHD), International Journal of Scientific Research in Education (IJSRE) and African Journal of Business Management (AJBM), amongst others. Prof. Ayo is an External Examiner to a number of Nigerian universities and has supervised about 200 postgraduate projects at Masters and Ph.D levels. He has published in several scholarly journals and academic conferences.

**Pattarin Chumnumpan** is currently pursuing her Ph.D in Management at The York Management School, University of York (UK). She is also the Director of Professional Training & Development at IKI-SEA and a full-time instructor at the department of International Business Management, School of Business Administration, Bangkok University. She holds an MBA from Fairleigh Dickinson University (USA) in Global Business Management as well as a Bachelor of Business Administration - 1st class Honours from Chiang Mai University (Thailand). She has worked as a Human Resources and Training Coordinator at the Hilton Hua Hin Resort and Spa, and as a secretary to the Director of Sales and Marketing at the Sukhothai Bangkok Hotel. For the past years she has been involved in conducting research in the field of Knowledge Management, provided training and being involved with various KM projects at Bangkok University.

**Daniel Elemchukwu Egbezor** is currently a Senior Lecturer in the Department of Educational Foundations, Faculty of Education, University of Port Harcourt, Nigeria. His research focuses on sociological principles, institutional management and leadership, education effectiveness, teacher effectiveness and quality improvement, ICT in education and research methodology. Dr Egbezor have published in various international journals, chapters in books and leading international conference proceedings.

**Idongesit Efaemiode Eteng** Nee Idongesit Fidelis Essien has been a lecturer in the Department of Computer Science, University of Calabar, for five years having previously served in the same University as a programmer/systems analyst. She has served the University in a number of committees including one that inaugurated the International Journal of Pure and Applied Sciences. She has a BSc (Hons) (Computer Science) Degree, an MSc (Computer Science) from the University of Ibadan, Nigeria. She is currently tidying up her PhD (Computer Science) University of Ibadan under the supervision of Prof (Mrs) Adenike Osofisan. She is a member of NCS (Nigerian Computer Society) and CPN (Computer Professionals of Nigeria) and an author of several books and journal articles. Her primary interest areas are Software Engineering, Internet Computing, Cloud Computing, Artificial Intelligence, Database Management Systems, Web Security and Programming. She is a Christian and married with children.

**Uyinomen O Ekong** received an M.Sc. in Management Information Systems (MIS) with specialization in mobile computing from Covenant University, Ota, Nigeria in 2006. She obtained a B.Sc degree in Computer Science from Ambrose Alli University, Edo State Nigeria in 2002. She is currently working towards the Ph.D degree in the Department of Computer Science, University of Benin, Benin City Nigeria. Her current research interests include that application of Artificial Intelligence methods and techniques for network security, human interactive proofs, mobile computing, E-commerce, and E-government. She is a member of Nigeria Computer Society (NCS), Computer Professionals of Nigeria (CPN) and Institute of Electrical and Electronic Engineers (IEEE). Uyinomen O Ekong has published in scholarly journals and academic conferences.

**Ray Hackney** is Chair in Business Systems, Director of the Doctoral Programme and Head of the Information Systems Evaluation research group at Brunel University, UK. He has contributed extensively to research in information systems and management with publications in numerous national and international conferences and journals. He has taught and examined Doctoral and MBA programmes including Manchester Business School and the Open University. He is Associate Editor of the JGIM, JEUC, JLIM, ACITM, EJIS and case editor for IJIM. His research interests: the strategic management of information systems within a variety of organisational contexts, with an increasing speciality in government sectors; and has contributed to several EPSRC and European funded research projects. He was President of the Information Resource Management Association (IRMA) 2001/2002 and is now an Executive Member of the Information Institute www.information-institute.org; and serves on the European Doctoral Association for Management & Business Administration (EDAMBA) Executive Committee.

**Airi Ifinedo** works as an IT Consultant for a US-based, Enterprise Resource Planning (ERP) solutions provider. She holds six professional certifications in Microsoft Business Solutions (NAV) applications. She received her BBA from Oulu Polytechnic (Oulu University of Applied Sciences), Finland and an MBA from Tallinn University of Technology, Estonia. She is familiar with the business and IT climates in the Baltic and Nordic countries. Her current areas of interests include e-business development, ERP systems use in organizations, EDI, logistics, Global IT issues, and project management. Airi Ifinedo has published in scholarly journals such as Computers in Human Behavior (CHB), Baltic Journal of Management (BJM), and International Journal of Business and Systems Research (IJBSR). She is affiliated with APICS.

**Ernest G Kitindi** is currently a Senior Lecturer in the Department of Accounting at the University of Dar Es Salaam. He has held positions as Senior Lecturer and Lecturer at that University and, for about ten years, was with the University of Botswana both as Senior lecturer and Head of Department. Dr Kitindi is a prolific scholar and has more several scholarly publications in international and local journals and conference proceedings. His research interests are: agency theory and its applications, corporate governance in public entities, SMEs and microfinance issues/SACCOS, gender issues in accounting, and personnel issues.

**Peter James Kpolovie** is a Senior Lecturer and current acting head of the Department of Educational Psychology, Guidance and Counselling, Faculty of Education, University of Port Harcourt. He earned his B.A (Ed) 2; 1, M.Ed with 4.44 CGPA and PhD with 5.00 CGPA from University of Port Harcourt in 1991, 1996, and 2002 respectively. Kpolovie is a specialist in test and measurement and in research. His PhD dissertation, titled "validation and standardization of culture fair intelligence test for use in Nigeria", in 2002 won NUC's best doctoral thesis award which is the highest academic award in Nigeria. Other awards include common wealth scholarship award of excellence at the University of Port Harcourt Graduate School Silver Jubilee Celebration. Kpolovie have researched and published widely with major contributions in intelligence testing application of information technology (SPSS in particular) in data analysis, better ways of human learning, educational statistics and research method.

**Klodwig Venant Mgaya** is a senior lecturer in Business Information Systems at the Faculty of Business, University of Botswana. He also taught at the University of Botswana and worked as a Systems Librarian at the Michael Somare Library, University of Papua New Guinea. His main research interests are in the areas of corporate information systems, systems security, information systems personnel, business process management and accounting information systems. Klodwig holds a BCom(Accounting) degree from University of Dar es Salaam, MSc (Information Systems) from University of London (London School of Economics) and is currently a PhD researcher at the Department of Informatics, University of Pretoria in South Africa.

**Aniebiet Ntui** lectures in the Department of Educational Foundations Guidance and Counselling, University of Calabar, Nigeria. Her current research interests are information use and users studies. She has published over twenty five articles in reputable national and international journals and book chapters, in refereed texts. She is also a chartered librarian and a member of the Nigerian Library Association Contact: ntuinju@yahoo.com

**Nwachukwu Prince Ololube** earned a Ph.D. in Education and Teacher Education with focus in Eduactional Management and Planning from the University of Helsinki, Finland. In addition, he holds a Post graduate Diploma in Human Resources Management, M.Ed. in Educational Management and Planning, and B.Sc. in Political Science. He is currently a Senior Lecturer in the Department of Educational Foundations and Management, Faculty of Education, University of Education, Port Harcourt, Nigeria. His research focuses on institutional management and leadership, education effectiveness, teacher effectiveness and quality improvement, ICT in education and research methodology. Ololube has published 4 books, and has published in various refereed international journals, chapters in books and leading international conference proceedings. You can contact him via his email(s): ololubeprince@yahoo.com, ololubenp@gmail.com, ololube@ololube.com, and access his profile via his website: www.ololube.com.

**Aderonke A. Oni** holds B.Sc. and M.Sc.in Management Information System from Covenant University. She is currently a PhD student in the Department of Computer and Information Sciences, Covenant University, Ota, Nigeria. Her current research interests are in the following areas: e-commerce, e-business, e-government, theoretical investigation of users' acceptance of information system, design theories for information system, and software engineering. She also lectures in the Department of Computer and Information Sciences, Covenant University.

**Adenike Oyinlola Osofisan (FNIM, FNCS)** was a pioneer student of Computer Science, University of Ile-Ife and the first Nigerian woman PhD holder in Computer Science after a Master's degree at Atlanta in 1979. She had unprecedented nine distinctions in MBA (Finance & Accounts). She joined University of Ibadan as a Senior Lecturer and in 2006 became the first female black Computer Science Professor in Sub-Saharan Africa. She presided over the Computer Professional Registration Council of Nigeria; is a Board member, Nigeria Internet Registration Association and OMATEC Computers; Coordinator of four Nigerian universities and France Collaboration Programmes; and Director of Computerise Nigeria Project. She holds many prizes, scholarships and fellowships in UK, USA, Australia and India. She is a Fellow, Nigerian Institute of Management and Nigeria Computer Society; Life Member, Nigerian Economic Society; Member, Computer Society of IEEE; Member, ACM; and authors over 70 publications in journals and conference proceedings.

**Eno Joseph Ottong** teaches Library and Information Science at the University of Calabar, Nigeria. She is also heads the Department. Her current research interest is in Library and Information Science, which include organization of resources, user-instruction and information literacy, and information dissemination to user groups. She presents at various national and international conferences, recently the International Federation Library Association Conference at Puerto-Rico. A local chair on the conference on Information Technology and Economic Development a Conference jointly organized by University of West of Scotland and University of Calabar, she educates and trains Librarians as well as is involved in consultancies. She is a Chartered Librarian (LRCN), a Council member of the Nigerian Library Association (NLA), and the current Chair of NLA Cross River State Chapter. She is also in the Editorial Boards of the Library and Information Practitioner Journal, Heartland Journal and the Information Science Journal.

**Alice Phiri Shemi** is a senior lecturer in Business Information Systems at University of Botswana, Faculty of Business. Her research and publication areas are in E-commerce in small firms, ICTs and financial inclusion in marginalized communities, E-learning, IS/IT outsourcing, Strategic information systems and Career orientations of IS personnel in developing countries. Alice is a member of the Association for Computing Machinery (ACM). Alice is currently a PhD researcher at Salford Business School, University of Salford, Greater Manchester, UK.

**Dimitrios I Tseles** is professor of Automation Department of Technology Education Institute (TEI) of Piraeus, Athens. He has a B.Sc in Physics, M.Sc in Electronic Control, M.Sc in electronics and Communication Systems and a PhD in Control Systems. He is the chair and founder of the annual eRA (International Scientific conference for the contribution of Information Technology to Science, Economy, Society and Education. He is the publisher of two scientific books (CAD/DAM and Data Acquisition Systems) for tertiary education, several books about technical subjects and notebooks for postgraduate students. He has also published widely in international scientific journals. He has also presented and published in many scientific conferences. He has led many inter-institutional collaborations including with University of the West of Scotland (when it was University of Paisley). Contacts: infotech@teipir.gr dtsel@teipir.gr.

**Faith-Michael E Uzoka** is a faculty member in the Department of Computer Science and Information Systems, Mount Royal University, Canada. He obtained MBA (1995), MS (1998) and PhD (2003) in Computer Science with focus on Information Systems. He also conducted a two-year postdoctoral research in the University of Calgary (2004–2005). He is on the editorial/review board of a number of information systems and medical informatics journals/conferences. He is currently the president of the Canadian Institute for Medical and Organizational Informatics. His research interests are in medical decision support systems, evaluation systems using soft-computing technology, organizational computing and personnel issues, and technology adoption/innovation.

**Vasileios (Billy) Yfantis** holds a BA honours degree in Marketing from the Technological Education Institute of Athens and an MSc in Information Technology with Web Technology from the University of the West of Scotland. Mr. Yfantis is currently employed within the Greek Government in a position that is related to the use of ICT for the citizen's service. He has also been a freelance journalist for more than 15 years by contributing content to both electronic and printed media. As a conference speaker, he in 2011 presented innovative research on the reduction of "Digital Divide in the Music Industry" at the International Scientific Conference eRA. The main areas of his research interests feature: Information Communications Technology, e-Tourism, Digital Divide in Developing Countries, e-Government and in the Digital Entertainment Industry. Contact: Byfantis@yahoo.com

# Index

## F



## G



## H



## I



## K



## L



## M

## N



## O



## P



## R



## S

## T



## U



## V



## W